Governing through Standards

International Political Economy Series

General Editor: **Timothy M. Shaw**, Professor and Director, Institute of International Relations, The University of the West Indies, Trinidad & Tobago

Titles include:

Timothy Cadman
QUALITY AND LEGITIMACY OF GLOBAL GOVERNANCE
Case Lessons from Forestry

Andrew F. Cooper
INTERNET GAMBLING OFFSHORE
Caribbean Struggles over Casino Capitalism

Andrew F. Cooper and Timothy M. Shaw (*editors*)
THE DIPLOMACIES OF SMALL STATES
Between Vulnerability and Resilience

Anthony Leysens
THE CRITICAL THEORY OF ROBERT W. COX
Fugitive or Guru?

Valbona Muzaka
THE POLITICS OF INTELLECTUAL PROPERTY RIGHTS AND
ACCESS TO MEDICINES

Stefano Ponte, Peter Gibbon and Jakob Vestergaard (*editors*)
GOVERNING THROUGH STANDARDS
Origins, Drivers and Limitations

Mireya Solís, Barbara Stallings and Saori N. Katada (*editors*)
COMPETITIVE REGIONALISM
FTA Diffusion in the Pacific Rim

Peter Utting and José Carlos Marques (*editors*)
CORPORATE SOCIAL RESPONSIBILITY AND REGULATORY GOVERNANCE
Towards Inclusive Development?

International Political Economy Series
Series Standing Order ISBN 978–0–333–71708–0 hardcover
Series Standing Order ISBN 978–0–333–71110–1 paperback
(*outside North America only*)

You can receive future titles in this series as they are published by placing a standing order. Please contact your bookseller or, in case of difficulty, write to us at the address below with your name and address, the title of the series and one of the ISBNs quoted above.

Customer Services Department, Macmillan Distribution Ltd, Houndmills, Basingstoke, Hampshire RG21 6XS, England

Governing through Standards

Origins, Drivers and Limitations

Edited by

Stefano Ponte
Senior Researcher, Danish Institute for International Studies

Peter Gibbon
Senior Researcher, Danish Institute for International Studies

and

Jakob Vestergaard
Senior Researcher, Danish Institute for International Studies

First published 2011 by
PALGRAVE MACMILLAN

Palgrave Macmillan in the UK is an imprint of Macmillan Publishers Limited, registered in England, company number 785998, of Houndmills, Basingstoke, Hampshire RG21 6XS.

Palgrave Macmillan in the US is a division of St Martin's Press LLC, 175 Fifth Avenue, New York, NY 10010.

Palgrave Macmillan is the global academic imprint of the above companies and has companies and representatives throughout the world.

Palgrave® and Macmillan® are registered trademarks in the United States, the United Kingdom, Europe and other countries

ISBN 978–0–230–29540–7

This book is printed on paper suitable for recycling and made from fully managed and sustained forest sources. Logging, pulping and manufacturing processes are expected to conform to the environmental regulations of the country of origin.

A catalogue record for this book is available from the British Library.

Library of Congress Cataloging-in-Publication Data
    Governing through standards : origins, drivers and limitations / edited by Stefano Ponte, Peter Gibbon, Jakob Vestergaard.
        p. cm.
    Includes index.
        ISBN 978–0–230–29540–7
        1. Total quality management in government. 2. Performance standards. 3. Public administration. I. Ponte, Stefano. II. Gibbon, Peter. III. Vestergaard, Jakob.

JF1525.T67.G68 2011
352.3'57—dc23   2011021117

10 9 8 7 6 5 4 3 2 1
20 19 18 17 16 15 14 13 12 11

Printed and bound in Great Britain by
CPI Antony Rowe, Chippenham and Eastbourne

Contents

Tables and Figures

Tables

Figures

Acronyms

4C	Common Code for the Coffee Community
ABNT	National Standards Organisation of Brazil
ACP	African, Caribbean and Pacific Group of Countries
AESC	American Engineering Standards Committee
AICPA	American Institute of Certified Public Accountants
AOEFM	Association of Furniture Making Firms of Oaxaca (Mexico)
ASF	American Securitization Forum
ASQ	American Society for Quality
A-IRB	Advanced Internal Ratings Based
B2B	Business-to-Business
BCBS	Basel Committee on Banking Supervision
BCI	Better Cotton Initiative
BDB	Association of German Banks
BIS	Bank for International Settlements
BRC	British Retail Consortium
BSCI	Better Sugar Cane Initiative
BSI	British Standards Institute
CAG	Consultative Advisory Group (of IFAC)
CAR	Corrective Action Requests
CB	Certification Body
CCMSS	Consejo Civil Mexicano de la Silvicultura Sostenible (Mexico)
CDI	National Commission for the Development of Indigenous Peoples (Mexico)
CDO	Collateralized Debt Obligation
CIRAD	Centre de Coopération Internationale en Recherche Agronomiquepour le Développement (France)
COC	Chain of custody
CONAFOR	National Forestry Department (Mexico)
COP15	15th Conference of the Parties to the UN Framework Convention on Climate Change
COPOLCO	Committee on Consumer Policy (ISO)
CRD	Capital Requirements Directive
CRDS	Certified Reliability Data Sheets
CSR	Corporate Social Responsibility

CWG	Criteria Working Group
DFID	Department for International Development (UK)
DQAB	Defence Quality Assurance Board (UK)
EC	European Commission
EEC	European Economic Community
ERA	Estudios Rurales y Asesoria (Mexico)
ESF	European Securitization Forum
ETI	Ethical Trading Initiative (UK)
ETP	Ethical Tea Partnership
EU	European Union
FAM	Fisheries Assessment Methodology
FAO	Food and Agriculture Organization
FASB	Financial Accounting Standards Board (US)
FBF	Banking Federation of France
FEA	Failure Effect Analysis
FEE	Féderation des Experts Comptable Européens (Federation of European Accountants)
FETRAF-SUL	Federation of Family-Based Agricultural Workers of the South (Brazil)
FFP	Fair Flowers Fair Plants
FIRA	Trust Funds for Rural Development (Mexico)
F-IRB	Foundation Internal Ratings-Based (Basel II)
FIRCO	Shared Risk Trust Fund (Mexico)
FLO	Fairtrade Labelling Organizations International
FLP	Flower Label Program
FPEAK	Fresh Produce Exporters Association of Kenya
FSA	Financial Services Authority (UK)
FSAP	Financial Sector Assessment Program
FSB	Financial Stability Board
FSC	Forest Stewardship Council
FSF	Financial Stability Forum (forerunner of FSB)
G7	Group of seven 'leading industrialized nations'
G8	Group of eight 'leading industrialized nations'
G10	Group of 10 countries that participated in the original General Agreement to Borrow
G20	Group of 20 'major advanced and emerging economies'
GLOBAL-GAP	Global-Good Agricultural Practices
GMO	Genetically Modified Organism
GPPC	Global Public Policy Committee (international accounting network)

GPPS	Global Public Policy Symposium (of the largest international accounting and audit networks)
GTZ	International Technical Cooperation Authority (Germany)
HACCP	Hazard Analysis Critical Control Points
HEBI	Horticultural Ethical Business Initiative (UK)
IAASB	International Auditing and Assurance Standards Board
IAG	International Auditing Guidelines
IAIS	International Association of Insurance Supervisors
IAS	International Accounting Standard (later IFRS)
IASB	International Accounting Standards Board
IASC	International Accounting Standards Committee (now IASB)
ICAEW	Institute of Chartered Accountants of England and Wales
ICAS	Institute of Chartered Accountants of Scotland
ICBA	Independent Community Bankers of America
ICC	International Code of Conduct for the Production of Cut Flowers
ICOFOSA	Integradora Comunal Forestal de Oaxaca S.A. de C.V. (Mexico)
IEC	International Electrotechnical Commission
IEEPO	Instituto Estatal de Educación Pública de Oaxaca (Mexico)
IFA	International Financial Architecture
IFAC	International Federation of Accountants
IFIAR	International Forum of Independent Audit Regulators
IFOAM	International Federation of Organic Agriculture Movements
IFRS	International Financial Reporting Standard
IFS	International Featured Standards (mainland Europe food standard)
IIF	International Institute of Finance
IMF	International Monetary Fund
IMO	Institute for Market Ecology (Switzerland)
IOSCO	International Organization of Securities Commissions
IRB	Internal Ratings Based
ISA	International Standard on Auditing
ISDA	International Swaps and Derivatives Association
ISEAL	International Social and Environmental Accreditation and Labelling Alliance

ISO	International Organization for Standardization
IT	Information Technology
JAS	Japanese Organic Agricultural Standard
JBA	Japanese Bankers' Association
KFC	Kenya Flower Council
LCR	Liquidity Coverage Ratio
LDC	Least Developed Country
LTCM	Long-Term Capital Management (US hedge fund)
MIT	Massachusetts Institute of Technology
MNC	Multi-national company
MoD	Ministry of Defense (UK)
MPS	Milieu Programma Sierteelt (Netherlands)
MSC	Marine Stewardship Council
MSI	Multi-stakeholder Initiatives
NAFEC	North American Fund for Environmental Cooperation
NASA	National Aeronautic and Space Agency (US)
NATO	North Atlantic Treaty Organization
NGO	Non-governmental Organization
NSFR	Net Stable Funding Ratio
NSMD	Non-State Market Driven
PCAOB	Public Company Accounting Oversight Board (US)
PEFC	Programme for the Endorsement of Forest Certification
PIOB	Public Interest Oversight Board (of IFAC)
PROCYMAF	Proyecto de Conservación y Manejo Sustentable de Recursos Forestales en México
PRODEFOR	Mexican Forestry Development Program
PYME	Secretariat of the Economy, Small Business Section (Mexico)
QIS	Quantitative Impact Study
RAF	Royal Air Force (UK)
RBF	Risk-Based Framework
ROSC	Report on Standards and Codes (World Bank)
RPN	Risk Priority Number
RSB	Round Table on Sustainable Biofuels
RSPO	Roundtable on Sustainable Palm Oil
RTRS	Round Table on Responsible Soy
SCS	Scientific Certification Systems (certification body)
SEC	Securities and Exchange Commission (US)
SEDAF	State Agriculture and Forest Development Agency (Mexico)

SIV	Structured Investment Vehicle
SMEs	Small and Medium Enterprises
TAC	Transnational Auditors Committee (of IFAC)
TREES	Training, Extension, Enterprises and Sourcing (Rainforest Alliance programme)
TSMO	Transnational Social Movement Organization
UN	United Nations
UNOFOC	National Union of Community Forestry Organizations (Mexico)
US GAAP	Generally Accepted Accounting Principles (US)
VaR	Value-at-Risk
VCSS	Voluntary Consensus Standard Setting
WOCCU	World Council of Credit Unions
WWF	World Wide Fund for Nature (formerly the World Wildlife Fund)

Contributors

Emmanuelle Cheyns is a senior researcher at the French Agricultural Research Centre for International Development (CIRAD). She has been involved in research on food quality perception by consumers in African cities, the impacts of liberalization in the oil palm value chain in Côte d'Ivoire, forms of participation and negotiation between stakeholders involved in sustainable voluntary standards, and the inclusion of minority voices in the elaboration of standards.

Marcel Djama is a senior researcher at the French Agricultural Research Centre for International Development (CIRAD). His research interest is centred on regimes of governing, globalization and social change. He has published on standards and certifications and on indigenous movements.

Eve Fouilleux is a senior researcher at the French National Center for Scientific Research (CNRS – CEPEL, Montpellier) and an associated senior researcher at the French Agricultural Research Centre for International Development (CIRAD). She is interested in understanding how and why policies and regulations emerge, stabilize and change (or do not change). She has researched the European Common Agricultural Policy and, more generally, international bargains and controversies related to agriculture and rural policies. She is now mainly interested in the rise of transnational private policy tools in agriculture and their organizational, institutional and political dimensions.

Peter Gibbon is a senior researcher at the Danish Institute for International Studies (DIIS). His interests include standards, commodities and large-scale farming in Africa. He is co-author of *Trading Down: Africa, Value Chains and the Global Economy* (2005) and co-editor of *Global Agro-food Trade and Standards: Challenges for Africa* (2010) and of recent special editions of *Development Policy Review* on 'Africa and the WTO Doha Round' (2007) and of *Economy and Society* on the 'Governance of Global Value Chains' (2008).

Lasse Folke Henriksen is a fellow at the Department of Business and Politics, Copenhagen Business School and formerly a research assistant at DIIS. His research has so far revolved around the role of experts and expert knowledge in driving the construction and regulation of global markets. He is involved in a project examining how professions form strategies to influence transnational policy-making in the areas of financial and environmental governance.

Christopher Humphrey is Professor of Accounting at Manchester Business School. His main research interests are in the areas of international financial regulation and auditing practice. He is an associate editor of the *European Accounting Review* and serves as an academic representative on both the Technical Strategy Board and governing Council of the Institute of Chartered Accountants in England and Wales (ICAEW). He is also the chair of the UK's Conference of Professors of Accounting and Finance (CPAF).

Martin Højland was a research assistant at the Danish Institute for International Studies (DIIS) in 2009–10. In addition to his contribution to this volume, he is the co-author of a DIIS Policy Brief on 'Reforming Global Banking Rules'. The empirical focus of Martin's Master's thesis, completed in 2009, was the international banking standard known as the Basel 2 accord.

Ranjit Lall is a research associate at St John's College, Oxford University. His primary research interests are in the area of domestic and international financial regulation. He is a former economist at the Bank of England, where he worked in the Financial Stability Directorate, and editorial writer for the *Financial Times*.

Anne Loft is Professor at the School of Economics and Management, Lund University, Sweden. Her primary research concerns the regulation of accounting and auditing, and their role in global financial governance. Together with Christopher Humphrey she is writing the official history of the International Federation of Accountants (IFAC), the global association for the accounting profession. She is vice-president (Education) of the International Association for Accounting Education and Research, and one of the editors of the *International Journal of Auditing*.

Dan Klooster is Professor of Latin American Studies at the University of Redlands. His PhD is in Geography from the University of California, Los Angeles. His research and publications address the intersections of conservation and development in Latin America, especially Mexican community forestry and the role of forest certification as an instrument of global environmental governance.

Craig N. Murphy is Professor of Global Governance at the University of Massachusetts Boston's McCormack Graduate School of Policy and Global Studies and M. Margaret Ball Professor of International Relations at Wellesley College. He is author of *The International Organization for Standardization, Global Governance through Voluntary Consensus*, with JoAnne Yates (2009) and *The UN Development Programme: A Better Way?* (2006).

Stefano Ponte is a senior researcher at the Danish Institute for International Studies (DIIS) and head of the research unit 'Global Economy, Regulation and Development' (GEARED). His research interests include the dynamics of governance in global value chains and the role played by standards and celebrities in mobilizing 'ethical consumption'. His most recent co-authored books and edited collections include *Brand Aid: Shopping Well to Save the World* (2011), *Global Agro-food Trade and Standards: Challenges for Africa* (2010) and 'Governing Global Value Chains', a special issue of *Economy and Society* (2008).

Lone Riisgaard holds a PhD in International Development Studies from Roskilde University, Denmark. She is a project researcher at the Danish Institute for International Studies (DIIS). She has researched and published on sustainability standards, labour rights issues and Global Value Chain analysis, with focus on the cut flower value chain originating in Kenya and Tanzania.

Isabelle Vagneron is a researcher at the French Agricultural Research Centre for International Development (CIRAD). She is interested in how sustainability standards (re)shape agro-food chains, with a special focus on smallholders in developing countries. Her work also involves analysing the specific strategies developed by private certification bodies involved in organic and fair trade certification. She has published widely on global value chains and sustainability standards.

Jakob Vestergaard is a senior researcher at the Danish Institute of International Studies (DIIS). His publications include *Discipline in the Global Economy: International Finance and the End of Liberalism* (2009), 'More Heat than Light: On the Regulation of International Finance' (*Economic Sociology*, 2010), and 'The Asian Crisis and the Shaping of "Proper Economies"' (*Cambridge Journal of Economics*, 2004). Before taking up his current position at DIIS, Jakob was ESRC post-doctoral fellow at the London School of Economics and Political Science (LSE) and assistant professor at the Copenhagen Business School, Department of Management, Politics and Philosophy.

JoAnne Yates is Deputy Dean and Sloan Distinguished Professor of Management at the Sloan School of Management, MIT. She is author of *The International Organization for Standardization, Global Governance through Voluntary Consensus* (2009) and *Structuring the Information Age: Life Insurance and Technology in the Twentieth Century* (2005).

Kevin L. Young is LSE Fellow in Global Politics at the London School of Economics, where he teaches global governance and international political economy. His primary research is on the role of private sector groups in the formation of financial regulations at the national and global levels.

1
Governing through Standards: An Introduction

Stefano Ponte, Peter Gibbon and Jakob Vestergaard

A 'world of standards'?

In this book, we use a broad definition of standards as norms selected as a model by which people, objects or actions (including government regulation itself) can be judged and compared, and which provide a common language to evaluators, the evaluated and their audiences.[1] By governance we mean the shaping of the conduct of others through network forms of organization involving a wide range of non-state actors but also government, mainly through exchange and negotiation rather than through traditional state-led regulation.

While in the past standards were mainly developed to address technical, metrological and compatibility issues and operated as tools of simplification, unification and specification (Ewald, 1990), they now perform key functions of governing conduct of people and institutions (including governments) within an increasing number of domains of contemporary economies and societies (Brunsson and Jacobsson, 2000; Tamm Hallström, 2004; Fransen and Kolk, 2007; Pattberg, 2007; Lampland and Star, 2009; Vestergaard, 2009; Tamm Hallström and Boström, 2010; Higgins and Larner, 2010a; Gibbon *et al.*, 2010; Timmermans and Epstein, 2010; Cadman, 2011). Standards define constraints but also enable interaction by providing common language and means of communication. They are set and managed within a system of norms, conventions and values that are revisable and negotiable, rather than absolute (Ponte and Gibbon, 2005; Henman and Dean, 2010). They involve classification and categorization, exclusion and inclusion thresholds, choice of measurement devices and intervals – in other words they perform 'boundary work' that needs maintenance, and produces new identities, subjectivities and forms of social organization (Higgins and Larner, 2010b).

While adopting a broad definition of standards, we do differentiate between standards set by public authority (and thus embedded in regulation) and those that are voluntary, thus are not based on the sovereign authority of the state, so not requiring compliance and state sanction in case of non-compliance. We also acknowledge that the two categories are porous and overlapping: (1) voluntary standards can and have been embedded in regulation; (2) existing regulations have provided input into the formation of voluntary standards; (3) standards are sometimes legally recognized as risk mitigation devices (especially in food safety); and (4) 'proper' regulation is itself increasingly the object of standards and standardization (Vestergaard, 2009); and (4) states respond in very different ways to the voluntary features proposed by standard initiatives (Cashore *et al*.,. 2004; Gale and Haward, 2011).

We also differentiate between formal standards and other norms and conventions that arise from unintentional action, repetition and habit (Brunsson and Jakobsson, 2000; Ponte and Gibbon, 2005). Formal standards are usually linked to governing authorities (standard setting organizations or networks, often but not always certifiers and accreditation agencies) (Hatanaka *et al.*, 2005; Loconto and Busch, 2010) and are accompanied – or are expected to be accompanied – by a set of sanctions in case of non-compliance, such as losing a certification, applying corrective actions, or to exposure in name-and-shame lists and expectations that the market will 'punish' non-compliance. Voluntary, formal standards and standards setters are said to be in constant need to achieve, maintain and manage legitimacy to exert authority, since they need to convince standards users to adopt them and 'audiences' to see such adoption as something acceptable (Cashore *et al.*, 2004; Tamm Hallström and Boström, 2010; Bernstein, 2011). Again, the boundaries between formal standards and norms and conventions are not set in stone, as formal standards can build upon conventions and standards setters can even try to carry out 'normative work' to shape conventions (Gibbon *et al.*, 2008; Ponte, 2009; Timmermans and Epstein, 2010).

Voluntary standards seek to overcome the limits of state capacity to regulate these realms, but also arose from the increasing willingness of public authority under neoliberalism to delegate such regulation to private actors or multi-stakeholder initiatives. The rise of idealized market paradigms provided a new model for regulation in emerging areas of public concern, and for reforming existing models in established ones.

In emerging areas of public concern such as climate change, pseudo-market systems may be created; in established ones like food safety, authority tends to be fragmented, re-bundled and distributed to new actors. In both cases, business is devolved major new responsibilities but at the same time granted substantial discretion in how these are fulfilled. Rather than occurring through a combination of trust and direct operational inspection, verification of fulfilment increasingly demands documentation of managerial controls (Power, 2003) or the discipline of the market (Vestergaard, 2009).

While at national level within Europe[2] this tendency has gone furthest in the historically liberal United Kingdom, against the background of a different set of circumstances it is also evident within the EU governance system. Here, the establishment of a single market has necessarily entailed legal harmonization. However, given the EU's limited centralized authority the latter process normally has had to take the form of re-stating laws in terms of 'essential requirements', often defined only in terms of outcomes. Thus, a strong element of discretion in implementation has again become the rule, alongside forms of conformity verification emphasizing managerial system requirements (Majone, 1996). In both national and EU-level public sector governance, such requirements explicitly or implicitly involve benchmarking the performance and integrity of systems against standards, both managerial and sectoral.

Voluntary international standards are one of the instruments of private governance that have emerged as a result of perceived governmental failures in addressing global problems on the basis of bounded jurisdiction. Three aspects of inter-governmental governance stand out in relation to this: (1) international agreement formation is a complex and time-consuming process requiring consensus building and thus is prone to deadlock (the current status of the Doha round of trade negotiations and the failure of COP15 in Copenhagen are only two recent manifestations); (2) while powerful states can deliberate or recommend actions within 'exclusive clubs', these tend to function effectively only when participation is limited or when facing imminent catastrophe (the G20 head of state forum at the height of the financial crisis in 2008–09 is one example); yet, when participation is too limited, exclusive clubs suffer from a representation and legitimization deficit (for example, the G8, but currently also the G20, Vestergaard, 2011a), while when participation is widened, efficiency tends to decrease (Hüllse and Kerwer, 2007); (3) inter-governmental governance has legitimization problems of its own (Best, 2007; Seabrooke, 2007; Bernstein, 2011; Brassett and

Tsingou, 2011; Vestergaard, 2011b) that may provide additional space for non-governmental forms of governance.

The increasingly global scope of economic activity and the challenges it raises in governing relates to changes in industrial organization and the increased mobility of finance. Production shifted from the domestic domain or within vertically integrated multinational companies (MNCs) to more dispersed locations, organized in network forms, and from developed to developing countries, thus mostly beyond the reach of national regulators (in the North) and within the reach of weaker regulators (in the South). Where international regulation has succeeded, it has been mostly in relation to facilitating trade (and even here, it is now facing problems in moving further ahead). But a restructuring of industrial organization has at the same time facilitated the emergence of alternative responses to traditional regulation, for example, protest campaigns and the use of market pressure to shape the behaviour of business – the latter has been particularly effective against MNCs with a high brand profile (Mayer and Gereffi, 2010).

Standards, types of authority and the re-articulation of governance

Standards are part of a broader set of instruments that are said to be advancing 'private authority' in governing economic, social and environmental phenomena (Cutler *et al.*, 1999a; Hall and Biersteker, 2002a; Rittberger and Nettesheim, 2008). But they also play an important role in shaping regulation and 'proper' policy making (Vestergaard, 2009). The literatures on global governance and private authority suggest that governments are increasingly unable to regulate economic, social and environmental life because of the increasing complexity and rapidity of change, the transnational and global scope of economic activity, and the delegitimating effect of neoliberal ideology on the state. The extent to which this has led to a wholesale retreat of the state or to a re-configuration of public and private spheres is a contentious issue (Hall and Biersteker, 2002a; Pattberg, 2007; Clapp and Fuchs, 2009; Büthe, 2010; Cadman, 2011). While there is broad recognition that private authority is on the rise, it may actually apply to areas that were never regulated by the state to begin with; when it addresses transnational problems it can actually enhance state capacity by allowing the state to escape innate constraints and to focus more effectively on other areas of regulation; also, private authority often actively interacts with public authority in a variety of ways, thus making it difficult to disentangle the two (Cashore *et al.*, 2004; Büthe, 2010).

The literature on 'private authority' seeks to identify emerging structures and sources of international political and rule-making authority. Authority is said to 'exist when an individual or organization has decision-making power over particular issues and is regarded as exercising that power legitimately' (Cutler *et al.*, 1999b, p. 5). Such literature, spanning political science, international relations and international political economy, looks at the reconfiguration of governing and the limits and possibilities of global economic and environmental governance (among many others, see Levy and Newell, 2005; Rittberger and Nettesheim, 2008; Clapp and Fuchs, 2009; Cadman, 2011). Parallel to this is another, also large, literature dealing specifically with the role and authority of business in global governance. Broadly speaking, such literature looks at how business governs through its lobbying power in shaping public regulation; how, conversely, governments and international organizations attempt to shape business behaviour through global business regulation; and how business either through self-regulation or in partnership with other actors (NGOs, governments) establishes standards, codes of conduct and other CSR initiatives and with what consequences on societies, the environment and development (for recent contributions, see Utting and Marques, 2009; Ougaard and Leander, 2010; Marques and Utting, 2010).

Prominent in many discussions are attempts at categorizing the sources of private authority. Cutler *et al.*, (1999b) identify three: perceived expertise (see also Brunsson and Jacobsson, 2000), historical practice that builds acceptability and appropriateness for the exercise of authority; or grant of power from the state. Hall and Biersteker (2002b) identify market, moral and illicit authority, arising respectively from inter-firm co-operation, non-governmental organizations and organized violence. Rosenau (2003) enlarges this palette to include knowledge, reputational, issue-specific and affiliate authority (arising from epistemic communities, credit agencies, non-governmental organizations (NGOs) and cultural or religious groups).

But because private authority is not exercised through the traditional rule-making mechanisms and sovereign legitimacy of the Westphalian state, it must be based on other forms of legitimacy – so the literature argues. New actors 'claim to be, perform as, and are recognized as legitimate by some larger public (that often includes states themselves) as authors of policies, of practices, of rules, and of norms' (Hall and

Biersteker, 2002b, p. 4). Legitimacy in this context implies that 'there is some form of normative, uncoerced consent...on the part of the regulated or governed' (*Ibid.*) based on market, tradition, expertise and/or moral claims that are asserted through a variety of political and rhetorical practices.

As these new forms of governance lack the traditional enforcement capacities associated with the state and democratic representation, legitimacy is often seen as relational and deriving from the perceptions of stakeholders and 'audiences' (Boström and Tamm Hallström, 2010). Those claiming authority need to achieve support, approval and legitimization from a broad group of actors, including the state. Therefore, in multi-stakeholder initiatives, for example, (see below), much effort is geared towards mimicking democratic representation through the setting up of different expert groups and stakeholder councils, and the promotion of openness, transparency and accountability (*Ibid.*).

In the institutionalist literature emerging from management and organization studies, one of the main tenets is that standard setting organizations build rule-making authority and legitimacy through expertise so that standards can actually be seen as 'expert knowledge stored in the form of rules' (Jacobsson, 2000, p. 41; see also Brunnson and Jacobsson, 2000; Tamm Hallström, 2004). Expertise is a kind of knowledge that claims to be correct, embodies practical advice, is produced by specialists and can be challenged only by specialists (Jacobsson, 2000). It covers both content and procedures (*Ibid.*, p. 48). Experts from this point of view are not influential because they can present arguments that persuade, but because they can avoid argument (Hüllse and Kerwer, 2007). In this approach, focus is on *what* knowledge is used to create standards and provide them with legitimacy. But more recent contributions have also attempted to understand *how* that happens (Tamm Hallström and Boström, 2010).

Legitimacy concerns may be important in some realms of standard making and management, and especially in multi-stakeholder initiatives. But when private governance acquires quasi-compulsory features (for example, when retailers require Global–GAP certification from all their fresh produce suppliers) it is not clear why legitimacy should play such an important role. Private standards or requirements set by business may actually not require constant legitimacy-making that is based on acceptance by consumers and governments (contrary to what is argued in Fuchs and Kalfagianni, 2010). Consumers are rarely aware of business-to-business standards such as Global–GAP or basic codes of conduct because such information is not transmitted to them via a label.

Governments have little power to shape whether a retail chain demands that its suppliers are certified against one or another standard.

The existing literature on governance in global value chains (including previous work of two of the editors of this volume; Gibbon and Ponte, 2005; Ponte and Gibbon, 2005; Gibbon *et al.*, 2008; Gibbon and Ponte, 2008; Ponte, 2009) shows that private authority is often applied by business outright and outside the frame of formal institutions or organizations. Here, issues of legitimacy and authority are less ambiguous: lead firms in value chains, for example, demand that their suppliers match specific standards (technical specifications, processing methods, volumes and quality, logistics, time to market). These standards govern the daily lives of producers, traders, and workers. And even demands for business to behave more ethically in relation to social and environmental issues have been addressed increasingly via standards and certifications that eventually require suppliers (rather than retailers) to conform to them.

All in all, rather than an outright transfer of authority from the public to the private realm as part of a broader trend towards deregulation, it is more appropriate to see the current configuration of government of the economy as part of a process of re-regulation, or more precisely a 're-articulation of regulatory authority' (from Utting, 2008). Within this re-articulation, public regulation has indeed retreated in some areas of the economy, but at the same time other forms of governmental and inter-governmental regulation are actually being strengthened (relating, for example, to intellectual property rights, trade and investment, and 'crimes against humanity') (Utting, 2008). This is happening as more 'collective' or 'socialized' forms of private authority are also appearing, themselves increasingly supported by the state and international organizations (O'Rourke, 2003). So while co-regulation efforts (for example, multi-stakeholder initiatives) are on the rise, we may also be witnessing the 'coming together of different regulatory approaches in ways that are complementary, mutually reinforcing and synergistic, or at least less contradictory' (Utting, 2008, p. 249). Re-articulated regulation is thus based on different forms of regulatory interaction (Ibid.).

Whether this is indeed leading to complementary, mutually enforcing and synergistic outcomes is an empirical question that this book seeks to address. Given the less hierarchical configuration of re-articulated regulation, and its more negotiated nature, we prefer to subsume this phenomenon under our use of the term 'governance'. In this book, we focus on standards as one of the most important devices that are at play in such re-articulation of governance.

The place of this book vis a vis existing approaches to the study of standards

Standards have been approached in the literature from a variety of perspectives. Focus has been on the material construction of standards and their material effects. *Realist* and *institutionalist* perspectives, as seen above, have focused much of their effort in identifying sources of private authority and specifically how standards and the organizations that drive them achieve legitimacy. Contributions within *political economy* have examined standards from a variety of angles within a materialist field: (1) in terms of their content, coverage and proliferation; (2) their governance, adoption and issues related to conformity; (3) the costs and benefits of compliance; the dynamics of negotiation, content setting, certification procedures and accreditation; (4) how standards arise from (or shape) value chain restructuring, inclusion/exclusion dynamics and welfare outcomes. Much attention has been placed on the development outcomes in the South and on weaker players (among others, in the field of agro-food standards, see Swinnen, 2007; Gibbon *et al.*, 2010; Sneyd, 2011).

But other literature has also examined the discursive, ideational and normative dimensions of standards. *Actor-network* perspectives have been particularly interested in understanding how materials and techniques are deployed by actors (scientists, managers and so on) to enrol other actors, extend the range of application of standards beyond localized spaces and to apply, adapt and 'translate' standards locally (Timmermans and Berg, 1997; Lampland and Star, 2009; Higgins and Larner, 2010a). From such perspective, standards entail 'acting at a distance' (Latour, 1987) and are one of the ways of governing through the application of calculative devices (Callon, 1986). *Convention theory* has also been used in standards work to understand the 'normative work' behind standard formation and management (Ponte and Gibbon, 2005; Ponte, 2009). *Governmentality* approaches have seen standards as technologies for the governing of conduct (Vestergaard, 2009; Gibbon and Ponte, 2008; Higgins and Larner, 2010a), where standards construct fields of visibility that reconstitute the social domains of the knowable and governable. From a governmentality perspective, standards aspire at shaping conduct and are underpinned by rationalities for the organization and governing of social life (Miller and O'Leary, 1987; Henman and Dean, 2010).

This collection brings together scholars studying both the historical development of standards and their new forms and roles, across the substantive areas of: banking and financial reporting; quality management and organizational social responsibility; and social, environmental and labour issues ('sustainability standards'). The contributions are from social scientists working within sociology, economics, accounting, political science and geography, with a common interest in how and why standards are used as governance tools in the economy, how they are internally governed, and what effects they have in the real world. The authors combine political economy and governmentality approaches to varying degrees. They do so, on the one hand, to address the limitations of a purely material approach in much political economy. On the other hand, they seek to go beyond a narrow programmatic focus in much of the governmentality literature by examining whether – and, if so how – programmes of government are made workable in practice.

Three of the four chapters dealing with banking and finance take a more explicit political economy approach (Chapters 2, 3 and 4). Chapter 2 shows how the use of international standards on banking has become extensive and integrated into banking operations themselves, facilitating the emergence of a neoliberal regime of self-regulation as opposed – quite literally – to a more pro-active kind of regulation by public authorities. Chapter 3 argues that key provisions of these standards allowed banks to be more exposed to risk, with the cumulative effect of destabilizing (rather than stabilizing) the financial sector – thus facilitating the emergence of the current financial crisis. Chapter 4 shows that these standards were subject to 'regulatory capture' by prominent international banks in the standard setting process, explaining their specific content and why they were unable to achieve their intended effects.

Chapters 5 to 10 deal in part or *in toto* with governmentality issues in the sense that they examine the role of expert knowledge, epistemic communities, professions and technologies of governing. Chapter 5 examines the entanglements between private and public in the making of standards for corporate financial reports, and the role played by the auditing profession in particular. Chapter 6 (on the pre-history of ISO 9000) and Chapter 8 (on the Roundtable on Sustainable Palm Oil) apply a governmentality approach most explicitly. Chapter 7 (on ISO 26000) draws from social movements theory, while Chapter 9 (on two sustainability roundtables) draws from the sociology of engagements (a body of work closely related to convention theory). Chapter 10 (on sustainability standards in fish and cut flowers) and Chapter 11 (on sustainability standards in forestry) are mainly concerned with the exclusionary, distributional and network formation effects of sustainability standards. Chapter 10 also examines the role of expert knowledge in standard formation and management. Chapter 11 goes beyond existing political economy accounts on how standards govern global value chains to show how local networks can use these standards instrumentally for their own purposes.

Most chapters deal with the *origins* of 'governing through standards' in their respective fields. Two chapters (6 and 7) have a long duration perspective looking at the precursors of such standards, but many others go back at least to the beginning of a standard-making process. All of them highlight the *drivers* that are behind the setting, development, management and application of standards, be these actors (experts, social movements, epistemic communities, professions, stakeholder groups, industry representatives, business, government and any combination/alliance of these), motivations (pressures towards self-governing, governmental failures in regulating, opening of new areas of governing) or processes (profession driven vs. stakeholder driven; hegemonic vs. contested; transparent vs. opaque; national/local adoption vs. adaptation). Finally, all chapters highlight the *limitations* of 'governing through standards', which are discussed collectively in the conclusion.

Governing through standards in banking and financial reporting (Part I)

It is generally agreed in the literature that standards are increasingly used not only to govern conduct by private actors in the economy, but also to govern 'proper regulation' of such conduct itself. In previous work, Vestergaard (2009) showed how in the aftermath of the Asian crisis the IMF and World Bank promoted the setting and voluntary adoption of standards on how to 'properly' organize and regulate economies and how Asian economies were constructed as 'improper' forms of capitalism. Under an initiative called International Financial Architecture (IFA), standards of 'best practice' and crisis prevention measures were devised with the expectation that financial markets would reward and punish economies according to their degree of compliance with such standards. The Financial Sector Assessment Program (FSAP), first launched in 1999, entailed the development of standards in twelve areas falling into three main categories: policy transparency (data dissemination, and transparency of fiscal, monetary and financial policy), financial sector integrity (banking supervision, security, insurance and anti-money laundering), and market integrity (accounting, auditing, corporate governance, and insolvency and creditor rights). Attached to these standards was a system of surveillance that included the production of 'Reports on the observance of standards and codes' (ROSCs) by the IMF and the World Bank.

Vestergaard (2009) argues that FSAPs rendered economies visible, accountable and governable via hierarchical observation and normative judgment. Deviations from standards, norms and benchmarks were to be made visible with the expectation that markets would provide rewards and punishment. This would lead subjects to discipline themselves and thus economies would behave *as if* financial markets observe, assess and reward or punish. In addition to the market, formal enforcement mechanisms were also envisaged, such as conditionality, contingent credit lines and IMF Article IV consultations, but were never made to function well, if at all. But even in relation to market discipline, no clear link between compliance with these standards and the behaviour of financial markets can be established. In the first half of the 2000s, FSAPs had achieved considerable coverage (they were carried out in 120 countries between 2001 and 2006), although emerging markets and East Asian economies were under-represented and those countries that did carry out FSAPs have been reluctant to engage in updates. With the onset of the financial crisis, very little activity followed in this realm. Despite severe conceptual and operational problems in its first decade of existence, the FSAP was identified as one of the main pillars of the G20 crisis response in autumn 2008 and onwards. With respect to banking and finance, international standards very much remain the preferred mode of global economic governance in other words, as witnessed also by the much debated revisions of the international standard for banking supervision, the so-called Basel 3 accord.

Vestergaard (2009) argues that the IFA marked the emergence of a new regime in international economic governance driven by standards and codes of practice – 'from a regime predicated on the binary division between economies that are in crisis and economies that are not, to one predicated upon the binary branding of proper vs. improper economies, from localised and confined interventions dealing with economies transgressing the permitted-prohibited boundary to the constant measuring and governing of economies against the norm of a "proper" economy' (Vestergaard, 2009, p. 177).

In Part I of this book, we build on this overall picture to examine what happened to two of the twelve sets of standards that were part of the IFA: (1) the Basel committee standards on banking; and (2) standards on financial reporting.

Given the importance of international standards on banking in view of the most recent financial crisis, three chapters are dedicated to this topic. The Basel Committee on Banking Supervision was originally composed of financial regulators and central bankers of the 'G10' club but has been expanded to include all 'G20' countries.[3] Its members are not elected, in many cases not even delegated to take decisions on behalf of governments, and such decisions are not subject to approval by governments. The Basel Committee establishes standards on the financial soundness of banks and on 'proper' financial regulation. Basel standards formally only apply to member countries, but even for member countries they are voluntary in the sense that they are subject to ratification via sovereign authority of governments. Despite their voluntary nature, international standards of banking regulation constitute a remarkable case of convergence on international standards. Since their first launch in 1988, Basel standards have been implemented not only by the Basel member countries but by virtually all countries outside the membership. This voluntary implementation of Basel standards by more than 100 countries not party to the agreement is remarkable (Tarullo, 2008, p. 65). Although the private sector does not formally participate in the deliberations of the Basel committee, it has strong influence on its outcomes.

The three chapters on Basel standards can be read individually as self-standing, therefore contain some degree of repetition on the basics of the standards they deal with. But they also have a clear division of labour in terms of their aims.

In Chapter 2, Kevin Young shows how the use of industry-wide standards has been a critical component of banking regulatory regimes over the last 20 years. Drawing from both national and international contexts, his chapter analyses 'governance through standards' by focusing on both the rise of the use of standards as a governance practice and the limitations of this practice. The rise of standards in banking has facilitated three interrelated but contradictory dynamics already at play within the industry: first, these standards have facilitated the construction of liberal regulatory regimes; second, they have allowed regulators to mitigate competitive deregulation at the international level; and third, they have facilitated a market-based metric for the evaluation of risk, which acts as a functional substitute for active regulation by public authorities. At the same time, Young also shows that governing through standards has made it easy for powerful states and parts of the financial sector to 'carve-out' special exceptions to meet their particular preferences. Also, some countries have simply 'opted out' of adherence – either by not implementing them or by not enforcing their content.

In Chapter 3, Jakob Vestergaard and Martin Højland argue that, in public debate, the story of the current financial crisis has largely been one of deregulation, complex financial products and greedy financiers. However, a growing consensus has emerged among economists and regulators, that the international standard for the regulation and supervision of banks – the so-called Basel II Accord – played a key role in the crisis. Vestergaard and Højland highlight in particular the pro-cyclicality of some of the key provisions of Basel II that led to the current state of affairs in banking. In response to the growing recognition of the limits of Basel II, the leaders of the G20 countries have made a revision of international banking standards a core element of its deliberations over measures to be taken to reduce the likelihood and severity of financial crises in the future. Vestergaard and Højland argue that the Basel III accord address only marginally and superficially the shortcomings of Basel II. They see Basel III as an intensification of Basel II rather than a revision of it, which gives rise to considerable scepticism with regard to the Basel Committee's current objective of ensuring a 'better balance between banking stability and sustainable credit growth' in the future.

In Chapter 4, Ranjit Lall supplements the contribution by Vestergaard and Højland by chronicling in detail how key standards included in the Basel II accord were directly shaped by industry interests and lobbying. Lall shows how regulatory capture by large banks took place and how it was consolidated through first-mover advantage. These standards not only failed to improve the safety of the international banking system, but also effectively instituted a system where large banks had an in-built advantage over smaller banks. Lall explains not only why Basel II failed, but also why the latest set of proposals to regulate the international banking system through standards – the so-called 'Basel III' Accord – is likely to meet a similar fate.

In Chapter 5, Christopher Humphrey and Anne Loft examine standards on corporate financial reporting – including standards on accounting and auditing carried out in relation to the preparation of annual financial reports. In this field, private authority in the form of the international accounting profession and public authority in the form of international regulators are coming together in a global network that aims at making financial statements reliable and comparable globally. Such standards are spreading and converging, despite the complexity of the instruments they deal with. They are being included in regulation, used as benchmarks, and endorsed and encouraged by international organizations.

Humphrey and Loft disentangle the complex and often tense interactions between public and private actors in standard making, and the role played by a powerful internationalized profession – auditing. Because international standards on auditing are based on principles rather than rules or a set of instructions, 'professional judgment' and 'professional scepticism' play a key role. The auditing profession in this way is given some flexibility in how it yields authority over its jurisdiction, a space where its historical propensity for 'self-regulation' can be exercised. However, pressure is also mounting to reduce such space to avoid inconsistency. However, Humphrey and Loft conclude that it is not more rule-based standards that are needed, but more transparency on actual practice.

Historical perspectives on quality management and organizational social responsibility standards (Part II)

As reflected in the content of this book, most work on standards focuses on standards that are contemporary or which have emerged only in the last few years. Standards history, particularly from a critical socio-economic perspective, is a relatively undeveloped field – and one moreover where accounts of standardizing *organizations* predominates (cf. Tamm Hallström, 2004; Higgins, 2005; Murphy and Yates, 2009). Thus, while there is a growing literature on how and why standards are proliferating, there are few or no attempts to interpret this question in terms of whether there are 'model' standards, or ideals of standard setting, or communities of standard setters that have served as much more general blueprints and whose influence has proved decisive in this process – or why this should be the case, and what it might tell us. The two papers in Part II of this volume, although contrasting in their approaches, provide complementary efforts at such interpretations. Broadly, they identify ISO 9000 (or, more specifically its earlier form of UK Defence standards) as providing a template for an extremely broad range of subsequent standards development. Second, they identify consensus formation and maintenance as the defining ideal of technically-based standard-setting since its inception. And third, they identify the 'social movement of engineers' – and its contemporary descendents – as the leading protagonist of the promotion of technical standards as an emancipatory social mission.

In Chapter 6, Peter Gibbon and Lasse Folke Henriksen thus apply a governmentality framework to construct a technological pre-history of ISO 9000 via an analysis of quality management standards in the UK and US. Given that the standards in the two countries are related and that the British Standard promulgated in 1979 provided both the content and form for the subsequent ISO 9000 series, they are of particular relevance. The emergence of quality management standards represents a key moment in the unfolding the more general trend towards 'governing through standards'. For the first time, standards were promulgated that required evidence for a series of managerial controls, instead of for conformity to substantive procedures and outcomes, while allowing managers the discretion to define the content of these controls in their own terms – as long as their presence could be verified.

The evolution of quality management standards in the US and the UK since the 1940s that Gibbon and Henriksen trace emerged from interactions between the military and its suppliers. The 'translations' involved in this process were shaped mainly by the radically different relations between the military and civil contractors in the two locations. These differences were reflected in UK civil contractors gaining *de facto* control over how quality standards were defined and applied. As a result, modern quality management standards came to incarnate a 'freeing of capital' that in turn facilitated their uptake in the Thatcherite programme of 'marketization'.

In Chapter 7, Craig Murphy and JoAnne Yates examine the role of epistemic communities in the formation of technical standards in the past century, and of ISO 26000 more recently. They argue that standard setters should be seen as a 'social movement of engineers' dating back over a century, a movement based on a common conviction that humanity could benefit from the multiplication of objective, technical and consensus-based standards. Murphy and Yates show that, from the outset of standard setting, standards activists from across the political spectrum started speculating that the processes for establishing industrial standards could with benefit be extended to social regulation.

Today, ISO is completing a social responsibility standard through that very mechanism. The standard may have advantages over similar attempts to create private social regulation because participation in the ISO standard-setting process sometimes convinces companies to focus on longer-term and more civic goals. Also, the centrality of standard setters within global firms in lead industries may give ISO 26000 unusually powerful advocates there. At the same time, Murphy

and Yates highlight that the current 'social movement' of standard setters (where IT engineers play a major role and prefer open-source style
standard setting) may be incompatible with the increasingly bureaucratized and conservative nature of ISO. This points to an increasing separation between the 'spirit' of international technical standardization
and its organizational embodiment.

Governing through sustainability standards (Part III)

This last part of the book deals with sustainability standards, which
in many but not all cases take the form of multi-stakeholder initiatives (MSIs). MSIs have received much attention in recent standards
literature, particularly in relation to legitimacy concerns. What some
identify as MSI, others have termed 'non-state market-driven' (NSMD)
governance (Cashore *et al.*, 2004; Bernstein and Cashore, 2007). The
features of NSMD systems are that: (1) they do not derive policy-making
authority from the state, although the state may influence them or even
participate; (2) they drive towards collective goals and values over time
for a wide range of stakeholders, and justify this drive via specific design
forms (based on claims of openness, transparency, accountability); (3)
authority is granted to them by players in the supply chain; (4) they
reconfigure markets by seeking to address global problems that firms
otherwise would not address; and (5) they demand verification of compliance and set consequences for non-compliance (Cashore *et al.*, 2004;
Bernstein and Cashore, 2007).

Cashore *et al.* (2004) argue that market actors drive certification
schemes (and thus enable a 'governing through markets') because they
fear more demanding government regulation, search for competitive
advantage, and try to achieve corporate social responsibility objectives.
They argue that if certification schemes are too demanding, the market will reject them. Under this set of definitions, NSMD governance
is seen as different from broader processes of CSR, industry self-regulation, political consumerism and public–private partnerships because
it is based on the 'acceptance of shared rule by a community as appropriate and justified' (Bernstein and Cashore, 2007, p. 348). Codes of
conduct are not NSMD governance instruments because they are not
verified and simply provide a social license to operate. The reason posed
for such restrictive definition on what constitutes NSMD is a normative
one for these authors – they argue that such form is the one that has
most potential to address social and environmental problems.

In Part III of this book, the contributors question whether these NSMD instruments are indeed delivering to such expectations (see also Sneyd, 2011) and whether the market is really rejecting 'stricter' standards. Gale and Haward (2011), for example, highlight that if standards are too lax, social and environmental *demandeurs* of standards will reject them, posing threats to their legitimacy (see also Ponte and Riisgaard this volume). The contributions to this book, however, cover a broader set of phenomena than the restrictive definition of the tools of NSMD governance, to include codes of conduct as these also play important parts in the re-articulation of governance and in 'governing through standards' more specifically.

These chapters focus on understanding the process of establishing and maintaining legitimacy rather than deciding whether legitimacy exists or not (along with Tamm Hallström and Boström, 2010). They approach the legitimacy issue beyond the quality of output (market uptake) to also cover internal arrangements (input and process legitimacy). Output legitimacy itself is not just about market uptake, but rather about a balancing of market impact and stringency of standard and the capacity to solve problems. Input legitimacy is about balanced representation, the creation of stakeholder categories, the inclusion of expertise and high profile actors, and negotiating who can be considered a stakeholder to begin with (see also Pattberg, 2007). Procedural legitimacy is about facilitation of effective participation, transparency, accountability of decision-making procedures, and consensus building (Tamm Hallström and Boström, 2010).

Boström and Tamm Hallström (2010) also argue that legitimacy in MSIs is always preliminary, related to a contested construction of a problem and its solution(s), characterized by a balancing act with state actors and international organizations. Such a setup is inherently fragile because legitimacy needs to be repeatedly fostered, re-built and re-asserted and power balance maintained. As standards become more complex and bureaucratic, some stakeholders will find it difficult to follow the process. This undermines the inclusiveness of the multi-stakeholder form. MSI secretariats also tend to assume more powers and to assume greater first-hand control of processes, transmuting into a stakeholder itself. This further undermines the multi-stakeholder nature of the arrangement and provides new challenges.

The chapters in Part III suggest that while this balancing act is indeed taking place, the difficulties in maintaining it should not be overblown. In the formation stage, input legitimacy can be managed in subtle ways to achieve set objectives (see Djama *et al.* this volume; Cheyns this volume). It may not even be seriously attempted when an initiative does not face any competition in the market for standards (Ponte and Riisgaard this volume). And it may not be even necessary when local actors instrumentally use certification to achieve their own objectives (Klooster this volume).

In Chapter 8, Marcel Djama, Eve Fouilleux and Isabelle Vagneron apply a governmentality approach to examine sustainability standard setting, certifying and benchmarking – with particular focus on the Roundtable on Sustainable Palm oil (RSPO). While recognizing the value of institutionalist approaches in understanding the spread of MSIs and their apparent convergence in terms of organizational structure (Dingwerth and Pattberg, 2009), Djama *et al.* ask the 'how' questions that often escape the analysis of MSIs: How are MSIs governed? How are internal conflicts managed? How can different agendas and ideas coexist within the same organization?

Djama *et al.*'s main argument is that a technology of government called 'managerialism' permeates these new initiatives. They define managerialism as 'the collection of knowledge and practices initially intended for corporate management but now systematically aimed at increasing the efficiency of collective action'. They argue that in the academic literature to date, multi-stakeholder standards have been mostly analysed from the viewpoint of how external legitimacy is created and sustained for private global governance mechanisms. Their chapter establishes and addresses an alternative research agenda on these standards. In addressing the political rationalities that standards promote and the technologies of internal governance they deploy, it shows how a series of potentially serious political conflicts concerning economic and environmental sustainability are neutralized in practice. Particular attention is given to the patterns of decision making involved in consensus building, auditing and benchmarking.

In Chapter 9, Emmanuelle Cheyns examines two multi-stakeholder initiatives in sustainable agriculture and tests the limits of their 'inclusiveness' paradigm. She argues that a key trend in the evolution of agro-food standards in the past decade has been the development of open participation and negotiation processes referred to as 'multi-stakeholder' initiatives. These are aimed at creating 'sustainable' voluntary standards for agricultural goods (coffee, cocoa, oil palms, soya beans, bio-fuels, sugar cane, cotton are the main ones) and have been developed through a series of Roundtables. Intended to be private and voluntary in nature, these initiatives are founded on a rationale focusing on 'government failure', in particular in Southern countries, to take responsibility for 'environmental goods'. In large part, their claims to legitimacy are founded on assuring the balanced participation (and representation) of all categories of stakeholders in a participatory and inclusive process resting on dialogue.

However, while participation of certain categories of actor – such as local communities and small-scale producers – is desired in principle, in practice they are incorporated in ways that delegitimize their arguments and interests. Referring to the specific cases of two Roundtables (those on 'sustainable palm oil' and 'responsible soy'), a detailed analysis is undertaken of how a 'strategic' regime of engagement is at play in the standard-setting process, rather than other possible engagement regimes, such as one based on the qualification of a common good, or one based on 'familiar' and personal attachments and relations. Cheyns examines the tensions relating to different forms of representation and participation. While speaking for a large number of voices and founded on the principle of inclusion, these initiatives find it difficult to define a common good (in terms of values and principles of justice) in a pluralistic way and thus resort to urgency, expediency and pragmatism in order to provide short-term solutions. They also experience difficulties in taking account of how those communities directly affected by unsustainable and irresponsible practices experience and articulate their losses, their attachments and their demands.

In Chapter 10, Stefano Ponte and Lone Riisgaard examine cooperation and competition dynamics in the market for sustainability standards. The point of departure in their analysis are two common understandings arising in the literature: that 'best practices' in the governance of standards and specific forms of governance (for example, the multistakeholder form) are becoming more common; and that competition is leading to a 'race to the bottom' in the field of standard content and to a differentiation between standard organizations that focus on market size and those that focus on high standard content. The literature argues that the two aspects are also mutually reinforcing, as conflicts that earlier might have concerned governance are now expressed in terms of standards content.

In their chapter, Ponte and Riisgaard raise a series of questions about this consensus. They question whether competition among different standards actually matters in determining standard content; whether the general proliferation of standards is leading towards a 'race to the bottom' in standard content; and whether there is a clear-cut differentiation between different kinds of standard setting bodies in terms of principles and the number of actors complying with the standard. They also ask the additional questions of whether 'best practice' pressure in standards governance is actually leading to improved practices and finally whether raising or lowering standard levels has a positive outcome for the inclusion of Southern suppliers. In order to reflect upon these points, they examine the development of standards in two sectors: wild capture fish (dominated by one sustainability initiative) and cut flowers, where a large number of parallel initiatives were started or implemented in a relatively short period of time, thus defining a context of high competition from the start and strong influence from best practice expectations.

In Chapter 11, Dan Klooster continues the examination of the role of weaker actors and local communities in standard setting and adaptation (and the possible exclusionary effects of standards) that permeated the previous two chapters. Klooster, however, provides a more optimistic note for the future of standards as a tool of social justice, showing that global standards can be used instrumentally at the local level. He argues that standards are often captured in the literature using a linear narrative in which Northern decisions about certification procedures determine Southern actions. In such a picture, certification serves the interests of big retailers in buyer-driven commodity chains and places significant barriers to entry on Southern producers. The case study examined in his chapter suggests that under some circumstances, certification can leverage qualitative changes in production patterns that are co-determined by local, strategic actors, and therefore have regionally and locally-specific outcomes.

Klooster examines the way strategic actors in community forest enterprises, government and NGOs used forest certification to develop wood furniture manufacturing capacity in Southern Mexico. While forest certification did not dramatically improve timber exports, and while community forest enterprises were unable to meet buyers' demand for large volumes, high quality and low prices, community forest advocates and promoters in government and NGOs facilitated other venues for using certification in beneficial ways. Indigenous forest-owning communities formed a consortium that manages forests, produces wood furniture, and markets it to the state public school system and to consumers in community-owned factory outlet stores. For producers in this network, forest certification improved forest management and signified the social and environmental benefits of forest management practices. In this case study, certification built credibility, facilitated inter-community cooperation, legitimated preferential government purchases, and helped educate and recruit individual consumers.

Chapter 12 provides a general conclusion. It sketches a collective picture on the origins and drivers of 'governing through standards', reflects on whether such governance may be reaching its limits, and suggests ideas for a future research agenda.

Notes

We would like to thank the participants of the international conference 'Governing through Standards' (Copenhagen, 24–26 February 2010) where first drafts of some of the chapters included in this collection were first presented. The conference was funded by the Danish Development Research Council (FFU) and the Danish Institute for International Studies. We would also like to thank Nynne Warring for her invaluable editorial assistance.

1   This is a merger and reformulation of definitions of standards by Henman and Dean (2010, p. 79) and Loconto and Busch (2010, p. 508) with the addition of evaluating regulatory practices themselves as constituting a 'standard' (Vestergaard, 2009).
2   Outside Europe it is perhaps most noticeable in Australia and New Zealand.
3   The member countries of the Basel committee are the nineteen member countries of the G20 plus a handful of additional European countries (Belgium, Luxembourg, the Netherlands, Spain, Sweden, Switzerland) and two countries that are financial hubs in Asia (Hong Kong and Singapore).

References

Bernstein, S. (2011) 'Legitimacy in intergovernmental and non-state global governance', *Review of International Political Economy*, 18(1), 17–51.
Bernstein, S. and Cashore, B. (2007) 'Can non-state global governance be legitimate? An analytical framework', *Regulation & Governance*, 1, 347–371.
Best, J. (2007) 'Legitimacy dilemmas: The IMF's pursuit of country ownership', *Third World Quarterly,* 28(3), 469–488.
Boström, M. and Tamm Hallström, K. (2010) 'The fragile authority of multi-stakeholder standards', presented at the conference *Governing through Standards*, Copenhagen 24–26 February.
Brassett, J. and Tsingou, E. (2011) 'The politics of legitimate global governance', *Review of International Political Economy*, 18(1): 1–16.
Brunsson, N. and Jacobsson, B. (2000) 'The contemporary expansion of standardization' in N. Brunsson, B. Jacobsson and associates (eds) *A World of Standards* (Oxford: Oxford University Press).
Brunsson, N., Jacobsson, B. and associates (eds) (2000) *A World of Standards* (Oxford: Oxford University Press).

Büthe, T. (2010) 'Private Regulation in the Global Economy: A (P)Review', *Business and Politics*, 12(3), Article 2.

Cadman, T. (2011) *Quality and Legitimacy of Global Governance: Case Lessons from Forestry* (Basingstoke and New York: Palgrave Macmillan).

Callon, M. (1986) 'Some elements of a sociology of translation: Domestication of the scallops and the fishermen of St Brieuc Bay' in J. Law (ed.) *Power, Action and Belief: A New Sociology of Knowledge?* (London: Routledge).

Cashore, B., Auld, G. and Newsom, D. (2004) *Governing through Markets: Forest certification and the emergence of non-state authority* (New Haven: Yale University Press).

Clapp, J. and Füchs, D. (eds) (2009) *Corporate Power in Global Agrifood Governance* (Cambridge, MA and London: MIT Press).

Cutler, A.C., Haufler, V. and Porter, T. (1999b) 'Private Authority and International Affairs' in A.C Cutler, V. Haufler and T. Porter (eds) *Private Authority and International Affairs* (Albany: State University of New York Press).

Cutler, A.C., Haufler, V. and Porter, T (eds) (1999a) *Private Authority and International Affairs* (Albany: State University of New York Press).

Dingwerth, K. and Pattberg, P. (2009) 'World politics and organizational fields: The case of transnational sustainability governance', *European Journal of International Relations*, 15(4), p. 707–743.

Ewald, F. (1990) 'Insurance and Risk', in G. Burchell, C. Gordon and P. Miller (eds) *The Foucault Effect: Studies in Governmentality* (London: Harvester).

Fransen, L.W. and Kolk, A. (2007) 'Global rule-setting for business: A critical analysis of multi-stakeholder standards', *Organization* 14(5), p. 667–684.

Fuchs, D. and Kalfagianni, A. (2010) 'The causes and consequences of private food governance', *Business and Politics*, 12(3), Article 5.

Gale, F. and Haward, M. (2011) *Global Commodity Governance: State Responses to Sustainable Forest and Fisheries Certification* (Basingstoke and New York: Palgrave Macmillan).

Gibbon, P. and Ponte, S. (2005) *Trading Down: Africa, Value Chains and the Global Economy* (Philadelphia: Temple University Press).

Gibbon, P. and Ponte, S. (2008) 'Global Value Chains: From Governance to Governmentality?', *Economy and Society*, 37(3), 365–392.

Gibbon, P., Bair, P. and Ponte, S. (2008) 'Governing Global Value Chains: An Introduction', *Economy and Society*, 37(3), 315–338.

Gibbon, P., Ponte, S. and Lazaro, E. (eds) (2010) *Global Agro-food Trade and Standards: Challenges for Africa* (Basingstoke and New York: Palgrave Macmillan).

Hall, R.B. and Biersteker, T.J. (2002b) 'The emergence of private authority in the international system' in R.B. Hall and T.J. Biersteker (eds) *The Emergence of Private Authority in Global Governance* (Cambridge: Cambridge University Press).

Hall, R.B. and Biersteker, T.J. (eds.) (2002a) *The Emergence of Private Authority in Global Governance* (Cambridge: Cambridge University Press).

Hatanaka, M., Bain, C. and Busch, L. (2005) 'Third-party certification in the global agrifood system', *Food Policy*, 30(3), 354–369.

Henman, P. and Dean, M. (2010) 'E-Government and the production of standardized individuality' in V. Higgins and W. Larner (eds) *Calculating the Social: Standards and the reconfiguration of governing* (Basingstoke and New York: Palgrave Macmillan).

Higgins, J. W. (2005) *Engine of Change: Standards Australia since 1922* (Blackheath: Brandl & Schlesinger).

Higgins, V. and Larner, W. (2010b) 'From standardization to standardizing work' in V. Higgins and W. Larner (eds) *Calculating the Social: Standards and the reconfiguration of governing* (Basingstoke and New York: Palgrave).

Higgins, V. and Larner, W. (eds.) (2010a) *Calculating the Social: Standards and the reconfiguration of governing* (Basingstoke and New York: Palgrave Macmillan).

Hüllse, R. and Kerwer, D. (2007) 'Global standards in action: Insights from anti-money laundering legislation', *Organization*, 14(6), 625–642.

Jacobsson, B. (2000) 'Standardization and expert knowledge' in N. Brunsson and B. Jacobsson and associates (eds) *A World of Standards* (Oxford: Oxford University Press).

Lampland, M. and Star, S.L. (eds) (2009) *Standards and Their Stories: How quantifying, classifying, and formalizing practices shape everyday life* (Ithaca and London: Cornell University Press).

Latour, B. (1987) *Science in Action: How to Follow Scientist and Engineers through Society* (Cambridge, MA: Harvard University Press).

Levy, D. and Newell, P.J. (eds) (2005) *The Business of Global Environmental Governance* (Cambridge, MA and London: MIT Press).

Loconto, A. and Busch, L. (2010) 'Standards, techno-economic networks, and playing fields: Performing the global market economy', *Economy and Society*, 17(3), 507–536.

Majone, G. (1996) *Regulating Europe* (London and New York: Routledge).

Marques, J.C. and P. Utting (eds.) (2010) *Business, Politics and Public Policy* (Basingstoke and New York: Palgrave Macmillan).

Mayer, F. and Gereffi, G. (2010) 'Regulation and economic globalization: Prospects and limits of private governance', *Business and Politics*, 12(3), Article 11.

Miller, P. and O'Leary, T. (1987) 'Accounting and the construction of the governable person', *Accounting, Organizations and Society*, 12, 235–265.

Murphy, C. and Yates, J. (2009) *ISO, the International Organisation for Standardisation: Global governance through voluntary consensus* (London and New York: Routledge).

O'Rourke, D. (2003) 'Outsourcing regulation: Analyzing nongovernmental systems of labour standards and monitoring', *Policy Studies Journal*, 31(1), 1–29.

Ougaard, M. and Leander, A. (eds.) (2010) *Business and Global Governance* (London and New York: Routledge).

Pattberg, P.H. (2007) *Private Institutions and Global Governance: The new politics of environmental sustainability* (Cheltenham: Edward Elgar).

Ponte, S. (2009) 'Governing through Quality: Conventions and Supply Relations in the Value Chain for South African Wine', *Sociologia Ruralis*, 39(3), 236–257.

Ponte, S. and Gibbon, P. (2005) 'Quality Standards, Conventions and the Governance of Global Value Chains', *Economy and Society* 34(1), 1–31.

Power, M. (2003) 'Evaluating the audit explosion', *Law and Policy*, 25(3), 185–202.

Rittberger, V. and Nettesheim, M. with Huckel, C. (eds) (2008) *Authority in the Global Political Economy* (Basingstoke and New York: Palgrave Macmillan).

Rosenau, J. (2003) *Distant Proximities: Dynamics beyond Globalization* (Princeton: Princeton University Press).

Seabrooke, L. (2007) 'Legitimacy gaps in the world economy: Explaining the sources of the IMF's legitimacy crisis', *International Politics*, 44(2): 250–268.

Sneyd, A. (2011) *Governing Cotton: Globalization and Poverty in Africa* (Basingstoke and New York: Palgrave Macmillan).

Swinnen, J.F.M. (2007) *Global Supply Chains, Standards and the Poor: How the Globalization of Food Systems and Standards Affect Rural Development and Poverty* (Wallingford and Cambridge, MA: CABI).

Tamm Hallström, K. (2004) *Organizing International Standardization: ISO and the IASC in quest of authority* (London: Edward Elgar).

Tamm Hallström, K. and Boström, M. (2010) *Transnational Multi-stakeholder Standardization: Organizing fragile non-state authority* (Cheltenham: Edward Elgar).

Tarullo, D.K. (2008) Banking on Basel: The Future of International Banking Regulation (Washington DC: Peterson Institute for International Economics).

Timmermans, S. and Berg, M. (1997) 'Standardization in action: Achieving local universality through medical protocols', *Social Studies of Science*, 27, 273–305.

Timmermans, S. and Epstein, S. (2010) 'A World of Standards but not a Standard World: Toward a Sociology of Standards and Standardization', *Annual Review of Sociology*, 36, 69–89.

Utting, P. (2008) 'Rearticulating regulatory approaches: Private-public authority and corporate social responsibility' in V. Rittberger and M. Nettesheim (2008) *Authority in the Global Political Economy* (Basingstoke and New York: Palgrave Macmillan).

Utting, P. and Marques, J.C. (eds) (2009) *Corporate Social Responsibility and Regulatory Governance: Towards Inclusive Development?* (Basingstoke and New York: Palgrave Macmillan).

Vestergaard, J. (2009) *Discipline in the Global Economy? International finance and the end of liberalism* (London and New York: Routledge).

Vestergaard, J. (2011a) 'The G20 and beyond: Towards effective global economic governance', *DIIS Report* 2011: 04 (Copenhagen: Danish Institute for International Studies).

Vestergaard, J. (2011b) 'The World Bank and the emerging world order: Adjusting to multipolarity at the second decimal point', *DIIS Report* 2011: 05 (Copenhagen: Danish Institute for International Studies).

2
The Rise of Banking Standards and Their Limits

Kevin L. Young

Introduction

The development and deployment of industry-wide standards has been a critical component of governing finance over the last 20 years. Standards are perhaps nowhere so widespread and yet so contradictory as in the domain of banking. Policy debates surrounding the proper conduct of banking regulation, at either the global or national level, focus on reforming existing standards. Meanwhile, organized banking lobbyists have increasingly focused their attention on responding to, and attempting to shape, such standards. The relationship between the particular content of international standards and objectives of efficiency and equity in financial regulation is often employed as part of policy and governance critiques of the existing system of financial governance (Wade, 2009; Blackburn, 2008; Financial Services Authority, 2009; Walter, 2010 The ground less well traversed is how the use of international standards became so extensive and so fundamentally integrated into banking as such.

In this chapter, I examine governance through standards by focusing on both the rise of the use of standards as a governance practice and the limitations of this practice in the area of banking regulation. I divide my analysis into three sections. In section one, I outline the history of the use of international regulatory standards in banking. I focus on three of the most seminal developments in international banking standards: the Basel Capital Accord of 1988, the Basel Core Principles of 1997, and the Basel II Capital Accord of 2004. The trend across these developments highlights the growing extensiveness and detail standard-setting agendas.

In the second section, I argue that the rise of standards in banking has contributed to a number of interrelated but contradictory dynamics at play within the industry and its governance. On the one hand, governing through standards has enabled regulators to mitigate competitive deregulation at the international level. On the other hand, however, standards have facilitated the construction of liberal regulatory regimes, and have in some ways acted as a functional substitute for more pro-active regulation by public authorities. Finally, in section three I illustrate a number of ways in which the use of standards in banking has been limited, using examples from recent national policy-making, as well as the negotiation of international banking standards. I point out the unevenness not only in implementation but also the variegated way in which international standards are adapted to suit local circumstances.

The rise of standards in banking

The governance of banking through international standards cannot be understood outside the institutional context in which such standards are developed. Put simply, every major banking standard has been generated by one institution: the Basel Committee on Banking Supervision (BCBS). As an informal group within the Bank for International Settlements in Basel, Switzerland, the BCBS was formed in 1974 in response to the re-emergence of global finance, a phenomenon which was causing policy dilemmas that could not be addressed at the national level alone.[1] For most of its history, the Basel Committee has been composed of financial regulators and central bankers from what is known as the 'G10', a club of countries which actually includes 13 states: Belgium, Canada, France, Germany, Italy, Japan, Luxembourg, the Netherlands, Spain, Sweden, Switzerland, the United Kingdom and the United States. After recent calls by the G20 to 'review' the memberships of the international standard-setting bodies, in March 2009 regulators and central bankers from seven additional states were added: Australia, Brazil, China, India, Mexico, Russia and South Korea. In June 2009, a second expansion took place in which regulators from the remainder of the G20 member states were added, along with Hong Kong and Singapore.

The BCBS is consistently identified as the archetypal example of a transnationally organized technical institution setting the pace of financial regulation, and is considered central to the system of global financial governance.[2] As Alexander, Dhumale and Eatwell have noted, '[t]he Basel Committee has become the most influential international financial standard-setting body' in the world today (Alexander *et al.*, 2006, p. 54; Porter, 2005, pp. 57–65; Davies and Green, 2008, pp. 32–47). The governance of the BCBS has been a particular point of fascination for social scientists for some time due to its peculiar structure. The particular institutional design of the BCBS has meant that its decisions are several steps removed from sovereign authority. The participants within the BCBS are not elected representatives, and in most cases they have not even been formally delegated to take decisions within the BCBS on behalf of governments. Rather, participants are senior bureaucrats within regulatory agencies and central banks. Although such institutions are a part of the formal state apparatus, they are, by design, highly independent from elected legislatures and executives.[3] Additionally, the decisions of the BCBS itself are not subject to approval by any national government or external authority.[4] As Underhill and Zhang have correctly asserted, the BCBS is characterized 'by virtual separation from any accountable political process'. (Underhill and Zhang, 2006, p. 29). Most decisions are made on the basis of technical discussion in a manner commensurate with 'deliberation', meaning that most engagement is informal in character, and the *de facto* decision-rule is implicit consensus.[5]

The output of the BCBS has far-reaching consequences in terms of how financial regulation is conducted all over the world. In addition to establishing regulatory standards for the G10, and because of strong incentives for states to emulate BCBS standards, it exercises global influence.[6] International capital markets use Basel-based standards to evaluate the financial soundness of banks, and international institutions, such as the IMF, have also used BCBS standards as a crucial metric (Alexander *et al.*, 2006). National regulatory agencies outside the G10 attempt to make their banking systems Basel-compliant to signal the good health of their financial systems to international markets (Alexander *et al.*, 2006; Brownbridge and Kirkpatrick, 1999). For these reasons, and because of the peculiarities of the BCBS' governance structure discussed above, the output of the BCBS has been regarded as a prime example of 'soft law', as its standards are enforced, but not through legal, sovereign authority (Panourgias, 2006; Delonis, 2004; Abbott and Snidal, 2008). Additionally, Basel standards have a profound effect on the internal operations of banks around the world. They affect the daily practices of risk management, and are integrated into the culture of firms. The output of the BCBS thus indirectly constitutes, as one US banker put it, 'the lingua franca of capital'.[7]

The BCBS has developed four major regulatory standards, each of which constituted the high water mark in banking standards for their time: the Basel Concordat of 1975 (revised in 1983), the Basel Capital Accord of 1988, the Basel Core Principles of 1997, and the Basel II Accord of 2004. A brief review of the development and content of each of these international standards demonstrates that the trend across time is toward an ever greater extent and detail of standard setting within the banking industry.

The 1988 Basel Capital Accord

In 1987 and 1988, the BCBS formulated and produced what would become the most famous regulatory standard in the history of banking: the Basel Capital Accord. Domestic pressures within the US political economy led to a strong preference among the US Federal regulatory agencies (and the US Congress) to address the declining state of capital adequacy not through new domestic regulation, or through a new national regulatory standard for US banks, but rather through a new multilateral initiative. Joined by the UK in this endeavour (which was itself pressured by its domestic banking institutions (Oatley and Nabors, 1998)), the US members of the BCBS proposed to generate a radical new standard with which to regulate banks. The 'Cooke ratio' (named after the Chairman of the BCBS at the time, Peter Cooke of the Bank of England) specified that banks had to have a 'capital to assets ratio' of 8 per cent. Substantively, this meant that for every dollar a bank lent out, it had to maintain a minimum of eight cents of regulatory capital in case of unexpected losses. This meant that banks could not operate with third party funds alone, but rather had to rely in part on their own capital, to a minimal degree. Such a standard constituted a real constraint on *de facto* banking practices at the time, since it involved reallocations of capital within banks, and thus changed internal practices (De Carmoy, 1990).

The details of this new international regulatory standard were not very controversial and cooperative agreement at the technical level was not difficult, especially with two major economies like the US and the UK taking the initiative. There was, however, a major obstacle to international agreement: Japan. Japanese Banks had secured an extremely dominant place in markets in Manhattan and London; moreover, eight out of the top ten largest banks in the world were Japanese, and Japanese banks were extremely profitable during the period of Japan's great financial bubble). This contemporary reality was not unknown to the US and UK regulators, and some have interpreted the Accord as partly motivated by these competitiveness concerns (Kapstein, 1992;

Genschel and Plümper, 1997). When the US and UK failed to convince Japan that they should agree to the Accord, regulators from the US and UK declared a bilateral pact in which capital adequacy standards were specified. This move put Japan in an intolerable position, since such a standard effectively excluded their banks; thus Japan was effectively forced to concede to agreeing the Basel Accord.

While the Basel Capital Accord was not intended to be a 'global' standard, but rather an agreement among the G10, it soon became the *de facto* global standard in banking regulation. As such the Basel Accord of 1988 has been widely heralded within the IPE literature as the strongest example of cooperative agreement within the world of financial diplomacy (see, for example, Singer, 2007; Simmons, 2001; Kapstein, 1992). As Kerwer notes, '[w]hen compared to other ventures in international rule making, the BCBS's capital-adequacy standard is often considered one of the biggest success stories of global regulation'. (Kerwer, 2006, p. 620). This success is evinced not only in the reversal of the decline of capital adequacy standards at the time, but also in the widespread adoption of the standard. By 1998, over 120 countries had adopted this international regulatory standard (Alexander *et al.*, 2006; Genschell and Plümper, 1997). Furthermore, the Basel Capital Accord was integrated into the metrics of how bank safety and soundness were assessed by market actors and industry periodicals.[8]

With a considerable success in standard generation in hand, but international financial stability clearly not secured, the BCBS expanded the depth and breadth of their activities as the international standard setters in banking. By the end of the 1990s, new concerns had arisen which prompted the generation of new international regulatory standards, exemplified in the Basel Core Principles, and the Basel II Capital Accord, a wholesale revision of the original Basel Capital Accord.

The Basel Core Principles

After the G7 Summit in Lyon in June 1996 called for more attention to improving and strengthening the financial system, the BCBS sought to replicate its successful model of standard generation, this time in a more principles-based way (BCBS 1997).[9] This led to the release of the second of the BCBS's major standards, the Basel Core Principles. The Basel Core Principles included 25 different standards for the effective supervision of banking activities. The bulk of the Principles involved a number of technical and institutional standards, such as principles of how to assess bank ownership, the management structure of banks, and different kinds of risk in the banking sector. The bedrock metric for assessing the latter is, perhaps not surprisingly, the Basel Capital Accord (BCBS 1997). However, the Basel Core Principles are unique in that they argue not only for compliance with technical and risk-based standards, but also sought to emphasize the importance of the institutional precon-ditions for 'sound' regulation of the banking sector. For example, they state that effective banking supervision requires operational independ-ence of regulators, a clear set of responsibilities and objectives, and legal protection for supervisors (BCBS, 1997). In addition, they also ascribe resource requirements, such as sufficient financial resources for bank-ing regulation and the power to enforce compliance (*ibid*, pp. 38–39). What is fascinating is that the BCBS even acknowledged that these institutional reforms might, in some cases, require 'substantive changes in the legislative framework and in the powers of supervisors' in order to implement the Core Principles (*ibid*, p. 3).

As Walter has argued, the BCBS drew heavily upon the institutional designs and practices in countries like the US and the UK, which pro-vided the key regulatory benchmarks of transparency and regulatory independence (Walter, 2008, p. 22) . However, the actual process of generating the Core Principles involved a sea change in the standard-generating process. While the formation of the Basel Capital Accord (and its revision, Basel II, described below) did not involve participa-tion of regulators outside the G10, the generation of the Core Principles did. As Porter and Wood have pointed out, by the late 1990s the BCBS had already institutionalized more vigorous engagement with countries outside its membership, such as through the regionalized groupings of financial supervisory authorities and its biannual conferences of super-visors from all over the world (Porter and Wood 2002). The drafting of the Core Principles for Effective Banking Supervision involved a for-mal process of consultation which included 15 LDCs in the drafting group and the establishment of a Liaison Group with representatives from 20 countries in addition to a Consultation Group of outsiders as well. Gaining the participation of these Regional Supervisory Groups not only encouraged local banking supervisory communities to pro-vide their consent, but also facilitated implementation, which the BCBS interpreted as urgent (BCBS, 1997).

Whereas the Basel Capital Accord was intended to be an international standard for the G10, which then became a *de facto* global standard, the Core Principles had global ambitions from the beginning. This can be seen as part of the motivation for the extension of participa-tion to agencies and institutions outside the BCBS for the first time.

The Core Principles were designed explicitly to be general and verifiable by national supervisors, regional supervisory groups and international financial markets (BCBS, 1997). In addition, the BCBS actively encouraged the IMF and the World Bank to use the Core Principles as part of their activities. These institutions did so enthusiastically, especially following the new governmental strategies pursued following the East Asian crisis of 1997–98, as part of larger efforts to constitute 'proper economies' (Vestergaard, 2004). The IMF and World Bank began including the Core Principles in its Article IV consultations through the emerging system of financial sector surveillance at the time, as part of Financial Sector Assessment Programs (FSAPs). The Core Principles also became part of the IMF's Reports on the Observance of Standards and Codes (ROSCs). Thus in the Basel Core Principles we can observe the greater extensiveness and detail at the core of the standards promoted by the BCBS. These noticeable shifts from the 1988 Capital Accord are striking; however, they pale in comparison to the Basel II Capital Accord, the next major standard developed by the BCBS.

The Basel II Accord of 2004

Despite the BCBS' attempts to expand the use and efficacy of international standards in banking, by the late 1990s, it was clear that they were themselves failing to heed the standards they had set for themselves. Several BCBS members were allowing their banks to count financial instruments as 'Tier 1' capital, a practice that was questionable by their own international standards.[10] While these issues were addressed by a new agreement (and détente on the definition of capital),[11] they raised the spectre of further problems concerning slippages in the standards that regulators were willing to agree with one another. In the context of the contemporaneous East Asian and Russian financial crises, such slippage was not seen as a positive development.[12]

To compound these concerns, members of the BCBS were becoming increasingly aware of banks' active subversion of the Basel Capital Accord – that is, regulatory capital arbitrage. A BCBS working group commissioned at the time concluded that 'over time the banks have learnt how to exploit the broad brush nature of the [1988 Basel Accord] requirements' (Jackson, 1999, p. 26). The most substantial concern in this respect was the growth of securitization – the bundling together of assets and packaging them as large, alienable securities in the open market. The challenge of regulating securitization was a common one throughout the G10 and beyond, and was particularly marked in the

US, where such markets were most developed (Costello, 1998; Jackson, 1999, p. 26). Because the 1988 Basel Accord did not differentiate much in its treatment of loans, large banks had begun to securitize their highest quality credit while leaving the lower quality loans on their balance sheet. In other words, banks were proportionately hoarding riskier assets – and the use of new financial innovations such as 'special purpose vehicles' allowed banks to do so (Harris, 1998). As one commentator in the *Financial Times* put it in 1998, 'Banking regulators and supervisors can be forgiven for regarding private banking as being devised by a malevolent spirit to torment them' (Prest, 1997).

It was decided within the BCBS that the Capital Accord needed to be revised to deal with these challenges, in an effort to strengthen international banking standards. While the entire BCBS agreed that there needed to be a dramatic overhaul of the Accord, there was a spectrum of views regarding exactly how this should be done. A consensus, however, agreed that the new Accord should better weight the riskiness of bank practices to the level of capital adequacy required, thus maintaining the original spirit of the original Accord but making regulatory capital adequacy more 'risk sensitive'. Some BCBS participants were particularly enthusiastic in regard to utilizing the advances in quantitative risk management from within the banking industry itself in order to generate the new regulatory standard.[13] International financial sector advocacy associations such as the Institute of International Finance and the International Swaps and Derivatives Association promoted the idea that banks should be able to utilize *their own* internal models to generate their own risk sensitive levels of capital adequacy.

Ultimately, however, a series of intense deliberations and research conducted by the BCBS beginning in 1998 decided that such a move would be neither prudent nor wise; thus, a middle path was decided, in which banks with advanced risk management techniques would be able to estimate their own risk parameters, but the models in which capital adequacy would be calculated would be determined by the BCBS itself. Over the course of the next five years, the new Basel Capital Accord, 'Basel II' as it was known, evolved from a preliminary set of ideas about how to make banking regulation more risk sensitive into an extremely detailed 239 page document. Beginning in 1999, the BCBS posted drafts of the Accord on its website, and solicited detailed comment through a 'consultative process.' Basel II set out to develop detailed regulatory minimum standards concerning how banks were to assign regulatory capital. It developed such standards by attempting to ensure that regulatory capital allocation was 'risk sensitive.' Rather than specifying a simple set of risk categories that modulated the amount of regulatory capital that banks had to hold, as the original Accord did, Basel II attempted to evaluate, on a microeconomic basis, the specific level of risk associated with particular internal processes of banks.

Basel II is seen as a central example of either everything that is wrong with the current structure of global financial regulation, or everything that is right about it. Regardless, Eatwell's recent remark that '[t]he analytical foundations of regulation over the past three decades are clearly defined in the structure of Basel II' seems appropriate (Eatwell, 2009, p. 37). It is also illustrative of the fact that standards within a single industry are quite strongly defined by one single system of governance. Basel II represents the most extensive and detailed approach to banking standards yet produced. Like the Basel Core Principles, it was intended from the outset to be utilized as the *de facto* global regulatory standard. Such a goal was, in many respects, achieved: one month following the finalization of Basel II in 2004, surveys suggested that 88 non-BCBS countries had indicated they intended on implementing Basel II (BIS Financial Stability Institute, 2004).

The consequences of governing by standards

Now that some of the tendencies in international banking standards development have been elaborated, it remains to be established what the rise of international standards in banking actually *means*, substantively. While we have seen that the extent and detail of the standards have increased over time, what more can be said of the rise of standards as a governance practice? In this section I argue that the rise of standards in banking has facilitated a number of interrelated but contradictory dynamics within the banking industry. Through the promotion of governance by standards, banking regulators have been able to mitigate some of the effects of 'competitive deregulation' at the international level. However, standardization has facilitated the construction of liberal regulatory regimes, and has acted as a functional substitute for more pro-active regulatory governance by public authorities.

The rise of international standards in banking has discouraged competitive deregulation in a number of ways. Since the creation of the 1988 Basel Capital Accord, international banking standards have facilitated the generation of minimal standards of practice that are, in most instances, observed. In this way, governance by standards can be seen as a cooperative solution to a global prisoner's dilemma game faced by banking regulators. In an environment of ever-increasing financial competition, national financial regulatory authorities are locked into a prisoner's dilemma: The rational strategy of each individual national regulator is to loosen regulatory standards in order to facilitate a more competitive environment for its nationally-embedded financial sector. Given the reality of global financial interdependence, pursuing such individual strategies means that each national regulator is faced with the possibility of also dealing with the effects of a riskier international financial environment, which could potentially lead to adverse consequences for them as a well-given financial contagion. The incentives to pursue a collective solution to the problem of financial contagion given economic interdependence are thus substantial. Multilateral agreement on minimal standards, such as Basel I and II, and the Basel Core Principles, can thus be seen as the institutionalization of a cooperative 'way out' of such a dilemma.

As we have seen above in each of these standards, the motivation has been to *increase* the floor of regulatory standards – that is, to decrease the race to the bottom, rather than to accelerate it. Basel I sought to address declining capital adequacy standards; the Basel Core Principle set to establish broad institutional parameters for comprehensive banking supervision; and Basel II prescribed detailed regulatory requirements for the assessment of risk in the assignment of regulatory capital. It is hardly surprising then that many scholars have identified the rise of governance by standards in banking (in particular the seminal first monumental step of the 1988 Basel Capital Accord) as an example of how regulatory cooperation countervails some of the adverse consequences of financial globalization. In this regard, Macey has used the BCBS as an example of 'regulatory cartelization', whereby regulators collude to generate standards and codes that increase their domestic bargaining power relative to their domestic constituents (Macey, 2003). Following both Simmons and Genschel and Plümper, Vogel and Kagan have noted that the BCBS's output as an example of increasing regulatory standards, specifically as an example of the 'California Effect' of a race-to-the-top (Genschel and Plümper, 1997; Simmons, 2001; Vogel and Kagan, 2004). Coming from a completely different paradigm, Rude observes the neoliberal character of some of the BCBS's most recent output, but argues nevertheless that it is indeed an example of increased regulatory standards (Rude, 2008).

As each of these assessments suggests, there is some truth to the narrative which represents international standards in banking as forces discouraging regulatory competition. It might be said that such a representation of the rise of standards in banking is 'most true' when considering the basic *form* of international banking standards. Each of the standards reviewed above was, after all, a regulatory floor which constrained the behaviour of banks, not ceilings. However, when we examine in more detail the actual *content* of international standards in banking, a more complex story emerges.

The rise of standards in banking has facilitated the construction of liberal regulatory regimes. Such a trend can be seen in the actual content of the most recent international standards discussed above, the Basel Core Principles and the Basel II Accord. The Basel Core Principles facilitate liberal regulatory regimes through the minimalist nature of standards. In this regard it might be said that the rise of standards in banking has facilitated the transition from a 'developmental' state approach to regulation based on active intervention, to one characterized by a neoliberal 'regulatory state' in which regulatory action conforms to basic frameworks of action, themselves dictated by global standards (Jayasuriya, 2005; Majone, 1994). In other words, the rise in banking standards, and indeed many international financial standards in general, has been characterized by a transition to a more arms-length, liberal approach where regulatory discretion is in some ways both constrained and enabled by international governance standards. Walter has demonstrated the empirical case for this transition through case studies in East Asia (Walter, 2008). This can also be seen in the actual content of the Basel II Accord, although recent changes in supervisory practices following the global financial crisis may have countervailed such trends.

Moreover, the actual application of the Basel Core Principles illustrates how the use of this international standard has operated within most countries. Some evidence suggests that the actual implementation of the Core Principles has used the standard as a means of achieving external credibility with international financial markets and with the international financial institutions like the World Bank and IMF, with the more institutionalist reforms neglected in relative terms. Through an extensive review of the actual application of the Core Principals throughout the developing world, the World Bank and IMF suggested that of all the Core Principals that have been applied, the preconditions were not addressed adequately (Calari and Ingves, 2002, pp. 4–5). A recent IMF-based empirical study suggests that compliance with the Basel Core Principles has no measurable effect on the riskiness of banks, either at the individual or systemic level (Demirgüç-Kunt and Detragiache, 2010).

Basel II's highly complex and detailed content is less general, but has promoted liberal regulatory regimes much more explicitly. Basel II is actually composed of three different 'Pillars'. In the first of these, Pillar I: Regulatory Capital Requirements, incredible mathematical detail is brought to bear on how risk should be calculated, and which models can be employed to assess a whole panoply of risks facing banks. In this Pillar of the Accord, considerable autonomy is given to banks' own internal practices. Banks with sophisticated risk management systems can use their own estimates of risk parameters (such as the probability of default of a loan) to compute the allocation of their regulatory capital. The way that many risk parameters within Basel II's complex regulatory models also reflect confidence in liberal market practices. In many of the simpler approaches to risk measurement, risk estimates are based on the evaluation of external rating agencies, rather than the discretion of regulators. Indeed, even in the more advanced approaches to risk measurement within Basel II which do not rely on external, but rather *internal* (that is, bank-generated) ratings of risk exposures and losses, the gradations of risk are themselves based on practices and standards of external rating agencies. The second pillar, 'Supervisory Review' places emphasis on the standards by which regulators can intervene in banking practices – in effect establishing parameters for intervention and regulatory discretion. Basel II's third 'Pillar' is market discipline, and constitutes a series of minimal standards for the disclosure of information, transparency, and the like, which are believed to help condition bank safety and soundness by means of external market-based evaluation.

In addition to reflecting great confidence in 'market-based' practices and neoliberal beliefs about risk (self-)management, the shift to Basel II represents a noticeable transfer of autonomy from regulators to banks in many ways commensurate with the objectives of the liberal regulatory state. The complexity of practices of many large banking organizations is considerable, and as such Basel II provides a way for the actual labour of regulation to be shared between regulators and banks. The market itself produces many of the parameter inputs that go into risk modelling. In this way, Basel II can be seen as an example of governance through standards in which they act as a functional substitute to more pro-active regulatory governance by public authorities. Standards in banking did not always have this flavour, however. The original Basel Accord was limited in the extent to which a necessarily liberal regulatory regime was being promoted. Its basic content meant that as long as the Cooke ratio was observed, a bank was in compliance with the Accord. Such a shift is perhaps exemplary of the (neo)liberalization of international banking regulation, and associated trends described in subsequent chapters of this book (see Chapter 3 by Vestergaard and Høyland, and Chapter 4 by Lall).

Limitations of governance by standards: exceptions and variegated implementation

While the rise of international standards has been extensive, and in some ways reflects a turn to liberal modality of governance, there are also distinct limitations of the trend of governance by standards. The rise of international standards in banking has been distinctly limited in two respects. Firstly, as governance by standards has become more intense over time, numerous exceptions and 'carve-outs' have been made in order to accommodate national institutional particularity. The second limitation concerns the considerable heterogeneity in implementation.

Standards and exemptionalism

Processes of standardization necessarily involve a movement from diversity to homogeneity in some way. In the case of international banking standards, this definition implies that there is a single set of processes or behaviours that must be conformed to. Yet in some respects this is not what has always come to pass, and what we can observe is a proliferation of exceptions made in order to accommodate specific and particularistic demands – what might be called 'exemptionalism'. Exemptionalism has been a prominent feature of the Basel II Accord, and exists on several different levels of the Accord itself. At the most basic level, Basel II provides a 'menu' of choices that banks and their national regulators can potentially pursue. There are choices in terms of which general approach to risk regulation a bank will employ. Banks can chose from a simple Standardized approach to credit risk regulation, an Advanced 'Internal Ratings-Based' approach, or a more intermediate Foundation approach. The number of options does not stop there, however. Banks can opt for different regulatory models based on their own discretion (or, in some cases, the discretion of their national regulators). For example, there are different ways of calculating a bank's risk exposure to securitization instruments, whereby Basel II provides two different overarching technical methodologies for such calculations to be made.

Exemptionalism within the Basel II Accord often emerged because of international negotiation dynamics, whereby BCBS members successfully bargained for a 'carve out', or in some instances a separate regulatory policy altogether, on behalf of their own particular national objectives and constituents. Consider the following example of a 'carve-out', the practice of putting aside special exemptions for a single country in a 'global' standard. At the very early stages of Basel II's development, in the spring of 1999, a row erupted within the Committee over the treatment of commercial real estate. While the majority of the BCBS saw banks' commercial real estate exposures as carrying a great deal of risk, justifying an increase in capital requirements for this part of bank activity, the German members of the BCBS flatly disagreed.[14] The Germans considered their banks' commercial real estate exposures to be very low risk because of special properties in the national loan underwriting standards, low historic rates of default, and sophisticated secondary markets for commercial real estate debt. After protracted conflict, delay, and the involvement of German national banking associations and the German Bundestag, the German delegation managed to acquire a special exception: a highly significant but generally elusive footnote in the Accord (BCBS 2001a, p. 11; BCBS 2003, p. 20; BCBS 2004, p. 20). Banks would be permitted to weight the risk associated with commercial real estate exposures by *half* the standardized level if their national banking regulators could demonstrate that certain criteria existed in the national banking system – criteria which, incidentally, are specific to the German banking system.

Another example of exemptions made in the Accord's development took the form of a separate regulatory policy to accommodate differences in national institutions. In the middle stage of Basel II's development, in 2001 and 2002, a series of difficulties arose in the construction of a standard treatment of banks' equity exposures, assets which banks hold which are essentially stakes in ownership in other firms, such as stock holdings. BCBS members broadly agreed that banks' equity exposures were particularly risky, and had to be addressed in a systematic fashion. Equity holdings were an increasingly important part of many banks portfolios, not only in Europe and Japan, but also increasingly in the United States.[15] Despite these efforts, they could not agree on just how equity should be regulated. US regulators argued for a relatively stringent approach based on existing practices in risk management. Japanese and German regulators, on the other hand, argued for a simpler approach which was less stringent in its capital requirements, citing both the size and importance of equity holdings within their banks. Japan had a particularly strong concern in this regard since Japanese banks' equity holdings were considered to be very high risk, and recent volatility in the Tokyo stock market suggested further risks in the future. Before the release of the January 2001 draft of the new Accord, it was decided that the BCBS would include *both* options, since international agreement could not be reached. What is remarkable is not only the differences in regulatory stringency in these two different approaches, but the fact that they constitute wholly different methodologies for the calculation of risk (Suarez *et al.*, 2006).

When domestic banking lobbies in Germany and Japan then became mobilized and involved their national parliaments, further changes soon followed. By October 2002, a number of changes were made to the equity regulations reflecting these pressures.[16] Loopholes were added, such as the fact that if equity investments were 'part of a long-term customer relationship' (of at least five years) and some other criteria such as the institution having 'general banking relationships with the portfolio company', the equity holding would be weighted two to three times lower than normal (BCBS, 2002). This reduced regulatory capital requirements for both German and Japanese banks, because banks in both of these countries have traditionally had such long-term relationships at the core of their equity strategies (Lütz, 2001). Equity holdings could receive a 0 per cent risk weight if the debt obligations were considered low risk, if the national regulator decided to allow this across the entire country (BCBS, 2002). Supervisors could *exempt* the equity investments of banks altogether, up to a maximum of ten years (BCBS, 2002; BCBS, 2004). These changes not only gave considerable national discretion to German and Japanese regulators, but this exemptionalism was itself shaped and tailored for these countries preferences. In the tension between standardization and exemptionalism, the latter clearly won.

Variegated implementation

Another way in which governance by standards in banking has been limited is with respect to implementation – the other side of 'exemptionalism', in which states have even greater discretionary power. Most of the political economy literature on international banking standards assumes, or actively argues, that states are systemically compelled to implement such standards. Alexander et al. for example have argued that national regulators employ Basel standards 'in order to prevent foreign capital flows from shifting out of their countries' to 'strengthen the soundness of their commercial banks' and to 'raise their credit ratings in international financial markets' (Alexander *et al.*, 2006, pp. 42, 229; Barth *et al.*, 2006, p. 71). Soederberg has argued that developing countries' compliance with the IMF and World Banks' Reports on the Observance of Standards and Codes (ROSCs), a substantial part of which includes banking standards, has an element of compulsion to it, since non-compliance would send adverse market signals to the international financial community.[17] While the incentives and international pressures to adhere to international banking standards may indeed be considerable in many contexts, such tendencies should not suggest a universal trend. National banking regulators have been shown to exercise considerable degrees of discretion, in turn raising questions about how far standards can reach, and how 'global' governance by standards actually is.

Numerous studies have illustrated that the national implementation of international banking standards has been limited. As Chey has convincingly demonstrated, in East Asia the first Basel Accord (of 1988) was only implemented in a 'cosmetic', rather than a substantive fashion. Imperfect monitoring meant that considerable autonomy was granted to domestic regulators (and their banks) to signal compliance, but not to conform to the international standard in substantive terms (Chey, 2006). More recently Walter's analysis of a variety of financial standards' implementation in East Asia suggests a strikingly similar conclusion. His empirical study of 'mock compliance' suggests that meaningful implementation of international banking standards is conditional on particular configurations within domestic politics. While 'outright non-compliance' can have negative economic consequences, especially for developing countries, 'mock compliance' does not necessarily entail such costs (Walter, 2008).

Existing practices have also shown that some countries can indeed 'opt out' of implementing standards, so long as they signal this when the standard is still being developed. In the summer of 2003, for example, both the People's Bank of China and the Reserve Bank of India publically criticized the Accord's appropriateness for their own economies. India indicated that it would not implement all of the Accord, and China stated publically that it would adapt the Accord on some of its own domestic principles (McGregor and Pretzlik, 2003; Minkang, 2003). Another way in which implementation of international standards in banking has been limited is in respect to *adaptation* of the international standard. The EU translated the 1988 Basel Capital Accord more or less directly into their Capital Requirements Directive (CRD), effectively making a global regulatory law – since the CDR is legally binding for all EU member states. Basel II was also translated into European law, but there were changes made in the translation. The US implementation of Basel II reflects adaptation most acutely. In February 2003 (notably under Congressional scrutiny at the time), US financial regulators publically announced that only a small number of very large 'core' banks have to implement Basel II – a number which was initially posited at 12, and then to 20. It was decided that they would apply only the most advanced approaches within the Accord, and could not select from the different 'menu' of approaches mentioned above. This stands in strong contrast to the European Economic Area, where every bank must be Basel II compliant, and banks can choose which approach they employ.

Conclusion: governance through standards in banking

This chapter has examined governance by standards by focusing on the rise, development and deployment of international regulatory standards in banking. I first outlined the history of the use of international regulatory standards in banking, focusing on three seminal developments in international banking standards: the Basel Capital Accord of 1988, the Basel Core Principles of 1997 and the Basel II Capital Accord of 2004. These developments suggest a growing extensity and detail of standard-setting agendas over time. I then argued that the rise of standards in banking has contributed to a number of interrelated but contradictory dynamics within the banking industry and its governance. While governance by standards has helped to mitigate competitive deregulation among states, it has also facilitated the construction of liberal regulatory regimes. The rise of international standards has also been characterized by an important tension between standardization and what I have called exemptionalism.

Despite the extensity of governance by standards in banking, there have been a number of limitations in the way in which standardization has actually operated over the period examined. In particular, I described the unevenness not only in the implementation of standards, but also in the adaptation of international regulatory standards to local circumstances. As governance by standards has become more intense over time, numerous exceptions and 'carve-outs' have been made to accommodate the particularity of national institutions. Interest groups of various kinds and national institutions have influenced international standards on many occasions. However, international standards in banking are implemented rather unevenly across the world.

The consequences of this tension between standardization and exemptionalism are best reflected in the political responses to banking regulatory standards, both past and present. During the formation of the Basel II Accord, there were numerous demands by outsiders to change and adapt the Accord in order to accommodate different stages of economic development and levels of technological sophistication. The Basel Committee itself was forced to manage these demands; as we have seen, if such demands were made from within the Committee's membership, then they were sometimes met with the desired response. Yet for many constituents of the global community that did not have any means of representation in the Basel Committee, calls for exemptionalism were not heeded. Financial regulatory agencies within developing countries exerted a very cautious voice regarding the implementation costs of Basel II. Many countries' regulators complained of their lack of internal resources to implement an international standard that, while not necessarily very technically demanding from the perspective of G10 countries, would represent significant costs for them.[18] Some developing country regulators even argued that such asymmetries would unevenly distort the competitive playing field in banking (Bank of Thailand, 2001, p. 6; Bank of Mauritius, 2001, p. 2). Other developing country regulators (especially in Latin America) argued that Basel II should allow for 'partial use' of the internal ratings-based approaches to credit risk, thereby allowing their banks to select the advanced parts of the Accord that they could use while still employing the simpler 'Standardized Approach' parts of the Accord for most purposes (Banco de Mexico, 2001, p. 2; Joint Submission, 2001, p. 1). New ideas were also offered by 'outsiders' at the time. For example, regulators from both India and China implored the BCBS to build a scaled down approach of Basel II for developing countries (People's Bank of China, 2001, p. 2; Reserve Bank of India 2001, p. 7). None of these proposals was heeded at the time. This is hardly surprising, given the fact that none of these country's regulators had formal representation on the Basel Committee. It also underscores that even forms of exemptionalism that would have increased implementation rates were not heeded given the lack of political weight behind them.

The defence of exemptionalism is of course the need for flexibility given the possible costs of 'shoehorning' to fit one completely homogenous and rigid approach. There may be excellent reasons for flexibility in this regard, especially if the core principles of an international standard are themselves problematic. But what does it mean when the 'insiders' are able to realize their special demands while 'outsiders' are not? As the Basel Committee has recently completed a 'Basel III' Accord to address perceived shortcomings in the existing standards, this question has been particularly pressing. Following the G20's calls for expanded membership in international standard-setting bodies in

November 2008, the Basel Committee was expanded to include regulators and central bank authorities from developing countries for the first time. In March 2009, representatives from Australia, Brazil, China, India, South Korea, Mexico and Russia were added, which was followed by a second expansion in June 2009 to include all G20 country members plus Hong Kong and Singapore. What this membership expansion means at least on one level is that formally represented voices are more diverse than ever. Not only has the total number of country representatives increased significantly, but the extent of institutional diversity is now much greater than before. On one level of course, banking in China, Brazil, Mexico and Germany all follow some basic similar principles. However, given the need to sometimes focus on very specific forms of bank behaviour when considering financial risks and contagion while generating standards, the tension between standardization and exemptionalism will likely be stronger than ever.

Notes

1   These included a series of international banking crises that challenged then-prevailing conceptions of national jurisdiction in banking, such as the Bank Herstaat Crisis, the Franklin National crisis and the Banco Ambrosiano crisis. See Barth, Caprio and Levine, 2006.

2   See, for example, Jordan and Majnoni, 2003; Porter, 2003; Pauly, 2008; Alexander *et al.*, 2006.

3   This strong, but not complete, separation is well established within the existing literature on regulatory agencies and central bank independence. See Gilardi, 2007; Gilardi, 2002; McNamara, 2002.

4   The G10 Governors within the Bank for International Settlements approve major policy outputs of the BCBS, but this role is largely ceremonial, and in any case is composed of some of the same institutions as the BCBS itself. See Davies and Green, 2008.

5   See, for example, Slaughter, 2004; Kussin and Kette, 2006. These observations are also substantiated by interviews conducted with BCBS participants.

6   See Kerwer, 2005; Ho, 2002. By 1998, over 120 countries either claimed to have adopted the 1988 Basel Accord or were in the process of doing so. See Alexandar *et al.*, 2006; Genschell and Plümper, 1997.

7   Confidential interview with industry participant.

8   As evinced by the changes in *The Banker* magazine at the time, which changed the construction of their league tables of the banking industry after the Basel Capital Accord came into effect. The definition of Tier 1 capital, as well as the Cooke ratio itself, became standard metrics through which risk was assessed across institutions, not just to BCBS members, but to market participants as well. See also Mullineux, 1992.

9   The onset of the East Asian financial crisis in 1997 also motivated these endeavours further, but it is important to point out that the initial motivations for the Basel Core Principles arose before the Thai economy began to plunge into crisis.
10 Under the original Basel Accord of 1988, half of the loans and investments were to be in the form of 'Tier 1' capital, the superior form of capital which for the most part composed the bank's equity and retained profits. First in Japan the Ministry of Finance was allowing its banks to count forms of equity as capital that were of very low value. Then more systemic problems of regulatory competition began occurring. After the US Federal Reserve allowed American banks began to issue 'hybrid securities' (a financial instrument that is essentially a debt obligation but is counted as capital) and count these securities as Tier 1 capital, this soon spread to Dutch, German, and Japanese banks as well. Standards then fell even further, with banking regulators in Germany and Luxembourg and the UK following the US' lead. See Boland, 1998; Graham, 1998a.
11 At the International Conference of Banking Supervisors conference held in Sydney in October 1998, it was decided that such 'innovative capital instruments' such as hybrid securities could account for no more than 15 per cent of Tier 1 capital, and compliance guidelines were outlined for the kinds of securities that would be permitted to count toward capital adequacy. See Graham, 1998b.
12 Anonymous interview with BCBS member. See also Bonte, 1999.
13 Interviews with various BCBS members.
14 Based on accounts from interviews with BCBS participants from a variety of countries
15 In particular, the BCBS wanted to 'remove the possibility that banks could incur a lower capital charge as a consequence of holding the equity of an obligor rather than its debt' – a loophole that the BCBS was keen to close. See BCBS, 2001b, pp. 22–23.
16 This account is based on interviews conducted with BCBS participants from a variety of BCBS countries.
17 See Soederberg, 2003, p. 13. Walter has critiqued these claims on empirical grounds. See Walter 2008, pp. 11–12.
18 See Bank of Indonesia, 2001, p. 1; Bank of Mauritius 2001, p. 4; Central Bank of Sri Lanka 2001, p. 2; Bank of Thailand 2001, p. 6; People's Bank of China 2001, p. 4. All these submissions and others are publicly available at http://www.bis.org/bcbs/cacomments.htm

References

Abbott, K.W. and Snidal, D. (2008) 'The Governance Triangle: Regulatory Standards Institutions and the Shadow of the State' in W. Mattli and N. Woods (eds) *The Politics of Global Regulation* (Princeton: Princeton University Press).
Alexander, K., Dhumale, R., and Eatwell, J. (2006) *Global Governance of Financial Systems: The International Regulation of Systemic Risk* (Oxford: Oxford University Press).

Bank of Indonesia (2001) *Letter to BCBS Secretariat.* 31 May.

Bank of Mauritius (2001) *Letter to BCBS Secretariat.* 4 June.

Banco de Mexico (2001) *Letter to BCBS Secretariat.* May.

Bank of Thailand (2001) *Letter to BCBS Secretariat.* May.

Barth, J., Caprio, G., and Levine, R. (2006) *Rethinking Banking Regulation: Till Angels Govern* (Cambridge: Cambridge University Press).

BCBS (1997) *Core Principles for Effective Banking Supervision* (Basel: BCBS, September).

BCBS (2001a) Second *Consultative Paper* (Basel: BCBS, January).

BCBS (2001b) *Overview of the New Basel Capital Accord* (Basel: BCBS, January).

BCBS (2002) *Quantitative Impact Study Three Technical Guidance* (Basel: BCBS, October).

BCBS (2003) *Consultative Document: Overview of the New Basel Capital Accord* (Basel: BCBS, April).

BCBS (2004) *International Convergence of Capital Measurement and Capital Standards: A Revised Framework* (Basel: BCBS, 26 June).

BIS Financial Stability Institute (2004) *Implementation of the new capital adequacy framework in non-Basel Committee member countries,* Occasional Paper No. 4, July.

Blackburn, R. (2008) 'The Subprime Crisis', *New Left Review,* March–April, 63–106.

Boland, V. (1998) 'Banks Show Preference for New European Asset Class', *Financial Times,* 19 August 1998, 30.

Bonte, R. (1999) 'Supervisory Lessons to be Drawn from the Asian Crisis', *Basel Committee on Banking Supervision Working Papers,* No. 2, June.

Brownbridge, M. and Kirkpatrick, C. (1999) 'Financial Sector Regulation: The Lessons of the Asian Crisis', *Development Policy Review,* 17, 243–266.

Calari, C. and Ingves, S. (2002) 'Implementation of the Basel Core Principles for Effective Banking Supervision, Experiences, Influences, and Perspectives', *World Bank and International Monetary Fund Working Paper,* 23 September.

Central Bank of Sri Lanka (2001) *Letter to BCBS Secretariat.* May.

Chey, H-K. (2006) 'Explaining Cosmetic Compliance with International Regulatory Regimes: The Implementation of the Basle Accord in Japan, 1998–2003', *New Political Economy,* 11(2), 271–289.

Costello, P. (1998) 'Opening Address' to *the International Conference of Banking Supervisors,* Sydney, 21 October.

Davies, H. and Green, D. (2008) *Global Financial Regulation: The Essential Guide* (Cambridge: Polity).

De Carmoy, H. (1990) *Global Banking Strategy: Financial Markets and Industrial Decay* (Cambridge: Basil Blackwell).

Delonis, R. P. (2004) 'International Financial Standards and Codes: Mandatory Regulation Without Representation', *NYU Journal of International Law and Politics,* 36, 563–634.

Demirgüç-Kunt, A. and Detragiache, E. (2010) 'Basel Core Principles and Bank Risk: Does Compliance Matter?' *IMF Working Paper,* March.

Eatwell, J. (2009) 'The Future of International Financial Regulation' in S. Burke (ed.) *Re-Defining the Global Economy* (New York: Friedrich Ebert Stiftung Occasional Paper No. 42).

Financial Services Authority (2009) *The Turner Review: A regulatory response to the global banking crisis* (London: Financial Services Authority), March.

Genschel, P. and Plümper, T. (1997) 'Regulatory Competition and International Co-operation', *Journal of European Public Policy*, 4(4), 626–642.

Gilardi, F. (2002) 'Policy Credibility and Delegation to Independent Regulatory Agencies: A Comparative Empirical Analysis', *Journal of European Public Policy*, 9(6), 873–893.

Gilardi, F. (2007) 'The Same, But Different: Central Banks, Regulatory Agencies, and the Politics of Delegation to Independent Authorities', *Comparative European Politics*, 5, 303–327.

Graham, G. (1998a) 'Banking Industry Divided Over Type of Buffer Against Losses', *Financial Times*, 6 April, 20.

Graham, G. (1998b) 'Banking Supervisors Relax Rules on Hybrid Securities', *Financial Times*, 28 October, 21.

Harris, C. (1998) 'Call to Revise Banks' Capital Adequacy Rules', *Financial Times*, 22 September 1998, 4.

Ho, D. (2002) 'Compliance and International Soft Law: Why Do Countries Implement the Basel Accord?', *Journal of International Economic Law*, 5, 647– 648.

Jackson, P. (1999) 'Capital Requirements and Bank Behaviour: The Impact of the Basel Accord', *Basel Committee on Banking Supervision Working Papers*, No. 1, April.

Jayasuriya, K. (2005) 'Beyond Institutional Fetishism: From the Developmental to the Regulatory State', *New Political Economy*, 10(3), 381–387.

Joint Submission of the Banking Regulatory Authorities of Argentina, Bolivia, Columbia, Costa Rica, Honduras, Paraguay, the Dominican Republic, Uruguay, Venezuela (2001) 30 May.

Jordan, C. and Majnoni, G. (2003) 'Regulatory Harmonization and the Globalization of Finance' in J. A. Hanson, P. Honohan, and G. Majnoni (eds) *Globalization and National Financial Systems* (Oxford: World Bank and Oxford University Press).

Kapstein, E. (1992) 'Between Power and Purpose: Central Bankers and the Politics of Regulatory Convergence', *International Organization*, 46(1), 265–387.

Kerwer, D. (2005) 'Rules That Many Use: Standards and Global Regulation', *Governance*, 18(4), 632–661

Kerwer, D. (2006) 'Governing Financial Markets by International Standards' in M. Koenig-Archibugi and M. Zürn (eds) *New Modes of Governance in the Global System: Exploring Publicness, Delegation and Inclusiveness* (London: Palgrave Macmillan).

Kussin, M. and Kette, S. (2006) 'Making Use of Cognitive Standards: On the Logic of a New Mode of Governance in International Finance' in T. Strulik and H. Willke (eds) *Toward a Cognitive Mode in Global Finance: The Governance of a Knowledge-Based Financial System* (Frankfurt: Campus Verlag).

Lütz, S. (2001) 'From Managed to Market Capitalism? German Finance in Transition', *German Politics*, 9(2), 149–170.

Macey, J. (2003) 'Regulatory Globalization as a Response to Regulatory Competition', *Emory Law Journal*, 52(3), 1353–79.

Majone, G. (1994) 'The Rise of the Regulatory State in Europe', *West European Politics*, 17(3), 77–101.

McGregor, D. and Pretzlik, C. (2003) 'China Formally Rejects Basel II Rules', *Financial Times*, 16 August, 5.

McNamara, K. R. (2002) 'Rational Fictions: Central Bank Independence and the Social Logic of Delegation' in Mark Thatcher and Alex Stone Sweet (eds) *The Politics of Delegation* (London: Frank Cass).

Mingkang, L. (2003) 'Testing Times Lie Ahead for Supervisors', *The Banker*, 1 December.

Mullineux, A. (1992) 'Introduction' in A. Mullineaux (ed.) *European Banking* (Oxford: Blackwell).

Oatley, T. and Nabors, R. (1998) 'Redistributive Co-operation: Market Failure, Wealth Transfers, and the Basle Accord', *International Organisation*, 52(1), 35–54.

Panourgias, L. E. (2006) *Banking Regulation and World Trade Law* (Oxford: Hart Publishing).

Pauly, L. (2008) 'Financial Crisis Management in Europe and Beyond', *Contributions to Political Economy*, 27, 73–89.

People's Bank of China (2001) *Letter to BCBS Secretariat*, 30 May.

Porter, T. and Wood, D. (2002) 'Reform without Representation? The International and Transnational Dialogue on the Global Financial Architecture', in L. E. Armijo (ed.) *Debating the Global Financial Architecture* (Albany: SUNY Press).

Porter, T. (2003) 'Technical collaboration and political conflict in the emerging regime for international financial regulation', *Review of International Political Economy*, 10(3), 520–551.

Porter, T. (2005) *Globalization and Finance* (Cambridge: Polity).

Prest, M. (1997) 'A Vice as Well as a Virtue', *Financial Times*, 26 November, 3.

Reserve Bank of India (2001) *Letter to BCBS Secretariat*. May.

Rude, C. (2008) 'The Role of Financial Discipline in Imperial Strategy' in M. Konings and L. Panitch (eds) *American Empire and the Political Economy of Global Finance* (London: Routledge).

Simmons, B. A. (2001) 'The International Politics of Harmonization: The Case of Capital Market Regulation', *International Organization*, 55(3), 589–620.

Singer, D. A. (2007) *Regulating Capital: Setting Standards for the International Financial System* (Ithaca: Cornell University Press).

Soederberg, S. (2003) 'The Promotion of 'Anglo-American' Corporate Governance in the South: Who Benefits from the New International Standard?' *Third World Quarterly*, 24(1), 7–27.

Slaughter, A-M. (2004) 'Disaggregated Sovereignty: Towards the Public Accountability of Global Government Networks', *Government and Opposition*, 39(2), 159–190.

Suarez, F., Dhaene, J. and Vandufel, S. (2006) 'Basel II: Capital Requirements for Equity Investment Portfolios' *Belgian Actuarial Bulletin*, 5, 37–45.

Underhill, G. and Zhang, X. (2006) 'Norms, Legitimacy, and Global Financial Governance' *World Economy and Finance Research Program Working Paper Series* No. 13, September.

Vestergaard, J. (2004) 'The Asian crisis and the shaping of 'proper' economies', *Cambridge Journal of Economics*, 28, 809–827.

Vogel, D. and Kagan, R. (2004) 'Introduction' in D. Vogel and R. A. Kagan (eds) *Dynamics of Regulatory Change: How Globalization Affects National Regulatory Policies* (Berkeley: University of California Press.

Wade, R. (2009) 'Financial Regime Change', *New Left Review*, September–October, 5–21.

Walter, A. (2008) *Governing Finance: East Asia's Adoption of International Standards* (Ithaca: Cornell University Press).

Walter, A. (2010) 'Chinese Attitudes Toward Global Financial Regulatory Cooperation: Revisionist or Status Quo?' in E. Helleiner, S. Pagliari, and H. Zimmerman (eds) *Global Finance in Crisis: The Politics of International Regulatory Change* (London: Routledge).

3
The New Standard in Banking Regulation: From Basel II to Basel III

Jakob Vestergaard and Martin Højland

Introduction

The international standard for the regulation and supervision of banks – the so-called Basel II Accord – played a key role in the recent global financial crisis. The G20 countries therefore made a revision of international banking standards a core element of their crisis response: a revision of Basel II was thought to be of paramount importance in efforts to reduce the likelihood and severity of financial crises in the future. At their first gathering in Washington, November 2008, the G20 leaders tasked the Basel Committee with preparing a report on possible revisions to the Basel II accord. At that point, the Basel committee had already been in full motion on these issues for a year. The Basel Committee thus came to play a central role in crafting the first international report trying to outline the causes of the crisis and the needed responses to it (FSF, 2008). The report was the first in a series of reports produced jointly by the Financial Stability Forum (FSF) and the Basel Committee to provide leaders of the G8 and G20 countries with inputs on how to understand and respond to the crisis.[1] With respect to the revision of the Basel standards, this work culminated with the release of a comprehensive package of revisions in late summer 2010 – the proposed Basel III accord – which was endorsed by the G20 leaders a few months later at their summit in Seoul in November 2010.

Against the general background of this process of international re-regulation in banking, the present chapter addresses the following empirical questions: What has been the role of standards in the governance of banking since the mid-1980s?; How did the new generation of banking standards launched in 2004 – the Basel II Accord – contribute to the current global financial crisis?; What are the main novelties of the proposed Basel III Accord, not least in light of the global financial crisis?; Are these re-regulation efforts likely to achieve their stated objectives of making financial crises fewer and milder in the future by better balancing credit growth and economic growth?

The chapter demonstrates that the Basel II Accord was a key contributory cause of the global financial crisis in two main ways. First, it reinforced and institutionalized the industry-wide use of quantitative risk management models which inadvertently undermined the resilience and stability of international financial markets. Second, by introducing lower capital reserve requirements for assets on banks' trading book, as compared to assets on their banking books, the Basel II Accord accelerated processes of securitization, by which banks repackaged and sold loans to other financial market participants. While this 'originate-and-distribute' model of banking was initially thought to disperse risk in the system in fact it created a complex interconnectedness of risk, rendered it more than difficult to ascertain where various forms of risks ended and contributed considerably to the accumulation of liquidity risk, and the subsequent credit crunch.

The Basel III Accord seeks to address the shortcomings of the Basel II accord in a number of ways. The core elements of the new approach are higher levels of better quality capital, improved risk coverage, the introduction of leverage and liquidity risk ratios and a counter-cyclical buffer. Unfortunately, the general pattern is that the new measures introduced are insufficient and inadequate *vis-à-vis* the stated objectives of the new Accord.

This chapter is structured as follows. First, we briefly summarize the history of the Basel Committee and the first Basel standard, Basel I, launched in 1988 (section one). We then look at the main features of Basel II (section two) and discuss its main shortcomings, not least in light of the global financial crisis (section three). This is followed by a description of the main elements of the new Basel III standard (section four). We conclude by arguing that while Basel III does address some of the shortcomings of Basel II, it is not a satisfactory regulatory response to the global financial crisis. We should see Basel III as an intensification of its predecessor rather than a departure from it – which is rather disturbing from a banking sector stability perspective.

Historical background

The establishment of the Basel Committee

The Basel standards are developed by the Basel Committee, named after the Swiss city that hosts its secretariat within the Bank of International Settlements. The Basel Committee was originally established by the central-bank governors of the G10 countries in 1974, but back then the objective was not to develop standards for banking regulation. The Basel committee was established in response to turbulence in international currency markets following the breakdown of the Bretton Woods system in the early 1970s and the objective was to ensure adequate supervision of banks that were internationally active. The closing of the German Bankhaus Herstatt in 1974 is often depicted as having been particularly important in convincing policy-makers at the time of the need for internationally coordinated supervision of internationally active banks (Tarullo, 2008). Bankhaus Herstatt had speculated aggressively on the international currency markets with money borrowed from banks around the world, and when these investments turned bad it went bankrupt and was closed by the German authorities. Because of time-zone differences Bankhaus Herstatt ceased its operations when a number of American banks had released payments in Deutschemark in exchange of USD before having actually received the corresponding amount in dollars. This led to a series of panic actions on the euro-dollar market and a greater liquidity crisis was only avoided when a number of American banks chose to provide the needed liquidity for the banks under stress. At the time there were no rules or procedures for supervision of internationally active banks, nor for handling bankruptcy cases with severe international ramifications. The first key objective of the Basel Committee therefore was to ensure that no bank operating internationally would escape supervision (BCBS, 1975). The Committee's work on these issues resulted in the *1975 Basel Concordat*, which established rules determining the responsibilities of home and host country supervisors.

The focus on capital requirements

It was in the course of the 1980s that the question of capital reserve requirements became increasingly central to international deliberations on banking regulation and remained so ever since. The centrality of this measure in the regulation of banks is related to a specific set of dynamics between banks, its customers and their governments.

For all companies, banks or other, capital put aside is expensive in the sense that it entails foregoing a profit that could otherwise have been made from deploying that capital actively. Generally, market actors are expected to demand and hence ensure that their counterparties maintain sufficient capital buffers, but in the case of banks, there is reason to expect that market-induced capital reserves will tend to be insufficient (Tarullo, 2008). This is due to both demand- and supply-side factors. The widespread existence of deposit insurance schemes, which protect depositors in the case of bank failures, tend to weaken the disciplining of banks from the demand-side. Depositors cannot reasonably be expected to observe the capital adequacy practices of their banks as diligently as they would have, had their deposits not been insured. On the supply-side, the repeated experience of banks being bailed out by governments is more than likely to tempt them to maintain less prudent capital buffers than they would have done otherwise. The gradual institutionalization of government bail-outs of banks may be said to go as far back as the Great Depression of the 1930s (Holten, 2004), where it was first seen, at full scale, how devastating the ramifications of bank collapses can be for the wider economy. Although it made perfect sense for governments to make it a high priority to avoid major bank collapses, the institutionalization of government bail-outs of banks greatly enhanced the problem of moral hazard. Not only did depositors have little reason to worry about the credit worthiness of their bank, given various forms of deposit insurance schemes; now big banks had every reason to pursue high risk strategies in the search for the highest possible yields, for they could calmly rely on being bailed out by governments should they run into trouble.

In sum, weak demand-side disciplining of banks (cf. insured depositors) and moderate self-disciplining (given government bailouts) in combination can be expected to result in insufficient capital reserves in the banking sector. The regulatory response to this predicament became that of capital adequacy requirements, stipulating that banks had to put aside a certain level of capital for them to be able to absorb unexpected losses and secure their own solvency in troubled times. Such capital requirements were imposed by national regulators in all the major, developed countries. But in the absence of any mechanism of international coordination, the capital requirements imposed on banks by national regulators were not identical, of course. It was not clear therefore what to do with internationally active banks. Were banks operating under foreign jurisdictions to comply with the capital requirements of the home or the host country? How should one deal with the competitive advantage that some banks operating in foreign jurisdictions enjoyed over their domestic competitors because of capital requirement differentials? And did such internationally active banks not represent a potential threat to the stability of the banking systems of the foreign jurisdictions in which they operated when able to take on greater risks at lower price (Davies and Green, 2008)? These issues led Paul Volcker, then Governor of the American Federal Reserve Bank, to push for the development of a common framework for capital regulation of internationally active banks. Many first considered such international regulation unfeasible because banks were operating in very different national financial systems. Moreover, for many it was it was a politically undesirable way to go since it was widely seen as an infringement on national sovereignty (Marcussen, 2007). But after convincing his counterpart at the Bank of England, Volcker nevertheless succeeded in getting the G10 to develop an international standard for the capital requirements of international banks. The result was the *1988 Accord on Capital Adequacy* – or *Basel I*.

Basel I: The 'risk-bucket' approach to capital requirements

The two key objectives of Basel I were to secure a safe international banking system and to create a level playing field for banks internationally, and the main instrument to achieve this was capital adequacy requirements. The capital requirements of Basel I focused exclusively on the type of risk considered particularly important for banks, namely *credit* risk; the risk of a debtor defaulting on his loan. Banks were required to reserve capital of at least 8 per cent. of their *risk-weighted* assets. This reserved capital had to include core capital – Tier 1 capital – of at least 50 per cent. (BCBS, 1988). The risk weighting was a way to make the capital requirements risk-sensitive – sensitive, that is, to risks in the portfolios of banks. If a portfolio included high-risk loans, the amount of capital held in reserve had to be correspondingly high. It was based on five categories, or so-called risk buckets, each carrying a weight of 0, 10, 20, 50 or 100 per cent. Cash and OECD–government bonds, for example, had a 0 per cent risk weighting and didn't require a capital reserve while traditional corporate loans had a 100 per cent risk weighting and required the full 8 per cent in reserve (BCBS 1988, §29 & Annex 2).

In the beginning of the 1990s, Basel I came to be seen as too crude. The realities of the financial sector were thought to have outdated the Basel I accord (Alexander *et al,*. 2006). Two main problems were identified. First, the crudeness of the risk-bucket approach inadvertently incentivized high-risk investment behaviour. The same risk weighting applied for all corporate loans, for example, and this created incentives for banks to invest in the most risky assets, as they didn't require higher capital reserves but produced a higher yield. Second, Basel I was criticized for its exclusive focus on credit risk. Why focus so narrowly on credit risk when banks were increasingly active in capital markets and thus were getting more and more exposed to *market* risk, that is, the risk of losses in a portfolio due to movements in market prices?

In parallel, the notion was spreading in the banking sector, and among regulators and policy makers, that governments were not well equipped to regulate banks. Given the increasing complexity and sophistication of risk management in large banks, many saw it as preferable to rely as much as possible on bank *self-regulation*. Alan Greenspan, for instance, then Chairman of the Federal Reserve, asserted that banks as well as other financial institutions would have to be increasingly self-regulated 'largely because government regulators cannot do that job' (cited in Tarullo, 2008, pp. 15–16).

The first major step in the direction of increased bank self-regulation was taken in 1996 with the *Market Risk Amendment* to the Basel I agreement, which introduced capital requirements for market risk. Banks were permitted to use their internal quantitative risk management models to produce estimates of their so-called value-at-risk as a basis for measuring their market risk capital requirements (BCBS, 1996). Soon after the implementation of the Market Risk Amendment, along with a couple of other amendments, it was decided, however, that a more radical revision of Basel I was necessary. Important impetus for this contention resulted from the financial crisis in Asia in 1997–98 and the near collapse of the US-based Long-Term Capital Management hedge fund in the immediate wake of the Asian crisis.[2] In June 1999, the Basel Committee released the first set of proposals for a new framework for banking regulation. In June 2004, after five years of negotiations, consultations and impact studies, the Basel II accord was published.

Basel II: sophisticated 'risk-sensitivity'

The fundamental aim of Basel II was to secure the soundness and stability of the international financial system and prevent competitive inequality among internationally active banks, as had been the case with the Basel I agreement.[3] But the manner in which Basel II pursued this objective was fundamentally different. First, the Basel II agreement introduces a three-pillar regulatory framework. Second, a differentiated approach was introduced, by which several distinct approaches for the calculation of capital reserve requirements are sanctioned for the same type of risk.

The three pillars of the Basel II accord are (i) minimum capital requirements; (ii) guidelines on regulatory intervention by national supervisors; and (iii) guidelines on disclosure standards for banks. The gradual integration of market risk which began with the market risk amendment in 1996 was completed with the full integration of market risk in Pillar 1. Further, the Basel II accord integrates a third type of risk, operational risk – the risk of losses resulting from inadequate or failed internal processes, people and systems, or from external events (BCBS, 2006; Power, 2005) – in its core provisions defined in Pillar 1.[4] While credit, market and operational risk were now addressed in and through the capital requirements of Pillar 1, a host of other risks – including reputational risk, liquidity risk, pension risk, systemic risk, and concentration risk – were relegated to Pillar 2 and hence rendered non-binding.

The required amount of capital that banks had to put aside in Basel II was maintained at 8 per cent of their risk-weighted assets. One might get the impression then that with respect to minimal capital requirements, the Basel II accord resulted in little substantial change. The *methodologies* promoted for the calculation of capital reserves changed the capital adequacy practices of banks rather significantly, however. The new methodologies aimed to make capital adequacy requirements as 'risk-sensitive' as possible; they aimed, in other words, to enable banks to put aside an amount of capital that reflected as accurately as possible the specific risk characteristics of its portfolio (BCBS, 2006, §5 and §10). The new methodologies constituted an appealing improvement not only from the perspective of banks, who stood to enhance their profitability, but also from the perspective of politicians, who envisaged increased economic growth through more efficient resource allocation and enhanced credit creation.

The new accord thus was more complex not only in terms of the types of risks it sought to take into account, but also in terms of the methodologies allowed to calculate those risks and the corresponding levels of capital to be held in reserve against them. For both credit, operational and market risk different approaches were sanctioned depending on the size and sophistication of the bank.

Table 3.1   Risk management approaches sanctioned by the Basel II accord

	Simple	**Medium**	**Advanced**
Credit risk	Standardized Approach	Foundation Internal Ratings-Based (F-IRB) Approach	Advanced Internal Ratings-Based (A-IRB) Approach
Operational risk	Basic Indicator Approach	Standardized Approach	Internal Measurement Approach
Market risk	Standardized Approach	Standardized Approach	Internal Models Approach

Note: Authors' elaboration based on BCBS (2006).

Value-at-risk models

At the heart of the new methodologies for calculating risk was the notion of value-at-risk (VaR). For market risk, all large banks were required to use VaR models. Indeed, even in the more advanced approaches to credit risk and operational risk it was the logic of VaR modelling that came to predominate.

The appeal of VaR models, both to banks and to regulators, was that they expressed risk as a single number, a dollar figure (Nocera, 2009). This single number measures what the maximum loss will be – with a certain high probability (usually 95 or 99 per cent probability) – for a given trader, portfolio or firm. If, by the end of a trading day, a trader has ten million dollar VaR, this means that with 99 per cent probability the maximum short-term loss of that trader will be ten million dollars, on the assumption that market fluctuations remain within the boundaries of what is statistically normal. Central to the appeal of VaR models is that they allow for aggregation as well as decomposition of financial risk: they can measure the aggregated risk of an investment bank as well as the risk carried by any individual trader.

VaR models allowed not only for aggregation of risk from the individual to a trading desk, but also for aggregation of risk across asset classes. The risk characteristics of a portfolio consisting of a complex mixture of bonds, equities and derivatives could be summarized in one single measure, the aggregate value-at-risk of that portfolio. By implication, the overall financial risk of an entire financial institution could equally be expressed in terms of its aggregate VaR across the full range of asset classes. Within minutes after the closing of markets, CEOs of financial institutions know their firms' aggregate value-at-risk.

Basel standards had allowed banks to use their own advanced risk management systems as the basis for calculating capital reserves for market risk since 1996. The first big boost for VaR models, however, occurred a year later with the near-collapse of the LTCM fund in 1997.[5] The LTCM boom and bust debacle convinced many on Wall Street that there was an urgent need for financial institutions to develop an in-depth understanding and monitoring of the aggregate risk of a firm, across its many complex positions. The only game around that could deliver this was VaR. Regulators moved in the same direction. In 1997, the US Securities and Exchange Commission decided that it was of paramount importance that the risk posed to the financial system by derivatives trading was made visible to market participants as well as to regulatory authorities. Investors were to be required to disclose these risks, it was decided, and VaR would be the measure and the method-ology delivering this 'visibilization'. Following this, many banks and financial institutions began including VaR information in their finan-cial statements. With the agreement on the Basel II Accord in 2004, VaR estimations were required on a daily basis, with a confidence level of 99 per cent, a timeframe of minimum ten days, and historical data inputs going back at least one year (BCBS, 2006, §718 LXXVI).

From 2004, the use of banks 'advanced internal ratings-based' (A-IRB) models was allowed for the calculation of credit risk. Contrary to mar-ket risk, the fundamental problem in assessing credit risk is that there are no easily observed market prices for most credit exposures, however. This means that credit risk models must be predicated upon other types of data than market prices, such as various forms of ratings, to arrive at VaR figures for total credit risk (Nickell *et al.*, 2001).[6]

According to the Basel Committee, the overall aim of the Basel II Accord in general and the predication of capital reserve requirements upon banks' internal risk management models in particular was to reward 'the improvements in risk measurement and control that had occurred' and provide 'incentives for such improvements to continue' (BCBS, 2009, p. 3). By predicating banking regulation on banks own risk management practices, VaR models inevitably and irresistibly became the name of the game in international banking.

Separating the bank balance sheet

Basel II introduced lower capital reserve requirements for assets on banks' trading books than for assets on their banking books. The underlying rationale of this was that assets in the trading book could always be sold if the banks experienced problems and that, hence, less capital was needed to be held against these assets. Making the fact that balance sheets were separated in a banking book and a trading book one of the most essential building blocks of the Basel II Accord was to have significant ramifications for the business of international banking. With the assets related to the traditional activities of banks (ex. private deposits) placed in the banking book, and assets subject to trading on the capital markets placed in the trading book, lower capital requirements for the latter gave banks a strong incentive to move assets from the banking book to the trading book through the financial process of *securitization*. In and through the process of securitization banks transform non-tradable loans into securities tradable on the financial markets. In addition to reducing the capital adequacy requirements for banks, securitization was thought to transfer credit and market risks from banks to capital markets, and hence result in a benevolent dispersion of risk.

Securitization works by aggregating debt instruments in a pool and then issuing new securities backed by the pool – so-called mortgage-backed or asset-backed securities. In the case of what was called 'structured' securitization, a large group of loans (typically sub-prime mortgages, student loans or credit card debt) were pooled and then split into 'tranches' each reflecting the predicted riskiness of the loans. The tranches carried not a group of specific loans, but a proportion of loans based on their default rate. In the lowest tranches you had the loans that defaulted first, in the highest tranches the loans that defaulted latest. The holders of the safest tranches would therefore only be subject to losses when all the subordinated tranches stopped performing. The different tranches carried a credit rating and a risk premium related to their risk profile. The lowest tranches got the lowest credit rating and hence carried a higher risk premium (Jobst, 2008).

Processes of securitization involved a host of actors in a complex network of relations. At the centre of this process usually was an off-balance sheet vehicle – also called a structured investment vehicle (SIV) or a 'conduit' – set up by the originating bank to facilitate the process. The SIV would first take over the payment stream of the loans that the originating bank wanted to securitize and pay the bank in return. Because the SIV was regarded as a legally autonomous entity by Basel II the transfer of loans between the originating bank and the SIV removed the loans from the balance sheets of the originating bank and reduced its capital requirements. The SIV then packaged and sold the tranches to end-investors in the form of Collateralized Debt Obligations (CDOs).

In order to be able to sell the CDO, the SIV needed an underwriter to guarantee the underlying loan and this job was typically done by another bank or in some cases even by the originating bank itself. The end-investors would typically be other financial institutions – commercial banks, investment banks, pension funds or hedge funds – financing their investments short term on the interbank money markets, taking on high amounts of leverage in the process.

The advantages of securitization were many for the actors involved (Engelen *et al.*, 2010). It generated a series of fees, and boosted the short-term bonuses for bankers. It created more liquidity in the financial system as illiquid non-tradable assets were transformed into liquid tradable assets. It lowered the capital requirements for the banks because the risk of the original loans was transferred from their banking book to their trading book. This meant credit expansion, which is always popular with politicians, because of its tendency to boost short-term economic growth. Finally, and perhaps most importantly, securitization was believed to make the financial system more stable and resilient because banks credit risks were dispersed throughout the financial system. In the words of the IMF, 'There is growing recognition that the dispersion of credit risk by banks to a broader and more diverse group of investors, rather than warehousing such risk on their balance sheets, has helped to make the banking and overall financial system more resilient (...) The improved resilience may be seen in fewer bank failures and more consistent credit provision. Consequently, the commercial banks, a core segment of the financial system, may be less vulnerable today to credit or economic shocks' (IMF, 2006).[7]

The shortcomings of Basel II

At the core of Basel II in general, and the notion of risk-sensitive capital requirements in particular, was the assumption that market prices were a good indicator of financial risk. Unfortunately, they turned out not to be so. While efforts to enhance the 'risk-sensitivity' of capital reserves were thought to improve the risk management practices of banks, the result was the opposite. The new methodologies turned out *not* to reflect the actual risks in the portfolios of banks. Moreover, the lower capital reserve requirements for assets on the trading book as compared to those on the banking book gave banks strong incentives to engage in regulatory arbitrage in ways that created new kinds of risk in the system.

Securitization and the booming of liquidity risk

The process of securitization turned the banking system into an increasingly complex maze of interconnectedness. Banks securitized mortgages, invested in CDOs and insured each other in numerous crosscutting ways, and the same bank would typically act as securitizer in one process, credit enhancer in another (through the issuance of Credit Default Swaps on CDOs), investor in a third and underwriter in a fourth. Instead of acting as intermediaries between borrowers and investors and transferring the risk from the mortgages to the capital market, banks became primary investors in these products on the basis of short-term funding and excessive leverage. This created a maturity mismatch where the creditor side was made up not by deposits from bank customers but from short debt financed daily on the interbank markets by banks. The combination of high leverage and a growing maturity mismatch greatly increased a type of risk not adequately dealt with in the Basel II accord; namely liquidity risk. Ironically, the massive accumulation of liquidity risk was a more or less direct result of attempts by banks to circumvent the capital requirements of Basel II.

Value-at-risk models

An important problem with the use of VaR models for financial risk management was that their risk estimations were based on data inputs going back only one year, and hence inevitably reflected the economic cycle. When the economy was booming in the years up to the crisis, data inputs going into VaR calculations reflected a booming market and therefore progressively *reduced* risk weightings and capital adequacy requirements. This created a false sense of security, more risky behaviour and thus further fuelled the boom. In the course of the economic downturn, however, data going into the VaR estimations reflected a market under stress, which resulted in *increasing* risk weights and *increasing* reserve capital requirements – at a time when credit was needed the most. Hence, VaR models exacerbated both the boom and the bust.

At a more fundamental level, VaR models have been criticized on the grounds that they tell you nothing about the most important financial risks. An estimate of what your maximum loss will be with 99 per cent probability, simply doesn't tell you anything about your potential loss should an 'extreme' event occur. In the words of David Einhorn, founder of the hedge fund Greenlight Capital, VaR is like an 'airbag that works all the time, except when you have a car accident' (Einhorn and Brown, 2008).[8]

Industry-wide adoption of quantitative risk management models

The fact that the same type quantitative risk management models were adopted across the board in the banking sector further exacerbated the problem of procyclicality. The encouragement of the adoption of quantitative risk management models reflected and accelerated a growing fashion in risk management away from discretionary assessments of risk towards quantitative and market-sensitive approaches (Persaud, 2001). This approach did not take adequate account of herding, one of the most salient features of globally integrated financial markets.[9] In a herding environment, the widespread use of risk-management models that are standardized, quantitative and market sensitive will tend to destabilize markets, making them less rather than more resilient. When everyone searches out investment positions which had high returns, low volatility and low correlation in the past, these will inevitably become overvalued assets – and hence turn sour and become the exact opposite of what made investors chase them in the first place. 'In this way', Avinash Persaud (2004, p. 98) explains, market-sensitive risk-management systems 'manufacture risk' and 'add to the pro-cyclicality of capital flows'. By predicating capital regulation on a bank's own quantitative risk management models, Basel II reinforced, intensified and institutionalized an ongoing homogenization of investment behaviour, with banks and other financial institutions identifying and selecting investment portfolios on the basis of the same data, using the same quantitative models to evaluate those data. In so doing, the Basel II agreement exerted a significant procyclical and destabilizing effect on the international financial system, the resilience of which it undermined rather than enhanced.

Microprudential vs macroprudential financial regulation

The failure to acknowledge and take into account the dynamic effects of industry-wide adoption of the same type of risk management models reflects the predominance of a microprudential as opposed to a macroprudential approach to financial regulation. The latter acknowledges that investment behaviours that 'appear compelling and fully rational from the perspective of individual market participants' may well lead to 'undesirable aggregate outcomes for the market as a whole' (Borio, 2004, p. 234). Unfortunately, the Basel II Accord further intensified and institutionalized the predominance of a microprudential approach to financial regulation. Little progress has been made with respect to devising new modes of financial regulation based on in-depth understanding of the effects of the collective actions of individual market participants on financial market dynamics.

Basel III: balancing growth and stability

In its efforts to develop a new international banking standard, the Basel Committee has released a comprehensive set of regulatory proposals in the form of eight consultative papers, five sets of principles, two impact studies and a number of guidance papers. The proposed Basel III Accord consists of revisions of the Basel II framework as well as of completely new regulatory measures. In the former category, the key changes are provisions to ensure higher levels of better quality capital and enhanced risk coverage. In the latter category, the main regulatory innovations are the introduction of a leverage ratio, a liquidity ratio and a countercyclical buffer. The three new regulatory measures are all introduced in the hope that they will help ensure 'a better balance between banking sector stability and sustainable credit growth' (BCBS, 2010a).

Higher levels of better quality capital

The capital bases of many banks were insufficient to absorb the losses incurred in the crisis; the levels of high quality capital were simply too low. In response to this, the Basel Committee has raised the requirements for the most loss-absorbing types of capital, and made changes to the definitions of different kinds of capital. This implies a more complicated framework for the calculation of capital reserves. As one financial market observer noted at the release of the new framework:

> There's a lot to unpack and explain. But the first thing to note is that we've moved from a simple 'Tier 1 has to be 4 per cent., Tier 2 has to be 8 per cent' to a 3x3 matrix with all manner of different minima (Salmon, 2010)

The minimum capital requirement remains at 8 per cent of risk-weighted assets, as in Basel I and II. However, 75 per cent of capital reserves have to be Tier 1 capital, so that reserves in the form of Tier 1 make up 6 per cent of total assets (as opposed to 4 per cent in Basel II). Moreover, 75 per cent of this Tier 1 capital must take the form of common equity, regarded as the highest quality form of loss-absorbing capital, so that common equity capital makes up 4.5 per cent of total assets. In addition to this, banks will be required to hold a so-called 'capital conservation buffer' of 2.5 per cent, also in the form of common equity, in order to withstand periods of stress. When banks draw upon this buffer, they will be subject to a set of constraints on their earnings distributions (dividends and bonus payments, for instance) (BCBS, 2010a, §50). This brings the total common equity requirements to 7 per cent., as compared to 2 per cent under Basel II.

A large number of changes are made with respect to the definition of capital. Capital is now divided in two overarching categories: *Tier 1 Capital*, which is split further into the two sub-categories of *Common Equity* and *Additional Going-Concern Capital*, and *Tier 2 Capital*. To each of these categories corresponds a set of criteria that instruments are required to meet in order to be included in the relevant category – no less than 37 criteria in total. In addition to this comes a long list of details on the eligibility of specific kinds of instruments, such as minority interests, deferred tax assets and mortgage servicing rights that are now restricted not to exceed 15 per cent of a bank's common equity capital in total (BCBS, 2010a). These changes reflect an effort to address the inadequacies of the previous framework in predicting the loss-absorbing quality of a number of asset types. The general trend of the introduced changes thus is a tightening of what counts as capital and a more elaborate and sophisticated conceptualization of capital.

Improved risk coverage

Despite the sophistication of the risk management systems promoted in and through the Basel II Accord, a situation developed in which there was 'huge uncertainty as to where risk resides' (Guha and Tett, 2007). It was as if risk somehow escaped the risk management framework. Thus, the Basel III agreement proposes quite a few measures to ensure an improved 'risk coverage'. Most of these changes consist of adjusting the risk-weights and capital charges for the activities that proved to be much more risky than anticipated and introducing new capital charges for risks not previously accounted for. The changes include (i): higher risk-weights for securitization and re-securitization exposures; (ii) raised credit conversion factors for short-term liquidity facilities to off-balance sheet conduits (that is tougher treatment for the use of structured investment vehicles); (ii) the introduction of capital charges for mark-to-market losses due to credit valuation adjustments; (iii) higher capital charges for over-the-counter exposures such as complex illiquid derivatives; (iv) higher capital charges for counterparty credit risk arising from derivatives and securities financing activities; and (v) an increase in the correlation assumptions for exposures to other financial institutions (BCBS, 2010a, §14).

With respect to the value-at-risk-based trading book framework two key changes are suggested. First, an *incremental risk charge* is proposed as a supplement to existing VaR calculations, to make provision for a number of risks not captured by VaR models, such as the risk of an asset being downgraded or defaulted. Second, new *stressed* value-at-risk requirements are proposed, by which banks are required to include a one-year observation period of significant financial stress in their value-at-risk calculations (BCBS, 2010a, §12). Each of these changes in the risk coverage is expected to lead to higher capital levels, reduced incentives for arbitrage between the trading and banking book and reduced pro-cyclicality of the minimum capital requirements for market risk.

New proposals on leverage and liquidity risk ratios

Basel II made it possible for banks to vastly increase their leverage on the basis of supposedly highly liquid assets with correspondingly low risk weights. But as banks were forced to deleverage by selling off these assets – which soon turned out to be highly *illiquid* – prices went down and this exacerbated the negative spiral of losses, declines in capital levels and contraction in credit. In order to constrain the build-up of leverage and avoid destabilizing processes of deleveraging, the Basel III agreement proposes a leverage ratio as a supplementary measure to the risk-based requirements in Basel II. This would have the form of a non-risk-based, 'backstop' measure based on gross exposure (BCBS, 2010a, §16).[10] In essence, this means that as much capital would need to be held back for a government bond as for a much riskier loan. The leverage ratio is in-sensitive to risk.

In the years preceding the crisis liquidity was ample, funding was easy and liquidity risk just wasn't much of an issue in the risk management practices of banks. But the crisis demonstrated how quickly liquidity risk can materialize and funding evaporate. The Basel III agreement thus includes a set of *Principles for Sound Liquidity Risk Management and Supervision* along with proposals for two minimum standards for funding liquidity. The principles include guidance on the use of liquidity risk management tools such as comprehensive cash flow forecasting, liquidity scenario stress testing and the development of contingency funding plans. The minimum standards include minimum requirements for the quality and quantity of liquid assets to be held by banks in the long and short term. The short-term standard – the so-called

Liquidity Coverage Ratio – identifies the amount of high quality liquid assets needed by a bank to offset the cash outflow that can be encountered under acute short-term stress scenarios lasting one month. This measure is intended to promote short-term resilience to potential liquidity disruptions (BCBS, 2010a, §40). The long-term standard – the so-called Net Stable Funding Ratio – establishes a minimum acceptable amount of stable funding based on the liquidity characteristics of a bank. It is aimed at changing the liquidity risk profiles of banks away from short-term funding mismatches toward more stable, long-term funding (BCBS, 2010a).

Measures to address pro-cyclicality

Although many of the measures mentioned above – including the capital conservation buffer, the stressed value-at-risk requirement and the leverage ratio seek to ameliorate the problem of procyclicality, the central measure in this regard is the counter-cyclical buffer. The basic idea behind a counter-cyclical buffer is to slow banking activity when it is overheating and to encourage lending in times of stress. The countercyclical buffer will be imposed 'when, in the view of national authorities, excess aggregate credit growth is judged to be associated with an excessive build-up of system wide risk' (BCBS 2010a, §137). When credit in the economy is growing so much faster than the economy itself that authorities get concerned with 'system-wide risk', they may thus decide to impose a countercyclical buffer. Conversely, the countercyclical buffer will be released as soon as the credit cycle turns, in order to help absorb losses and reduce the risk of credit being constrained by capital requirements. The size of the countercyclical buffer will be set by national authorities between 0–2.5 per cent of risk-weighted assets and will be required to be made up of common equity (BCBS, 2010a, §139 and §142).

The countercyclical buffer comes with an elaborate set of guidelines. These include principles and methodologies for making judgments about credit growth to guidelines for selecting the authority to operate the buffer (home or host country). Thus, to assist national authorities in deciding when the buffer should apply, the Committee has devised a 'common reference point' for measuring excessive credit growth. When credit/GDP exceeds its long-term trend with an amount assessed to be associated with a build-up of system-wide risk the counter-cyclical buffer should be activated and vice-versa. The Committee warns, however, that such calculations may sometimes be misleading, and therefore recommends that authorities assess their validity by taken into account other indicators, such as various asset prices, funding spreads, credit condition surveys, real GDP growth and data on the ability of non-financial entities to meet their debt obligations on a regular basis (BCBS, 2010b).

Discussion: limitations of Basel III

Inadequate increase of capital reserve requirements

On the release of the provisional agreement on Basel III in September 2010, the *Financial Times* reported that global banking regulators had agreed to 'triple the size of the capital reserves that the world's banks must hold against losses' (Masters, 2010). Although this does indeed appear substantial, 'tripling almost nothing' still leaves you with almost nothing, as Martin Wolf (2010) noted. To appreciate the insignificance of the proposed increases in capital reserve requirements consider the following two perspectives. First, with respect to Tier 1 capital, Basel III raises requirements to 8.5 per cent (if all measures are counted), which is below the 10 per cent held on average by US banks in recent decades (Johnson, 2010a, 2010b). This modest requirement for Tier 1 capital does not match well with US Treasury Secretary Timothy Geithner's repeated emphasis on 'capital, capital, capital', as the appropriate response to the crisis. Second, and perhaps more importantly, the proposed capital reserve requirements are considerably below what the emerging consensus in mainstream financial economics would suggest. Scholars argue that between 15 and 20 per cent Tier 1 capital should be held by banks in good times (Hanson *et al.*, 2010) and influential observers have gone as far as to suggest that we would be well advised to consider the new Basel III requirement a 'capital *inadequacy* ratio' (Wolf, 2010, emphasis added).

The marginalization of countercyclicality

In the immediate aftermath of the onset of the global financial crisis, there was substantial emphasis on the need for countercyclical financial regulation (Brunnermeier *et al.*, 2009). On the surface of things, we may see the introduction of a 'countercyclical buffer' as the regulatory expression of this concern and hence a highly welcome regulatory innovation. In reality, however, Basel III has relegated the concern with counter-cyclicality to the margins. What was needed was a fundamental revision of capital reserve requirements to make them countercyclical at their root, not a marginal 'add-on' to the existing framework. 'Counter-cyclicality needs to be at the heart of the new regulatory regime and not an optional extra', in the words of Avinash Persaud (2010). The combination of a modest increase in capital reserve requirements and the introduction of a 'countercyclical buffer' when credit growth is deemed excessive will achieve very little in terms of moderating boom and bust cycles.

No alignment of risk taking with risk absorption capacity

A perspective completely ignored by the proposed Basel III accord is that financial institutions differ in terms of the types of risk that they are best suited to absorb, and that regulation should encourage an alignment of risk taking with risk absorption capacity. The focus of regulation needs to be shifted away from the current emphasis on sensitivity to the market price of risk and the insistence on 'equal treatment' of all financial institutions, towards a much greater 'sensitivity to risk capacity and a better appreciation that diversity is the key to liquidity' (Persaud, 2008; 2010). Financial institutions are not equally suited for absorbing the three main types of risk; liquidity risk, credit risk and market risk. For an institution to be able to absorb liquidity risk it must operate on a long-term horizon, which is what long-term investors, such as pension funds, should be doing. To be able to absorb credit risk, a financial institution should have a diversified and uncorrelated pool of loans. The universal promotion of quantitative risk management models in and through the Basel II accord helped create a situation, however, where long-term investors were not playing their 'natural' role of absorbing liquidity risk and banks were selling on credit risk to institutions not suited for it. For the international financial system to be resilient, specific types of risk must be taken by institutions that have a 'natural capacity' for that type of risk. In order to achieve this, financial regulation must be diversified in the sense that different types of risk-management approaches are sanctioned and promoted for different types of financial institutions. In such diversified financial regulation lies, Persaud argues, a 'potential for a virtuous cycle' (Persaud, 2004, p. 102). 'The more short-run and long-term investors behave differently', he argues, 'the shorter market disruptions will be and the more this different behaviour would be profitable for long-run investors' (*ibid.*). A more effective regulation of international finance would need to promote such diversity and segmentation of risk, as opposed to the current homogenizing approach.

The 'grandfathering' of Basel III

Since early 2010, the banking industry has lobbied to postpone the implementation of whatever Basel III agreement would eventually be reached. Thus, during a meeting in South Korea in the spring of 2010 the G20 ministers agreed, on the advice of the Basel Committee, that implementation of Basel III was to be postponed from end-2012 to between 2014 and 2016. By September, the deadline had been further postponed to between 2015 and 2019. The key argument made by the banking industry to achieve a postponement has been that premature implementation of new capital regulations could threaten the fragile economic recovery (Lall, this volume). The main lobbying group of large international banks, the International Institute of Finance (IIF), thus released an impact assessment on 10 June, stating that the Basel III proposals would cause a cumulative reduction in GDP of 920 billion dollars – equivalent to 4.3 per cent of GDP by 2015 in the Eurozone alone. The US would see a reduction of 951 billion dollars or 2.7 per cent of GDP. Together this would amount to more than nine million fewer jobs created, the IIF stressed (Bryant and Masters, 2010). These assessments have not been confirmed by independent analysis. The chief economic advisor to the Bank of International Settlements, Steven Ceccheti, for instance, suggested in May 2010 that 'the net impact of the Basel committee reforms on growth will be negligible' and 'our preliminary assessment is that improvements to the resilience of the financial system will not permanently affect growth – except for possibly making it higher' (Giles, 2010).

The most troubling aspect of this 'grandfathering' is the considerable risk that even the limited revisions agreed upon in the form of the Basel III Accord will ultimately never come into effect. In each of the last seven international financial crises, plans for a 'radical shake up of international regulatory of monetary arrangements have made surprising progress, only to be tidied away and stuffed in the bottom drawer once the economy recovered' (Persaud, 2010).

Concluding remarks

Three trends in the history of international banking regulation from the mid-1970s to the mid-2000s stand out. First, minimal capital adequacy requirements gradually became the most important mode of banking regulation and international standard setting. Second, from the mid-90s, a shift took place from a rules-based approach towards a supervisory approach, focusing on ensuring the integrity of banks' own risk management systems in and through particularized review procedures. From a regulatory perspective, the Basel II Accord was a milestone in the sense that it unified these two trends into a common regulatory framework. The concern with capital adequacy requirements was integrated in the review-based approach to banking regulation by stipulating that capital reserves were to be calculated on a case-to-case basis, with reference to the particular risk management systems operated by the bank in question (Tarullo, 2008, p. 15). Third, these new methodologies for the calculation of capital reserves were characterized by a heavy reliance on market inputs (banks' own risk management models, credit ratings, market prices and so on.).

While these developments have proved to be problematic from a banking sector stability point of view, the Basel II Accord served well the short-term interests of the main parties involved. Banks successfully gamed the rules to the effect of considerably reducing capital reserves. Regulators, on the other hand, were convinced – with the persuasive assistance of international bankers' associations (Lall this volume) – that aligning capital requirements as closely as possible to the underlying risks in the portfolios of banks was key to striking the best possible balance between credit growth and banking stability.

Unfortunately, two of the core components of the Basel II accord – the sanctioning of various forms of VaR models for the calculation of capital reserves for market and credit risk and the introduction of lower capital reserve requirements for assets on banks' trading book as compared to their banking books – were key contributory causes of the global financial crisis that evolved only a few years after agreement on Basel II had been reached.[11] Although Basel II aimed at securing financial stability, in effect it contributed to excessive credit expansion in the banking system, which proved to be highly destabilizing for the global economy.

According to Jean-Claude Trichet, Chairman of the Basel Committee Group of Governors and Heads of Supervision, the Basel III accord will 'promote the long-term stability of the banking system' by launching 'a new regulatory landscape' that 'reflects the key lessons of the crisis' (BCBS, 2010c). The overall objective of the Basel III agreement is to strike a balance between credit growth and economic stability, it is said. This marks a new emphasis in international banking regulation. For the first time, it is explicitly acknowledged that credit growth should be kept in line with growth in the real economy if financial and macroeconomic stability is to be ensured. Unfortunately, the Basel III committee does not put its feet where its mouth is: the concern with excessive credit growth is cosmetic rather than substantive. This seems indeed to be the general pattern. While Basel III does address some of the key shortcomings of its predecessor, it does so in ways that are insufficient and inadequate if not immaterial.

The new measures introduced by the Basel III framework suffer from a range of conceptual and methodological limitations. The success of a *countercyclical buffer*, for instance, depends on the ability of national authorities to assess when risk is building in the system. But are the methodologies for assessing and predicting the future trajectory of financial risk that we have at our disposal much better now than they were before the crisis? Likewise, the success of the *liquidity ratio* depends on the ability to predict which assets are liquid. But the global financial crisis demonstrated how ample liquidity one day can be followed by its evaporation on the next. Even the leverage ratio, praised as a non-risk 'backstop' measure, suffers from the shortcomings of market-sensitive calculation and computation. Its success depends on the ability not only to set the ratio at the exact level where banks have enough capital, but also on being able to value assets 'correctly'. The Basel III agreement continues to rely on the principle of risk-weighted capital reserve requirements, based on a bank's own quantitative risk management models. This testifies to a continued belief in the possibility of knowing, calculating and managing financial risk on a day-to-day basis. 'Our goal is to ensure that all material risks are captured', proclaimed Nout Wellink, Chairman of the Basel Committee (BCBS, 2010d). Irrespective of the global financial crisis, the conviction still is that risks may be known, calculated and successfully managed by the use of sophisticated quantitative risk management models. The fundamental problem is, however, that we don't have a good grip on the dynamics of financial risk. 'No financial or bank crisis has ever occurred from something *ex-ante* perceived as risky', observes Per Kurowski (2010). On the contrary, 'they have all resulted, no exceptions, from excessive lending or investment in something perceived as not risky' *(ibid.)*.

These are just a few examples of a number of fundamental limitations of the Basel III accord, which may be briefly summarized as follows.

First, the agreed increase of capital reserve requirements is far from sufficient. Second, the provision for counter-cyclicality is only marginal, an add-on, when what is needed is for counter-cyclicality to be at the heart of capital reserve requirements. Third, concerns with monitoring and governing credit growth and capital market inflation are also relegated to the margins of the new Accord, despite the centrality of such efforts to macroprudential financial regulation. Fourth, there is no effort to adopt a differentiated approach to financial regulation that ensures that different types of financial institutions take the kinds of risk that they are most capable of absorbing. Fifth, implementation of revised and new regulatory measures has been postponed until the period from 2015 to 2019, as a result of intense banking industry lobbying.

The global financial crisis presented a unique opportunity to substantively revise the regulation of international banking and finance. Basel III effectively closed this historical window of opportunity. The Basel III Accord is, essentially, an intensification of Basel II rather than a substantial break with it. This does not bode well for the future financial stability of the world economy.

Notes

1   A key milestone in this work was the release of three reports setting the guidelines for the re-regulatory response to the crisis, prepared for and endorsed by the G20 leaders at their London summit in April 2009 (G20, 2009; FSF, 2009a, 2009b, 2009c).

2   The financial crisis in Asia in 1997–98 was widely believed to have been caused by 'bad banking' (Krugman, 1999), and thus played a key role in instigating a revision of banking standards in and around wider efforts to 'strengthen the international financial architecture' (Vestergaard, 2009; Kenen, 2001).

3   'The fundamental objective of the Committee's work to revise the 1988 Accord has been to develop a framework that would further strengthen the soundness and stability of the international banking system while maintaining sufficient consistency that capital adequacy regulation will not be a significant source of competitive inequality among internationally active banks' (BCBS 2006, §4).

4   Operational risk was added to Basel II in order to make provisions for events such as the breakdown of computer systems, natural disasters and fraud.

5   VaR emerged as a distinct concept in the late 1980s, in the wake of the stock market crash of 1987. But until the mid-1990s, VaR was a development project run by a limited number of 'quants' employed at the large US investment bank, JP Morgan. In 1994, JP Morgan published and gave free access to the methodology.

6   Scholars distinguish between two main approaches to producing VaR data for credit risk: ratings-based methods versus equity-based models (Nickell *et al.*, 2001).

7   A similar conviction was expressed by the Basle Committee in their first consultative paper on Basel II: "[T]he Committee recognizes that asset securitization can serve as an efficient way to redistribute the credit risk of a bank to other banks or non-bank investors" (BCBS, 1999).

8   Defenders of VaR say, in response, that VaR was never intended as a tool for the management of the financial risks associated with extreme events – for the rather obvious reason that extreme events per definition cannot be probabilistically modeled on the basis of historical data. The problem lies, they argue, not in the technology, but in misguided use of it: VaR models are one tool of analysis among many and financial institutions must deploy supplementary strategies for dealing with the occurrence of extreme events.

More specifically, strategies for dealing with extreme events should be developed on the basis of a combination of stress-testing and qualitative reasoning.

9 'Herding' denotes financial market behaviour where investors or bankers buy what others are buying and sell what others are selling, and hold on to what others hold on to, rather than making investment decisions based on their own risk assessments.

10 A leverage ratio is basically a measure of total assets or exposure to capital, but there are many variants for the design of a leverage ratio, which is illustrated by the long list of details on the definition of capital and exposure in the proposal.

11 Since Basel II was not formally ratified before early 2007 in the EU and in course of 2007 and 2008 in the US, some observers argue that it couldn't possibly have been a key contributory cause of the global financial crisis. But the perspective of this paper is that with respect to the risk management practices of internationally active banks, the date of international agreement on Basel 2 – reached in June 2004 – is far more decisive than the formal ratification dates in national parliaments.

References

Alexander, K., Dhumale, R. and Eatwell, J. (2006) *Global governance of financial systems – the international regulation of systemic risk* (Oxford: Oxford University Press).

BCBS, Basel Committee on Banking Supervision (1975) *Basel Committee: Report on the supervision of banks' foreign establishments – Concordat* (Basel: Bank of International Settlements).

BCBS, Basel Committee on Banking Supervision (1988) *Basel Committee: International convergence of capital measurement and capital standards* (Basel: Bank of International Settlements).

BCBS, Basel Committee on Banking Supervision (1996) *Amendment to the capital accord to incorporate market risks* (Basel: Bank of International Settlements).

BCBS, Basel Committee on Banking Supervision (1999) *A new capital adequacy framework. Basel Bank for International Settlements* (Basel: Bank of International Settlements).

BCBS, Basel Committee on Banking Supervision (2006) *Basel II: International convergence of capital measurement and capital standards: A revised framework – comprehensive version* (Basel: Bank of International Settlements).

BCBS, Basel Committee on Banking Supervision (2009) *History of the Basel Committee and its Membership* (Basel: Bank of International Settlements).

BCBS, Basel Committee on Banking Supervision (2010a) *Basel III: A global regulatory framework for more resilient banks and banking systems* (Basel: Bank of International Settlements).

BCBS, Basel Committee on Banking Supervision (2010b). *Guidance for national authorities operating the countercyclical buffer* (Basel: Bank of International Settlements).

BCBS, Basel Committee on Banking Supervision (2010c) *Press Release: The Group of Governors and Heads of Supervision reach broad agreement on Basel Committee capital and liquidity reform package* (Basel: Bank of International Settlements).

BCBS, Basel Committee on Banking Supervision (2010d). *A new regulatory landscape – remarks of Nout Welling*. Speech by Chairman of the Basel Committee on Banking Supervision, Nout Wellink, at the 16th International Conference of Banking Supervisors in Singapore, September 2010 (Basel: Bank of International Settlements).

Borio, C. (2004) 'Market stress and vanishing liquidity', in A. Persaud (ed.) *Liquidity black holes. Understanding, quantifying and managing financial liquidity risk* (London: Risk Books).

Brunnermeier, M., Crockett, A., Goodhart, C., Persaud, A. and Shin, H.S. (2009) *The fundamental principles of financial regulation* (London: Centre for Economic Policy Research).

Bryant, C. and Masters, B. (2010) 'Bankers fear effects of Basel rules', *Financial Times*, 10 June 2010.

Davies, H. and Green, D. (2008) 'Global financial regulation – the essential guide', (Cambridge, Polity Press).

Einhorn, D. and Brown, A. (2008) 'Private profits and socialized risk', *GARP Risk Review*, June/July 2008.

Engelen, E., Erturk, I., Froud, J., Weaver, A. and Williams, K. (2010) 'Reconceptualizing financial innovation: frame, conjuncture and bricolage' *Economy and Society*, 39 (1), 33–63.

FSF, Financial Stability Forum (2008) *Report of the Financial Stability Forum on Enhancing Market and Institutional Resilience* (Basel: Bank of International Settlements, Financial Stability Forum).

FSF, Financial Stability Forum (2009a) *Report of the Financial Stability Forum on addressing procyclicality in the financial system* (Basel: Bank of International Settlements, Financial Stability Forum).

FSF, Financial Stability Forum (2009b) *FSF principles for sound compensation practices* (Basel: Bank of International Settlements, Financial Stability Forum).

FSF, Financial Stability Forum (2009c) *FSF principles for cross-border cooperation on crisis management* (Basel: Bank of International Settlements, Financial Stability Forum).

Giles, C. (2010) 'Bankers' 'doomsday scenarios' under fire from Basel study chief', *Financial Times*, 31 May 2010.

G20, Group of Twenty (2009) *Leaders statement – the global plan for recovery and reform*. The Group of Twenty, London, April 2009.

Guha, K. and Tett, G. (2007) 'Turmoil tests a system that slices up and disperses risk', *Financial Times*, 15 August 2007.

Hanson, S., Kashyap, A.K. and Stein, J.C., (2010) 'A macroprudential approach to financial regulation', Manuscript, submitted to *Journal of Economic Perspectives*.

Holten, G.A. (2004) 'Capital calculations: Has the CCRO missed the point?', *Energy Risk*, 1(3).

IMF (2006) *Global Financial Stability Report – Market Developments and Issues* (Washington, International Monetary Fund).

Jobst, A. (2008) 'What is securitization?', *Finance and Development* (Washington, D.C.: International Monetary Fund).

Johnson, S. (2010a) 'Why higher capital standards are needed', *New York Times*, 29 July 2010.

Johnson, S. (2010b) 'Basel III: the fatal flaw', *The Baseline Scenario*, 16 September 2010.

Kenen, P. (2001) *The international financial architecture: What's new and what's missing?* (Washington, D.C.: Institute for International Economics).

Krugman, P. (1999) 'What happened to Asia?', in S. Ramachandran (ed.) *Global competition and integration* (Dordrecht: Kluwer Academic Publishers).

Kurowski, P. (2010) *The bare-naked Basel Committee* Blogpost on 28 September 2010 downloaded on 10 October 2010 at http://subprimeregulations.blogspot.com/2010/09/bare-naked-basle-committee.html

Marcussen, M. (2007) 'The Basel Committee as a transnational governance network', in M. Marcussen and J. Torfing (ed.) *Democratic network governance in Europe* (Palgrave Macmillan).

Masters, B. (2010)'Basel rewrites capital rules for banks', *Financial Times*, 12 September 2010.

Nickell, P., Perraudin, W. and Varroto, S. (2001) 'Ratings- vs equity-based credit risk modeling', Bank of England, *Working Paper 132*.

Nocera, J. (2009) 'Risk mismanagement', *The New Yorker*, 2 January 2009.

Persaud, A. (2001) 'The disturbing interactions between the madness of crowds and the risk management of banks in developing countries and the global financial system', in S. Griffith-Jones and A. Bhattacharaya (eds.) *Developing countries and the global financial system* (London: Commonwealth Secretariat).

Persaud, A. (2004) 'Liquidity black holes', in A. Persaud (ed.) *Liquidity black holes. Understanding, quantifying and managing financial liquidity risk* (London: Risk Books).

Persaud, A. (2008) *What needs to be done – and by whom.* Dani Rodrik's weblog. http://rodrik.typepad.com/dani_rodriks_weblog/2008/10/what-is-to-be-done–and-by-whom.html

Persaud, A. (2010) 'The empire strikes back', *VOX*, 14 September 2010.

Power, M. (2005) 'The invention of operational risk', *Review of International Political Economy*, 12(4), 577–599.

Salmon, F. (2010) 'Basel 3 arrives', Felix Salmon's Reuters blog, http://blogs.reuters.com/felix-salmon/2010/09/12/basel-iii-arrives/.

Tarullo, D. (2008) *Banking on Basel: the future of international financial regulation* (Washington, D.C.: Peter G. Peterson Institute of Economics).

Vestergaard, J. (2009) *Discipline in the global economy. International finance and the end of liberalism* (London: Routledge).

Wolf, M. (2010) 'Basel: the mouse that did not roar', *Financial Times*, 14 September 2010.

4
Reforming Global Banking Standards: Back to the Future?

Ranjit Lall

Introduction

The recent financial crisis has prompted widespread calls for more robust regulation and supervision of the international banking system. The crisis laid bare a flawed financial architecture, designed by a handful of nations and limited to a small fraction of cross-border activity, which did little to prevent the catastrophic buildup of systemic risk. One of the key elements of this failed architecture was the Basel II Accord, a set of standards to govern the international banking system drawn up by the Basel Committee on Banking Supervision (BCBS), a group of G10 banking supervisors. 'After the current crisis', the economist Joseph Stiglitz has declared, 'it is clear that Basel II is dead' (Stiglitz, 2008, p. 21). Nouriel Roubini, meanwhile, argues that, 'All the pillars of Basel II have already failed even before being implemented' (Roubini, 2009). Some have even suggested that Basel II, although adopted only in the European Union in mid-2007, was itself one of the underlying causes of the crisis (Blundell-Wignall and Atkinson, 2008). The shortcomings of Basel II are especially puzzling given that the fundamental aim of the Basel II Committee, when it set out to reform banking rules in 1999, was to craft an Accord that significantly *improved* the safety and soundness of the international banking system. In this chapter, I ask why Basel II fell so short of its creators' aspirations. In answering this question, I also hope to explain why the latest attempt to regulate the international banking system, the so-called 'Basel III' Accord, is meeting a similar fate.

Basel II's failure, I argue, lies in regulatory capture, *'de facto* control of the state and its regulatory agencies by the "regulated" interests, enabling these interests to transfer wealth to themselves at the expense of society' (Mattli and Woods, 2009, p. 10). Large international banks systemically manipulated the provisions of Basel II in their favour, extracting rents at the expense of their smaller competitors and, above all, the stability of the international financial system. They did this by exploiting their personal links with the Basel Committee to secure 'first-mover advantage' in the regulatory process. Arriving first at the decision-making table gave them disproportionate influence over regulatory outcomes, since policy decisions made at an early stage tend to be self-reinforcing.[1] As more resources are invested in a given policy, the costs of abandoning that policy in favour of once-possible options increase commensurately.[2] Unfortunately, the banking industry's relationship with the regulatory community – the basis of its ability to gain first-mover advantage – has only strengthened since the publication of the Accord in 2004. It helps us to understand not only why the Basel Committee failed to achieve its original objectives for Basel II, but also why the latest attempt to reform global banking rules, despite the tremendous political will behind it, is likely to enjoy no more success. The fate of Basel III, my analysis warns, is very much a case of history repeating itself.

There are few areas of regulation as closely linked to broader macroeconomic stability and efficiency as banking regulation. Banks occupy a pivotal position in the economy, both as the basis of an efficient payments system and the key agents of financial intermediation – transforming the savings of those with a surplus (lenders) into productive investment by those with a deficit (borrowers). In part to protect the deposit insurance fund and in part to minimize the often enormous negative externalities associated with bank failures, regulators tend to impose a variety of prudential standards on banks aimed at ensuring their safety throughout the economic cycle. Over the past 25 years, capital adequacy requirements have emerged as the dominant form of prudential regulation. The rationale for holding regulatory capital – mostly made up of shareholders' equity – against bank assets is to provide a buffer against unexpected losses, allowing the bank to continue to operate during periods of stress. Where requirements are not high enough, banks will not have sufficient capital to cover their losses; liabilities will quickly come to outweigh assets, rendering them insolvent.

Unfortunately for banks, capital requirements come at a cost. Since equity is significantly more expensive than debt as a source of financing, when banks are forced to maintain capital buffers exceeding their preferred level they tend to regard these requirements as a form of 'regulatory taxation' (Jackson *et al.*, 1999a, p. 22.). By lowering their capital levels, banks can reduce funding costs, increase leverage and boost their return on equity. For banks with sizeable asset bases, a tiny percentage reduction in capital requirements can represent a windfall of billions of dollars. As I show later, the incentive to minimize capital has proved too strong to resist. By hijacking Basel II negotiations, large international banks effectively rewrote the standards on international capital regulation to give themselves free rein to set their own capital requirements. The result was an Accord that allowed those institutions that posed the *greatest* threat to the stability of the financial system to hold the *least* capital – a recipe for economic disaster.[3] Understanding why Basel II failed to achieve the proper goals of capital regulation has important implications for subsequent efforts to create standards governing the international banking system, including Basel III.

The chapter is organized as follows. Section two begins with a brief history of the Basel Committee and the transition from the first Basel Accord to the second. This is followed by a more detailed account of the gap between the Basel Committee's objectives for Basel II and the outcome of the regulatory process. I attempt to explain this gap in section three. I show how personal contacts within the Basel Committee enabled large international banks to arrive first in the regulatory process and secure their favoured provisions in Basel II. Section four turns to the latest attempt to revise international capital adequacy standards, Basel III. I provide compelling evidence that the very same factors that caused Basel II's failure are now preventing any meaningful progress for its successor.

The failure

Although the Basel Committee's initial work focused on determining the responsibilities of home and host country regulators *vis-à-vis* cross-border banks, its mandate soon expanded to capital requirements. The first framework for the capital regulation of internationally active banks was the 1988 Accord on Capital Adequacy, or Basel I (BCBS, 1988). Minimum capital requirements were based on two ratios: a ratio of Tier 1 (mainly equity) capital to risk-weighted assets of 4 per cent; and a ratio of Tier 1 plus Tier 2 (undisclosed reserves, loan-loss provisions, subordinated debt) capital to risk-weighted assets of 8 per cent. Assets were risk-weighted weighted according to the credit risk of the borrower – that is, the risk that the borrower will default on a loan. Government bonds, for example, had a zero risk weighting, which entailed that no capital needed to be held against them. Traditional corporate loans, meanwhile, had a 100 per cent risk weighting, which entailed that capital constituting the full 8 per cent of the value of a loan must be held against it.

By the late 1990s, the Accord had come to be seen as a blunt instrument that was 'useless for regulators and costly for banks' (quoted in Wood, 2005, p. 129). It provided easy opportunities to engage in regulatory arbitrage: exploiting the difference between economic risk and regulatory requirements to reduce capital levels without reducing exposure to risk. Its crude risk buckets for different categories of borrower entailed, for instance, that a loan to a secure blue chip company was treated the same as a retail customer's overdraft. This gave banks an incentive to move towards riskier, higher-yielding assets within a given bucket (from blue chip loans to retail overdrafts). Further, Basel I's narrow focus on the traditional 'originate-to-hold' model of banking encouraged banks to shift assets off the balance sheet, typically securitizing them.[4] By securitizing a pool of loans and selling the tranches on to third parties with partial recourse or financial guarantees, banks were able to lower capital requirements while retaining the full risk associated with the original pool (Jackson *et al.*, 1999a). The consequence of these activities was that overall capital levels in the banking system, which had risen sharply after Basel I came into effect in the early 1990s, were now beginning to decline.[5]

In September 1998 the Basel Committee announced that it would officially review the 1988 Accord with the aim of replacing it with more flexible rules. In June 1999 it released its first set of proposals for the new framework. According to the Committee, the new accord would have the following objectives: (1) The Accord should continue to promote safety and soundness in the financial system and, as such, the new framework should at least maintain the current overall level of capital in the system; (2) The Accord should continue to enhance competitive equality; (3) The Accord should constitute a more comprehensive approach to addressing risks (BCBS, 1999).

After five years of negotiations, notice-and-comment rounds and impact studies, the Committee finally announced that it had agreed on a new capital framework, the Basel II Accord. The accord rested on three 'pillars'. In addition to specifying minimum capital requirements (Pillar 1), the new accord provided guidelines on regulatory intervention to national supervisors (Pillar 2) and created new information disclosure standards for banks with a view to enhancing market discipline (Pillar 3).

As the regulatory process drew to a close, however, it became painfully clear that the Accord had failed to achieve *any* of its stated objectives.

With respect to the first and second objectives, the Committee's decision to establish an 'advanced internal ratings-based (A-IRB) approach' in Pillar 1 was crucial. Under the A-IRB approach, banks were for the first time permitted to use their own models to estimate various aspects of credit risk, an innovation that would ostensibly more closely align regulatory capital with underlying risk.[6] Smaller banks lacking the resources to operate in-house models would adopt the 'standardized approach', essentially a more refined version of Basel I which linked more fine-grained risk buckets to external ratings provided by credit rating agencies. As well as failing to improve the accuracy of credit risk assessments, the use of internal ratings would result in large capital reductions relative to Basel I. The fourth official 'Quantitative Impact Study' (QIS) showed that A-IRB banks would experience an average drop in minimum capital requirements of 15.5 per cent and a median reduction in Tier 1 capital of 31 per cent (OCC, FRS, FDIC, and OTS, 2006). Since the large banks adopting this approach hold a significant share of the market, overall capital levels in the banking system would almost certainly decline – on QIS-4 estimates by as much as 20 per cent in the United States – in explicit contradiction to Basel II's primary objective.

The introduction of internal ratings would also give the largest banks an enormous competitive advantage over their smaller rivals, breaching the Committee's second objective of enhancing competitive equality amongst banks. The 2006 QIS-5, for example, shows that A-IRB banks would experience a capital reduction of up to 26.7 per cent, while banks under the standardized approach would experience a 1.7 per cent *increase* in overall capital requirements (BCBS, 2006). Under Basel II, these larger institutions would be able to free up capital, expand their asset bases and maximize profits, at the same time as other banks were forced to deleverage and liquidate assets. These discrepancies would almost certainly reduce the profitability of smaller banks, causing them to lose market share and making them more vulnerable to takeovers from larger banks. Indeed, a 2006 survey of over 300 banks by Ernst and Young found that 75 per cent believed Basel II would benefit the largest banks employing the most advanced risk modelling systems at the expense of those unable to adopt them (Thal Larsen, 2006) Basel II, despite the Committee's original intentions, would create clear winners and losers.

Finally, Basel II cannot be seen to constitute a more 'comprehensive' approach to addressing risks. The Accord decisively failed to capture the three previously unregulated types of risks earmarked by the Committee at the beginning of the regulatory process: trading book risks, market risk and securitization risk. Provisions for trading book risks were conspicuously absent, despite the Committee's awareness that the size of trading portfolios had mushroomed as a result of Basel I.[7] The treatment of market risk was little better.[8] Under Basel II, banks would be allowed to use sophisticated mathematical models to produce estimates of 'value-at-risk' (VaR), even though these models had been revealed in the late 1990s to vastly underestimate the probability of 'extreme' market events.[9] Finally, banks were allowed to hold negligible levels of capital against securitized assets, largely on account of the extremely low risk weights assigned to highly rated tranches, precisely those positions that incurred the largest losses in the recent crisis. According to QIS-5, A-IRB banks would see their securitization capital requirements fall by between 0 per cent and 17.3 per cent, while other banks would experience an increase of between 7.7 per cent and 10.2 per cent – figures that also have serious implications for the competitive equality (objective 2) that the Committee had aimed to achieve.[10]

What explains the astonishing gap between the Committee's initial aims for Basel II and the final product of the regulatory process? In the next section, I attempt to test the hypothesis that Basel II's failure was the result of the excessive influence of large international banks in negotiations for the Accord.

Why Basel II failed: an in-depth examination of the standard-setting process

To test my account of Basel II's failure, I propose to use the method of process-tracing. A close examination of Basel Committee documents, press releases, interview transcripts and other sources will help to determine whether the implications of the capture hypothesis are borne out in the sequence of events comprising the Basel process (George and Bennett, 2005, p. 6). The first part of the section focuses on the Basel Committee's failure to achieve its first and second aims for the Accord, the result of its decision to allow the largest banks to use internal ratings. The second part will turn to the third aim, and the developments in the treatment of market risk, the trading book, and securitization that caused Basel II to fall short of providing a more 'comprehensive' approach to risk management.

Internal ratings

The Basel Committee's decision to create an A-IRB approach to credit risk represents perhaps the clearest example of excessive industry influence in the Basel process. It should be evident by now that the attraction of internal ratings for large international banks lies in their potential for bringing about significant capital reductions. This can occur for two reasons. First, internal ratings are largely derived from historical data, which tend to understate the level of capital needed against future losses. Historical default rates of asset classes are often poor indicators of future default rates, and during financial crises assets which were previously uncorrelated tend to become correlated, generating much larger losses than anticipated.[11] Second, internal ratings provide banks with an easy opportunity to engage in regulatory arbitrage – reducing capital without reducing risk. The irony, of course, is that internal ratings were introduced as a *solution* to regulatory arbitrage.

Central to the introduction of an A-IRB approach to credit risk was the Institute of International Finance (IIF), a powerful Washington-based lobby representing major US and European banks. The IIF had long enjoyed a close relationship with the Basel Committee based on its personal contacts in national regulatory agencies. The longest-serving Chairman of the Basel Committee, the Bank of England's Peter Cooke (1977–88), was in fact one of the co-founders of the IIF.[12] The Chairman of the Committee in the mid-1990s, the Bank of Italy's Tommaso Padoa-Schioppa, was a close associate of Charles Dallara, Managing Director of the IIF since 1993. Indeed, it was after meeting at a social occasion in March 1995 that the two agreed to establish an 'informal discussion' on regulatory issues between financial institutions and bank supervisors. This led to the creation of the Market Risk Amendment in 1996 (see below), the product of close cooperation between Committee members and the IIF under agreed 'ground rules' of strict confidentiality. These links became even stronger under the chairmanship of William McDonough (1998–2003), a president of the New York Federal Reserve who presided over almost all of the Committee's work on Basel II. Another close friend of Dallara's from his 22 years at the First National Bank of Chicago, McDonough gave the IIF unprecedented access to the Committee from the earliest stage of the reform process. The institute even went as far as to establish a Steering Committee on Regulatory Capital in June 1999 specifically to make recommendations regarding the new Accord, a body that remained the Basel Committee's principal interlocutor throughout negotiations. The advantages of privileged access to standard setters were clear from the early stages of the Basel process. As early as the Second Consultative Paper in 2001 the IIF was able to identify seven different areas in which the Basel Committee had adopted its recommendations.[13]

One of these areas was the introduction of an internal ratings-based approach to credit risk. The IIF had lobbied aggressively for greater recognition of banks' own risk measurement systems since November 1997, on the grounds that they were more risk-sensitive than Basel I's arbitrary risk weights and had the crucial advantage of being already in use by banks (IIF, 1997). This proposal was initially met with skepticism by standard setters. At the September 1998 conference at which the Committee announced its agenda for revising Basel I, Bank of England staff stated that there were 'significant hurdles' to using internal systems to set capital requirements (Jackson *et al.*, 1999b, p. 100.) Similarly, a study by two Federal Reserve economists found the state of ratings systems in large American banks far less advanced than had been widely assumed (Treacy and Carey, 1998). Nevertheless, by the release of the first consultative paper for the new Accord the IIF had succeeded in convincing enough of the Committee of the merits of an A-IRB approach to credit risk for 'some sophisticated banks' (BCBS, 1999, p. 37.) There were, however, only a few paragraphs devoted to the idea, and the focus of the paper was how *external* ratings provided by credit rating agencies would be formally incorporated into the Accord. What changed between the release of the first paper in June 1999 and the second in January 2001, in which a full specification of a new A-IRB approach was given?

The answer lies in the persistent lobbying of the IIF, which took advantage of its intimacy with the Committee to ensure that the advanced approach, almost an afterthought in the first paper, became a reality. During 2000, the Steering Committee published a report specifically urging the Basel Committee to permit banks to use their internal risk rating systems as a basis for assessing capital requirements. Sir John Bond, then Chairman of the IIF, suggested that the measure was 'important for enhancing the competitiveness of banks by bringing individual banks' capital requirements more in line with actual risks' (Ibison, 2000). Revealingly, a credit risk manager at the UK's Financial Services Authority (FSA) at the time admitted that 'more regulators around Europe are coming round to the view that a large number of banks should be able to qualify for internal ratings' (Mackintosh, 2000). By mid-2000, it seems, every member of the Basel Committee had come around to the IIF's view, and the working group on credit risk began informal work with the IIF to incorporate internal ratings into the new framework.[14] The second draft's detailed exposition of the A-IRB approach was 'welcomed' by the IIF's Steering Committee as one of seven areas in which its recommendations had been taken on board (IIF, 2001a, p. 6).

By the time small and non-G10 banks became aware of the likely impact of these developments, the release of the second consultative paper in 2001, negotiations were at such an advanced stage that an overhaul of the Committee's proposals was near impossible. As the vice president of a leading association of American community banks, put it, 'We didn't get involved until quite a late stage... And when we did, the modelling (A-IRB) approach was already set in stone. The [Basel] Committee had been convinced by the large banks.'[15] The few comments on the paper left by small banks reflected serious apprehension about the potential competitive inequities of Basel II. Among the loudest voices were the Second Association of Regional Banks, a group representing the Japanese regional banking industry, and Midwest Bank, an American regional bank catering to consumers in Missouri, Iowa, Nebraska and South Dakota. The latter protested that the few banks qualifying for the A-IRB approach 'will not be required to keep the same level of capital against financial instruments as 99 per cent of the financial institutions in this nation who cannot qualify under these standards' (Midwest Bank, 2001, p. 1.) These concerns were perhaps best expressed by America's Community Bankers (ACB), another group representing community banks across the United States. The ACB made a strong case for the claim that 'the Accord will benefit only the most complex and internationally active banks, saddling the vast majority of financial institutions in the United States with a cumbersome and expensive capital regulatory scheme...' (ACB, 2001, p. 2). This was most pronounced, the group claimed, in Pillar 1, where 'the proposed bifurcation between the standardized and internal ratings-based approaches to establishing minimum capital requirements will competitively disadvantage many smaller banking institutions that lack the resources necessary for developing a finely calibrated IRB assessment system' (*Ibid*, p. 2).

Competitive fears were not confined to community banks. Several important emerging markets also expressed fears that they would be disadvantaged under the new arrangements. Commenting on the 2001 second consultative paper, the Reserve Bank of India complained that, by failing to qualify for internal ratings, emerging market banks would experience a 'significant increase' in capital charges (Reserve Bank of India, 2001, p. 2). The People's Bank of China, meanwhile, suggested that the proposals 'basically address the needs of large and complex banks in G10 countries' (People's Bank of China, 2001, p. 2). Similar worries were articulated by the Banking Council of South Africa, which pointed out that while 'the Accord aims at "competitive equality", the bigger, more advanced banks may have access to options that will give them a market advantage, whereas the smaller banks may find it difficult to afford the necessary infrastructure investments' (Banking Council of South Africa, 2001, p. 4) Like the objections of community banks, however, these came too late to influence proceedings. The costs of discarding years' worth of work on developing the A-IRB approach could not be borne by a Committee already under fire for breaching its deadline for finalizing the new Accord. It is no surprise that when a group of five major emerging markets protested about the Accord's competitive implications at a behind-closed-doors meeting in Cape Town in 2002, it was accused by Chairman McDonough of attempting to 'derail the whole process'.[16] By this stage the recognition of internal ratings was a well established feature of Basel II. Indeed, only very minor changes were made to Pillar 1's credit risk approaches between 2001's Second Consultative Paper and the final version of the Accord published in 2004.

Trading book, market risk and securitization

As mentioned in section two, the Committee's failure to achieve its third aim was a consequence of its refusal to properly regulate trading book risks, market risk and securitization risk. These developments can be traced to changes made both during negotiations for Basel II and in the mid-1990s shortly after Basel I came into effect.

Basel II's light treatment of the trading book had much to do with the International Swaps and Derivatives Association (ISDA), the largest global financial trade association, representing over 860 institutions in the privately negotiated derivatives industry. As one of the first organizations to comment on the new trading book framework, the ISDA managed to persuade standard setters to defer to its judgement on several key provisions. Perhaps the most important of the Committee's reversals was its September 2001 decision to drop an earlier proposal for an additional capital charge to cover the risks associated with credit derivatives. The ISDA had forcefully lobbied against the measure, dubbed the 'w factor', on the grounds that it was 'unjustified in light of market practice: losses experienced on repo or credit derivatives trades had been minimal, and the contracts used to document the transactions were enforceable and effective' (Boland, 2001). The Committee's reversal, as the *Financial Times* noted at the time, was at odds with concerns earlier expressed by its members about the possibility that the structure of some derivatives tended to concentrate risk rather than dispersing it (as they are in theory meant to do) *(Ibid)*.

The ISDA also had a hand in the Committee's failure to regulate those trading book risks that were not captured by standard market risk models, in particular counterparty credit risk. The Committee's trading book working group, which worked closely with the ISDA, bought into the association's argument that 'the assumptions regarding the calibration of credit risk requirements in the banking book may not be appropriate for trading book exposures, which are typically short term in nature, more liquid, and marked-to-market' (ISDA, 2001, p. 11). As one former member of the Committee admitted, 'We went too far on capital relief for the trading book. We were convinced by the industry that [instruments in the trading book] needed a lower capital charge because they were more liquid...In good times, it's hard to go against the banks.'[17] The recent financial crisis has shown this argument to be fatally flawed, with heavy losses on highly illiquid and opaque trading book instruments. In the end, the section devoted to the trading book was one of the shortest in the 2004 final Accord. Accusations of regulatory forbearance, which grew louder in 2004, once again came too late. While the Basel Committee was forced to admit that increased capital charges for trading book risks were needed, given 'the complexities of the trading book issues to be discussed', it was willing only to defer reform to a later date (Tiner, 2004).

The only aspect of the trading book that the Committee made a concerted effort to tackle was market risk, albeit in the mid-1990s rather than during official negotiations for Basel II. Even in this area, though, proposals were significantly watered down in the face of industry pressure. In 1993, the Committee proposed to amend the 1988 Accord to incorporate market risk, largely in response to the deregulation of interest rates and capital controls, which had increased banks' vulnerability to market fluctuations. The 1993 paper proposed a standardized methodology for measuring market risks which calculated capital requirements on the basis of certain characteristics of debt securities and derivatives, such as maturity, credit rating, and category of borrower (BCBS, 1993). These proposals were met with strong opposition from the IIF, which complained that they failed to recognize the most 'sophisticated' modelling techniques already in use (IIF, 1993). The IIF was soon joined by the Group of Thirty, a Washington-based association of senior bankers, which backed VaR models as 'much more analytically rigorous than the old rules of thumb that bankers used to use' (Gapper and Corrigan, 1994). Although at first reluctant to consider the use of VaR models, regulators began to give serious attention to the proposal after the establishment of an informal dialogue with the IIF in early 1995 (see above). By early 1995, the Committee fully endorsed the IIF's proposals, officially recognizing the use of in-house VaR models in a consultative paper released in April (BCBS, 1995).

This was a surprising development given the 'quite disparate' results from the Committee's testing exercise, which showed significant overall dispersion in capital charges for the same trading book even after the apparent factors causing systematic differences in model output were controlled for (*Ibid*, p. 5). It was also surprising given the serious doubts about these models that began to surface in 1995, such as the rating agency Standard and Poor's warning that the models only 'appear to offer mathematical precision' and that 'they are not a magic bullet' (Lapper, 1995). Most surprising, though, was the fact that these models passed into Basel II without question. At the time the Committee

Table 4.1   Initial aims and regulatory outcomes in Basel II

	Initial aim	Industry Lobby	Industry Recommendation	Final proposal
Internal Ratings	Incorporate external credit ratings into new framework	IIF	Recognize internal credit risk models of large banks	Recognition of internal ratings for large banks in A-IRB approach
Trading Book	Introduce capital charge for derivatives risk ('w factor'); capture counterparty credit risk	ISDA	Drop 'w factor'; do not apply credit risk capital requirements to trading book	'W factor' abolished in 2001; minimal regulation of trading book
Market Risk	Standardized methodology based on fixed risk parameters	IIF	Substitute standardized methodology for market risk (VaR) models	Recognition of VaR models in 1996
Securitization	Link risk weight categories to external credit ratings	ESF, ASF	Lower risk weights for rated tranches	Reduced weights for rated tranches

was formulating its first draft Accord in early 1999, banks were reporting widespread losses on Russian government bonds that were entirely unanticipated by their VaR models. Bankers Trust, an American wholesale bank, reported that on five days during the latest quarter its trading account losses had exceed its one day 99 per cent VaR calculation, a figure that statistically should be exceeded on just one day in a hundred (Graham, 1999). J.P. Morgan, too, reported that daily trading results had fallen below average far more often than its market risk models had predicted. Most damningly, a report published by the International Monetary Fund (IMF) in December 1998 had condemned VaR models for paying 'insufficient attention' to extreme market events and assuming that the processes generating market prices were stable (IMF, 1998). But despite widespread and persistent criticism, no questions were raised within the Committee about the continued use of VaR models in 1999.

Finally, Basel II's failure to create a more comprehensive approach to risk management also stemmed from its lenient treatment of asset securitization. In this case, the key actors were large forums for banks specializing in the trade of off-balance sheet instruments, in particular the European Securitization Forum (ESF) and the American Securitization Forum (ASF).[18] These forums persuasively argued that securitization facilitates prudent risk management and diversification by providing an efficient means for banks to redistribute their risks to those most willing to bear them. Securitization, the ESF claimed, 'has proven itself to be a source of safe, fixed income assets from the perspective of banks as investors' (ESF, 2001, p. 4). Although the credibility of these claims has been shattered by the recent crisis, the Committee proceeded to heavily dilute its securitization proposals, requiring progressively less capital for the same exposures as negotiations wore on. It even began to adopt the securitization industry's language, reiterating in several proposals that 'the Committee recognizes that asset securitization can serve as an efficient way to redistribute the credit risks of a bank to other banks or non-bank investors' (BCBS, 1999).

In its first draft in 1999, the Basel Committee proposed to directly tie capital charges for securitization tranches to external credit ratings. For all banks, tranches rated AAA or AA- would carry a 20 per cent risk weight, A+ to A- a 50 per cent weight, BBB+ to BBB- 100 per cent, BB+ to BB- 150 per cent, and B+ or below a deduction from capital. These proposals soon became the subject of intense industry opposition. In 2001, the ESF complained that the prescribed risk weights for rated tranches under the A-IRB approach were 'excessive', arguing that they should never be higher than identically-rated conventional corporate exposures (ESF, 2001). After the IIF stepped in to back the ESF's claim, protesting that the 'proposal's recommended treatment of securitiza-tion activities is too stringent and risks disrupting the valuable aspects of existing activities', the Committee acquiesced, almost halving risk weights for large banks in order to link them with corporate exposures with similar default probabilities (IIF, 2001b, p. 11). In the next two years, further reductions were made to A-IRB risk weights on the advice of the securitization forums. By the release of the final paper in 2004, they had reached dangerously low levels: risk weights for the senior positions of tranches rated AAA would be 7 per cent, AA 8 per cent, A+ 10 per cent, A 12 per cent, BBB+ 35 per cent, and BB 60 per cent (BCBS, 2004b). The risk weights for rated tranches under the standard-ized approach, meanwhile, remained the same as in the 1999 first draft. This was a startling reversal. The inadequate treatment of securitization under Basel I, after all, was one of the key reasons for updating it in the first place. It is hard to resist the conclusion that, had another set of actors been first on the scene, securitization proposals would have reflected a very different set of preferences.

A detailed examination of the Basel process, then, provides strong support for the capture hypothesis. By claiming first-mover advan-tage in negotiations for Basel II, large international banks were able to ensure that every one of their recommendations was incorporated into the final version of the Accord (as summarized in Table 1). The prefer-ences of second-movers, such as smaller and emerging market banks, were nowhere to be seen in Basel II. The ultimate consequence of these developments, regrettably for the Basel Committee, was an Accord that failed to achieve any of its original aims.

Implications for the fate of Basel III

Beginning in the subprime mortgage market in the United States in the summer of 2007 and quickly spreading to Europe and the rest of the world, the recent financial crisis has passed perhaps the most damn-ing verdict of all on Basel II. Whether or not they view it as a direct contributor to the crisis, supervisors have agreed that the fundamental tenets of the Accord – reliance on internal risk models, capital relief for the largest banks, and minimal regulation of the trading book – have been all but discredited by recent events. Something of a consensus has arisen in policymaking circles that a new approach to capital regulation is essential to the future stability of the global financial system. The

Financial Stability Forum (2008), an influential group of finance ministers and central bankers, issued a postmortem on the crisis in 2008 criticizing the 'significant weaknesses' in the existing capital framework (FSF, 2008, p. 12). The February 2009 Larosière Report, a framework for the future of European financial regulation, demanded 'fundamental review' of Basel II on the grounds that it 'underestimated some important risks and over-estimated banks' ability to handle them' (De Larosière Group, 2009, p. 16). The FSA's much anticipated Turner Review called for minimum standards to be 'significantly increased from [the] current Basel II regime' (FSA, 2009, p. 54). These efforts culminated in a 'regulatory tsunami' of new and far-reaching proposals issued by the Basel Committee in December 2009, dubbed 'Basel III'. The reform package shook the finance industry and in some eyes heralded a new era in the history of banking regulation – an era of 'more capital, more liquidity, and less risk' (PricewaterhouseCoopers, 2010, p. 6).

Such conclusions are too hasty. In this section, I argue that the same factors that led to Basel II's failure have resurfaced to undermine its successor. Despite the immense political will behind an overhaul of the global financial architecture, it is once again large international banks that have seized control of the regulatory process, effectively closing the window of opportunity for far-reaching reform. The first part of the section describes the favourable conditions, namely the shift of regulatory authority from the Basel Committee to the G20, under which Basel III was conceived. In the second part, I show how changes to these conditions in late 2009 lead us to expect an outcome of regulatory capture. In the final part, I test this prediction against the events of recent months, finding compelling evidence that large banks have enjoyed considerable success in diluting the reform proposals.

The origins of Basel III

To understand how large financial institutions have been able to regain control of the Basel process, we have to return to the origins of Basel III in late 2008. The unexpected collapse of investment bank Lehman Brothers in September saw the financial crisis spill over into the real economy. GDP growth in the Euro area ground to a halt in the third quarter of 2008 and fell to 1.3 per cent in the fourth; in the United States, 0.9 per cent growth in the second quarter turned into 0.3 per cent in the third and –1.3 per cent in the fourth.[19] With public anger at the financial sector mounting and banking regulation becoming an increasingly politicized issue, capital adequacy standards soon became the prerogative of the G20. Unlike the Basel Committee, the G20 is a forum of elected political leaders whose decisions are informed by a wide range of constituencies. Agreements reached by the group are therefore not expected to solely reflect the preferences of large international banks.

Indeed, the G20 was an effective advocate for capital adequacy reform. Two months after the Lehman collapse, the group called for international standard setters to 'set out strengthened capital requirements for banks' structured credit and securitization activities' (G20, 2008, p. 2). This prompted the Basel Committee, which had failed to make a single change to Basel II since the crisis broke out, to approve a set of enhancements to the Basel II trading book framework in July 2009 (BCBS, 2009). At the Pittsburgh Summit in September 2009, the G20 moved beyond the trading book, extending its demands to the whole of the Basel II framework. Setting a deadline of end-2010, the group ordered the Committee to formulate a new set of capital rules that would form the centerpiece of an 'international framework for reform' (G20, 2009, p. 8). These rules would include an international leverage ratio, countercyclical capital buffers, surcharges for 'systemically important' institutions, more restrictive definitions of capital, and short- and long-term liquidity ratios. In December 2009, the Committee took the first steps towards realizing the G20's vision for a new capital regime, issuing a set of preliminary proposals whose details would be filled in over subsequent rounds of negotiations during 2010 (BCBS, 2009). In a telling sign of the industry's frustration, IIF Managing Director Charles Dallara protested that 'political forces are driving the reform agenda, and central bankers have been marginalized in their role'(Chong, 2009). Chairman Joseph Ackermann, meanwhile, complained that he was not 'properly consulted' before the Pittsburgh Summit, and called on his fellow bankers to 'start again with an intensive dialogue between the private sector and the public sector on the strategic questions, on the technical details, including what is the economic price of certain things we are doing' (Guha, 2009a).

Fortunately for banks, the December reform package was only the beginning of the story for 'Basel III'. Rule-making soon returned to the Basel Committee, creating a major risk that the latest international capital Accord would once more fall short of its creators' aims. This is because the Committee formulating Basel III remains closely connected to the banking industry. One of the most prominent members of the Committee, the New York Federal Reserve's Marc Saidenberg, was head of regulatory policy at Merrill Lynch and a member of the IIF Committee on Market Best Practices until 2008. As recently as October

2007, the same month Merrill Lynch announced a record $7.9bn loss on subprime-related investments, Saidenberg was busy lobbying regulators to 'avoid a knee-jerk reaction to recent events' (Callan *et al.*, 2007). Senior figures in the Basel Committee, meanwhile, have moved in the opposite direction. Darryll Hendricks, formerly of Federal Reserve Bank of New York, chairs the IIF Working Group on Valuation; Patricia Jackson, formerly of the Bank of England, chairs the IIF Working Group on Ratings; Roger Ferguson, a former vice chairman of the Federal Reserve's Board of Governors, sits on the institute's board of directors. In perhaps its greatest coup, the IIF managed to recruit Jacques de Larosière, author of the abovementioned Larosière Report and former governor of the Bank of France, to head its newly formed Market Monitoring Group. Despite acknowledging in the report that the crisis 'has shown that there should be more capital, and more high quality capital, in the banking system, over and above the present regulatory minimum levels', Larosière has in recent months enthusiastically taken up the IIF's cause (De Larosière Group, 2009, p. 16). 'Capital ratios,' he claimed in October 2009, 'if they are not well conceived, could substantially harm our economies. I see a great danger here. Regulators must not start piling new ratios on the existing ones, adding further requirements (leverage ratios, special ratios on large systemically important institutions, anti-cyclical capital buffers) to the normal – and revamped – Basel II risk-based system... Together, their impact could be lethal.' (De Larosière, 2009).

Leverage ratio, capital surcharge, countercyclical buffers and liquidity ratios

Although the standard-setting process has yet to be concluded, there is strong evidence that large international banks have arrived first in the latest Basel process and that they are already enjoying considerable success in diluting Basel III. As well as being pushed back from their original 2012 starting date, key provisions of the Accord have been relaxed or even dropped in response to industry pressure. In the rest of this subsection, I examine five such provisions: the international leverage ratio; the capital surcharge on 'systemically important' institutions; countercyclical capital buffers; liquidity requirements; and restrictive definitions of capital.

The most contested element of the reform package has been the international leverage ratio, a simple ratio of equity to total (non-risk-weighted) assets introduced to provide a backstop against the risks inherent in the use of internal ratings. With some version of the ratio already in place in Canada, Switzerland and the United States, the

Committee's proposal to extend a leverage cap to all G20 countries has met with fierce resistance from European banks. Just one week after the publication of the December reform package, Denmark's largest financial institution Danske Bank protested that a leverage ratio would fail to capture the low risk of its large mortgage portfolio (Shanley, 2009). The Association of German Banks (BDB), meanwhile, called for the measure to be scrapped on the grounds that it 'would force banks to scale back their lending and therefore slow down the economic recovery' (BDB, 2010). Counterbalancing efforts by large American, Canadian, or Swiss banks to level the playing field have failed to materialize, largely a consequence of the perceived stringency of the Committee's proposal (unlike existing ratios it would capture all off-balance sheet assets and would not permit the netting of derivatives exposures).[20] With even banks such as JP Morgan and UBS opposed to the measure, regulators have been able to mount little resistance to the industry's offensive. In July 2010, the Committee announced that it would provisionally set the ratio at a mere 3 per cent, allowing banks to accumulate assets an incredible 33 times the value of their Tier 1 capital (BCBS, 2010, p. 3). It also refused to make compliance mandatory, proposing that the ratio form part of Pillar 2 – leaving its implementation at the discretion of national regulators – until at least 2018. It is no coincidence that almost one year before, as news of the G20's latest plans emerged, IIF managing director Charles Dallara had specifically called for 'leverage [to] be considered in this context under the so-called "Pillar 2" of the Basel II Accord' (Guha, 2009b).

The proposed capital surcharge on 'systemically important' banks has run into similar problems. After failing to influence the G20 with a lengthy report in July 2009 deeming it 'counterproductive', the IIF in recent months has intensified its lobbying efforts against the proposal, warning regulators as early as September 2009 of the dangers of 'setting up artificial categories of systemic firms' (IIF, 2009; Guha, 2009c). The banking industry, however, has not been united in its opposition to the surcharge. Smaller institutions, seeking to neutralize the capital advantage enjoyed by large banks under Basel II's A-IRB approach, have strongly supported the surcharge. The Independent Community Bankers of America (ICBA), an association representing 5,000 American community banks, has claimed that the 'largest financial institutions in the United States that are now considered "too big to fail" should be subject to a more rigorous set of leverage and risk-based capital requirements than other institutions and that are not determined by the institutions themselves based on internal risk-ratings formulas' (ICBA, 2010,

p. 3). Similarly, the World Council of Credit Unions (WOCCU), a trade association representing 54,000 not-for-profit credit unions around the world, has argued that the greater interconnectedness of A-IRB banks 'demands higher, not lower, capital requirements for large financial institutions, as the current calibration of Basel II suggests' (WOCCU, 2010, p. 2). Unfortunately, these actors may once again have arrived too late. By the time they registered their support for a capital surcharge – the end of the comment period in April 2010 – the Committee had already reached its own conclusions about the proposal. As early as March 2010, a month before the end of the comment period, one member noted a 'deeply-held scepticism around the table' regarding a rule-based capital add-on.[21] By mid-April, one week before the end of the comment period, the subcommittee charged with overseeing the proposal had already begun developing approaches for incorporating the surcharge into Pillar 2 of the new Accord (*Ibid*). The Committee confirmed fears that a potential surcharge would be non-binding in July, when it pledged to develop a 'guided discretion' approach to setting capital requirements for systemically important institutions (BCBS, 2010, p.5).

The Committee's attempt to mitigate the pro-cyclicality of the existing capital framework is likely to face more mixed fortunes. The proposed adoption of 'forward-looking provisioning' – an accounting practice that entails setting aside reserves for *expected* losses rather than actual losses – has been strongly supported by the Spanish banking industry, in particular Europe's largest bank Santander, which has been subject to a similar requirement since July 2000. Consequently, despite opposition from HSBC, UBS and the American Bankers Association, forward-looking provisioning is likely to feature in the final version of Basel III, with one Committee member describing the proposal as being 'warmly embraced' at a plenary in March 2010.[22] Other measures to tackle pro-cyclicality, however, look considerably less likely to survive the consultation process. The Committee's proposal to introduce 'countercyclical capital buffers' – buffers which are raised above regulatory minima in economic upswings and subsequently drawn upon as losses are incurred during periods of stress – has been contested by almost all segments of the industry. Several banks have followed the IIF's lead in arguing that 'such buffers must be determined, under flexible guidance, through a Pillar 2 approach, avoiding rigid triggers that are likely to be ineffective or counterproductive to a firm's recovery' (IIF 2010, p. 2). These views appear to be gaining currency. At its March 2010 plenary, a month before the deadline for public comments, the

Committee was said to have given a 'lukewarm reception' to preliminary proposals to include the add-on (linked to a credit-to-GDP ratio) in Pillar 1.[23] Although a formal version of the proposals was released for consultation in July, the Committee explicitly stated that the need for 'jurisdictional judgment makes [the proposals] distinct from the current Pillar 1 approach' (BCBS, 2010, p. 12).

Finally, efforts to introduce tighter definitions of capital and minimum liquidity requirements have suffered a significant setback in recent months. The Committee had originally proposed to exclude certain assets, such as minority interests and tax deferred assets, from the common equity component of Tier 1 capital because they had not proved sufficiently loss-absorbing during the crisis (BCBS, 2009, p. 13). Faced with the prospect of raising substantial amounts of new equity, a broad coalition of banks has mobilized to press the Committee to loosen its proposed definition of capital. The French Banking Federation (FBF), whose members depend heavily on equity provided by overseas shareholders, warned in April 2010 that the exclusion of minority interests would 'penalize the business model of cross-border groups' (FBF, 2010, p.4). The Japanese Bankers' Association (JBA), meanwhile, denounced the proposed treatment of tax deferred assets as 'one-sided' and 'rash', calling for it to be modified 'to ensure international comparability based on the differences in accounting standards and tax regime of each country' (Nakamoto, 2010; JBA, 2010, p. 13). In July 2010, the Committee yielded to industry pressure, allowing banks to include both types of assets in their common equity base. Echoing the FBF, the Committee justified its decision on the grounds that 'certain deductions could have potentially adverse consequences for particular business models and provisioning practices'.[24]

A similar reversal has characterized the Committee's stance on the liquidity coverage ratio (LCR) and net stable funding ratio (NSFR), provisions aimed at ensuring banks hold enough liquid assets to meet their short- and long-term funding needs. In its April submission to the Committee, the IIF protested that the stress scenarios used to calculate the ratios were 'implausible' and 'excessively restrictive', arguing for 'a more realistic approach, with the changes of assumptions that would follow from it' (IIF, 2010, p. 6). The institute also advised the Committee to expand its 'too-restrictive' definition of liquid assets under the LCR to include corporate and covered bonds, and to shift the NFSR to Pillar 2 because it was 'far from granular enough to support a highly prescriptive regime' (*Ibid*, p. 16). Remarkably, just three months later the Committee fully embraced the institute's recommendations.

Table 4.2 Initial proposals and likely regulatory outcomes in Basel III

Initial Proposal	Industry Recommendation	Likely outcome (Basel III)
Introduce international leverage ratio in Pillar 1 (i.e. binding)	Move to Pillar 2 (i.e. non-binding)	Ratio made non-binding until at least 2018; set at only 3%
Create capital surcharge for 'systemically important' institutions in Pillar 1	Drop surcharge	Removal or adoption in Pillar 2
Introduce countercyclical capital buffers in Pillar 1	Move buffers to Pillar 2	Adoption in Pillar 2
Exclude minority interests and tax deferred assets from common equity base	Drop proposal	Proposal abolished in July 2010
Introduce short-term liquidity coverage ratio (LCR) and longer-term net stable funding ratio (NSFR)	Use less demanding stress scenarios for both ratios; widen definition of liquid assets under LCR; shift NSFR to Pillar 2	Relaxed stress scenarios for both ratios; wider definition of liquid assets under LCR; NSFR moved to Pillar 2 until at least 2018

As well as instituting less demanding stress scenarios for both measures, it permitted banks to count corporate and covered bonds as part of their portfolio of liquid assets for LCR, and shifted the NSFR from Pillar 1 to Pillar 2 until at least 2018 (BCBS, 2010, p. 6).

To summarize, this section offers a pessimistic assessment of the likely outcome of Basel III negotiations. As the first to contribute to the post-crisis regulatory discourse, large international banks have managed to regain control of the Basel process, with devastating consequences for the latest efforts to create an effective international capital regime (see Table 2). With such conditions in place, only one outcome remains likely. Just as the Basel Committee of the late 1990s failed to meet its objectives for a new capital Accord, the Basel Committee of the late 2000s – ten years and one global financial crisis later – is set to meet a similar fate.

Conclusion

When the Basel Committee decided to update the original Basel Accord in 1998, it had high hopes for a new international standard for capital regulation. The new Accord, the Committee claimed, would remedy the defects of the existing regulatory framework and significantly improve the safety and soundness of the international banking system. Why did Basel II fail to live up to these expectations?

Basel II's failure, in a nutshell, was the result of excessive influence by the banking industry. By claiming first-mover advantage in the Basel process, a small group of well-connected international banks were able to overhaul the rules of international capital regulation to maximize their profits at the expense of those without a seat at the decision-making table. Community banks and emerging market institutions had little choice but to accept what was in effect a *fait accompli*.

Unfortunately, as we have seen, these very same factors may have also jeopardized the latest attempt to reform international capital requirements, Basel III. Given the importance of reform in this area for the health of the global economy, it is crucial therefore that we heed the lessons of the analysis presented here. Future efforts to revise capital adequacy standards must both observe ensure that access asymmetries between different stakeholders are as small as possible – principally, but not exclusively, by maintaining some kind of distance between supervisory bodies and the banking industry. Though difficult in practice to achieve, if implemented faithfully, such changes would go a long way towards ensuring that the next time regulators set out to revise international capital standards, they achieve every one of their aims.

Notes

1　There is an important caveat. Early participation will only confer a decisive advantage on actors when negotiators have little accountability to domestic constituents. It has little consequence when agreements reached at the international level must be endorsed by domestic constituents in a separate 'ratification phase'. This effectively nullifies the potential gains from early participation, since any deal can be later rescinded by domestic groups.
2　As Paul Pierson puts it (2004, p. 71), 'If early competitive advantages may be self-reinforcing, then *relative timing* may have enormous implications... groups able to consolidate early advantages may achieve enduring superiority. Actors arriving later may find that resources in the environment are already committed to other patterns of mobilization'.
3　As Andrew Haldane, Executive Director for Financial Stability at the Bank of England, colourfully puts it: 'Basel vaccinated the naturally immune at the expense of the contagious: the celibate were inoculated, the promiscuous intoxicated.' (Haldane, 2009, p. 27).
4　Securitization is a way of financing a pool of assets which involves transferring them to a third party conduit, usually a 'special purpose vehicle' (SPV),

which then issues asset-backed securities that are claims against the asset pool.

5   A July 1998 survey found that the average Tier 1 capital of the largest 1,000 banks made up only 4.48 per cent of total assets, its lowest level since 1992. Cited in Wood, 2005, p. 124.

6   The different aspects of credit risk include probability of default, expected loss given default, and exposure at default. Estimates are fed into a formula which determines the amount of capital that should be held against a given exposure. See BCBS, 2004a.

7   The trading book is the portfolio of financial instruments which are purchased or sold on the stock market to facilitate trading for a bank's customers or hedge against risk.

8   Market risk is defined by the BCBS as 'the risk of losses in on and off-balance sheet positions arising from movements in market prices' (BCBS, 2004a, p. 157).

9   VaR is the probability that losses on a portfolio of assets will exceed a certain amount within a given time horizon, for example $1m over the next ten days.

10   BCBS, 2006. For some banks the drop was as much as 43 per cent.

11   Author's interview with former BCBS member 1, Oxford, December 2008.

12   Author's interview with former BCBS member 2, Oxford, October 2008. The IIF was founded in 1983.

13   IIF, 2001a. The most frequent meetings with banking executives appear to have been conducted by the Federal Reserve trio of William McDonough, Roger Ferguson and Darryll Hendricks – all of whom had a private-sector background and went on to work at major banks after leaving the Basel Committee. Author's interview with former BCBS member 3, Washington D.C. January 2009.

14   Author's interview with former BCBS member 3, Washington D.C., January 2009.

15   Author's interview with vice president of community bankers' association, Washington D.C., January 2009.

16   Author's interview with former BCBS member 4, Washington D.C. January 2009.

17   Author's interview with former BCBS member 3, Washington D.C., January 2009.

18   Author's interview with former BCBS member 5, London, December 2008.

19   Data from IMF World Economic Outlook Database. Available at http://www.imf.org/external/pubs/ft/weo/2009/01/weodata/index.aspx (accessed 22/04/2010).

20   In the words of one credit analyst at Moody's, the proposal is 'far more draconian than the version currently being used in the US and Switzerland'. (Westlake, 2010).

21   Author's interview with BCBS member 6, London, February 2010.

22   *Ibid.*

23   Author's interview with BCBS member 7, London, February 2010.

24   BCBS, 2010, p. 1. These assets can now constitute up to 10 per cent of common equity each.

References

ACB, America's Community Bankers (2001) *Submission to the Basel Committee on Banking Supervision*. Available at www.bis.org/bcbs/ca/amcobare.pdf

Banking Council of South Africa (2001) *South African banks' response to BIS*. Available at http://www.bis.org/bcbs/ca/thbacosoaf.pdf

BCBS, Basel Committee on Banking Supervision (1988) *International Convergence of Capital Measurement and Capital Standards* (Basel: Bank of International Settlements).

BCBS, Basel Committee on Banking Supervision (1993) *The Supervisory Treatment of Market Risks* (Basel: Bank of International Settlements).

BCBS, Basel Committee on Banking Supervision (1995) *An Internal Model-Based Approach to Market Risk Capital Requirements*. (Basel: Bank for International Settlements).

BCBS, Basel Committee on Banking Supervision (1999) *A New Capital Adequacy Framework. Consultative Paper Issued by the Basel Committee on Banking Supervision* (Basel: Bank for International Settlements).

BCBS, Basel Committee on Banking Supervision (2004a) *International Convergence of Capital Measurement and Capital Standards: A Revised Framework* (Basel: Bank for International Settlements).

BCBS, Basel Committee on Banking Supervision (2004b) *Changes to the Securitization Framework* (Basel: Bank for International Settlements).

BCBS, Basel Committee on Banking Supervision (2006) *Results of the Fifth Quantitative Impact Study (QIS-5)* (Basel: Bank for International Settlements).

BCBS, Basel Committee on Banking Supervision (2009) *Strengthening the Resilience of the Banking Sector* (Basel: Bank for International Settlements).

BCBS, Basel Committee on Banking Supervision (2010) *Annex* (Basel: Bank for International Settlements).

Blundell-Wignall, A. and Atkinson, P. (2008) 'The Subprime Crisis: Causal Distortions and Regulatory Reform', paper presented at the *Reserve Bank of Australia Conference*, July, Kirribilli, Australia.

Boland, V. (2001) 'ISDA welcomes Basle decision', *Financial Times*, 25 September 2001.

BDB, Bundesverband deutscher Banken (2010) 'Association of German Banks warns of negative consequences of a leverage ratio'. Available at http://www.german-banks.com/html/15_press/press_00_100305.asp

Callan, E., Wighton, D. and Guha, K. 'Regulators urged to take back seat', *Financial Times*, 25 October 2007.

Chong, F. (2009) 'Bank fragmentation fears as politics overwhelms finance', *Asia Today Online*, 5 November 2009.

De Larosière Group (2009) *The High-Level Group on Financial Supervision in the EU* (Brussels).

De Larosière, J. (2009) 'Financial regulators must take care over capital', *Financial Times*, 16 October 2009.

ESF, European Securitisation Forum (2001) *Submission to the Basel Committee on Banking Supervision*. Available at http://www.bis.org/bcbs/ca/eursecfor2.pdf

FBF, French Banking Federation (2010) *FBF comments on the consultative documents*. Published by the Basel Committee on Banking Supervision (BCBS 164 &165). Available at http://www.bis.org/publ/bcbs165/frenchbankingfe.pdf

FSF, Financial Stability Forum (2008) *Report of the Financial Stability Forum on Enhancing Market and Institutional Resilience*, 7 April 2008.

FSA, Financial Services Authority (2009) *The Turner Review: regulatory response to the global banking crisis*.

Gapper, J. and Corrigan, T. (1994) 'Byte of the new bank managers', *Financial Times*, 7 September 1994.

George, A. and Bennett, A. (2005) *Case Studies and Theory Development in the Social Sciences* (Cambridge, MA and London, England: MIT Press).

Graham, G. (1999) 'Scientific certainties have taken a beating', *Financial Times*, 29 January 1999.

G20, Group of Twenty (2008) *Declaration of the summit on Financial Markets and the World Economy*. Washington D.C., November. Available at http://www.g20. org/Documents/g20_summit_declaration.pdf

G20, Group of Twenty (2009) *Leaders' Statement: The Pittsburgh Summit. September 24–25*. Available at: http://www.g20.org/Documents/pittsburgh_summit_ leaders_statement_250909.pdf

Guha, K. (2009a) 'Bankers warn on regulation's threat to growth', *Financial Times*, 2 October 2009.

Guha, K. (2009b) 'Bankers fight back against regulatory overkill', *Financial Times*, 2 October 2009.

Guha, K. (2009c) 'IIF warns on lack of global banking rules', *Financial Times*, 14 September 2009.

Haldane, A. (2009) 'Rethinking the Financial Network'. Speech delivered at the Financial Student Association, Amsterdam.

Ibison, D. (2000) 'IIF outlines banks' worries over Basel Accord reform', *Financial Times*, 13 April 2000.

ICBA, Independent Community Bankers of America (2010) *Submission to the Basel Committee on Banking Supervision*. Available at http://www.bis.org/publ/ bcbs165/icboa.pdf

IIF, Institute of International Finance (1993) *Report of the Working Group on Capital Adequacy*.

IIF, Institute of International Finance (1997) *Report of the Working Group on Capital Adequacy: Recommendations for Revising the Regulatory Capital Rules for Credit Risk*.

IIF, Institute of International Finance (2001a) *Report of the IIF Steering Committee on Regulatory Capital*. Available at http://www.bis.org/bcbs/ca/iistctonreca.pdf

IIF, Institute of International Finance (2001b) *Report of the Working Group on Capital Adequacy*. Available at: http://www.bis.org/bcbs/ca/iiwgoncaad.pdf

IIF, Institute of International Finance (2009) *Restoring Confidence, Creating Resilience: An Industry Perspective on the Future of International Financial Regulation and the Search for Stability*.

IIF, Institute of International Finance (2010) *Re: "Strengthening the Resilience of the Financial Sector" and "International Framework for Liquidity Risk, Measurement, Standards and Monitoring"*. Available at http://www.bis.org/publ/bcbs165/ioif.pdf

IMF, International Monetary Fund (1998) *World Economic Outlook and International Capital Markets: Interim Assessment*.

ISDA, International Swaps and Derivatives Association (2001) *Response to the Basel Committee on Banking Supervision's Consultation on the New Capital Accord*. Available at http://www.bis.org/bcbs/ca/isdaresp.pdf

Jackson, P., Furfine, C., Groeneveld, H., Hancock, D., Jones, D., Perraudin, W., Radecki, L., Yoneyama, M. (1999a) 'Capital Requirements and Bank Behavior: The Impact of the Basle Accord', *BCBS Working Paper no.1 (April)* (Basel: Bank for International Settlements).

Jackson, J., Nickell, P. and Perraudin, W. (1999b) 'Credit Risk Modelling', *Financial Stability Review (Bank of England)*, Issue 6, 94–121.

JBA, Japanese Bankers Association (2010) *Comment on the Basel Committee's Consultative Documents: "Strengthening the resilience of the banking sector," and "International framework for liquidity risk measurement, standards and monitoring"*. Available at http://www.bis.org/publ/bcbs165/japanesebankers.pdf

Lapper, R. (1995) 'Work ahead for quality controllers – banks', *Financial Times*, 12 April 1995.

Mackintosh, J. (2000) 'Banks may get right to assess own risk', *Financial Times*, 31 March 2000.

Mattli, W. and Woods, N. (2009) *The Politics of Global Regulation* (Princeton: Princeton University Press).

Midwest Bank (2001) *Submission to the Basel Committee on Banking Supervision*. Available at http://www.bis.org/bcbs/ca/midindbk.pdf

Nakamoto, M. (2010) 'Japan's banking chief hits at 'rash' capital proposals', *Financial Times*, 21 April 2010.

People's Bank of China (2001) *Comments on the Second Consultative Package on the New Capital Accord*. Available at www.bis.org/bcbs/ca/pebkofch.pdf

Pierson, P. (2004) *Politics in Time* (Princeton: Princeton University Press).

PricewaterhouseCoopers (2010) 'Basel Committee proposals for 'Strengthening the resilience of the banking sector: New rules or new game?' *Banking and Capital Markets*. Available at http://www.pwc.com/gx/en/banking-capital-markets/assets/PwC-basel-proposal.pdf

Reserve Bank of India (2001) *Comments of the Reserve Bank of India on the New Basel Capital Accord*. Available at www.bis.org/bcbs/ca/rebkofin.pdf

Roubini, N. (2009) 'Nouriel Roubini on prospects for 2009', *Financial Times*, 9 February 2009.

Shanley, M. (2009) 'Swedish FSA against binding bank leverage ratio', *Reuters*, 22 December 2009.

Stigtliz, J. (2008) 'Government Failure vs. Market Failure: Principles of Regulation', *working paper prepared for the Tobin Project's conference on "Government and Markets: Toward a New Theory of Regulation"*, 1–3 February 2008, Yulee, Florida.

Thal Larsen, P. (2006) 'Basel II best for biggest in banks' view', *Financial Times*, 10 April 2006, p. 23.

Tiner, J. (2004) 'The Practical Implications of SEC Regulation outside the United States', speech delivered at the Marriott Hotel, London.

Treacy, W. and Carey, M. (1998) 'Credit Risk Rating at Large US Banks', *Federal Reserve Bulletin* (November), 898–921.

OCC, FRS, FDIC, OTS: US regulatory agencies (Office of the Comptroller of the Currency, Federal Reserve System, Federal Deposit Insurance Corporation, Office of Thrift Supervision) (2006) *Summary Findings of the Fourth Quantitative Impact Study*.

Westlake, M. (2010) 'Heated debate seen likely over leverage ratio', *Global Risk Regulator*, 8(2), February 2010.

Wood, D. (2005) *Governing Global Banking: The Basel Committee and the Politics of Financial Globalization* (Aldershot: Ashgate).

WOCCU, World Council of Credit Unions (2010) *Re: Consultative document on Strengthening the Resilience of the Banking Sector.*

5
Moving Beyond Nuts and Bolts: The Complexities of Governing a Global Profession through International Standards

Christopher Humphrey and Anne Loft

Introduction

In the world of international financial reporting, standards are king! In this chapter we explore governance of financial reporting through the key instrument of standards. For both international and national organizations concerned with the global financial reporting[1] arena the vision is clear – that business enterprises, especially listed companies, will prepare their financial reports using International Financial Reporting Standards (IFRS[2]) produced by the International Accounting Standards Board (IASB). These financial reports will then be audited in accordance with International Standards on Auditing (ISA) produced by the International Auditing and Assurance Standards Board (IAASB) of the International Federation of Accountants (IFAC).

One of the reasons that this standard-setting arena is so interesting to study is that, as a case of private global standards, it seems relatively quite advanced in terms of adoption, implementation, oversight and compliance. This is despite the complexity of the global governance arena in which it operates and the fact that the character of the work itself makes it difficult to make and to use standards. This can be seen in the problems of, for example, sorting out how to apply the relevant IFRS to generate values for financial assets for which there is no market, how to audit such valuations and whether sufficient reliable audit evidence can be found. There is an expectation that convergence to one global set of standards for financial accounting and auditing will soon be achieved for listed companies and public interest entities – most recently fuelled by the G20, who in the leaders' statement made in Pittsburg in September 2009, called on 'our international accounting bodies to redouble their efforts to achieve a single set of high quality, global accounting standards within the context of their independent standard setting process, and complete their convergence project by June 2011'.[3]

Understanding the developing regime of international accounting and auditing standards demands a sound awareness of the institutions active in·this area, the wider global financial regulatory context and knowledge of the standards themselves. The key institutions are considered in the first part of the chapter, while in the latter part the focus is specifically on the international standards for auditing (ISAs), which involves looking not just at the standard setting process but also into the nature of the standards themselves – and how they get used in practice. Opening the 'black box' of the standards allows assessments of the extent to which standards are principles-based and rely on 'professional judgements' on the part of the auditor. This ultimately emphasizes the importance of studying not just standard setting, but also what happens as standards are implemented and enforced in practice.

Our interest in such issues derives from over a decade of research engagement with international auditing and related financial regulation (for example,. see Loft *et al*,. 2006; Humphrey *et al.*, 2009) and especially the work we have done in studying the history of the history of the International Federation of Accountants (IFAC). This has enabled us to build up an extensive collection of primary (original documents) and secondary (academic, professional and journalistic articles) source material on the development of international standards on auditing standards, as well as aspects of their adoption and implementation. In our role as IFAC historians, we have interviewed around 90 individuals who have been involved in IFAC; dealt with regulatory and governance issues in the big audit firms, and international regulators[4]; observed a variety of IFAC standard setting, executive board and council meetings, attended the most recent two World Congresses of Accountants (2006 and 2010); and participated in various professional conferences, including those organized by the Federation of European Accountants, the European Commission, and some national professional accounting associations.

Theoretically, our perspectives are rooted in those of Held and McGrew (2002) and others such as Brunsson and Jacobsen (2000) and Hülsse and Kerwer (2007, p. 629) who 'take seriously the fact that global regulation increasingly consists of standards' and insist on the importance of understanding how standards are being produced and used in the context of a developing global governance. Of particular interest in the field of political science are the interactions between a whole host of national, regional and international organizations active on the global scene and the respective strength and balance of authority between professional bodies and their regulators. Political scientists (see Cutler *et al.*, 1999; Biersteker and Hall, 2002; Porter, 2005; Büthe, 2010 and Cutler, 2010) routinely contrast private (non-governmental) authority and public authority. Thus the IASB and IFAC are described as private organizations, while the World Bank, IMF, Basel Committee on Banking Supervision (BCBS) the International Organization of Securities Commissions (IOSCO) and the Financial Stability Board (FSB) are described as public organizations. The case of accounting and auditing is especially significant here because the accounting profession is invariably held out as being a very powerful profession (for example, see Nolke, 2005) and capable of shaping the way in which global governance through standards takes place. This is important as professional authority has certain defining characteristics beyond technical expertise and private interest – in particular to do with exercising professional judgement and acting in the public interest. How important this 'professional' element is to the regime of standards forms a central focus of this chapter.

The rise in importance of standards for accounting and auditing

Classically the word 'standard' in the context of rule making is defined as 'something set up and established by authority as a rule for the measure of quantity, weight, extent, value, or quality'.[5] A typical example is the development of standards for industrial products such as nuts and bolts, and more recently, through the voluntary consensus standard setting represented by such organizations as the International Organization for Standardization (ISO) (Murphy and Yates, 2009). The modern standardization movement in the financial reporting field can be dated back to the Wall Street crash of 1929. The most important regulatory initiative made in the wake of in the wake of the crash was the establishment of the US Securities and Exchange Commission (SEC) in 1934. The enacting legislation charged the SEC with setting the accounting standards which should be used by US listed companies,[6] and auditing standards duly followed. However, the SEC did not set the standards themselves; they allowed the US accounting profession, through their professional association the American Institute of Certified Public Accountants (AICPA) to do so. In other Anglo-Saxon countries self-regulation by the profession without state oversight was the norm, and this included the development of accounting and auditing guidelines and standards. However, even until the 1980s, with the exception of the US, these were fairly short and general in nature – leaving much to professional judgement. The State had more say in some Continental European countries, such as Germany and Denmark, where the equivalent of the Anglo-Saxon accounting profession was established and regulated through law (often mitigated, however, by the possibilities the profession had of influencing this law).

The idea of international standards in the financial reporting arena developed in the wake of the growing integration of national economies into the world economy, it being thought that 'harmonization' would make life easier for both the producers and users of financial reports of cross-border entities. In the 1960s some initiatives were made, but it was not until the 1970s that international standards and guidelines for accounting and auditing began to be produced. In 1973, the International Accounting Standards Committee (IASC) as the IASB was then called, was formed, with headquarters in London, and began to produce International Accounting Standards (IASs).[7] In 1977 the International Federation of Accountants (IFAC) was formed with headquarters in New York, which had among its responsibilities producing guidelines for auditing; these became known as standards (ISAs) in 1991.

IFAC was given a much wider brief than the IASC. While producing auditing guidelines for practitioners was very important, it was also charged with establishing the basic principles for a code of ethics for member bodies to use, developing programmes for the education of accountants and helping management accountants to increase their knowledge and effectiveness. It was also responsible for organizing a World Congress every five years and engendering contacts between member bodies as well as representing the profession at an international level (Loft and Humphrey, 2006). It was no accident that these standard setters, the IASB and IFAC, were set up in the 1970s. Their formation seems to have been rooted in the increasing internationalization of commerce, where the inconvenience of there being different national ways of accounting became obvious. From being little known voluntary best practice standards in the 1980s, International Accounting Standards (IASs) and International Auditing Guidelines (IAGs) began to grow in importance, especially in the wake of the financial crisis in Asia in 1997–98.

The Asian crisis, global worries and a proposed 'cure' through standards

Of particular significance here is the form of the response made by the G7 to the crisis in Asia. Under the leadership of the UK chancellor, Gordon Brown, the G7 finance ministers sought to establish a 'new international financial architecture' which could help to prevent such crises occurring in future. Some commentators felt that some kind of 'World Financial Authority' should be set up (see Eatwell and Taylor, 2000); but it was not to be. What the G7 finance ministers proposed, was that a set of international standards could do the job; and this was accepted by the G7. The vision was that a global regime of 'economic discipline' could be established through the universal use of common standards for economies in every country throughout the world (Vestergaard, 2004, 2009; Wade, 2007). In 1999, twelve key standards, which included standards for accounting and auditing, were adopted by the newly formed 'Financial Stability Forum' (now Board). While ten of the standards were produced by international organizations in the public sphere, the other two, the international accounting standards produced by the IASC (now IASB), and the international auditing standards produced by IFAC, were distinguished by the fact that they were produced by private international organizations. The importance of this private status and its consequences for the regime of standards which has developed in financial reporting forms an important theme in this chapter.

One subtle but major change that came in the wake of the reactions to the Asian financial crisis was that as well as accounting and auditing being more visible and important, new connections were made between the creation of standards and the wider financial reporting context. This was reflected in the 'Concept Release on International Accounting Standards' issued by the US Securities and Exchange Commission (SEC, 2000) which stated that: 'while the accounting standards used must be high quality, they also must be supported by an infrastructure that ensures that the standards are rigorously interpreted and applied'. Elements that this infrastructure should include were:

- 'effective, independent, and high quality accounting and auditing standards setters;
- high quality auditing standards;
- audit firms with effective quality controls worldwide;

- audit profession-wide quality assurance;
- active regulatory oversight'.

The demand for 'audit firms with effective quality controls worldwide' is directly aimed at the then Big Five audit firms, whose audits in East Asia were considered to have been insufficient (see Rahman (1998). The issue here is that while the big audit firms were marketing themselves as global firms, they were actually networks of national partnerships, with varying degrees of independence from the global firm. During the last decade new controls within the firms themselves have made their practices (internal standards) much more similar, but it has seemingly been a struggle, both with firms in developed economies and especially in emerging economies" (see Tokar, 2005; Barrett *et al.*, 2005).

An example of the formalization of new structures of control in the wider regulatory environment can be seen in the diagram of the 'Financial Reporting Supply Chain' (Figure 5.1) produced by Philippe Danjou in 2005.[8] These developments further set the scene for the rise

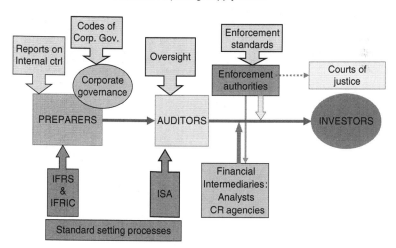

Figure 5.1   The financial reporting supply chain
Source: Danjou (2005).

of importance of accounting and auditing standards and the organizations which set them. IFRS and ISAs became seen not only as making life easier for transnational companies, but also capable of giving global investors a 'level playing field' at the same time as enhancing global financial stability. These benefits were reliant on achieving greater transparency – the argument being that if investors could clearly see correct figures (in economic terms), then market mechanisms would do the rest to keep the world economy on a smooth, efficient and productive track.

Today's standards – and the role of international regulators

The current international accounting and auditing standards are generally seen to be substantially more demanding and comprehensive in their coverage and reach than they were earlier, with regular assertions as to the value of progress in this area. As Sir David Tweedie, head of the IASB, puts it 'Global capital markets are already tightly integrated. Investors know it. The financial crisis has shown it. So why use more than one accounting language to describe it? Why should the same transaction be accounted for differently in Copenhagen and Chicago?'[9] According to the IASB, currently almost 120 countries have required or permitted the use of IFRS, and that the remaining major economies have agreed to converge with or adopt IFRSs in the very near future.[10] Since the autumn of 2008 the long global 'battle' to be the leading world accounting standards between US GAAP and IFRS has given way to what appears to be the inevitable convergence of US GAAP to IFRS, especially as the G20 have placed so much emphasis on the importance of this to global financial stability.

The support/endorsement of public international organizations for IFRS and ISAs has been crucial to their adoption; the three most important international organizations which support the adoption of IFRS and ISAs are the International Organization of Securities Commissions (IOSCO) the European Union (EU), through the European Commission (EC) and the World Bank[11]. At the same time as they have been involved in supporting adoption of the standards, they have also played a role in standard setting through making comment letters on exposure drafts. In particular in the case of IOSCO, this has also included getting quite involved with both the policies of the IASB, and those of IFAC's auditing standards board, the IAASB.

The membership of IOSCO is made up of national securities commissions, the largest and most influential of which is the US Securities and Exchange Commission (SEC). Formed in 1983 IOSCO currently (January 2011) has 114 ordinary members.[12] It has long advocated the production of international accounting and auditing standards, considering them to be important for global capital markets. It formally endorsed the use of IASs for the purpose of multinational offerings and cross- border listings in 2000 (although with conditions), and the IASB has continued to be active in discussions with IOSCO through a sub-committee of its Technical Committee.[13] In June 2009, after many years of discussion, IOSCO formally 'encouraged' securities regulators to accept audits performed and reported in accordance with ISA for cross-border offerings and listings.[14] As an association of national securities commissions, IOSCO has governmental authority behind each of its members; however, IOSCO itself has limited powers, relying on putting strong pressure on the national securities exchange authorities making up its membership for its recommendations to be accepted.

The European Commission has been particularly important in lifting the status of the international accounting and auditing standards. The Regulation (EC No 1606/2002) on the application of international accounting standards required, for financial years starting on or after 1 January 2005, listed companies and public interest entities in the EU to prepare consolidated accounts using IAS (now IFRS). This acceptance of such standards by a major public authority in the form of the EU was a significant event in moving them towards becoming global standards. For auditing, movement towards the adoption of ISAs as the EU standards for auditing has been somewhat slower, for although the Commission's statutory audit directive (2006/43/EC), adopted on 17 May 2006, supported the use of ISAs for financial audits carried out in member states, their formal adoption by the EU is still now, in May 2011, being discussed. In October 2010 a Green Paper entitled *Audit Policy: Lessons from the Crisis* was issued by the European Commission which explicitly sought views on the introduction of ISAs in the EU, and in particular on whether they should be legally binding and adopted through a process of endorsement like IFRS. As ISAs are already being used by many member states, the Green Paper also suggested that, instead of a Regulation, their usage could be further encouraged through a non-binding legal instrument such as a Recommendation.[15]

The World Bank has come to play a large role in getting the standards used in practice, with the development of this role going back to the Asian crisis, where, after the establishment of a set of twelve key standards for financial stability, a programme was set up to help developing and emerging economies to adopt and use the standards. A programme for making Reports on Standards and Codes (ROSC) was established in 1999, and the work was divided between the IMF and World Bank, with the latter organization taking responsibility for running the programme on accounting and auditing. An important part of the ROSC process involves using IFRS and ISAs as benchmark standards for assessing how well countries are getting on with the process of developing financial reporting – both in terms of adoption and use[16]. Related to the work of these three organizations, the Financial Stability Board,[17] under the auspices of the G20 takes a coordinating role in this arena which includes promoting usage of the standards, and communicating with the G20 concerning such usage.

Beyond encouraging/legislating for the adoption of the standards, there are other ways in which the international regulators discussed above interact with the standard setters. For example, the IASB has an IFRS Advisory Council whose members include the 'international regulators,[18] who also submit comment letters on discussion papers produced by the IASB. The IAASB has a Consultative Advisory Group (CAG), in which the international regulators take an active part (as observed by ourselves at meetings). In what follows, we seek to explore further this rather complex web of influences through the practical lens of the development of ISAs.

Public and private professional authority in the audit standard setting arena

ISAs introduction

IFAC is a private organization whose membership consists of professional accountancy bodies from around the globe (for instance, from the US, the American Institute of Certified Public Accountants, AICPA). As at 6 December 2010, IFAC had 164 members and associates in 125 countries and jurisdictions, representing approximately 2.5 million accountants in public practice, education, government service, industry and commerce (some jurisdictions have more than one association).[19] It is IFAC's aim that there should be a member body in every country. While there is some way to go to cover all 192 countries (according to the UN), the most powerful countries, including China and Russia, have member bodies. As discussed earlier, IFAC, even though classified as a private body, has a wide brief only to set standards, but also to lead the development of the global profession, all the time being committed to act in the public interest.

The development of ISAs and their adoption in many countries does mean that each professional association is involved in the adoption of ISAs nationally and the disciplining of audit practitioners. IFAC itself has no direct way to discipline individually the audit practitioners among the 2.5 million members of member bodies. However, member bodies themselves are now obliged take part in IFAC's compliance programme,[20] which has been set up to ensure that they live up to membership obligations which include making their 'best endeavours' to ensure, among other things, that ISAs and IFRS are used in their country (although clearly national law may prevent implementation, hence the clause 'best endeavors'). Member bodies must submit a self-evaluation, followed by an assessment of weaknesses, and an appropriate action plan. Information taken from this self-evaluation is placed on IFAC's public website; and it is expected that making it transparent will help to ensure that it is reliable.

IFAC is able to expel member bodies not living up to membership obligations, for example, not ensuring that ISAs are adopted and implemented in practice when it would be possible for them to do so. In practice expulsion is normally a last resort for dealing with professional bodies who are seriously inadequate, and seen as necessary in order to protect the IFAC 'brand'; membership of IFAC is increasingly being used by national professional associations to demonstrate that body's stature and development in their home country and on the global scene.

While, in regulatory terms, the auditing (and accounting) arena is often identified as one where 'private authority' dominates, we would argue that this is too simple an analysis. It significantly underplays the complex and dynamic relationship that has developed between the profession, international auditing (and accounting) standards-setting bodies, including the IAASB, and international regulators (especially the World Bank, IOSCO, BCBS and the European Commission).

Scandals wracked the US accountancy profession in the early part of the 21st century, in particular the collapse, with major financial problems, of the company Enron in 2002,[21] and the associated global collapse of their auditors, one of the then five largest audit firms in the world, Arthur Andersen. Andersen was accused, among other things, of a lack of independence from Enron, and of accepting Enron's misleading and fraudulent accounting practices. Andersen's audit of Enron was soon found to be not the only case of inadequate auditing of a large listed company, and the accountancy profession was in crisis. The result was calls for more regulation of the profession, both in the

US and internationally, inevitably leading to a greater role for public authority.

Public authority in the global field of audit regulation comes through the activities of the international regulators, now formalized as the Monitoring Group (following a reform of IFAC's organizational structure in 2003).[22] A Public Interest Oversight Board (PIOB) was also established, with the key task of overseeing IFAC's standard-setting processes including those of the IAASB. This involves monitoring each meeting of the committee, normally attending the whole meeting and commenting on due process when appropriate.[23] The Monitoring Group interacts with IFAC's leadership group and is responsible for appointing the members of the PIOB[24] (who are mainly senior regulators, the majority of whom are retired) and charged with the task of monitoring and overseeing IFAC's activities from a public interest point of view.[25] The objective of IFAC's reforms are, according to the Monitoring Group, '... to increase confidence that the activities of IFAC are properly responsive to the public interest and will lead to the establishment of high quality standards and practices in auditing and assurance'.[26] Stavros Thomadakis, the chairperson of the PIOB, has described this move as 'a landmark in the cooperation of world regulatory organizations for the oversight of international standard setting for auditors...' and 'represents a novelty for world-level public oversight'.[27]

For the parts of the profession where there had been extensive self-regulation, these changes brought with them regulation imposed by regulatory bodies connected to governmental authority, which Jim Sylph, technical director of IFAC, called 'direct regulation' for the 'sake of clarity' (Sylph, 2005, p. 4). While IFAC is a private authority in the international financial reporting arena, it has arguably entered into a complex, symbiotic relationship with the international regulators. In essence, we have public and private authority working together to establish international standards in the public interest. In an earlier piece of work, we used the term 'embedded oversight' as a way of emphasising the increasingly interlocking nature of the relationship between IFAC and the international regulatory community (Loft *et al.*, 2006).

The large accounting firms

There is another important source of private authority in connection with IFAC, and that is the Big Four accounting firms: PwC, Ernst & Young, Deloitte and KPMG. They work with IFAC through their membership of the 'Forum of Firms', which comprises audit firms that carry out transnational audits, and consists of 21 firms, including the Big Four.

The Forum of Firms' activities are carried out through the Transnational Auditors Committee (TAC). This has an important role in nominating members of the firms to be members of IFAC standard-setting committees, including the IAASB. Before this is discussed, it is worth noting that the Forum of Firms was established in 2001, not as a part of IFAC, but rather as a separate legal entity in Switzerland. The idea was that it should establish and supervise a self-regulatory peer-review system for audit firms carrying out transnational audits,[28] but this plan did not come to fruition due to the fact that the Enron scandal broke before the system could be started. As a consequence, peer review was subsequently no longer considered appropriate. Following the Sarbanes–Oxley Act (2002)[29] audit firms serving companies listed in the US, were to have their audits inspected by a new governmentally sponsored body, the Public Company Accounting Oversight Board (PCAOB).[30] The legislation had extra-territorial effects, and because of this, and their own national concerns about auditing quality, oversight of audit firms has generally come to be the responsibility of national regulators. In other words, self-regulation through peer review has generally been replaced by direct regulation.[31] The Forum of Firms has continued to operate, but not with the important peer-review role envisaged for it, but rather 'to promote consistent and high quality standards of financial reporting and auditing practices worldwide',[32] including the use of ISAs in the USA. The actions of the Forum have thus been reduced to 'promoting' and not disciplining in the field of audit firm oversight.

In connection with the establishment of the Forum, the big firms, under pressure from the World Bank and other international regulators, began to provide substantial funding for IFAC.[33] This funding was aimed particularly at supporting what is arguably its most important committee, namely the one making the auditing standards, the IAASB.

The Forum nominates members to the TAC, whose meetings deal with audit practice issues, and good practice in the wider matters of quality control of audits, staff training and independence. In doing this it acts 'as a formal conduit for interaction among transnational firms and international regulators and financial institutions with regard to audit quality, systems of quality control, and transparency of international networks'.[34] Importantly here, and in relation to the funding provided by the firms, the TAC also functions to identify qualified candidates for IFAC committees, including nominating five members of the IAASB.[35] Previously, before the reforms, it had been solely up to national professional associations of accountants to nominate persons for positions on IFAC's standard-setting committees, and usually these were persons from their own professional associations. The question arises to what extent membership of IAASB is dominated by the profession, in particular the large audit firms, although we emphasize that we are not arguing that the IAASB members associated with audit firms are not working in the public interest, rather, that a particular professional world view, for good or bad may come to dominate the thinking of the Board.

In 2010 of the total of 18 seats on the IAASB there were ten persons nominated by IFAC member bodies, five persons nominated by the TAC and three public members. Further inspection of the backgrounds of the members[36] revealed that in addition to the five TAC nominated members (which included one of each from the Big Four and one from the top of the next tier of firms, Grant Thornton), two of the ten nominated by member bodies were also from the Big Four. This means that seven members came directly from the six largest firms. Of the three public members, one was a governmental employee involved in public sector audit; one was a financial sector regulator, and one in banking and regulation, now retired, but who was a chartered accountant who had previously worked for one of the predecessor firms of KPMG and more recently been involved with the profession in other ways.[37] Arnold Schilder, current Chair of the IAASB, appointed in 2008, has an interesting history. He was a member of the Managing Board of the Dutch Central Bank immediately before becoming Chair of the IAASB, but earlier had been an international partner in what is now PwC (1985–1998).[38] He also has a PhD in auditing, and has taught part-time at the University of Amsterdam. Interestingly, and something which undoubtedly supported his candidacy for the position, is the fact that he has wide connections with many institutions and persons active in this regulatory arena, both public and private. Looking at the whole IAASB committee, and comparing the membership in 2010 with that of 2005, there is now less dominance by the large firms (as the international regulators have emphasized should preferably happen). In 2005, besides the five members from the TAC, seven out of the ten nominated by member bodies were working for the Big Four.

However, another factor which may have an influence on the way the committee thinks is that each member can bring one technical assistant, who also has speaking rights. The vast majority of these come from a professional accountancy background, either working for a big firm, or for a member body. As these persons may change (and are not listed formally on the website as are the members of the committee) then it is much harder to analyse their background.

Members of the IAASB sign a document certifying that they will work in the 'public interest' and they are frequently made aware of their public interest role (Simnett, 2007).[39] Although public members have been introduced to bring in an outside viewpoint, and a 'user' viewpoint is expressed through the IAASB's Consultative Advisory Group (CAG), the potential influence of large firm auditors on the IAASB has been criticized in a recent (2010) Monitoring Group assessment of the IFAC governance reforms.[40] The relationship between private and public authority in this regulatory arena reflects a delicate relationship between the make-up of the IAASB, its technical competence and external legitimacy.

The IAASB has the dilemma, which many other such standard setters have (Kerwer, 2010, p. 4), of the trade-off between having expert members who know the subject area inside-out, or more independent persons who have most likely got a lower level of expertise. Expertise is required to make effective and efficient standards (output legitimacy) while democratic control through the presence of independent members is needed to legitimize the standards (input legitimacy).

Large audit firms: creating their own global organization

There is another interesting feature in the private authority of the profession. That is the growth of cooperation between the 'Large Six' firms (namely, the Big Four firms plus the next two, Grant Thornton and BDO). This initiative started in the late 1990s, and out of this grew a Global Public Policy Committee (GPPC): 'a coordinating group for the six largest global accounting and auditing organizations focused on public policy, regulatory and professional matters'.[41] It operates through two working groups: the 'Standards Working Group'[42] and the 'Regulatory Working Group', and has held a fairly regular international symposium (GPPS), which is by invitation only. The GPPC is relatively secretive; having no official website. It is evident that the GPPC is working closely with international regulators – with one of its reports on fair value being shared in draft form with bodies such as the FSF (now FSB), BCBS, IASB and IOSCO (GPPC, 2006). In this connection Dick Kilgust, the then chair of the GPPC noted the importance of the large firms coming together to work on these issues, especially concerning valuation in the financial crisis, and commented that it is not their job to provide interpretation of standards, to draw attention to key issues to 'promote consistency and compliance'.[43]

Private and public authority

What this section of the chapter on public and private professional authority in the audit standard- setting arena has shown is that there are complex private/public relationships which need to be understood – especially since not only are regulators and the big audit firms involved in various ways in standard setting, embedded to a degree in IFAC's structure, but also they are involved in adoption and implementation of ISAs. In the case of adoption, the international regulators are involved through various forms of endorsement/recommendation of the standards by the World Bank, IOSCO, the European Commission and others. In the case of implementation, the big audit firms use ISAs. Beyond this, compliance is implicated in the World Bank, Reports on Standards and Codes on accounting and auditing.

The nature of standards: principle-based standards and the role of professional judgement

The complexity of the international audit standard-setting arena in structural terms is compounded by the practical complexities involved in the detailed specification of such standards. Auditing standards are not like standards for nuts and bolts, they do not give exact sizes and fittings so that they fit right every time. Rather auditing standards are process standards which inform the user of the standards of the procedures to carry out.[44] Following the procedures is expected to lead to an acceptable audit.

The nature of the standards

There is a tendency for those writing about standards not to tell the reader much about the form of the standards. In our opinion this is something which tends both to reflect (and reinforce) an impression that standards are something of an impenetrable 'black box' containing mysterious technical secrets. Following earlier work on auditing standards and methodologies, for example, Mennicken, 2008; Khalifa *et al.*, 2007; Barratt *et al.*, 2005; Eilifsen *et al.*, 2001 and Knechel, 2007[45]; it appeared to us that in the case of ISAs it is necessary to consider the form and nature of the standards in order to appreciate sufficiently the wider issues and factors that serve to influence their creation, adoption and usage. The aim of this section is to review the nature of the standards, how they are presented to the potential user, and the extent to which they define practice. ISA 500, which deals with audit evidence, will be used as an example, as it is one of the most important ISAs, both to practitioners and to academics seeking to understand the phenomenon of auditing (Power, 1997, pp. 69–70).

The latest published version of the ISAs is commonly referred to as the 'clarified' ISAs. The 'clarity project' was started in 2004 and involved redrafting, and also often revising the standards so that they are 'understandable, clear, and capable of consistent application. These aspects of clarity serve to enhance the quality and uniformity of practice worldwide'.[46] The project was completed in early 2009 and the clarity ISAs are now in effect. These 36 standards, which are stated to be 'principle based', are to be used for statutory audits (the normal year-end financial audits as envisaged by regulators such as the EU, IOSCO and the World Bank) and fill 735 pages in the IFAC Handbook (2010).

The first standard, ISA 200 acts as an introduction to the standards, dealing with '[t]he overall objectives of the independent auditor and the conduct of an audit in accordance with ISA'. Paragraph 7 of ISA 200 states that:

> The ISAs contain objectives, requirements and application and other explanatory material that are designed to support the auditor in obtaining reasonable assurance. The ISAs require that the auditor exercise professional judgement and maintain professional skepticism throughout the planning and performance of the audit and, among other things:
> - Identify and assess risks of material misstatement, whether due to fraud or error, based on an understanding of the entity and its environment, including the entity's internal control.
> - Obtain sufficient appropriate audit evidence about whether material misstatements exist, through designing and implementing appropriate responses to the assessed risks.
> - Form an opinion on the financial statements based on conclusions drawn from the audit evidence obtained. (IFAC Handbook, 2010, ISA 200: §7).

What is perhaps not clear to those who work outside the field of auditing is that many of the terms used here (and in general in the standards) are laden with special meaning to audit practitioners. In the glossary to ISAs to be found in the 'Handbook of international quality control, auditing, review, other assurance, and related services pronouncements' (IFAC, 2010, pp. 11–33) around 200 different terms and phrases are described. For example, professional judgement, professional scepticism, reasonable assurance and internal control are all defined. One possible analogy is to see such key terms and phrases resembling the steps of a horse performing dressage; they have all been carefully defined, and must be used with precision in the right place at the right time by the rider (the auditor). The auditor must perform the work appropriately, and, crucially, document what has been done and to what effect, so that the work can be inspected by either an immediate supervisor on the audit team, the audit partner in charge of the assignment, a review partner from another office in the firm, and, potentially, external inspectors from a regulatory oversight body. The outcome of any possible legal claims by investors (who lost money due to what they claim was a failed audit) will depend not so much on the work done, but crucially, the way in which such work was documented and justified – and the particular interpretation of expert witnesses concerning what they would regard as constituting 'sufficient appropriate audit evidence' in the case in question.

One important structural feature of the standards is that they are arranged in an order which follows the progression of work through the various stages of an audit. So after ISA 200, which deals more generally with the objectives of the audit, the next standard is, ISA 201, which concerns 'Agreeing the Terms of Audit Engagements'. Near the end of the series of standards, is ISA 700 on audit reporting.

ISA 500 and professional judgement

Under the 'Definitions' section of the standards, 'sufficiency of audit evidence' is defined as '[t]he measure of the quantity of audit evidence. The quantity of the audit evidence needed is affected by the auditor's assessment of the risks of material misstatement and also by the quality of such audit evidence' (ISA, 500 §5e). What is noticeable here is that the definition does not stand alone; there is a linked web of concepts, including the risk of material misstatement.

The requirements of ISA 500 fill just over one page and the application material is 13 pages in the Handbook. Requirement 11 will be used here to illustrate the nature of the linkages between the requirements of the standard and the application material requirement. Entitled 'Inconsistency in, or Doubts over Reliability of, Audit Evidence' (ISA, 500, §11) it reads that: 'If (a) audit evidence obtained from one source is inconsistent with that obtained from another; or (b) the auditor has doubts over the reliability of information to be used as audit evidence, the auditor shall determine what modifications or additions to audit procedures are necessary to resolve the matter, and shall consider the effect of the matter, if any, on other aspects of the audit' (ISA, 500, §11). The application material under A57 (referring to paragraph number) adds to this the statement that 'Obtaining audit evidence from different sources or of a different nature may indicate that an individual item of audit evidence is not reliable, such as when audit evidence obtained from one source is inconsistent with that obtained from another. This may be the case when, for example, responses to inquiries of management, internal audit, and others are inconsistent, or when responses to inquiries of those charged with governance made to corroborate the responses to inquiries of management are inconsistent with the response by management. ISA 230 includes a specific documentation requirement if the auditor identified information that is inconsistent with the auditor's final conclusion regarding a significant matter' (ISA, 500, § A57). What can be seen here is that even in the application part of the standard, what is suggested is not precisely defined, but involves processes to be set in motion; thought and professional judgement on the part of the auditor in practice.

Professional judgement – and on being a profession

In the preface to the standards it is stated under the heading 'professional judgement' that '[t]he nature of the International Standards requires the professional accountant to exercise professional judgement in applying them (Handbook, 2010, Preface §16). This is defined in the glossary of terms as the 'application of relevant training, knowledge and experience, within the context provided by auditing, accounting and ethical standards, in making informed decisions about the courses of action that are appropriate in the circumstances of the audit engagement' (Handbook, 2010, Glossary, p. 26). This is just one of a series of items in the glossary which relate to what it means to be a 'professional' in this field. Others include the terms *'professional accountant'* – which is defined as an individual who is a member of an IFAC member body, *'professional standards'* – which refers to International Standards on Auditing (ISAs) and relevant ethical requirements, and *'professional scepticism'*, which is defined as 'an attitude that includes a questioning mind, being alert to conditions which may indicate possible misstatement due to error or fraud, and a critical assessment of audit evidence' (Handbook, 2010, Glossary, pp. 26–27).

Being a member of a profession, using professional standards, making professional judgements, and retaining professional scepticism embodies a discourse of professionalism that has a range of implications for the production, adoption, usage and enforcement of the standards.

IFAC's Technical Director Jim Sylph comments that: '[i]n discussing methods of regulation, it is important to remember that accountancy is a profession. That means that professional accountants have an over-riding responsibility to the community in which they live, not just to their current clients or to themselves. So even in circumstances where there is total direct regulation, there is still a need for the profession to regulate the activities and conduct of its members to ensure that this responsibility to the community is fulfilled. The only caveat is that this regulation needs to be efficient and effective' (Sylph, 2005, pp. 5–6). Bringing in education he writes that 'education in values, especially through example and the appropriate use of experience and professional judgement, based on a solid educational foundation, and reinforced through continuing professional education, is essential to the future of the accountancy profession ...' (Sylph, 2007, p. 10).

The discourse of professionalism supports the 'filling out' of the ISAs in the context of practice through the use of the concepts of professional judgement and professional scepticism. As illustrated above, ISAs are strong on process and general procedures, but light on anything relating to the particular ways of exercising professional judgement as is required for overall realization of the ISAs programme. The emphasis on professional judgement and scepticism in ISAs fits with the nature of principle-based standards, which require interpretation and elaboration before they can be used. In essence, the notion of professional judgement, as expressed by Sylph and many others, is a concept or conceptual space which encapsulates the fundamental ideals of IFAC as to what it means to be a practicing auditor. At the same time it also links the micro-level of what goes on in the audit with the macro-level representation of auditing as a professional activity, something which among other things, reinforces the profession's 'ownership' of the audit jurisdiction.[47]

The value of focusing on the concept of professional judgement is that it serves to emphasize the complexity of regulatory systems that seek to secure governance through standardization in fields such as auditing, and the importance of analysis moving beyond studies of the adoption of standards to studies of the implementation and enforcement of standards. In the discussion section below, we give a flavour of some of the issues that have a particular pertinence in today's global audit regulatory arena.

Discussion and conclusion

In the age of economic globalization, information concerning the economic state of corporations and financial institutions is of crucial importance. In their role as 'financial technologists', accountants and auditors are the expert professionals with responsibility for the 'good financial reporting' which is seen as 'essential to the effective functioning of capital markets and the productive allocation of economic resources' (Volcker, 2002, p. 1).[48]

In this arena a complex form of global governance of financial reporting based on international standards seems to be emerging through the ongoing interactions and influences between international standard setters, the international accounting profession, large audit firms and the public authority of international financial market regulators and oversight bodies. The significance of international accounting and auditing standards has grown in the context of the growth of the international financial architecture, now more often referred to as global financial regulation. ISAs are on their way to becoming global standards, produced by the IAASB with a fascinating structural arrangement that engages and encompasses the large audit firms, international regulators and a Public Interest Oversight Board (PIOB). The setting of audit standards is focused on ensuring that auditors carry out audits in a competent way to ensure detection of significant errors and omissions in financial statements (Humphrey and Loft, 2009).

In today's post-Enron regulatory arena, it is common to talk of the demise of self-regulation and its replacement by various forms of independent public oversight and inspection processes undertaken by the numerous bodies identified in the preceding sections of this chapter. Our discussion of the concept of professional judgement, however, suggests that self-regulation in auditing has been reconfigured at a microlevel, wherein audit professionals retain a certain capacity to make substantial decisions of judgement in relation to the audits of their client companies. The regulatory reach of formal, external, monitoring systems, from such a standpoint, has definite limits in terms of how far it can penetrate the professional judgement-making processes associated with the audit.

The empirical question in relation to today's regulatory environment is to determine just how far such penetration has extended. While interpretations and usage of standards can vary depending on national business and regulatory cultural traditions, at a general level it is fair to argue that a primary impact of the Enron scandal (and other cases around this time) was to bring in a fundamental questioning of the level of trust that could be placed in processes and standards of auditors' professional judgement and expertise. The advent of independent public oversight and inspection regimes essentially meant that trust in auditors and their processes of judgement was in large part supplanted by trust in independent regulation and the methodologies and inspection approaches of independent regulators.

Such developments have, not surprisingly, seen some quite visible levels of disagreement between auditors and regulators in terms of whose interpretation of the application of auditing standards is most accurate and reliable. This can be seen on a regular basis in official regulatory inspection reports where the inspected audit firm has the capacity to provide counter-comments to the opinion of regulators (see PCAOB and AIU inspection reports[49]). Classic differences of opinion relate to the required level of documentation provided by audit firms in their working papers on specific audits. Regulators argue that such levels are not adequate for them to independently substantiate the judgements taken by auditors, while the firms counter that the judgements, while not documented to the regulators' satisfaction, were still the right ones. Additionally, regulators will comment that certain procedures were not undertaken (or at least not documented) and auditors will counter that they were not appropriate in the circumstances. At an overall level, regulatory reports will highlight specific areas where audits could improve, and the auditing profession will respond, in part by formally welcoming such reports, but emphasizing that the criticisms made were specific/relevant only to a minority of audits, that recommended changes would not have changed the given audit opinions and that the general quality of audit work remains satisfactorily high. In essence, while we may have in place additional, security-providing regulatory structures, we are still in the position of having to take on (someone's) trust whether auditor judgement is being exercised appropriately or not.

The CEOs of the big audit firms, have argued that the use of more high-level principle-based standards would 'need to rely on judgement from auditors because under that system they cannot look to rule-makers for constant clarifications, interpretations or exceptions'. For Deloitte CEO, James Quigley, changes in the standards would be less frequent. 'Those Standards would be almost timeless'[50]. This returns us to the nature of the 'black box' of standards – and the important need to open this up more through detailed research examining the connections between individual standards and the regulatory context in which they are developed. A particularly crucial test here is not so much standard setting, but standard use and, in particular, enforcement.

From a research perspective, such regulatory interactions provide a very lively site for future investigation. While 'professional judgement' may well be an essentially indeterminate or subjective concept, it is capable of being shaped by particular contexts and influences – and a priority for those interested in the international standardization of practices such as auditing is to investigate how regulatory actions are, indeed, reconstructing and reshaping what is deemed to be 'legitimate' audit work and the exercising of 'appropriate' professional audit judgement. We believe that such analysis can contribute to the literature on governance through standards and add another dimension to work carried out by political scientists on the authority and legitimacy of global standards (for example, see Kerwer, 2005).

There are some fascinating interactions, clashes and alliances to explore between different key players in the global regulatory arena, which collectively serve to emphasize how research into standard-setting processes has to go beyond the specification and adoption of standards, to studies of their implementation and enforcement. One intriguing aspect here in relation to professional auditor judgement is that while at one level it is the essential essence of a strong and vibrant profession, it can also be seen, in a world committed to global standardization, as a quite dangerous and risky concept – for it may lead to inconsistency. As an illustrative example, imagine an individual auditor 'judging' that the annual accounts of a bank do show a true and fair view –agreeing with the bank that although there are a lot of customers who are unable to pay the loans on their houses, the houses can be sold and the debt recouped, so there is no need for any special provisions in the accounts for the bad debts! Nothing seems to be wrong here – but just after the auditor signs off the accounts, and they are published and issued to shareholders, house prices take a dramatic fall...If this sounds familiar, well something very similar to this did of course occur in 2007 in the US. Another auditor might have judged differently – but who would have been 'right'? Another way of looking at this could be to consider that what the auditor said at the time might have been 'right' based on the evidence available at that time and that it could be not so much a question of whether or not another auditor would have come to a different conclusion, but whether auditors can predict the future?

Global commitments to high quality auditing standards and practices have arguably seen the transformation of conceptions of quality. While earlier it was about a competitive climb to an unreached and unrivalled 'top quality' summit by individual firms striving for competitive advantage, now quality is more about the collaborative enforcement of practices that consistently meet a pre-specified standard of quality practice. This is reflected in the use of the phrase 'promote consistency in performance and the use of professional judgement by auditors' by IAASB.[51] There is also a great concern among the large, multinational audit firms that they make 'consistent' judgements across their 'global' audits, not just because they are audits that are likely to be scrutinized carefully by external regulators, but because they are now required to define their own professional standing as leading international providers of auditing services on the basis that an audit by the firm in one country will be conducted to exactly the same standards as an audit by the firm in any other country. In short, a PwC or a KPMG audit is of the same standard no matter which country it is performed in. There is both a commercial imperative here in the sense that the large firms want to be seen as global entities but there is also a broader professional concern that major exposures of global inconsistencies in audit firms' practices will be damaging for the profession as a whole – and there is a heartfelt desire not to bear witness to the collapse of another international firm, as happened last with Arthur Andersen in the aftermath of the Enron scandal.

Empirically, it is worth asking exactly what terms such as 'independent' regulation mean and represent in practice, and whether we are in fact getting better quality and more innovative auditing practices through independently regulated regimes (for more discussion of the research imperatives with respect to audit quality, see Humphrey (2008) and for some competing analyses on the effectiveness of independent public oversight regimes, see Lennox and Pittman (2010) and Defond (2010). In this global regulatory context, it is particularly interesting to see national professional bodies, such as the ICAEW (2010) – bodies that used to lead the former self-regulatory audit regimes – recently emphasizing the 'deeply embedded features of national environments that pose challenges for international consistency in audit quality' (*ibid*, p. 3) and the importance of qualitative research in enhancing understanding of audit practice and the 'limits of global standards as a necessary but not a sufficient condition for international consistency in audit quality' (*ibid*, p. 32). Such differing standpoints and perspectives not only illustrate the increasing complexity of the field of international financial regulation but also the importance of continuing empirical research on the relationship between the nature and content of international standards and the global governance arena in which they are being developed, adopted, applied and enforced.

Notes

1 Here we use the term 'financial reporting' to include accounting and auditing carried out in the context of the preparation of the annual financial reports of companies. The abbreviation IFRS will be used to refer to the 'International financial Reporting Standards (formerly International Accounting Standards), and ISAs to refer to the 'International Standards on Auditing' (relating to financial auditing).

2 For a list of organizations and frequently used acronyms, see p. viii.

3   http://www.pittsburghsummit.gov/mediacenter/129639.htm
4   The term' international regulators' used in this chapter (following IFAC's usage) refers collectively to IOSCO, BCBS, World Bank, European Commission, IAIS (and the FSB in a coordinative role).
5   http://www.merriam-webster.com/netdict/standard
6   From speech given by Ethiopis Tafara (SEC,2005). http://www.sec.gov/news/speech/spch120105et.htm
7   For the history of the IASC, see Camfferman and Zeff (2007)
8   Danjou is currently a member of the IASB. Further details of his positions are available on http://www.ifrs.org/The+organisation/Members+of+the+IASB/Philippe+Danjou.htm The overheads referred to here have been removed from the internet. Note that CR Agencies stands for Credit Rating Agencies.
9   Sir David Tweedie, quoted in the *Financial Times*, 28 January 2010
10 http://www.iasb.org/NR/rdonlyres/0A5A767C-E7DE-49E5-8B12-499-F62F8870C/0/who_we_are.pdf (accessed July 2010)
11 The two not dealt with directly here are the International Association of Assurance Supervisors (IAIS) see http://www.iaisweb.org/ and the Basel Committee on Banking Supervision (BCBS) see http://www.bis.org/bcbs/
12 http://www.iosco.org/about/
13 http://www.iosco.org/annual_reports/annual_report_2009/pdf/annualReport2009.pdf
14 http://www.iosco.org/library/statements/pdf/statements-7.pdf
15 http://ec.europa.eu/internal_market/consultations/docs/2010/audit/green_paper_audit_en.pdf
16 http://www.worldbank.org/ifa/rosc_aa.html
17 http://www.financialstabilityboard.org/
18 http://www.iasplus.com/restruct/advisory.htm
19 http://press.ifac.org/news/2010/11/international-federation-of-account-ants-responds-to-monitoring-group-report
20 http://www.ifac.org/ComplianceProgram/
21 http://www.time.com/time/business/article/0,8599,193520,00.html
22 The members of the Monitoring Group are representatives from IOSCO (two), BCBS, the World Bank, and the International Association of Insurance Supervisors (IAIS); the European Commission has two observers.
23 See: Thomadakis (2009).
24 Concerning the formation of the PIOB see: http://www.bis.org/press/p050228.htm
25 See: Thomadakis (2009).
26 http://web.ifac.org/download/Monitoring_Group_Press_Release.pdf
27 Thomadakis quoted in press release (2005) http://www.bis.org/press/p050228.htm
28 It was based on the type of peer review established in the US, where audit firms carrying out the audit of listed companies checked each other's work following established procedures.
29 The Sarbanes-Oxley Act: http://www.gpo.gov/fdsys/pkg/PLAW-107publ204/pdf/PLAW-107publ204.pdf
30 http://pcaobus.org/Pages/default.aspx
31 IFAC has also used the term 'external regulation' (which appears to refer to the same concept as 'direct regulation') http://web.ifac.org/publica-

tions/ifac-policy-position-papers-reports-and-comment-letters/policy-positions#regulation-of-the-accountant

32   http://web.ifac.org/download/Forum_of_Firms_and_TAC_Fact_Sheet.pdf

33   Although the major source remains subscriptions from its member bodies, the national professional accounting institutes around the world.

34   http://www.ifac.org/TransnationalAuditors/. We consider that such 'conduits' (which our research suggests are numerous over the whole financial reporting arena, often informal) are crucial to the maintenance of global governance without a global government in this field.

35   http://web.ifac.org/download/Forum_of_Firms_and_TAC_Fact_Sheet.pdf

36   A short biography of members is provided by the IAASB, but we also used Google to search for further information.

37   It was possible to find out using a Google search that: 'chartered accountant, David Swanney spent his first 12 years in London on the London staff of a predecessor firm of KPMG, and on the technical staff of the Institute of Chartered Accountants in England and Wales'. David was a Council Member of the Institute of Chartered Accountants of Scotland from 1995 until 2001. He was also Chairman of ICAS England and Wales Area Committee between 1999 and 2001. http://www.bba.org.uk/about-us/contacts/d

37   http://www.ifac.org/IAASB/bios/bio.php?bio=arnold-schilder

39   Meetings are open to public observation, and are recorded and placed on the web, so transparency also can play a part in ensuring the independence of Board Members.

40   URL: http://ec.europa.eu/internal_market/auditing/docs/consultation-ifac-announcement_en.pdf

41   http://www.gta.am/mediacoverageview.asp?id=11 (accessed 10 August 2010). The members are the six largest international accounting and audit networks (PwC, Deloitte, Ernst & Young, KPMG, BDO and Grant Thornton).

42   While it is clear that important professional judgements are discussed at the top of the big firms, we have little knowledge of how the GPPC standards working group actually works – and it would be premature to see it as a decisive organ of global coordination in the field, for individual members of the committee cannot make decisions on behalf of the global firm.

43   *Accountancy Age*, 14 December 2007. http://www.accountancyage.com/accountancyage/news/2205772/big-six-issue-fair-value-paper The regulator/Big Four relationship has also been confirmed through our interviews.

44   See Mennicken (2008).

45   See also Humphrey (2008) for a general review of the audit research literature, and Cooper and Robson (2006) for a discussion of the audit profession literature.

46   http://web.ifac.org/clarity-center/index

47   Seen as a domain of knowledge and practice (Abbott, 1988).

48   Paul Volcker was, at the time, Chair of the IASC Foundation. Among his previous posts was that of chair of the US Federal Reserve 1979–1987. He is currently chairman of the US President's Economic Recovery Advisory Board.

49   For PCAOB, see http://pcaobus.org/Inspections/Reports/Pages/default.aspx For AIU, see http://www.frc.org.uk/pob/audit/

50 http://www.reuters.com/article/idUSN1554732620080116
51 See http://www.bis.org/bcbs/commentletters/ifac24.pdf (the original docu-
    ment is unavailable).

References

Abbott, A. (1988) *The System of Professions* (Chicago: University of Chicago Press).

Barrett, M., Cooper, D.J. and Jamal, K. (2005) 'Globalization and the coordinating of work in multinational audits', *Accounting, Organizations and Society*, 30, 1–24.

Biersteker, T.J. and Hall, R.B. (2002) *The Emergence of Private Authority in Global Governance* (Cambridge: Cambridge University Press).

Brunsson, N. and Jacobsson, B. and Associates (2000) (eds), *A World of Standards* (Oxford: Oxford University Press).

Büthe, T. (2010) 'Global private politics: a research agenda', *Business and Politics*, 12(3).

Camfferman, K. and Zeff, S.A. (2007) *Financial Reporting and Global Capital Markets. A History of the International Accounting Standards Committee 1973–2000* (Oxford: Oxford University Press).

Cooper, D.J. and Robson, K. (2006) 'Accounting, professions and regulation: Locating the sites of professionalization' *Accounting, Organizations and Society*, 31(4–5), 415–444.

Cutler, A.C., Haufler, V., and Porter, T. (1999) 'Private authority in international affairs' in A.C. Cutler, V. Haufler and T. Porter (eds) *Private Authority in International Affair* (New York: State University of New York Press).

Cutler, A.C. (2010) 'The legitimacy of private transnational governance: Experts and the transnational market for force' *Socio-Economic Review*, 8(1), 157–185.

DeFond, M.L. (2010) 'How should the auditors be audited? Comparing the PCAOB inspections with the AICPA peer reviews', *Journal of Accounting and Economics*, 49(1/2), 104–108.

Eatwell, J. and Taylor, L. (2000) *Global Finance at Risk: The Case for International Regulation*. (Oxford: Polity Press).

Eilifsen, A., Knechel, R.W. and Wallage, P. (2001) 'Application of the business risk audit model: a field study', *Accounting Horizons*, 15(3), 193–207.

GPPC, Global Public Policy Committee (2006) 'Global capital markets and the global economy: A vision from the CEOs of the international audit networks' http://www.globalpublicpolicysymposium.com/GPPC_Vision.pdf

Held, D. & McGrew, A.G. (2002) 'Introduction' in D. Held and A.G. McGrew (eds.) *Governing Globalization: Power Authority and Global Governance* (Cambridge: Polity Press).

Hülsse, R. and Kerwer, D. (2007) 'Global standards in action: insights from anti-money laundering regulation', *Organization*, 14(5), 625–642.

Humphrey, C. (2008) 'Auditing research: a review across the disciplinary divide', *Accounting, Auditing and Accountability Journal*, 21(2), 170–203.

Humphrey, C. and Loft, A. (2009) 'Governing audit globally – IFAC, the new international financial architecture and the accounting profession' in. D. Cooper, P. Miller, P. and C. Chapman (eds) *Accounting, Organizations, and Institutions: Essays in Honour of Anthony Hopwood* (Oxford: OUP).

Humphrey, C., Loft, A. and Woods, M. (2009) 'The global audit profession and the international financial architecture: understanding regulatory relationships at a time of financial crisis', *Accounting, Organizations and Society*, 34(6–7), 810–825.

IFAC Handbook (2010) *Handbook of International Quality Control, Auditing, Review, Other Assurance, and Related Services Pronouncements* (New York: International Federation of Accountants (IFAC), http://web.ifac.org/publications/international-auditing-and-assurance-standards-board/handbooks).

Kerwer, D. (2005) 'Rules that many use: standards and global regulation', *Governance: An International Journal of Policy, Administration, and Institutions*, 18(4), 611–631.

Kerwer, D. (2010) 'How do global standard-setters acquire rule-making authority?' Paper prepared for an International Symposium on 'Governing through Standards', Copenhagen, 24–26 February 2010.

Khalifa, R., Sharma N., Humphrey, C. and Robson, K. (2007) 'Discourse and audit change: transformations in methodology in the professional audit field', *Accounting, Auditing and Accountability Journal*, 20(6), 825–854.

Knechel, W.R. (2007), 'The business risk audit: origins, obstacles and opportunities', *Accounting, Organizations and Society*, 32(4–5), 383–408.

Lennox, C. and Pittman, J. (2010) 'Auditing the auditors: evidence on the recent reforms to the external monitoring of audit firms', *Journal of Accounting and Economics*, 49(1/2), 84–103.

Loft, A., Humphrey C. and Turley, S. (2006) 'In pursuit of global regulation: changing governance structures at the International Federation of Accountants (IFAC)', *Accounting, Auditing and Accountability Journal*, 19(3), 428–451.

Loft, A. and Humphrey, C. (2006) 'IFAC.ORG – Organizing the world of auditing with the help of a website' in H.K. Hansen and J. Hoff (eds) *Digital governance:// networked societies – creating authority, community and identity in a globalised world* (Copenhagen, Samfundslitteratur Press/NORDICOM).

Mennicken, A. (2008) 'Connecting worlds: the translation of international auditing standards into post-Soviet audit practice', *Accounting, Organizations and Society*, 33, 384–414.

Murphy, C.N. and Yates, J.A. (2009) 'ISO 26000 and the "Social movement of engineers" involved with standard-setting', prepared for the conference, *"Governing through Standards,"* at the Danish Institute for International Studies. Copenhagen, 24–26 February 2010.

Nolke, A. (2005) Introduction to the special issue: the globalization of accounting standards, *Business and Politics*, 7(3), 1–9.

Porter, T. (2005) 'Private authority, technical authority, and the globalization of accounting standards', *Business and Politics*, 7(3), 1–42.

Power, M. (1997). *The Audit Society* (Oxford: Oxford University Press).

Rahman, Z. (1998) 'The Role of Accounting in the East Asian Financial Crisis: Lessons Learned', *Transnational Corporations*, 7(3), 1–51.

SEC (2000) SEC *Concept Release: International Accounting Standards* Securities and Exchange Commission, File No. S7-04-00, http://www.sec.gov/rules/concept/34-42430.htm.

Simnett, R. (2007) 'A critique of the international auditing and assurance standards board', *Australian Accounting Review*, 17(2), 28–36.

Sylph, J. (2005) 'Transparency and audit regulation', speech given at the Fédération des Experts Comptables Mediterranéens Conference, Istanbul, Turkey, 13 December 2005.

Sylph, J. (2007) 'Accountancy regulation in the Mediterranean region'. Speech given at Fédération des Experts Comptables Mediterranéens Conference, Athens, Greece, 19 November, 2007.

Thomadakis, S. (2009) 'The public interest, the accounting profession and the turning point of the crisis'. Speech to *IFAC Council*, 1 September. http://www.ipiob.org/speeches/public-interest-accounting-profession-and-turning-point-crisis

Tokar, M. (2005) 'Convergence and the implementation of a single set of global standards: The real life challenge', *Northwestern Journal of International Law & Business*, 25(3), 687–710.

Vestergaard, J. (2004) 'The Asian crisis and the shaping of proper economies', *Cambridge Journal of Economics*, 28(6), 809–827.

Vestergaard, J. (2009) *Discipline in the Global Economy. International Finance and the End of Liberalism* (London: Routledge).

Volcker, P.A. (2002) 'Accounting, accountants, and accountability in an integrated world economy'. Remarks to the *World Congress of Accountants*, Hong Kong, 19 November 2002.

Wade, R. (2007) 'A new global financial architecture', *New Left Review*. 46 (July–Aug.), 113–129.

6
On the Pre-history of ISO 9000: The Making of a Neo-liberal Standard

Peter Gibbon and Lasse Folke Henriksen

Introduction

In a recent paper, Higgins and Tamm Hallström (2007) use a Foucauldian framework to discuss the relationship between neo-liberalism and standardization. They argue that governing through standards in general, and through quality management standards in particular, is a central neo-liberal technology of government. Governing through standards in general has this status because these standards embody the autonomous expert knowledge privileged by neo-liberalism, in a commodified form; and because the standardization process is based on the equally privileged practices of consensual public-private–decision making and voluntary private enrolment. At the same time, quality management standards in particular serve to propagate core bio-political 'practices of the self' – internalized discipline, self-reporting and inspectability – providing a neo-liberal legitimacy for organizations adopting them and allowing these and their own subjects to be 'governed at a distance'.

In the process of developing this argument, Higgins and Tamm Hallström sketch histories of both national and international standards bodies, and of quality management standards. Quality management standards (and certification mechanisms) are seen as emerging at the end of the 1970s. They appear through a 'culturalist' amalgamation-cum-transformation of 'mainstream management discourses' concerning optimal organizational controls and of 'hard engineering' quality control practices linked to inspection of military hardware using statistical techniques. This occurs initially 'in response to Japanese inroads into the markets of major Western consumer durable industries' (*ibid.*

p. 694). Later, it responds to a need to achieve arms' length coordination of international outsourcing.

This chapter accepts the framework of Higgins and Tamm Hallström's approach but challenges some aspects of their interpretation of Foucault's discussion of liberalism and neo-liberalism and, at greater length, their history of quality management standards as a governmental technology. Its central argument is that while indeed modern quality management standards emerged at the end of the 1970s, this process occurred entirely within the domain of military standards and was defined by contractors gaining control over how these standards were implemented. The definitive ISO 9000 series of standards on quality management, issued in 1987, was a word-for-word restatement of the British Standards Institute's BS 5750: 1979 standard, which in turn reproduced word-for-word the great bulk of the UK DEF series of military standards. The important transition was not that from a military to a civilian standard but during the process in the 1960s and early 1970s when US military standards for quality management 'travelled' across the Atlantic.

The remainder of this chapter is divided into five main sections. The first section briefly surveys Foucauldian work on liberal and neo-liberal governmental rationalities and technologies and the transition between them, and raises some questions about neo-liberalism for later discussion. The second, third and fourth sections provide a history of US and UK military quality standards as governmental technologies, covering their architecture, their development and the drivers of this development respectively.[1] Section five concludes. The chapter's empirical material is based on a combination of UK government papers and UK and US secondary sources.[2]

Liberal and neo-liberal governmentality

As Higgins and Tamm Hallström observe, Foucault distinguished between rationalities or programmes of government (normative discourses providing accounts of classes of persons, objects and behaviours to be governed) and technologies of government (strategies, techniques and procedures through which rationalities become operable). Liberalism's distinctive feature as a governmental rationality is that governing human behaviour occurs 'on behalf of society' rather than as simply an expression of sovereign power, and balances all substantive objectives specific against protection of the autonomy of the individual and civil society. Thus liberal government always 'suspects that (it) govern(s) too much' and always asks 'why there has to be a government ... to what extent it can be done without and in which cases it is needless or harmless ...' (Foucault, 1994, pp. 74–75).

On the other hand, the dominant liberal governmental technology is disciplinary power. This involves analysing, breaking down and rearranging the population in order to 'generate forces, making them grow and ordering them ...' (Foucault, 1998, p. 136), thus minimizing the need for more extensive governmental intervention, 'generating forces', entails supervision, correction and training. It generates and mobilizes expert knowledge of the population and applies this to increase human aptitudes – thus allowing 'government at a distance'.[3]

This suggests a tension between constraint, as implied by the disciplinary apparatus, and freedom as facilitated by its outcomes. Foucault alludes to this in terms of disciplinary power's incorporation of two 'dreams of society', that of the military and that of 'philosophers and jurists'. The former's reference is 'to the meticulously subordinated cogs of a machine ... permanent coercions (and) indefinitely progressive forms of training' (Foucault, 1991, p. 169), while the latter's is to a social contract and an otherwise unfettered exercise of political and economic rights.

Foucault alludes directly to a second tension of disciplinary power. This is between the scale of the disciplinary apparatus required to 'generate forces', and its cost. One of disciplinary power's guiding principles is to secure the exercise of power at 'the lowest possible cost', political and economic. This may be achieved, for example, through 'hierarchical' application of observation and penalties (*ibid..*, pp. 170–182), thus sorting out actors requiring less, rather than more, application of external power. Foucault's main emphasis here, however, is on the savings entailed by panopticon mechanisms, which putatively secure the 'automatic functioning of power' (*ibid.,* pp. 200–09).

Implicitly at least, Foucault (2008) and most of the wider governmentality literature distinguish neo- or advanced liberalism from liberal rule in terms of a modification in governmental rationality. Neo-liberalism's normative discourse prescribes reconstructing the state and the wider socio-political environment in terms of the image of the market. Less change is evident in respect of governmental technologies, although some new ones emerge and others increase or diminish in centrality.

Foucault noted these processes but never followed them in much detail. Neo-Foucauldians however, notably Rose (1993, 1996, 1999), have sought both to explain their occurrence and spell out what they entailed. For Rose (1996, 1999 and Dean 1999), two elements are crucial in explaining the success of 'advanced' liberalism in the late 1970s and 1980s. First, intellectual criticisms of the welfare state arose from both ends of the political spectrum, although with different aims and arguments. This questioned the logic of a state apparatus divided into a series of separate bureaucratic structures with related expert specialisms delivering distinct 'substantive rationalities of rule', largely insulated from external control (Rose 1996, pp. 52–4). Such an apparatus was inefficient, expensive and unaccountable.

This political criticism became effectively 'governmental' by linking up with a second element, namely technologies of marketization or market governance (Rose and Miller, 1992; Rose, 1996, 1999; Dean, 1999; see also Larner, 2000). Not only the economy, but all areas of life, were to be reconstituted as markets. This involved deployment of expertise facilitating marketization, either through outsourcing of management and service tasks formerly performed publicly, or by transforming public agencies into entities operating according to principles of financial sustainability/profitability, price and quality competitiveness and accountability.

The technologies of marketization were not 'substantive', but mostly 'performance', such as auditing, accounting and quality and risk management. Their propagators translated them into their new settings and used them to apply standardized forms of calculation, monitoring and evaluation in order to 'announce the market's verdict' (Rose 1996, p. 54; Dean 1999, p. 267). The highly mobile technology of auditing, in particular, proved an effective means of rendering complex locales and contexts manageable for governments. It did so through generating newly calculative and result-oriented subjects, and promoting 'new distantiated relations of control between political centres of decision and the "non-political" procedures, devices and apparatuses' (Rose 1996, p. 55; Power 1997).

While this analysis of the neo-liberalism transition is impressive in its combination of theoretical sophistication and historical insight, it leaves unanswered several questions. This section concludes by mentioning three of these, each of which is touched on in the succeeding empirical sections and returned to in the paper's conclusion.

The first concerns the histories of the principal governmental technologies through which neo-liberalism materialized. Despite Foucault's (2007) injunction that these should form the basis of a research programme, this has only materialized patchily. Even Power's (1997, 2007) writings on audit and risk management technologies are mainly surveys of applications rather than histories. Some such technologies and the standards they are based on are relatively old and mirror the instruments of disciplinary power described by Foucault in *Discipline and Punish*. Others, like risk management, are more recent but originally had applications (mainly in insurance and engineering) very different from those assumed under neo-liberalism. How did these technologies 'travel' or become translated, and what was the nature of the transformations involved?

The second concerns similarities and differences across countries in neo-liberal experiences. The UK, Australia and to a lesser extent the US are the main national experiences drawn on in the governmentality literature, although both 'welfare liberalism' and neo-liberalism tend to be described in terms of a common 'Western' experiences. How much did national neo-liberal experiences diverge? Did some such experiences serve as more general models? If so, in what ways, and what facilitated this?

The third concerns the relation between the neo-liberal rationality of government as depicted in the governmentality literature and other political programmes associated with neo-liberalism. In the UK at least, besides marketization of the social sector, these included freeing capital from political controls in the markets for labour and for goods (abolition of policies on prices and incomes). They also included reducing public expenditure through channels other than marketization – for example, by rationalizing public functions, freezing recruitment of public employees, etc. These programmes may have had important implications for how marketization itself played out. Did they also shape the way that technologies associated with it travelled, and became implemented?

The architecture of military quality standards

The first element of the history of quality management standards presented here is a description of the formal architecture of military quality standards, as they were elaborated in the US and UK between 1940 and 1980. This introduces the vocabulary of this technology and provides a conceptual map of its main principles and instruments.

Military quality standards fell into two categories. The first was 'production standards'. These specified procedures for control of production, without designating who should perform them – military contractors, military/government employees, or others. The second was 'contracting standards'. These referred to systems of procedures – often covering activities over and above production – that contractors were solely responsible for performing. Conformity to 'Contracting standards' was established via second-party surveillance and recognized by the military through granting the contractor one or another form of 'Approved' status. Both categories of standards appeared first in the US.

Production standards

Formalized standards for control of production date from World War II and the associated conversion of mass civil production to military purposes. These standards mainly concerned physical inspection of output. Inspection standards were of varying levels of complexity. Following the more basic standards ('Standard Inspection Requirements') entailed the military and a given contractor first agreeing an 'Acceptable Quality Level' in terms of a specific percentage of pre-defined defects in a lot of a given size. End-of-line inspection with measuring instruments such as gauges was then performed for lots or batches according to standardized sampling plans. Lots with defect levels exceeding 'acceptable levels' were rejected.

Depending on the volume of production runs and nature of the products involved, requirements or recommendations were sometimes made for application of 'statistical control' to inspection. This method, first proposed by the American engineer W.A. Shewhart at Western Electric in the mid-1920s, involved collection of time series data and use of probability assumptions to differentiate 'chance' from 'assignable' causes of variation in output. Standardized 'control charts'[4] were used to perform this differentiation (Rees, 1980; Klein, 2000).

These standards were supplemented by requirements for control of non-conforming material. Defective production had to be physically segregated, documented and re-segregated into items for re-work, re-processing and scrap. In the second half of the 1950s they were further supplemented by the first generation of 'reliability standards', reserved for electronic components whose defects could not be detected using inspection or conventional measuring instruments. These standards laid down *fixed* acceptable levels and stringent sampling plans, as well as a sequence of physical tests that had to be performed for detection of the defects in question.

Until the mid-1950s, when external contractors produced US or UK military equipment, inspection was not only overseen but also directly performed by out-stationed or 'Resident' government inspectors. In the US after this date, resident inspectors remained only in an oversight role, but in the UK they were also to perform physical inspection for another 15 years. Besides having overall responsibility for a factory's inspection and materials controls, the resident inspector was the military's authority in approving derogations to production lots with defect levels above the 'acceptable quality level'. These, which were extremely common, were referred to as 'waivers' in the US and 'concessions' in the UK.

Contracting standards

At the end of the 1950s the first military standards were issued unambiguously attributing responsibility for performing quality-related functions to external contractors. At the same time, quality-related functions were specified (or re-specified) in terms of implementing and documenting an integrated set of procedures covering several – or, indeed, all – stages of the product cycle.

The first standard of this kind, 'Quality Program Requirements'[5], was issued as a joint US service standard in 1959. It stipulated that controls be defined and implemented for product design and development, purchasing, fabrication, processing, maintenance, packaging, storage and shipping or installation (in addition to production). Its use was reserved for contracts designated as 'complex', defined in terms of coverage of a combination of design and development, as well as production of a given item. US 'Quality Program Requirements' were to go through two amendments in the early 1960s. NASA published a very detailed and directive version in 1962[6], conformity to which was a requirement for all Apollo space programme contractors. The following year a less detailed version was re-published as a combined service standard, to be followed in the case of non-space applications.[7]

Two years after the first version of 'Quality Program Requirements' was issued, the US standards architecture evolved further. Contracting standards were now issued covering design and development alone, or production alone, for given *products* considered 'complex'. The need to issue these standards reflected the fact that, in the US, contracts for different activities in the preparation of a 'weapons system' were sometimes awarded separately, rather than a single contract(or) being used to cover all the activities or stages involved. Contracting standards for design and development alone took the form of a second generation of reliability standards.[8] Contracting standards for production alone consisted of elaborated statements of contractors' responsibilities in relation to inspection[9] and calibration of testing equipment.[10]

Development

This description of the architecture of military quality standards implies escalations in content, in breadth of coverage and in level of prescription. Escalation was indeed the dominant characteristic of these standards' development up to the mid-1960s. But from this time on, it was diluted or even displaced by another process that, for want of a better shorthand term, will be called simplification.[11] Since the evolving architecture was of US design, it was the US that led the way in escalation. However, simplification occurred mainly in the process of the dissemination and translation of US standards in the UK.

Escalation

Rather than document separately changes in the content, detail, breadth of coverage and level of prescription of military quality standards up to 1964, the best way of understanding the discussion here is in describing what escalation across these dimensions implied for how external military contractors had to be organized. The changes involved can be grouped under four headings, in ascending order of difficulty in terms of the challenges entailed.

First, explicitly where they followed the new requirements for inspection and calibration systems and implicitly when they followed Quality Program Requirements, contractors had to build or allocate segregated premises for use as bonded stores (for approved output), quarantine stores (for output that had failed final inspection) and calibration rooms, where in addition constant physical conditions had to be maintained.

Second, contractors had to follow a prescribed methodology in the process of design and development, in the name of securing product reliability. This was known as 'Failure Effect Analysis'[12] (FEA). In the case of military contracts this applied only to electronic components and devices, and assemblies incorporating them. In the case of NASA contracts FEA was obligatory for design and development of all inputs, including 'off the shelf' items and astronauts' food and drink (Sperber, 1973, p. 7).[13]

The first stage of FEA was to map a given component or assembly in terms of the inputs and outputs of each of its functions, resulting in a 'functional block diagram'. This was to be complemented by a 'sequencing diagram' showing for every component the order and times in which events in its 'mission' were supposed to occur. Having constructed these, the contractor had to imagine the different ways in which each component or assembly could fail, how likely each 'failure mode' was to occur, and what consequences each 'failure mode' would have. Subsequently, the contractor had to assign a ranking for each failure mode, in terms of its likely frequency, severity and ease of detection. On this basis a composite component 'Risk Priority Number' (RPN) was to be determined. Contracts specified 'limit' RPNs for each component, in the same way as they specified components' physical tolerances. If the contractor's RPN fell outside this, then design and development were to be progressively modified until an acceptable RPN had been attained.[14]

Third, contractors had to perform a series of new management task. These were to formalize existing working methods and procedures in writing (with an implied need for their rationalization where it became evident that they were not performed in a consistent way), and then to apply to them and document an unbroken chain of controls. This task subsumed maintaining records of results of controls, and establishing procedures for their internal review. Where reviews established the existence of problems, there was a further requirement to record resulting changes made. Contractors were also held responsible for assuring that their own sub-contractors followed adequate control procedures and that records existed of their results, prepared if necessary by contractors themselves.

US Military Quality Program Requirements demanded that contractors should document in the form of a plan how all these tasks were being followed, without specifying in detail the precise form this plan should take. The standard assumed that a Resident government inspector would be in a position to audit plans on the military's behalf on a contract-by-contract basis. NASA standards however required that contractors compile into a manual all documentation demonstrating an unbroken chain of controls for a given contract. The manual had to be approved by NASA authorities (rather than resident inspectors) in advance of any contract being awarded.

Finally, and most controversially, the scope of contractors' managerial prerogative was reduced when these standards were applied. Both Quality Program Requirements and Inspection System standards required a cadre of staff quarantined from production functions but with unlimited access to them, with sole authorization to 'sign off' output. The cadre was to have its own chain of command, headed by a Chief Inspector who was either a resident government inspector or who had been approved by government. Internally, the Chief Inspector was to report to a 'company senior officer' who was *not* a production executive. These structures reflected a central assumption of the military's approach to quality, namely that its achievement entailed creating a firewall between (those responsible for) output and (those responsible for) maintaining its integrity. The status of the Chief Inspector was underlined by a requirement that he/she had access to all company documents, including all contracts and modifications to them.

Simplification

By 1964 US military quality standards had unfolded to an unprecedented breadth, level of detail of coverage, and level of prescription. This was aimed both at producing a heightened level of predictability and control over output and at inculcating specific techniques such as statistical control and FEA. Heavy requirements for self-surveillance were added to an undiluted level of external surveillance in constituting a system resembling Foucault's (1991) category of 'permanent coercions'. However, shortly after this system had been completed it started to be loosened, simplified and subject to flexible interpretation. This process occurred as contracting standards were adopted in the UK.

UK military quality standards were not rationalized into the architecture described in section three until 1972–73. Before this, the UK military used six different and apparently inconsistent production standards referring only to inspection.[15] Furthermore, in contrast to the US, other large British state-owned enterprises such as the Central Electricity Generating Board and the General Post Office promulgated inspection standards. On certain contracts under US–UK military co-production arrangements some large UK contractors worked to US standards (including the Quality Program Requirements), but dissemination of this type of standard was otherwise limited. A 'Specification of Quality Management Requirements'[16], closely following US Quality Program Requirements, was issued by the UK Ministry of Technology in 1968 for application to 'complex' aircraft contracts for the Royal Air Force (RAF), but was never adopted by the Army or the Royal Navy.

Reluctant to directly borrow US standards since it was correctly considered that it could never have any influence over their current content or future development, the UK Ministry of Defence (MoD) instead decided to adopt NATO quality standards[17] as a framework. Canadian experts had written these in 1964–68, with the aim of promoting multilateral contract sharing and outsourcing between NATO countries, as opposed to only a series of bilateral arrangements between the US and other members. NATO standards had a similar architecture and content to US ones. But they were less detailed and the MoD considered their future development to be more open to non-US influence.[18]

Adopted by MoD alongside the new NATO-based UK Defence ('DEF') standards[19] was a joint military–civilian British Standards Institute (BSI) standard on reliability of electronic components[20], dating back to 1965 and promulgated at this time in deliberate distinction to the US 'Reliability System Assurance' standard of the previous year. The resulting combination of DEF standards and BSI reliability standards reversed the trend of escalation in most of its main dimensions.

First, UK standards on reliability of electronic components contained no requirement to use FEA or indeed to generate a quantitative estimation of component reliability. The terms of reference of the BSI committee set up by the military and leading contractors to write UK reliability standards had stated that due consideration should be given to this approach.[21] But the committee rejected it, arguing that production runs for UK electronic components were too short to allow sufficient measurements to be made for meaningful RPNs to be generated. Privately, officials commented sceptically on the underlying principles of US reliability standards and noted that all existing attempts to establish systematic quantitative estimations of reliability had ended in failure (as eventually became admitted in the US too – cf. Sapolsky. 1972, pp. 59, 105).

The Committee proposed instead that contractors producing complex electronic components should be subject to an approval or certification process. This involved demonstrating a capacity to perform a list of physical and environmental tests, accumulating the results of these tests over a six-month period, and generating summaries of them on 'Certified Reliability Data Sheets' (CRDSs). Certifiers and customers should have access to contractors' CRDSs and be given the opportunity to verify them against original acceptance test result records. The standard also required contractors to conform to an early version of Inspection System Requirements. Otherwise it differed from pre-FEA reliability standards mainly in its insistence on record keeping.

Second, the UK DEF version of 'Quality Program Requirements' was amended two years after they were issued to remove contractors' obligations in relation to sub-contractors' quality systems. Henceforth, more important sub-contractors were themselves required to meet Inspection and/or Calibration System requirements and became subject to MoD surveillance.[22]

Third, UK DEF standards involved a reduction in the volume of documentation required, particularly in relation to records of control results, in all three of its System Requirement standards (Quality Programme, Inspection System, Calibration System). In an internal discussion paper written during the preparation of UK DEF standards, the civil servant in charge of this process wrote that '(the MoD viewpoint) is that administration of (the) inspection requirements (embodied in existing standards) involves considerable effort backed up by extensive records whose value and contribution to product quality is highly dubious' and that therefore there was no intention to reproduce these in detail.[23]

As for specification of control systems, it will be recalled that US contractors were obliged to develop control plans for each contract performed. These had to be approved by resident government inspectors. As in the case of the BSI reliability standard just discussed, UK DEF standards were instead linked to a certification system that gave contractors Approved status for all 'complex contracts', or (in relation to Inspection and Calibration System standards) for all contracts for 'complex parts'. To gain approval, contractors had to write manuals describing their corporate system of instructions, controls and other procedures for each stage in the production cycle covered by the standard. The manual was evaluated directly by MoD, or the Ministry of Aviation Supply[24] in the case of aircraft manufacturers, who supplemented these processes with physical audits by non-resident staff. Approvals applied for a period of two years (after which re-audit was required).[25]

Two further, inter-related changes occurred during the 1970s that were to give UK quality management standards their unique character. These will be mentioned here but discussed in more detail below. These were a revision of the requirements found in US standards for inspection (and inspection staff) to be quarantined from other corporate operations, and (in 1980) the removal from 'select contractors' of the resident government inspectors who usually served as their Chief Inspectors. In both cases, a substantial restoration of managerial prerogative was entailed.

Thus by 1980 loosening, simplification and introduction of increased flexibility to military quality standards resulted in a UK standards architecture that mirrored that in the US, but whose content was stated – or at least applied – in more liberal way. Prescription of specific methodologies like FEA was eliminated, and external surveillance was reduced in favour of procedures under which contractors could independently demonstrate conformity.

Drivers of standards change

In understanding the rise and subsequent revision of military quality standards it is useful to consider the types of expert knowledge deployed in government and the military over the period, and the evolving division of labour and configuration of power between these entities. Useful contrasts may be made in both cases between the situations applying before and after 1970, and in the US and UK respectively.

Expert knowledge about military affairs

Both in the US and the UK militaries it became *de rigueur* during the 1950s to use the term 'weapon systems' rather than 'weapons'. 'Systems' thinking was enjoying increasing prestige at the time not only in the military but also in business, politics and social science – largely as a result of the apparent success from applying Operations Research to a series of technical military problems during World War II and the Korean War (cf. Bouyssou, n.d.; Mirowski, 2002; Sapolsky, 2003).

While the term was applied in both countries to the same range of objects (missiles, aircraft and ships), both the practical justifications for its use and the consequences thought to stem from using it differed markedly. In the UK, it appeared first in a government White Paper on *The supply of military aircraft* (UK Government, 1955). In the US it was used for the first time in 1952 in relation to the F-102 aircraft (McNaugher, 1987).

The UK White Paper presents pragmatic historical and technical justifications for the term, preferring it to 'weapons'. The Korean War forced the UK government to put a series of interim and research aircraft into accelerated production, before the first prototypes were flown. Two of the resulting aircraft proved problematic, due to problems of coordinating its engine and armaments. This was said to reflect a conceptualization of engine and guns as separate activities rather than as a system, 'the failure of any one of whose links can make the whole ineffective' (UK Government, 1955, p. 9).

The White Paper went on to represent the concept of weapons system in two ways. First the aircraft was represented as a combination of subsystems – 'airframe...engine, armaments, radio...and all the oxygen, cooling and other equipment which ensure its safety and efficiency' (*ibid.*). Second, aircraft *development* was represented as an integrated sequence of steps, where the duration and complexity of any given step

had effects on downstream production and the extent of later requirements for modification. Policy conclusions were derived in relation to
each representation. Based on the 'combination of sub-systems' representation, 'the ideal would be that complete responsibility for coordinating the various components of the system should rest with...the
designer (and)...it is the intention to move in this direction as far as
practical considerations allow' (ibid.). Based on the 'integrated development process' representation, '(adopting) a policy of shorter steps (that is,
fuller development of interim designs) would mean (fewer) subsequent
technical problems, (and thus greater availability) of up-to-date aircraft
that could enter production relatively quickly' (ibid., pp. 11–12).

The US weapons system concept was elaborated at length in 1959 in
the course of military officials' evidence to Congress, quoted at length
in Kast and Rosenzweig (1962, pp. 43–44). This embodies a different
problematic:

> Weapons systems comprise facilities and equipment in combination
> or otherwise, which form an instrument of combat. (This) definition
> is necessarily broad, as are all aspects of the concept, because (its)
> outstanding feature is flexibility...(A)n instrument of combat is des-
> ignated as a weapons system...when a determination is made that
> existing organizational structures are not adequate...to develop and
> produce the weapon...

The witness went on to state that organizational structures adapted to
the concept differed from others in two ways. First they incorporated
a distinct 'systems integration' role, and second they required a more
comprehensive type of military oversight, ideally taking a 'project'
form. However, no general implications were drawn for the length of
specific phases of the development process, or for who should carry out
systems integration:

> On the industrial side the (corresponding) procurement pattern may
> range from contracting with an organization which will handle only
> technical direction and systems management, to hiring a single con-
> tractor for performance of research, development and production as
> well as technical direction and systems management. In between
> these extremes are many patterns of contracting with several prime
> contractors, or jointly between prime contractors and the military
> organization.

In fact, the main legacy of the US application of the weapons system concept was a common military 'system oversight' tool. This combined a dedicated (project) management team with a logical framework of tasks, responsibilities and performances. When the development of new systems was approved, all the tasks this entailed could then be exhaustively specified, allocated and subjected to verification. Development of a weapons system thus meant 'reach(ing) down to any level of ... activity and find(ing) a plan and a performance report that logically and clearly (could) be related to the total job' (G. Pehrson of the Polaris Project team, quoted in Sapolsky, 1972, p. 99).

Contracting arrangements

Having observed that adopting a 'weapons system' approach had no direct implications for contracting arrangements, US officials went on to explain to Congress that the military's choices in this regard instead mainly reflected which of the services was given responsibility for a project. According to the Secretary of the Army, W. Brucke, if the US Army or Navy was awarded this role, then what he called 'the Arsenal Concept' applied. This prescribed that the military retain all key functions including system integration. Alternatively, if it were the Air Force, then normally a 'prime contractor' would perform design and development, as well as a large part of production and often also 'system integration'. This difference reflected the fact that while the branches of engineering relevant to the Army and Navy had developed hand-in-hand with military production, aircraft engineering was historically a civil activity. Brucke's own loyalty was to the 'Arsenal Concept', in whose justification he claimed that '... optimal performance of the weapons system management function requires the objectivity which is inherent within the defence establishment and not likely to be found in private industry. Only the Army and not private industry is capable of total integration of the completed weapon.' (cited in Kast and Rosenzweig, 1962, p. 63).

Thus the US Army and Navy retained extensive in-house capacity for design and development and, in 'their' weapons systems, project management subsumed system integration. One or more 'primes' would normally be responsible for fabricating the main assembly, but specification and even sub-contracting for components would be undertaken by the military itself.[26]

The Air Force instead depended on airframe manufacturers for a wide range of tasks from the 1920s through to the early 1960s. Even so, the role of Air Force primes should not be exaggerated. Until the 1950s a high proportion of components were procured directly by the military on primes' behalf under so-called 'Government Furnished Equipment' arrangements (Holley, 1964, p. 132) and even after 1952 when airframe manufacturers were allocated system integration roles, they had to submit for advanced approval an overall 'make-or-buy' plan for each contract. Later, when the Air Force gained responsibility for the Ballistic Missile System Programme, it too established in-house technical expertise and shifted towards an Arsenal Concept (Kast and Rosenzweig, 1962).

Restrictions on the role of primes reflected not only presence of the Arsenal Concept but also misgivings shared by the military and a considerable part of the US political class concerning over-dependence on large military contractors. From the 19th century onwards US politicians demanded that military expenditure should be spread across all states and small as well as large firms (McNaugher, 1987). The military itself expressed the fear that encouraging primes to vertically integrate would lead to a loss of the expertise found in more specialist areas of the contractor base (Holley, 1964; Kast and Rosenzweig, 1962).

In the UK, contracting arrangements where primes were delegated substantial design and development functions were common from the 1930s, not only for the RAF but also the Army (Ashworth, 1953; Postan *et al.*, 1964). Then, during the run up to World War II, leading contractors were given further responsibilities by the newly created Ministry of Supply, 'staffed mainly by recruits from industry' (*ibid*, 1964). The Ministry used a so-called Group Administration system for re-armament. Designated 'Main Contractors' were given responsibility to lead independent geographical networks of contractors and temporary government factories, in production sharing and subcontracting arrangements (Hornby, 1958). The coordination role was shared with government to varying degrees, according to which armed services was supplied. 'Mains'' responsibilities were fewest in Royal Navy contracts and greatest in those for Army armoured vehicles (Postan *et al.*, 1964).

After 1941, mains were less relied on for design and development. This followed the assumption by the Soviet Union of a fighting role in Europe and criticism of the performance of British tanks in the North Africa Campaign. Arguments now prevailed that the 'rigid production programme' necessary while Britain fought alone should give way to building capacity for 'continuous adaptation'. Research and Development and Technical Directorates mushroomed in the UK War Office, which (re-)asserted dominance over the Ministry of Supply (Postan *et al.*, 1964).

Over the following thirty years, mains usually functioned as system integrators for aircraft contracts (especially after the 1955 While Paper) but 'Arsenal Concepts' were applied in many non-aircraft projects (UK Government, 1971). However, the former responsibilities of mains remained part of government's institutional memory, to which recourse was made when the division of labour between government and contractors was subjected to critical reflection.

This occurred in 1970–71 when the incoming Conservative government proposed a clearer demarcation of the central government role from those of private industry and local government (UK Government, 1970). In the defence area, this played out in terms of decisions to confine military technical activity to research and quality assurance, and to redefine the government's procurement role to writing specifications and letting contracts. This restored a 'concept of partnership (with) industry', whereby 'much of the design (could be) done...by outside contractors who generally have greater access to civil technology and more experience in matching design to production possibilities' (UK Government, 1971, p. 22).

By 1971 it was clear that US and UK military procurement, while sharing a language of weapons systems, were otherwise pulling in different directions. In the US the Arsenal Concept was mobilized to support an in-house systems oversight function distinct from systems integration. Fed by a mainly populist opposition to over-dependence on large contractors, this justified standards that were not only expansive in scope and detail but which could be used as an instrument of external management of contractors. In the UK the Arsenal Concept, system oversight and integration functions were never clearly differentiated and the pattern of military procurement was politically uncontroversial. This led to a different approach to standards – one concerned with output's 'fitness for purpose', but within the framework of partnership with a highly concentrated industry.[27]

Inspection costs and responsibilities

Inspection requirements, as they were laid down in military standards throughout the period, implied the need for large numbers of inspectors. According to Lamprecht (2000, p. 102), the US Air Force alone employed 14,000 at the end of World War II, while in the UK in 1967 the three services combined employed 21,700.[28] As such, the number of inspectors (or later, of all quality assurance staff) was a ready-made target when politicians or Treasury departments scrutinized military budgets and/or demanded higher priority within them for weapons systems and 'fighting forces'.

In the US, pressure to reduce military inspectorates' size emerged already in the late 1940s. In 1953, procurement regulations were published obliging contractors to maintain in-house inspectorates proportional to the size of the contracts they bid for – thus allowing military inspectorates to be reduced to a small number of staff in supervisory roles (Lamprecht, 2000). The steadily increasing range, and detail and prescription of US military standards from this time thus reflected not only American ideas about weapons systems and the role of contractors, but also an early withdrawal from basic inspection. Since all military contracting (up to the 1960s) was on a 'cost plus fixed fee' basis, the savings achieved were illusory. US contractors employed former military inspectors and the military hid their cost as additional expenditure on weapons.

UK contractors were not obliged to employ large numbers of inspectors, except when they worked on US or joint US–UK contracts like *Polaris* where functions not covered by UK standards were demanded (Drew, 1972). The size of UK military inspectorates first surfaced as an issue in the mid-1950s, when it was decided (by the Musgrave Committee[29]) to achieve savings by amalgamating the separate Army, Royal Navy and RAF inspectorates. In 1958 distinct inspectorates were re-established as a result of separation of the parent Ministries. After a further decade of Treasury complaints, the MoD Raby Committee was established in 1967.[30] The Committee heard from the Treasury that the inspectorates' annual direct cost was GBP 25 million[31] and recommended their reduction in number and the transfer all routine inspection to contractors.

In the UK a few hundred inspectors remained in MoD employment after this date. Some of these fell into the category of resident government inspectors while others were transferred to an external auditing role. Probably the largest proportion though were those performing routine inspection in government ordnance factories or in plants owned by small contractors deemed to lack the resources and expertise to perform inspection themselves.[32]

Unlike in the US, the UK reform occurred in the context of a shift away from 'cost plus fixed fee' contracts. By 1979 these represented only 22 per cent of military procurement by value. They were replaced by contracts with incentives, in the form of higher margins, for reducing costs (Smith, 1990). Moreover a discourse on UK manufacturing was emerging at the time that identified low productivity as a problem attributed in part to employment of excessive numbers of non-productive workers, or 'indirects'.[33] As will be seen, this led to proposals from the contractors' side for re-interpretation of how inspection functions should be performed.

The number of government-paid inspectors was subject to further substantial reduction in 1980, as part of the incoming Thatcher government's programme to shrink the UK civil service.[34] As noted earlier, oversight by resident government inspectors was withdrawn from a MoD list of 'select' Approved suppliers. In addition, MoD inspectors were withdrawn from routine inspection across most of the smaller contractors where they had remained performing this task.

Contractors' rights

Contractor dissatisfaction with military standards was expressed from the outset both in the US and the UK, mainly in the shape of what Taylor (1911) famously called 'soldiering'. When statistical control became a 'recommendation' rather than explicit requirement in inspection standards after World War II, US contractors simply stopped using it (Lightstone, 1993). Later, they implemented even the first generation of reliability standards only in 'diluted and truncated' forms (MacGuigan, 1960), while in the UK few electronic component manufacturers bothered to seek Approved status under their UK version (Blanks, 1973). Most prospective NASA contractors failed to submit documented quality programmes for advance approval (Sperber, 1973), and the MoD feared the same would happen in the UK after preparation of corporate quality manuals was mandated under DEF Quality Programme Requirements (Jones, n.d.).

These responses had rather different consequences in the US and the UK. In the NASA case, and probably more widely in the US, the authorities had to abandon rigorous enforcement in favour of 'face-to-face meetings, troubleshooting particular concerns' (Sperber, 1973). In the UK, via a rather tortuous process, contractors were granted formal rights in relation to interpretation of standards.

The institutional framework for this process was the Defence Quality Assurance Board (DQAB) formed in 1970. This followed a recommendation by the Raby Committee that a special MoD apparatus was necessary to write and administer UK DEF standards[35]. While DQAB consisted only of MoD staff, its workplan included a series of annual residential conferences with Directors from the main contracting companies and a Panel of industry representatives was set up to advise it. At its first meeting the DQAB Chief Executive,

H. Drew, set out the Board's philosophy. Firstly, quality was going to be viewed as the responsibility of suppliers rather than the MoD, and the standards that the Board adopted would be interpreted in ways that promoted this. Secondly, and as a logical correlate, 'quality requirements' would henceforth rest on 'mutual agreement between purchaser and supplier'.[36]

Thus, although UK DEF Quality Programme Requirements would follow those of their US counterpart in stipulating a quarantined inspection staff reporting to a Chief Inspector who was a resident government representative, Drew intimated at the time of their release that DQAB did not intend to enforce this. Indeed, he observed, a literal interpretation of this rule 'would detract from the contractor's responsibility for quality... Quality failures attributable to his system (would) cease to be his responsibility. This is true whether we reserve to (government) the right to monitor and supervise while making detailed requirements, or whether we insist that the inspection function must be undertaken solely by inspection personnel, (thus) militating against the introduction of operator control.'[37]

While the role of the Panel proved rather passive, DQAB annual conferences saw contractor representatives reporting 'what we really do' in areas like inspection and challenging DQAB to endorse these practices as falling within a liberal interpretation of the rules. For example, contractors should be allowed to designate heads of production divisions as having overall responsibility for quality, while the role of Chief Inspectors or 'quality managers' as they were beginning to be called, should be 'providing advice, standing back and thinking and occasionally checking to make sure inspection is adequate'.[38]

Contractors also seized gratefully upon Drew's explicit opening to 'operator control'. The 1973 residential conference featured a paper by a Director of Rolls-Royce describing how inspection 'could be done by making operators (rather than inspectors) sign off output as conforming to specification'.[39] The subsequent discussion focused entirely on problems of getting trade unions to agree with this procedure, while it was taken for granted that it was acceptable to DQAB.

Such was the confidence of the contractors that the same paper concluded by demanding that 'MoD auditors should be instructed to use contractors' quality assurance systems wherever possible, with requests for extra actions only where needed, rather than automatically seeking changes to the norm (where this departed from standards).'[40] Broadly, it appears that this too was accepted by DQAB. MoD files on the results of the audits remain closed, but a contemporary paper by Drew's successor at DQAB (Sauch, 1976) suggests that while significant departures from DEF standards were picked up in a majority of cases, non-Approval was the exception rather than the rule.

Conclusions

Quality management standards date, in their modern form, from the early 1970s. They emerged in this form as UK military standards. These took their architecture and much of their content from the US military standards of a decade before. US standards did embody 'hard engineering' quality control practices and were also shaped by contemporary US management discourses, in particular 'systems thinking' and its incarnation in project management methods. However, when these standards were disseminated in the UK these foundations were eroded.

UK military officials were intellectually sceptical about some claims of these discourses. They were also highly dependent on large contractors, with whom their relations were closer than in the US. Furthermore, they had less leeway to finance the standards' literal implementation than their US colleagues. They therefore adopted a more 'liberal' approach to their promulgation. A decision was made to obtain UK contractors' consent to 'responsibilization'. The *quid pro quo* was that UK contractors were freed from some US requirements and allowed to re-define others in their own terms. Modern quality management standards as they then emerged thus recognized managerial prerogative and cost as principles equally important as discipline, self-reporting and inspectability. Arguably, it was this combination that made UK DEF standards in their civil incarnation[41] successful as neo-liberal technologies of government.

This train of events became possible not because UK DEF standards truly balanced 'freedom' with 'control', but because they resulted from a testing and re-definition of the 'boundaries of government' by concerned parties in a specific context. As a result, corporate entities were formally responsibilized, enabling their 'government at a distance', but in a manner extending their freedom from substantial public control.

Foucault's governmentality framework offers a conception of standardization that goes beyond mainstream 'global governance' perspectives focusing on decision-making processes and the achievement of legitimacy for standards, that is, on standards as 'expertise-based rules that can be adopted voluntarily' (Kerwer, 2001, p. 8). Instead, it views standards as technologies operating through a combination of traditional forms of 'sovereign power' such as legal sanctioning and – more importantly – disciplinary mechanisms such as surveillance, inspection, hierarchization and segregation. More recently available work by Foucault (2007, p. 11ff) can be used to show that in some cases they further operate through what he describes as 'technologies of security' – mechanisms that govern through rendering intelligible the physical regularities of objects, for example, by using statistical control.

Foucault believed that standards or norms were a core liberal governmental technology. Presumably they retained this role under neo-liberalism, particularly where – as in the case of quality management standards – they had applicability not only to economic activity but also to the 'conduct of conduct' generally. But Foucault's analysis of neo-liberalism did not get this far.

The post-Foucault governmentality literature has moved in this direction though. It has done so by examining the role of a number of standards-based practices (auditing, accounting....); though not necessarily the actual standards they are based upon, as technologies of 'marketization'. This literature tends to assume that off-the-shelf forms of these technologies, compatible with the neo-liberal project, were readily available for use. The question this begs is how it was that *these* technologies came to play this role and not others such as Operations Research-based project management, which also allowed conduct to be specified in terms of responsibilities, and then allocated and verified. The answer must be that some technologies travel better than others, since they have already undergone modifications that make it more likely that neo-liberal actors such as firms and governments will take them up later. The conditions under which this occurs clearly matter, and demand careful specification.

This point is related to the second and third questions about neo-liberal governmentality raised in section one. Neo-liberal standards – or at least, neo-liberal quality management standards – arose significantly earlier in the UK than in the US. This partly reflects the UK's less highly formalized and rationalized institutional structures. This point is alluded to in the comparative capitalism literature (for example, Lazonick, 1990; Chandler, 1990), although not in a way that connects the pragmatic informality of UK institutional arrangements to a more explicit national recognition of capitalist prerogative. This in turn was more pronounced in some sectors than others. Again, the bureaucratic context in which the standards evolved seems to matter greatly, not only in respect of nation-state path dependencies but also in terms of the characteristics of the sectors in which they arose.

Vogel (1996, pp. 131–2) states that, during the 1980s, UK regulatory reform involved on the one hand a drastic increase in juridification and codification and on the other a fragmentation of the state's regulatory authority into a range of new 'independent' agencies. Similar arguments may be found in the governmentality literature (Rose, 1996). However, in certain spheres of government such as defence, regulation remained both highly centralized and organized along much more traditional liberal principles. This – and the reasons for it – is key to understanding how standardization in this particular sector ended up locking-in, spilling-over and eventually becoming the global benchmark for quality management.

Critical to at least some of the governmentality literature on 'the new regulation' is the assumption that the competitive conditions on which it is founded can be constructed regardless of context. This is evident, for example, in recent institutionalist interpretations of neo-liberal reforms as 'pro-competitive disengagement' (Vogel, 1996; see also Jordana and Levi-Faur, 2005 and Levi-Faur, 2005). Yet in the defence sector, competition was not a central policy goal, even under Thatcher[42]. This reflected a variety of factors including the huge levels of investment that prospective competitors would have to make in order to challenge incumbents, the riskiness of such investment given the one-off nature of most large contracts, and government reluctance on security grounds to open procurement to foreign-based companies. Hence, a *de facto* monopoly situation prevailed enabling capital to domesticate the regulatory moment. In fact, it was precisely this transformation of military quality standards through capitalist domestication that would facilitate their spontaneous adoption by firms as generic technologies of neo-liberal regulation.

Because transformation of these standards only arose because of non-competitive conditions, and because this meant that it represented a 'freeing' of capital more than an elaboration of controls, it is more appropriate to characterize them as 'pro-capitalist' than as 'pro-competitive' or 'regulatory capitalist'. While we welcome the governmentality literatures' clarification that neo-liberalism is more than merely deregulation, the theses that 'freer markets' go hand in hand with 'more rules' and that a new 'regulatory state' has increased its rule-making authority in the era of neo-liberal globalization needs to be qualified.

'Marketization' emerged as a political programme in the UK under Margaret Thatcher alongside reducing public expenditure and freeing of capital from political controls. The history of military quality management standards shows that cutting spending and giving more power to capital took hold in the defence sector well before Thatcher came to power in 1979 and gave them the status of mantras. In this sector they directly provoked not pro-competitive re-regulation but an opening-out of disciplinary (and 'security') technologies in ways that allowed them to interlock with doctrines of management prerogative. It was this combination which was to truly define the Thatcherite project.

Notes

The authors thank participants for their comments at seminars at DIIS and Sciences Po in June 2009, where an earlier draft of the paper was presented. The usual caveats apply.

1 While this chapter focuses on the substantive origins of the standard, we elsewhere develop a detailed analysis of the political context of its appropriation to the UK (see Gibbon and Henriksen, forthcoming).
2 To leave the text as uncluttered as possible, reference throughout to specific standards and to government papers is made in footnotes only. References in the main body of the text refer only to published material.
3 Contrary to Higgins and Tamm Hallström, it is evident that Foucault considered expert knowledge (Foucault, 2007), standards – 'norms' in French – (Foucault, 1991, p. 184) and 'government at a distance' to play central roles in classical liberal, as well as neo-liberal, governmentality.
4 These charts can be found in US War Standard Z1.1-3 (1941), and later in MIL-STD-105D, 'Inspection by Attributes'.
5 MIL-Q-9858 (1959).
6 NASA 2002-2 (1962).
7 MIL-STD-9858A (1963).
8 MIL-STD-790 (1964).
9 MIL-I-45208 (1961). Some system-like inspection requirements were specified as early as 1950 in a US Air Force standard 'The control of aircraft and associated equipment' (MIL-Q-5923), although it is unclear to what extent this standard was ever applied (Lamprecht, 2000, pp. 102–04).
10 MIL-C-45662 (1961).
11 Our use of the term is similar to that of Latour and Woolgar (1986).
12 Later known as 'Failure Modes and Effects Analysis', and later still 'Failure Modes, Effects and Criticality Analysis'.
13 The NASA food and drink FEA became the prototype for Hazard Analysis and Critical Control Point standards in the food industry.
14 Coutinho, 1964; Blanks, 1973; Coppola, 1984; Saleh and Marais, 2006 provide historical accounts of FEA standards. The terminology applied to RPNs also changed over time.
15 Drew. H. 'Quality requirements for defence procurement' (May 1971), DQAB/P (71) 14 in DEFE 72/9.
16 Av. P. 92 (1968).
17 AQAP-1 to AQAP-9 (1969).
18 See the discussion of T. Mellin-Olsen's paper 'Quality assurance in NATO', presented to the 1972 Defence Quality Assurance Board Conference, DEFE 72/95.
19 DEF 05-21 to 05-32 (1972–73).

20   BS 9000 (1965).
21   Terms of Reference, (Burghard) Committee on Standards for Electronic Components (1963), FV 6/9.
22   Presentation by G. Bentley (Procurement Executive), DQAB 1975 Annual Conference, DEFE 72/87.
23   Drew. H. 'Quality requirements for defence procurement', (May 1971), DQAB/P (71) 14 in DEFE 72/9. See Sauch (1976) for similar arguments in favour of reducing calibration system requirements.
24   The aviation responsibilities of the UK Ministry of Technology were hived off into this new ministry in 1970.
25   Presentation by G. Bentley (Procurement Executive), DQAB 1975 Annual Conference, DEFE 72/87.
26   This model was sometimes varied, as in the Navy's Polaris project, by performing management tasks including contractor and sub-contractor selection through a project team, while contracting out systems integration to a private non-profit organization (Sapolsky, 1972).
27   By the 1980s there was only one UK producer each for several strategic types of equipment including airframes, missiles, ordnance and small arms, tanks, submarines, torpedoes, large aero and marine turbine engines, nuclear propulsion units, helicopters and warships. For electronics two producers accounted for 75% of procurement (Smith, 1990).
28   Raby Committee report ('Defence Department Review of Equipment Inspection Policy, 1967–69'), T225/4292.
29   The Musgrave Committee conducted an internal MoD enquiry in 1956. Its report was not consulted, since a summary of it is provided in the Introduction to Raby, T225/4292.
30   Raby Committee report ('Defence Department Review of Equipment Inspection Policy, 1967–69'), T225/4292.
31   This corresponded to between 1.5 per cent (RAF) and 6.1 per cent (Army) of the value of procurement expenditure by the different services (Jackson to Bancroft, 5/10/67, T225/4292). No comparable figure could be traced for the US.
32   Letter with Annex from Green to Controller of Aircraft, 13/5/80, DUS(POL) PE/232/11/2/11 in AIR 20/12692.
33   The literature propagating this view is critically reviewed by Nicholls (1986).
34   The reform reduced Civil Service numbers from 732,000 to 579,000 (Theakston, 1995).
35   DEFE 13/807.
36   DQAB/P (70)6, 28/9/70, in DEFE 72/8.
37   Drew. H. 'Quality requirements for defence procurement', (May 1971), DQAB/P (71) 14 in DEFE 72/9. In justification, Drew cited the recommendation of the Raby Committee 'that the overall responsibility for the design, development, production and quality assurance of an individual item...should be brought together at the lowest effective management level', Defence Department Review of Equipment Inspection Policy 1967–69, T225/4292. Considering 'operators' as managers clearly went beyond Raby's intentions, however.

38 Alexander, W. (Marconi Elliott) 'Management aspects of quality assurance in a manufacturing industry', 1972 Defence Quality Assurance Board Conference, DEFE 72/84.

39 Bowling, A. (Rolls-Royce) 'Quality in the market place', 1973 DQAB Conference, DEFE 72/85.

40 *Ibid.*

41 The British Standards Institute had already issued UK DEF standards verbatim in 1974 as 'guides' to quality management (rather than as standards). The 1979 version (BS 5750) changed nomenclature in a few places – including the titles from 'Guides' to 'Standards' – and dropped the UK DEF's sections providing instructions to Resident government inspectors, but was otherwise identical. This version was re-issued as ISO 9000 in 1987.

42 The Thatcher government did make greater use of competitive tendering (from 1983). By the end of the decade this resulted in a small measurable increase in the numbers of firms awarded contracts worth over £100 million and over £5 million respectively, but not to a change in the industrial structure. Five companies jointly accounted for almost half of all military expenditure in 1986 (Smith, 1990).

References

Standards

The standards referred to (from the US Z, MIL and NASA series; the NATO AQAP series; the UK DEF series; the British Standards Institute BS series; the International Organization for Standardization ISO series) were downloaded from the websites of ANSI, sqonline, everyspec, mynasa and dstan.

UK Government papers (National Archive, Kew)

AIR 20/12692. Royal Air Force quality assurance policy, 1976–80.

DEFE 13/807. Raby Committee II.

DEFE 72/8. Defence Quality Assurance Board I.

DEFE 72/9. Defence Quality Assurance Board II.

DEFE 72/84. Defence Quality Assurance Board Annual Conference 1972.

DEFE 72/85. Defence Quality Assurance Board Annual Conference 1973.

DEFE 72/87. Defence Quality Assurance Board Annual Conference 1975.

DEFE 72/95. Defence Quality Assurance Board Annual Conference 1971.

FV 6/9. Electronics standards, Burghard Report, 1965.

T225/4292. Defence department review of equipment inspection policy, Raby Committee, 1967–69.

Secondary literature

Ashworth, W. (1953) *Contracts and finance.* History of the Second World War Series (HMSO, London).

Blanks, H (1973) 'A review of new methods and attitudes in Reliability Engineering', *Microelectronics and Reliability,* 12, 310–39.

Bouyssou, D. (n.d.). 'Questionner le passé de la recherche opérationelle pour préparer son avenir', at www.hal.archives-ouvertes.fr/docs/00/02/86/.../cahierLamsade196.pdf (accessed 15 January 2010).

Chandler, A. (1990) *Scale and scope. The dynamics of industrial capitalism.* (Cambridge: Cambridge University Press).

Coppola, A. (1984) 'Reliability engineering of electronic equipment: A historical perspective', *Institute of Electronic Engineers Transactions on Reliability*, 33(1), 29–35.

Coutinho, J. (1964) 'Failure-Effect Analysis', *Transactions of the New York Academy of Sciences, Division of Engineering*, 564–585.

Dean, M. (1999) *Governmentality. Power and rule in modern society* (London: Sage).

Drew, H. (1972) 'Quality: Its origin and progress in defence procurement', *The Quality Engineer*, 36(1), 6–18.

Foucault, M. (1991) *Discipline and punish* (London: Penguin Books).

Foucault, M. (1994) *The order of things: An archeology of the human sciences* (New York: Vintage Books).

Foucault, M. (1998) *The will to knowledge* (London: Penguin Books).

Foucault, M. (2007) *Security, territory, population: Lectures at the Collège de France 1977–1978*, M. Senellart (ed.), (Palgrave Macmillan, Basingstoke).

Foucault (2008) *The birth of biopolitics: Lectures at the Collège de France 1978–1979*, M. Senellart, (ed.). (Basingstoke: Palgrave Macmillan).

Gibbon, P. and Henriksen, L. F, (2011). A standard fit for neo-liberalism. Forthcoming in *Comparative Studies in Society and History*.

Higgins, W. and Tamm Hallström, K. (2007) 'Standardization, globalization and rationalities of government', *Organization*, 14(5), 685–704.

Holley, I. (1964) *Buying aircraft. Materiel procurement for the Army Air Forces.* US Army in World War II Special Studies (Washington: Department of the Army).

Hornby, W. (1958) *Factories and plant.* History of the Second World War Series (London: HMSO).

Jones, J. (n.d.) *John Sutcliffe Jones.* at http://www.datanalysis.co.uk/industrial_career/rr_career/manufacturing/ (accessed 24 April 2009).

Jordana, J. and Levi-Faur, D. (2005) 'The politics of regulation in the age of governance', in J. Jordana and D. Levi-Faur (eds) *The politics of regulation. Institutions and regulatory reforms for the age of governance* (Cheltenham: Edward Elgar).

Kast, F. and Rosenzweig, J. (1962) *Management in the space age* (New York: Exposition Press).

Kerwer, D. (2001) 'Standardization as governance: The case of credit ratings agencies', Max Plancke Projektgruppe, Recht der Gemeinschaftsguter. Paper 2001/3, Bonn.

Klein, J. (2000) 'Economics for a client: The case of statistical process quality control and sequential analysis', *History of Political Economy*, 32 (Supp. 1), 25–70.

Lazonick, W. (1990) *Competitive advantage on the shop-floor* (Cambridge, MA: Harvard University Press).

Lamprecht, J. (2000) *Quality and power in the supply chain* (Amsterdam: Elsevier).

Larner, W. (2000)' Neo-liberalism: Policy, ideology, governmentality', *Studies in Political Economy*, 63, 5–25.

Latour, B and Woolgar, S. (1986) *Laboratory Life. The Construction of Scientific Facts* (New Jersey: Princeton University Press).

Levi-Faur, D. 2005 'The global diffusion of regulatory capitalism', *Annals of the American Academy of Political and Social Science*, 598, 12–32.

Lightstone, M (1993) 'The evolution of quality in the auto sector for the period 1940 to early 1950s', *ASQC Quality Congress Transactions*, 1993. 768/72.

MacGuigan, W. (1960) *Is anything new in reliability?*, Institute of Radio Engineers Transactions on Reliability and Quality Control, 1960, 81–83.

McNaugher, T. (1987) 'Weapons procurement: The futility of reform', *International Security*, 12(2), 63–104.

Mirowski, P. (2002) *Machine dreams: Economics becomes a cyborg science* (Cambridge: CUP).

Nicholls, T. (1986) *The British worker question: A new look at workers and productivity in manufacturing* (London: Routledge Kegan Paul).

Postan, M., Hay, D. and Scott, J. (1964) *Design and development of weapons: Studies in government and industrial organisation.* History of the Second World War Series (London: HMSO).

Power, M. (1997) *The audit society: Rituals of verification* (Oxford: Oxford University Press).

Power, M. (2007) *Organized uncertainty: Designing a world of risk management* (Oxford: Oxford University Press).

Rees, M. (1980) 'The mathematical sciences and World War II', *The American Mathematical Monthly*, 87(8), 607–21.

Rose, N. (1993) 'Government, authority and expertise in advanced liberalism', *Economy and Society*, 22(3), 282–300.

Rose, N. (1999) *Powers of freedom. Reframing political thought* (Cambridge: Cambridge University Press).

Rose, N. (1996) 'Governing 'advanced' liberal democracies' in A. Barry, T. Osborne and N. Rose (eds.) *Foucault and political reason. Liberalism, neo-liberalism and rationalities of government* (London: UCL Press).

Rose, N. and Miller, P. (1992) 'Political power beyond the state', *British Journal of Sociology* 43(2), 173–205.

Sapolsky, H. (1972) *The Polaris system development: Bureaucratic and programmatic success in government* (Cambridge, MA: Harvard University Press).

Sapolsky, H. (2003) 'Inventory systems integration', in A. Prencipe, A. Davies and M. Hobday *The business of systems integration* (Oxford: OUP).

Sauch, G. (1976) 'The evolution of defence procurement quality assurance', *Quality Assurance*, 2(4), 105–110.

Saleh, J. and Marais, K. (2006) 'Highlights from the early- (and pre-) history of Reliability Engineering', *Reliability Engineering and System Safety*, 91, 249–256.

Smith, R. (1990) 'Defence procurement and industrial structure in the UK', *International Journal of Industrial Organization*, 8, 185–205.

Sperber, K. (1973) Apollo experience report: Reliability and quality assurance. NASA Technical Note NASA TN D-7438.

Taylor, F. (1911) *The Principles of scientific management.* at http://www.eldritch-pressorg/fwt/ti.html.(accessed 28 October 2008).

Theakston, K. (1995) *The civil service since 1945* (Oxford: Blackwell).

UK Government (1955) *The supply of military aircraft.* HMSO, Cmd. 9388.
UK Government (1970) *The reorganization of central government.* HMSO, Cmd. 4506.
UK Government (1971) *Government organization for defence procurement and civil aerospace.* HMSO, Cmnd. 4641.
Vogel, S. (1996) *Freer markets, more rules* (Ithaca: Cornell University Press).

7
ISO 26000, Alternative Standards, and the 'Social Movement of Engineers' Involved with Standard Setting

Craig N. Murphy and JoAnne Yates

Introduction

The history of voluntary consensus standard setting (VCSS), from its emergence in the late nineteenth century to its current application both in the information technology (IT) industry and in social and environmental fields, is of interest, in part, because the pace of technological change in these new leading sectors is so rapid that the process may not be able to achieve its original purpose (Cargill,1997). At the same time, in the past 15 years, the process has been used to set environmental and social standards, something that advocates of VCSS from across the political spectrum began arguing for almost a century ago. Now that it has been tried, will the voluntary consensus process make the resulting social standards more legitimate and effective than the plethora of other private social and environmental regulatory standards that have been promulgated since 1985?

This chapter focuses on ISO's 2010 guidance standard for organizational social responsibility, ISO 26000, which covers labour, the environment, human rights, and other issues. We argue that if the social movement aspects of ISO standard setting had remained at the fore, ISO 26000 might have proved more effective than other similar standards. However, in the context of the lessons from the empirical literature on social movements, this may be unlikely. The choices ISO leaders have made about how to develop the social responsibility standard and the general dissatisfaction with ISO among some committed standard setters may undercut ISO 26000's effectiveness.

To make this case, we first demonstrate why it is useful to see VCSS as the product of a social movement rather than simply as a mechanism of cooperation among industrial firms relying on overlapping epistemic communities. We then turn to the ways in which the social movement aspect of VCSS could make ISO 26000 unusually legitimate and effective. Finally, we consider the conflicts within the VCSS social movement, many of which focus on the inadequacies of traditional VCCS and of national standard setting bodies and ISO itself.

Industrial standard setters as company representatives and as members of epistemic communities

The last decade has witnessed a significant increase of interest in standard setting among historians, political scientists, sociologists and economists due both to the rapidly expanding scope and high visibility of standards in telecommunications and information technology and to the explosion of private regulatory standards in all fields.[1] Much of the new research has focused on the outcome of standard setting with respect to governance or coordination. Political scientists and legal scholars have emphasized the emergence of private standards in fields where states and intergovernmental organizations have failed to regulate (Abbott and Snidal, 2009) while business and economic historians have looked at standard setting as part of their broader effort to take into account the wide array of economic coordination mechanisms that exist along the spectrum from 'market' to 'hierarchy' (Lamoreaux *et al.*, 2003).

Yet standardization, *per se*, need not be seen in opposition to the state (or to the market); standardization can be accomplished by institutions that lie anywhere along the line between 'market' and 'hierarchy,' whether the hierarchy be that of a firm or of the state. It is, therefore, worthwhile to study different *processes* of standard setting, to compare the circumstances under which they were developed, when and why they have been deployed, how effective they have been, and who they have served. VCSS, the process followed by the global network of standard-setting bodies that has ISO as its peak, is particularly worth investigating not only due to the vast scope and long history of that network, but also because the process has been emulated, to varying degrees, in other significant fields including international financial and accounting standards (Helleiner, 2010; Tamm Hallström, 2004), international labour standards (Tepper Marlin and Tepper Marlin, 2003), and even international standards for assessing the fairness of national elections (Stremlau, 2009).

A great deal of the literature that focuses on the process of VCSS has been by economists who model it as 'standard setting by committee,' an ideal type that lies between standard setting by the market and standard setting by the state. One of the most significant articles in this literature (Farrell and Saloner, 1988) suggests that the kind of technical committees that exist in ISO and other VCSS bodies are superior as standard setters to either states or to markets alone. 'Committees' actually achieve the desired outcome of setting a single standard. Moreover, even if significant value is placed on speed (not a virtue of VCSS), committees still outperform the market. Nonetheless, Farrell and Saloner point to a mechanism that is even more effective: standard setting by committees in a world in which powerful actors (dominant firms or powerful states) can leave the process at any time and set a standard that many others are likely to follow. Not coincidentally, this is a fairly accurate description of the real world of industrial standard setting in most sectors.

Nevertheless, despite the surface validity of the economists' models, they have at least one limitation. They treat the members of VCSS committees as made up of representatives of firms, as people only concerned with the specific interests of the companies for which they work. Yet, this has never been the self-understanding of many of the people involved in such committees nor is it the way that most standard-setting bodies officially define the role of the members of their technical committees. In the early 1900s, engineers established the original national VCSS bodies to create more effective systems of standard setting than what had gone before: standard setting done only by independent engineers who served no commercial interest. Historically, engineering knowledge, not the interest of the firm, came first. In contrast, the 1918 American Engineering Standards Committee's (AESC) Rules of Procedure described their aim as making standard setting 'fully representative'. Each new technical committee would include engineers from companies that produced the industrial product and engineers from companies that purchased the product, as well as representatives of 'the general interest,' that is, independent engineers. The Rules required that none of the three groups should predominate (Yates and Murphy, 2006). The same is true today. Moreover, while it is true that engineers on today's VCSS committees often describe themselves as, in part, serving the interests of their firms,[2] the rules of VCSS bodies invariably demand that members of technical committees serve a larger interest, either the general interest or that of the entire sector that produces or uses what is being standardized.

The engineering background of the participants in industrial standard setting, and their justification of the consensus norm with the argument that rational debate will lead to agreement on an optimal way of doing things, suggests that standard setters are not *just* representatives of particular stakeholders. They are also part of 'epistemic communities.' They are professionals who share knowledge, agree on criteria for validating new knowledge, and believe that humanity can benefit from the application of that knowledge (Haas, 1992, p. 3).

International relations scholars consider epistemic communities to be part of the explanation for international cooperation. They guide policy makers toward agreements on new international norms and toward similar national solutions to the same problems. The more that members of a specific epistemic community hold central roles in powerful governments, the more powerful the community. Thus, for example, the epistemic community of experts in public finance – whose members occupy central positions in the world's ministries of the treasury – is more broadly powerful than is the global community of experts in public education. Similarly, engineers associated with particular standards – say, the nineteenth-century electrical engineers who championed VCSS (Yates and Murphy, 2008) – have long helped industrial firms to cooperate with each other by guiding them toward shared standards (measurements of electricity, standard cable sizes, and so on.) and the most powerful of these communities consist of engineers who hold particularly important roles within powerful firms. These epistemic communities tend to be the most powerful within the most technologically dynamic sectors of any period, hence, perhaps, the relative prominence of the electrical engineers among all the standard-setting engineers of the late-nineteenth century.

The standards movement

Yet, members of VCSS committees are also not *just* representatives of companies or sectors who are also part of field-specific epistemic communities. They are also members of the community of 'standard setters,' a transnational group that has existed for more than a century, the group that founded AESC and the other early national standard-setting bodies in Great Britain, France, Germany, and other countries. This community is similar to an epistemic community in the sense that it consists of 'professionals who share knowledge' (about VCSS) and who 'believe that humanity can benefit from the application of that knowledge'.

Yet in one way, at least, 'standard setters' make up something *less than* an epistemic community: they have never really agreed on criteria for validating new knowledge about standard setting, *per se.* Over the last century, the greatest conflicts among standard setters have been over proposed changes in the voluntary consensus process – conflicts over *who should be at the table* (Independent engineers alone? Producing firms? Major purchasers? Retail consumers? Other stakeholders?) and over *the level at which consensus should be formed* (National? Global? Both?), and there has been no 'science' to which standard setters could turn to find a resolution.

Nevertheless, commitment to the broader idea of VCSS has kept a community of standard setters together. In his history of the Australian national standards body, Winton Higgins (2005, p. 39) calls the founders of today's global network of VCSS organizations 'evangelical engineers' who, 'in a spirit of internationalism ... generated enormous enthusiasm around the project of optimizing the application of mass-production principles, not least standardization, to civilian industries.' The early members of what Higgins calls the 'standardization movement' considered themselves to be *practical, internationalist, modest, democratic,* and *process-oriented* people who *served the common good* (Murphy and Yates, 2009b, pp. 14–17) and these same values continue to be central to many individuals working on VCSS committees.[3]

For the standardizers, their *practicality* is often associated with their identity as engineers and their commitment to creating standards that are likely to be adopted. The evidence of their *internationalism* includes commitments to the global diffusion of innovation as well as the many positive statements about the contemporary overarching intergovernmental organization (the League of Nations or the United Nations) by leading standard setters in every generation. The limited claims of standard setters about the significance of their work suggest, to them, their *modesty.* Nonetheless, as Samuel Krislov (1997, p. 21) notes, this 'nominal diffidence' may have a 'Uriah Heep aspect.' Standard-setting engineers, Krislov argues, typically believe that their knowledge and commitment to practicality make them uniquely qualified to design a better world. This is one reason, perhaps the main reason, that there have always been conflicts over expanding the range of stakeholders allowed to take part in VCSS (retail consumers, for example). Perhaps the most significant characteristic of the standards movement is its (self-perceived) *democratic process orientation*. Ian Stewart, head of the Australian national standards body in the 1970s put it this way:

> The dialogues associated with standardisation are a liberal education for all who participate in them. They involve an exchange of experience and of expertise of people who may not otherwise get together. They involve possibly conflicting interests who would otherwise stand in isolation with one another. All who emerge from the dialogues are wiser because mutual understanding is being strengthened. Participation in the preparation of standards is not a chore to be endured but an opportunity to be used, to benefit from the process of mutual education, and to influence the content of standards that will determine future practice. (Quoted in Higgins, 2005, p. 144)

Winton Higgins argues that 'standards produced by the typical standard setting body crystallise the communicative rationality that Habermas had in mind' (*ibid.*, p. 29). For Higgins, the continuity of this claim is the kernel of the worldview and political programme that link today's standard setters to the earliest proponents of VCSS.

According to these proponents, VCSS *serves the common good* both because it makes the participants wiser and because it creates 'better' standards than those achieved by any other methods. In the words of one of the most influential early proponents:

> In its broadest aspect it [standardization] may be said to imply, the introduction, through collective effort of economical measures of manufacture, not so much with the idea of gaining individual dividends as of unifying the needs of industry and thus bringing about the greatest good for the greatest number.' (Le Maistre, 1922, p. 1)

Taken together, these longstanding convictions of the 'evangelical engineers' and their followers suggest that it is appropriate to consider them as constituting a social movement. Perhaps, as the democratic theorist Jane Mansbridge has suggested, it should be called an 'epistemic social movement,'[4] a transnational movement of professionals who share knowledge and experience of VCSS and who are convinced that humanity can benefit from that knowledge.

The standards movement displays both similarities to, and differences from, the social movements – both national (Tarrow, 1998; Tilly, 2004) and international (Keck and Sikkink, 1998; Smith, 2001) – that have typically been the focus of studies by political scientists and sociologists. Like the modern labour movement, the socialist movement, and (arguably) even the abolitionists and the Chartists, the standards movement would have been all but inconceivable before the industrial revolution (c.f. Tilly, 2004, pp. 25–27). However, unlike most of the classic social movements of the nineteenth century, whether national (*ibid.*) or international (Keck and Sikkink, 1998, pp. 39–78), the standards movement has not focused on changing the law and state policies, except to urge that legislatures should delegate some of their own standard-setting powers to VCSS organizations.

The standards movement offered a partial alternative to parliamentary politics, but not the radical alternative of the anarchists or the utopian socialists. Standard setters have been reformist internationalists. In that way they are similar to the nineteenth century free trade movement in Britain, the Cobdenites, with whom many early standard setters shared significant goals and values. Some students of today's transnational social movements would reject treating organized advocates of free trade as a social movement. After all, 'social' movements are concerned with some larger, not-yet-fulfilled, or now-threatened social purpose. Today, free traders are in the driver's seat; their adversaries, the 'anti-globalization' movements are the quintessential transnational social movements of the moment (Chase-Dunn and Gills, 2005; Smith, 2001, 2008). In contrast, the early free trade movement centred on consumers, uniting working-class women, imperialists, and anti-colonial internationalists in a programme of social reform (Trentmann, 2008). Similarly, many early standard setters (and many of their more recent successors) embraced what we now call 'globalization' due to the capacity of larger markets to encourage economies of scale that can lower the cost of industrial goods and encourage innovation, both of which can contribute to social welfare.

Unlike the early free traders, and unlike most of the 'classical' social movements, standard setters have never aspired to create a mass following.[5] They have contented themselves with a community of like-minded professionals similar to that of the nineteenth century 'public systems builders' who promoted innovations in both government and international organization – for example, Rowland Hill, the inventor of the modern postal system (Murphy, 1994, pp. 62–74) or the later 'systematic management movement' that helped create the modern firm (Yates, 1989, pp. 6–20).

Like the public systems builders and like the systematic management movement, the standards movement has always been committed to broad utilitarian outcomes – efficiency and welfare. In that way, standards bearers are unlike the abolitionists, the peace movement, feminist movements, civil rights movements, and others that focus on much more specific goals. Instead, the standards movement (like the public systems builders and the systematic management movement) has been committed to a particular form of governance and to the application of a particular *process*, standard setting, especially standard setting by consensus. Winton Higgins (2005, pp. 28–29) explains that standards movement activists believe that this larger commitment to a 'democratic' process gives everyone involved the opportunity to see beyond the narrow interests of their employer or the even the disciplinary blinders of their expertise.

The standards movement's argument is attractive. It has always been the main claim of the social theorist and policy makers who have advocated using the rules of national and international standard-setting bodies to set needed social standards that have not been set through the regular parliamentary procedures and intergovernmental cooperation. That is why Sidney and Beatrice Webb (1920, p. 56) hoped for the 'further development' in 'the public service' of the processes devised within the British standards body. It is also why, more than 80 years later, the World Bank's Vice President for Europe called for resolving the world's most urgent problems – from poverty to global warming – through the application of ISO's voluntary consensus process (Rischard, 2002).

In fact, the centrality of the standards movements' commitment to 'democratic principles' makes it surprisingly similar to a number of more traditional social movements that the sociologist Francesca Polletta discusses in her study of twentieth century egalitarian politics in the United States, *Freedom is an Endless Meeting* (Polletta, 2004). Polletta's central argument is that American social movements made strategic, political choices when they chose participatory democratic procedures over other, more hierarchical, ways of making collective decisions. The standards movement makes similar strategic choices in favour of democratic procedures: Just as Polletta's activists argued that shared deliberation increased group ownership and commitment to decisions, advocates of VCSS argue that their open and thorough process results in more legitimate standards. Similarly, just as the activists pointed to the frequency with which their 'endless meetings' led them to discover fundamentally new ways to promote their goals successfully, standard setters point to the frequent discovery of better technical solutions in the course of committee debates.

Social movements that are convinced of the strategic value of democratic processes tend to avoid hierarchy and organization. Polletta (2004, pp. 27–30) identifies an almost anarchist theme in statements by US social movement leaders throughout the twentieth century and software engineers in the open source movement make similar statements, today (Weber, 2004, pp. 54–93 and see below). In contrast, the standards movement, at least in its early years, had little choice but to establish a network of organizations to advance its goals. As Jackie Smith (2005) argues, this organizational imperative is typical of *transnational* social movements. 'Transnational social movement organizations' (TSMOs) – such as Amnesty International, Greenpeace, and the World Social Forum – have been essential to overcome the transaction and information costs associated with the episodic collaboration among distant, voluntary activists who direct much of their action toward formal organizations – firms, governments and intergovernmental organizations. From the late nineteenth century through the foundation of ISO (in 1946), and even decades afterward, standards advocates pointed to the creation of standards bodies and cooperation among them as milestones in the advance of the 'international standards movement' (Coonley, 1956; Verman, 1973; Sturén, 1997). Many of the standards bodies themselves, especially ISO, have long provided the diverse transnational movement with its necessary organizational structure.

The social movement aspects of VCSS and the origin of ISO 26000

Critics of ISO's recent move into the field of social responsibility standard setting treat the organization as if it were a private firm whose managers decided to 'move into social and environmental standards is because it is a market opportunity' (Bernstein and Hannah, 2008, p. 599). As we discuss in this chapter's final section, there are good reasons for treating *some* of the VCSS standards bodies as if they have become profit-seeking firms. Nevertheless, ISO remains a relatively small organization that continues to have many of the characteristics of a TSMO. Therefore, social movement theory may provide better insight into ISO's move into the new field. Charles Tilly and Sidney Tarrow's concept of the 'political opportunity structures' faced by social movements is somewhat analogous to the 'market opportunities' that companies face. Just as profit-seeking firms react to market opportunities, social-change seeking movements react to the political opportunities created by increased access to state power, shifting social alignments (including new divisions among elites), and to the changing agendas of significant allies (Tarrow, 1998).

ISO's move into the social responsibility field responded to a major opportunity that emerged in the most recent phase of economic globalization when manufacturing shifted away from Europe, Japan, and North America to less-regulated countries in the developing world. Since the 1970s, repeated intergovernmental attempts to establish legally binding global regulation of manufacturing have failed, largely due to the opposition of the developing countries and of the United States (Ruggie, 2007; Murphy and Yates, 2009a). This failure created the space for the emergence since 1985 of dozens of international regulatory standard-setting schemes that involve cooperation among firms, intergovernmental organizations and TSMOs. These schemes range from Amnesty International's Human Rights Guidelines for Companies to the Worldwide Responsible Apparel Production labour code.

Between 1985 and 1994, most of the schemes were firm-dominated, for example, The Body Shop's 'Trade Not Aid' initiative of 1991. Post-1994, systems dominated by TSMOs (for example, Amnesty's Guidelines of 1997) and mixed firm-TSMO systems (for example, Social Accountability International's labour standard, SA 8000, also of 1997) became the most typical innovations (Abbott and Snidal, 2009, pp. 49–50).

The political opportunities seized by TSMOs arose not only due to the desire of many governments and international organization secretariats to establish some form of international regulation, but also due to emerging divisions among corporate elites. Within the deregulated world of global manufacturing, some companies found profitable niches as socially responsible firms. That is why company-generated schemes preceded those involving TSMOs, who later seized the opportunity created by the firms' desire to have neutral verification of their social responsibility claims.

ISO moved into the social responsibility field relatively late, in 2002. Its decision to do so reflected, in part, the accumulation of influences from other transnational movements going back to the 1950s when the United Nations and development activists encouraged ISO and some of the national standards bodies in Europe to provide technical assistance to developing countries that wanted to set up their own national standards bodies. In the late 1960s, ISO began to respond to demands from the new consumer movements in Europe and North America, and eventually (in 1978) created its Committee on Consumer Policy (COPOLCO). In 2002, COPOLCO recommended the creation of an

ISO social standard. Brazil's standards body, ABNT, and other national standard setting bodies interested in increasing developing country input into the creation of codes of corporate social responsibility enthusiastically endorsed the idea.[6]

ISO's earlier (mid-1990s) development of a set of environmental management systems standards (ISO 14000) opened the organization to pressure from other allied social movements, environmentalists and advocates of quality management. Initially, at least, the quality management movement had the greater impact. COPOLCO originally conceived of ISO 26000 as an auditable (monitored and verified) management system standard on the model of ISO 14000 and ISO's first set of management system standards, the ISO 9000 standards for quality management. Thus, COPOLCO thought of ISO 26000 as something of interest to the 'quality management movement,' another elite social movement like the nineteenth century public systems builders, the systematic management movement, and the international standards movement itself.

The quality management movement urges all organizations (public as well as private) to adopt a customer- or client-orientation and to monitor, and continuously to improve, all of the organization's practices. The ISO 9000 standards provide a system for documenting and monitoring almost everything that an organization does, an essential first step in any process of continuous improvement. Associations of quality management specialists (such as the American Society for Quality [ASQ] and the European Organization for Quality) became strong, if not uncritical, proponents of new ISO management systems standards (Murphy and Yates, 2009b, pp. 70–78). ASQ, for example, volunteered to be the convener of the US group that helped draft ISO 26000 (Bowers, 2006).

The final allied social movement that exerted some pressure on ISO to move into the social responsibility field was the corporate social responsibility (CSR) movement itself, especially in those countries in which it was closely allied with the national standards body, for example, in Brazil. There, the CSR movement has been particularly strong, in part, because the country's history of financial crises assured that those consumer banks that helped citizens buffer the wild fluctuations of inflation and devaluation would be the ones to survive. These 'socially responsible' firms (often privately-held banks headed by culturally conservative families that were, nonetheless, deeply committed to Catholic doctrine about responsibility to the poor) became models for others in the sector (Shanahan and Khagram, 2006). The power of the consumer financial sector, in combination with pressure from the democracy movement, unions, and UN agencies (Guedas and Faria, 2009), influenced firms in other sectors and the CSR movement organization, Instituto Ethos. Ethos played a central role in drafting the 2004 ABNT Social Responsibility Standard, which has served as a reference for the development of ISO 26000 (Backer, 2006). ABNT has also served with the Swedish standards body as the co-convener and secretariat of the ISO 26000 negotiations.

Through the Ethos Institute, the contemporary standards movement has even become linked to the quintessential 'anti-systemic' transnational social movements of the early twentieth-first century. Ethos is chaired by Oded Grajew who also founded the World Social Forum, a major site and organizational focus group opposing unregulated globalization (Smith *et al.*, 2007; Grajew, 2006). At the same time, others concerned with taming global capitalism have reached out the proponents of VCSS by adopting their methods, notably Alice Tepper Marlin whose monitored labour standard, SA 8000, has been adopted by manufacturing companies with over a million employees throughout the developing world (Tepper Marlin, 2006). Tepper Marlin points to the 29-member organization, ISEAL (originally named the International Social and Environmental Accreditation and Labelling Alliance), as a sign of the impact of VCSS methods and ideas in the new field of global private regulatory standards. ISEAL's own 'Standard-Setting Code' is based on VCSS methods (Mallett, 2010), and was developed through a voluntary consensus process among ISEAL members. VCSS, Tepper Marlin argues, has helped create new global social standards that work. The process leads to

> 'out of the box,' innovative solutions, because you don't get to consensus unless you address the key issues of everybody at the table and do so in a way that gets buy-in. If you've done a good job of identifying your key stakeholders and you've got them a standard that's got buy in from those different groups you accomplish something that will make the standard much more effective. (Tepper Marlin, 2009)

Professionals, overlapping movements, and the potential of ISO 26000

If ISO's move into social responsibility standard setting responded to the political opportunities created by the new, unregulated world of global manufacturing as well as to pressures from various social movements sympathetic to the standard setters, we should expect those same political opportunities and alliances to contribute to the success of the ISO standard. If the standard does indeed build on and extend existing social and environmental responsibility standards, we would expect that CSR advocates and environmentalists within organizations will embrace the new standard. It may be even more significant that the standard might be embraced and promoted by quality management enthusiasts and industrial standard setters within leading firms simply because men and women in those fields are often directly involved in fundamental corporate decisions.

Voluntary standards can only influence the entire global economy only if those standards are adopted by a vast number of organizations. Scholars of organizations study the emergence of organizational 'isomorphism,' the final result of adoption of similar practices. Paul J. DiMaggio and Walter W. Powell's (1983) classic article on collective rationality within groups of organizations identifies three sources of organizational isomorphism, all of which are relevant to adoption of 'voluntary' consensus standards. 'Coercive isomorphism' is what happens when clubs of certified compliers grow by enforcing a standard down a commodity chain. ISO also encourages the two other kinds of isomorphism. 'Mimetic' isomorphism when organizational leaders reason, 'We don't know what the right thing to do is in this case, so let's copy what others like us are doing.' 'Normative' isomorphism involves the invocation of an ideal to which organizational leaders wish to adhere: 'This looks like the *professional* way of doing things,' or, 'this looks like the *right* way of doing things.' The spread of ISO standards is often a matter of mimetic and normative isomorphism, a spread of practices facilitated by engineers following the lead of other engineers who provide an organic link between ISO standard setting committees and significant managers within firms.

When most other new social responsibility standards began, no organic connection existed between the standard setting body (for example, the UN Secretariat with the Global Compact or the NGO that initiated SA 8000[7]) and most companies around the world. That is not the case with ISO 26000. Each of the 100,000-plus organizations that conform to ISO's quality management standard are very familiar with ISO, as are the many companies in rapidly-developing technical fields in which standard setting has to be central to the company's strategy. Job titles tell the story: Oracle Systems has its 'Director of Standards Strategy and Policy,'[8] IBM its 'Vice President for Open Source and Standards' (Murphy and Yates, 2009b, p. 103). Whether the ISO-connected professionals are in quality management or in corporate strategy, they are much closer to the company's central decision making than are the corporate communications officers who typically provide an organ-ization's link to the UN's Global Compact.[9] Both the power within organizations of those managers familiar with ISO and those managers' professional identities lead some analysts to conclude that ISO 26000 will be taken up more rapidly than any of its CSR predecessors. Doing so will be considered a sign of professionalism and a logical extension of ISO 9000 and 14000 (Castka and Balzarova, 2008b).

Similar bonds of professionalism may encourage many otherwise reluctant small and medium enterprises (SMEs) to adopt the standard. One study indicates that managers in SMEs with quality management and standard-setting divisions are unusually willing to consider adopt-ing ISO 26000. The analysts argue that this is not just a matter of shared professional identity. Those professional links may offer SME produc-tion managers knowledge of ways to reduce costs as they implement the social responsibility standard (Perera, 2008). These expectations are consistent with the findings of a study of Nike garment suppliers who faced new standards imposed by Nike: benefits to workers tended to increase in factories where compliance was linked to improvements in work organization. The improved work organization created efficien-cies; the efficiencies encouraged the companies to internalize the costs of compliance (Locke and Romis, 2009). If, when ISO 26000 is finalized, the transnational network of ISO-conscious engineers can be tapped to provide knowledge about more efficient ways to organize production, the standard is likely to be widely adopted.

A 2008 survey of supply chain professionals in the UK suggests a final set of ways in an ISO standard may have unusual legitimacy within firms. The study was part of a project aimed at encouraging a more envir-onmentally sustainable world economy, 'where the emergence of regu-lations and consistent standards provide a global framework governing sustainable supply chain operations and clarity about specific actions'. In order to achieve that goal, the UK supply chain managers say that they need much more data on the environmental impacts down the entire supply chain; at present, only about half of the managers get relevant information even from the part of the chain that their company owns. They want clear, universally used benchmarks and 'smart containers' that would provide quick access to information from environmental audits of the entire production process of all the items in a shipment (Oracle Study, 2008). The ISO 26000 guidance standard may provide the basis for such benchmarks and ISO's recent work on standards for the electronic docu-mentation for containers and for supply chain security is, currently, the only game in town (Murphy and Yates, 2009b). ISO standards already solve some of the problems faced by supply chain professionals, which makes ISO the logical place to look for other solutions.

All of the factors above grow out of the professional roles played by quality managers and standard setters within firms. They treat these men and women as part of epistemic communities. However, it is also important to recognize that the same people are often part of overlapping and reinforcing social movements. The short-bio of one of IBM's chief standard setters, Nathaniel S. Borenstein describes him as, 'Distinguished Engineer with IBM Lotus Division, working on Internet standards and strategy and overseeing the Lotus research program. He is also the President of Computer Professionals for Social Responsibility' (Gutentag *et al,*. 2006, p. 1). Nokia's Pekka Isosomppi, who was 'heavily involved in the formation of the Open Mobile Alliance back in the turn of the millennium ... an attempt to reshape the industry through open standardization,' now directs the firm's Corporate Social Responsibility Division and is even pursuing a PhD study of ISO 26000.[10] And Oracle's head of standardization, Trond Undheim, is also the author of a recent book on socially responsible leadership (Undheim, 2008), and is married to a senior communication officer of the Asoka Foundation for social entrepreneurship,[11] which, among other things, has created TV documentaries highlighting the work of social standards promoters Alice Tepper Marlin (2006) and Oded Grajew (2006). As was the case with the early standard setters a century ago, many of the most socially-committed of today's 'evangelical engineers' seem to be in the technologically dynamic sectors of the day, and, arguably, that position may also bode well for the success of ISO 26000.

Bureaucratization of the social movement organizations, the likelihood of failure and the informal open source movement – activist alliance

Nevertheless, an alternative argument may be even more plausible. Unfortunately, for advocates of ISO 26000, engineers in the new leading sectors tend to be critical of ISO and the national standard-setting bodies that are its members. IT engineers involved in standard setting criticize ISO and its members for a kind of bureaucratization that, in part, also provides the more mundane explanation for ISO's recent entry into the social responsibility field – the argument that ISO members simply responded to a market opportunity. Many IT standards' engineers such as Undheim, Isosomppi and Borenstein question whether the traditional ISO VCSS process can respond to the pace of technological change in their field and they tend to endorse the principles of the open source movement as an alternative way to achieve the same progressive ends of the traditional standards movement. The development of new environmental and social standards outside the ISO framework (such as SA 8000), suggests that the future of voluntary standards in these fields may be linked to cooperation between social entrepreneurs and open source-oriented engineers.

Certainly, for standards engineers in some of today's leading industries, to know ISO's work is not necessarily to love it. Oracle's Undheim (2009) looks forward to a day in the near future when, 'ISO is either revitalized or disbanded... smaller, leaner, and not under the UN [idea of national representation] anymore. Industry has an equal seat, and there is ample funding for SMEs who want to participate'.

We will consider these details of Undheim's critique shortly, but will begin with his more general point: Undheim and others interested in CSR standard setting describe ISO and its members as if they had entered the stages of what social movement theorists call the 'bureaucratization' and 'decline' of a movement. 'Bureaucratization' is evident, in part, when social movement organizations can no longer rely on volunteerism 'to progress toward their goals and build constituencies.' Typically, they come to rely on paid staff to carry out functions of the organization (Christiansen, 2009, p. 3).

The need to create and pay for a professional staff has been a periodic problem not so much for ISO, but for the national standard-setting bodies. The problem emerged early in the United States (Yates and Murphy, 2006),[12] but it equally plagued other national standard-setting bodies that had once been centres of the social movement, including those in Australia and the United Kingdom, especially in the 1970s and 1980s (a central theme in Higgins, 2005). The Australian and British organizations, and those in many other countries, 'solved' the problem by becoming something like private, profit-making companies centred on the lucrative management systems standards business. Ever since the promulgation of ISO's quality management standard (ISO 9000) in the 1980s, some of the national standards bodies have become immensely wealthy from the profitable businesses of assessment and certification of various management systems. ISO's annual income is about 35 million dollars US, less than one-tenth of that of the aggressively income-seeking British standards body, BSI (Murphy and Yates, 2009b). ISO's series of environmental management systems standards (ISO 14000) further enriched many of its member bodies and because ISO 26000 was originally designed to take the same form as these two predecessors, its critics had some basis for their argument that ISO got into the field to exploit a profitable market niche for its members (Bernstein and Hannah, 2008).

ISO's own bureaucratization is more apparent when we look at its decision-making procedures. Bureaucratization is also evident when a social movement organization keeps adhering to outdated rules and procedures despite their perverse impact on the organization's larger goals. This is part of the complaint about ISO from IT standard setters who argue that the VCSS process cannot respond rapidly enough to their field's pace of technological change. Instead, many believe that, in their fields, the traditional 'evangelical engineers" goal of creating technologies that can be as widely used and as widely interconnected as possible can best be achieved by companies making their standards freely and publicly available (Weber, 2004). Members of the new generation of engineers are more likely to see themselves as part of the 'open source' movement not the 'standard-setting' movement, even if their jobs must involve attention to both issues. As David Clark, a leading Internet architect, famously put it, 'We reject: kings, presidents, and voting. We believe in: rough consensus and running code' (quoted in Russell, 2006, p. 104). According to telecommunications historian Andrew L. Russell, 'This phrase...represents a jab at the competing set of standards for internetworking created by...ISO [whose] process lacked experimental value and flexibility while at the same time suffering from excessive bureaucratic constraints.' (*ibid.*)

Social standard setter Alice Tepper Marlin (2009) believes that this problem of ISO adhering to outdated rules and procedures despite their having a perverse impact on the organization's larger goals has been evident in the negotiations on the ISO 26000 standard, but in a very different way. Instead of learning from social entrepreneurs like herself who have created social responsibility standards using a VCSS method modelled on ISO practices but amended to deal with the differences between technical and social problems, ISO attempted to follow its old rules. One of these requires that each national standards body must develop an internal consensus among different stakeholders (firms, unions, human rights organizations, environmentalists) before it takes a position. This is the 'UN 'character of ISO that seems so anachronistic to Oracle's Undheim. Not all national bodies actually enforce that rule in practice, but, in the ISO 26000 negotiations, the US body has. That has been particularly unfortunate because under ISO's again, somewhat anachronistic rules, many of the existing transnational social standard-setting bodies (like Tepper Marlin's) are represented through the US body simply because their headquarters are in the global financial capital, New York. This has the perverse effect that many of the people with the greatest practical knowledge of how to negotiate social responsibility standards are prevented from speaking in ISO 26000 meetings because their views do not correspond to the lowest-common-denominator consensus that exists within the US group. That consensus reflects the views of the many US firms that do not embrace global social responsibilities. Tepper Marlin (2009) argues that, as a result, ISO has alienated many of its strongest potential allies: CSR activists and companies that have made major commitments to the field. They now look to ISEAL, rather than ISO, as the major transnational organization supporting VCSS in their fields of interest.

The same groups have also been disappointed by the compromises that the ISO 26000 secretariat engineered to keep as many stakeholders as possible at the table. These compromises include changing the planned standard from a monitored and auditable management system standard (like ISO 9000 and 14000) to an advisory guidance standard (see Murphy and Yates, 2009a). That decision, Tepper Marlin (2009) argues, made the standard of little interest to firms that had actually embraced CSR. It also alienated many of ISO's allies in the quality management movement who had originally conceived of the standard as an extension of ISO 9000. Although, ironically, it may have created more business for Tepper Marlin's organization and other ISEAL members because they are in the position to help firms take the ISO standard, or elements of it, and turn it into something that can be monitored (SAI 2010).

A similar problem relative to the consumer movement has been created by the compromise language used to hold organizations responsible for conditions throughout the network of organizations over which they have influence – for example, throughout their whole supply chain. In 2008, Consumers International considered that language a victory. The language meant 'a corporation should not claim to be socially responsible if they produce their products in another country without considering working practices or how those goods are produced' (Consumers International, 2008). The language is important because as a 'guidance' standard, ISO 26000, could not include a simple mechanism found in ISO 9000: Certified companies are encouraged to seek supplies only from other certified companies and *must* keep track of the status of their suppliers.[13] However, in November 2009, John Ruggie, in his role as UN

Special Representative for Business and Human Rights, complained that the vaguer 'guidance' language in the current ISO 26000 draft actually ended up demanding too much. '[C]ompanies cannot,' in Ruggie's view, 'be held responsible for the human rights impacts of every entity over which they may have some leverage, because this would include cases in which they are not contributing to, nor are a causal agent of the harm in question. ... Asking companies to support human rights voluntarily where they have leverage is one thing; but attributing responsibility to them on that basis alone is quite another' (Ruggie, 2009, p. 2).

In light of the UN objection, the final standard will include much weaker language. That would disappoint many of ISO's consumer movement allies, some of them already disappointed by a 2009 decision to add language that ISO 26000 *was not* a 'standard' as understood in international law. If it were, references the World Trade Organization's 'Standards Code'[14] would tend to create both a floor and a ceiling for the social responsibilities of organizations involved in international commerce (Wirth, 2009).

Tepper Marlin (2009) maintains that ISO could have developed a standard that its potential allies in the CSR, environment, labour, human rights and quality management movements would have embraced if ISO had created a global VCSS committee that excluded organizations with no interest in an auditable social responsibility standard. ISO's commitment to its traditional procedures assured that it would create the much weaker standard that its strongest social movement allies find unsatisfactory.

What about ISO's traditional movement constituency, the 'evangelical engineers' in the leading technological sectors of the day, do they have similar grounds for disappointment? Undheim's critique of ISO's procedures certainly suggests that they might. Not surprisingly, given the social commitments of many of the IT engineers involved with open source and standard setting, Nokia's Pekka Isosomppi hopes that ISO 26000 will lead to the wide use of auditable social responsibility standards created by some of the social-movement oriented national standards bodies, such as ABNT. Yet, he worries that the ISO standard will become the basis for disparate systems of lowest-common-denominator national regulation, an outcome that would constrict the innovatory (one might say, 'open source') quality of the CSR movement (Isosomppi, 2009).

ISEAL, Tepper Marlin (2009) argues currently combines the strengths of both 'open source' and traditional ISO approaches to social standard setting: It fosters coalitions of businesses and NGOs that want to set new, higher standards in different social and environmental fields. At the same time, it promotes the consolidation of standards through its own voluntary consensus process among its members. If the century-old claims about the social promise of VCSS are ever actually fulfilled, it may be in these institutions, rather than in the standard-setting bodies that originated the process.

Notes

1   See Yates and Murphy (2006, pp. 2–4) on the range of literature. Abbott and Snidal (2009) document the global explosion of regulatory standards.

2   That is why one standard setter considers Machiavelli's *Prince* essential reading, 'It's short, sweet (well, not really) and gets you in the proper frame of mind for doing battle, er, gathering consensus,' (Nottingham, n.d.).

3   These values were apparent throughout the lives of two of the key figures in international standard setting, Charles Le Maistre (the British electrical engineer who played a central role in creation of standards organizations from the International Electrical Congress in 1904 through the establishment of ISO after the Second World War) and Olle Sturén, the Swedish engineer who was the longest serving head of the organization, from the 1960s through the 1980s. (See Yates and Murphy, 2006; Murphy and Yates, 2009b).

4   We are grateful to Mansbridge for suggesting this formulation.

5   That is, with the possible exception of advocates of Herbert Hoover's larger vision of an 'associative state' (Hawley, 1974).

6   Castka and Balzarova (2008a). In a survey of participants in the 2004 meeting on the proposed standard, developing country participants argued that, in the past, CSR standards had been designed in the North and 'imposed on suppliers from developing countries...with ISO, 'developing countries can at least influence the standard,'' (*ibid.,* p. 83. The contrast between the involvement of some Southern groups in ISO's work and the dominance of Northern groups in most corporate social responsibility standard setting bodies is significant. On the more typical cases, see Bendell (2005).

7   See Leipziger (2001) on the very small group that set the original standard.

8   The blog ('Trond's Opening Standard,' blogs.oracle.com/trond/) maintained by the current holder of the title is one of the most interesting sources of regular commentary on standards policy.

9   Each of the Compact's 'COP (Communications of Progress) Details' (found at www.unglobalcompact.org/COP/cop_search.htm) lists a contact person and his or her title.

10   Personal communication to CNM, April 2009.

11   Personal communication to JY, January 2009.

12   In the 1920s, the US national standard-setting body was dominated by academic engineers and unusually slow to embrace the principle of including all standard setters and standard users within the organization.

13   There are few good studies of the impact of this part of ISO 9000 and the related provisions in ISO 14000. A large 2001 survey of firms in Australia,

Canada, France, Hong Kong, Sweden, Taiwan and the United States found that most firms did not require all of their suppliers to be certified, that this was much more common relative to ISO 9000 than ISO 14000, and that there was significant difference across some sectors, but much less across others. Pharmaceutical, metals and plastics manufacturers were more likely to require certification down the supply chain. Textile, food, communications companies were less likely to do so (Corbett and Luca, 2001). Nonetheless, there is robust empirical confirmation of the often anecdotal claim that the global diffusion of ISO 9000 did move upstream in global supply chains (Corbett, 2006).

14 This is the way that ISO refers to the 1979 GATT Agreement on Technical Barriers to Trade. The current agreement obliges WTO members 'to ensure that technical regulations, voluntary standards, and conformity assessment procedures do not create unnecessary obstacles to trade.' Standards established through inclusively international voluntary consensus processes (essentially, those of ISO and its member bodies) have been considered by GATT and the WTO to be acceptable, *prima facie,* hence the potential significance of any ISO standard as both a ceiling and a floor that can be enforced through the WTO dispute process (ISO–IEC Information Center, 2009). ISO's head throughout the negotiation of the Standards Code, Olle Sturén, was, from the beginning, quite conscious of the way the Code would encourage the adoption of existing ISO standards and change the dynamics of negotiations for new standards, which would, thereby, become slightly less 'voluntary' for internationally traded products and services (Sturén, 1980).

References

Abbott, K. W. and Snidal, D. (2009) 'The Governance Triangle: Regulatory Standards Institutions and the Shadow of the State' in W. Mattli and N. Woods (eds) *The Politics of Global Regulation* (Princeton, N.J.: Princeton University Press).

Backer, L. C.(2006) 'Creating Private Norms for Corporate Social Responsibility in Brazil, 'Law at the End of the Day'' (25 June) lcbackerblog.blogspot.com/2006/06/creating-private-norms-for-corporate.html

Bendell, J. (2005) 'In Whose Name? The Accountability of Corporate Social Responsibility', *Development in Practice,* 15(June), 362–74.

Bernstein, S. and Hannah, E. (2008) 'Non-State Global Standard Setting and the WTO: Legitimacy and the Need for Regulatory Space', *Journal of International Economic Law,* 11 (September), 575–608.

Bowers, D. (2006) 'Making Social Responsibility the Standard', *Quality Progress* (April) www.asq.org/data/subscriptions/qp/2006/0406/qp0406bowers.html?s=qp

Cargill, C.F. (1997) *Open System's Standardization: A Business Approach* (Upper Saddle River, N.J.: Prentice Hall PTR).

Castka, P. and Balzarova, M.A. (2008a) 'ISO 26000 and Supply Chains – On the Diffusion of the Social Responsibility Standard', *International Journal of Production Economics,* 111(2), 274–86.

Castka, P. and Balzarova, M.A. (2008b) 'The Impact of ISO 9000 and ISO 14000 on Standardisation of Social Responsibility – An Inside Perspective', *International Journal of Production Economics*, 113(May), 74–87.

Chase-Dunn, C. and Gills, B. (2005) 'Waves of Globalization and Resistance in the Capitalist World System: Social Movements and Critical Global Studies' in R. P. Appelbaum and W. I. Robinson (eds) *Critical Globalization Studies* (New York: Routledge).

Christiansen, J. (2009) *Four Stages of Social Movements, an 'Academic Topic Overview'* (Ipswich, Mass.: EBSCO Publishing Inc).

Consumers International (2008) *ISO 26000 – Latest Developments,* 11 September www.consumersinternational.org/Templates/Internal.asp?NodeID=96544

Coonley, H. (1956) 'The International Standards Movement,' in D.Reck (ed.) *National Standards in a Modern Society* (New York: Harper and Brothers Publishers).

Corbett, C. J. (2006) 'Global Diffusion of ISO 9000 Certification through Supply Chains', *Manufacturing and Service Operations Management,* 8(Fall), 330–50.

Corbett, C. J. and Luca, A. (2001) 'Global Survey on ISO 9000 and ISO 14000: Summary of Findings', Anderson School of Management, UCLA.

DiMaggio, P. J. and Powell, W.W. (1983) 'The Iron Cage Revisited: Institutional Isomorphism and Collective Rationality in Organizational Fields', *American Sociological Review* 48(April), 147–160.

Farrell, J. and Saloner, G. (1988) 'Coordination through Committees and Markets', *RAND Journal of Economics*, 19(Summer), 235–52.

Grajew, O.(2006) 'Another World is Possible', *Ashoka Innovation Conversations* sic. conversationsnetwork.org/shows/detail3226.html

Guedas, A.L. and Faria, A. (2009) 'The Role of Global Development Organizations in the Diffusion of Corporate Social Responsibility in Brazil', *Revista de Gestão Social e Ambiental* 3(May-August), 124–40.

Gutentag, E., Sutor, B., Borenstein, N. and Schulz, C.H. (2006) 'Open Document, Open Revolution', *Opening Keynote Address to the OpenOffice.org Conference.* Villeurbanne, 13 September.

Haas, P. M. (1992) 'Epistemic Communities and International Policy Coordination', *International Organization*, 46(Winter), 1–35.

Hawley, E.W. (1974) 'Herbert Hoover, the Commerce Secretariat, and the Vision of the 'Associative State,' 1921–1928', *The Journal of American History*, 61(June), 115–40.

Helleiner, E. (2010) 'What Role for the New Kid in Town? The Financial Stability Board and International Standards', *paper presented at a workshop, 'New Foundations for Global Governance,'* Princeton University, 8–9 January.

Higgins, W. (2005) *Engine of Change: Standards Australia since 1922* (Blackheath, Australia: Brandl & Schlesinger Book Publishers).

ISO-IEC Information Center (2009) 'WTO, ISO, IEC and World Trade' www. standardsinfo.net/info/livelink/fetch/2000/148478/6301438/inttrade.html

Isosomppi, P. (2009) 'Voluntary Commitment to Social Responsibility: The Potential Mechanisms for the ISO 26000 Standard to Shape CSR', *paper presented at the Core IV Conference.* Berlin, 16 June.

Keck, M. and Sikkink, K. (1998) *Activists Beyond Borders: Activist Networks in International Politics* (Ithaca, N.Y.: Cornell University Press).

Krislov, S. (1997) *How Nations Choose Product Standards and Standards Change Nations* (Pittsburgh, Pa.: University of Pittsburg Press).

Lamoreaux, N. R., Raff, D. M. G. and Temin, P. (2003) 'Beyond Markets and Hierarchies: Toward a New Synthesis of American Business History', *American Historical Review*, 108(April), 404–33.

Le Maistre, C. (1922) 'Standardization: Its Fundamental Importance to the Prosperity of Our Trade', *paper read before the North East Coast Institution of Engineers and Shipbuilders* 24th March, reprinted by the order of the Council.

Leipziger, D. (2001) *SA 8000: The Definitive Guide to the New Social Standard* (London: Financial Times/Prentice Hall).

Locke, R. M. and Romis, M. (2009) 'The Promise and Peril of Private Voluntary Regulation: Labor Standards and Work Organization in Two Mexican Garment Factories' *MIT Sloan Research Paper No. 4734-09*.

Mallett, P. (2010) 'ISEAL in a Nutshell: Introduction to the ISEAL Standard-Setting Code' www.isealalliance.org/content/standard-setting-code

Murphy, C. N. (1994) *International Organization and Industrial Change: Global Governance since 1850* (Cambridge: Polity Press).

Murphy, C. N. and Yates, J. (2009a) 'ISO 26000: Fulfilling the Social Promise of Voluntary Consensus Standard Setting? Part I', *paper presented at the International Studies Association-Brazilian International Relations Association Joint International Meeting*, Rio De Janeiro, 22–24 July www.allacademic.com// meta/p_mla_apa_research_citation/3/8/1/1/3/pages381135/p381135-1.php

Murphy, C. N. and Yates, J. (2009b) *The International Organization for Standardization (ISO): Global Governance through Voluntary Consensus* (London: Routledge).

Nottingham, Mark (n.d.) 'So You'd Like to be a Standards Geek', www.amazon. com/gp/richpub/syltguides/fullview/1OL709EFLT7Y0

'Oracle Study Reveals the Shape of Tomorrow's Supply Chain' (2008) *Manufacturing and Logistics IT.* 25 July www.logisticsit.com/absolutenm/ templates/article-critical.aspx?articleid=3989&zoneid=31

Perera, O. (2008) 'How Material is ISO 26000 Social Responsibility to Small and Medium Enterprises?', *Winnipeg, International Institute for Sustainable Development with the support of the Swiss State Secretariat for Economic Affairs*, September.

Polletta, F. (2004) *Freedom is an Endless Meeting: Democracy in American Social Movements* (Chicago: University of Chicago Press).

Rischard, J.-F. (2002) *High Noon: Twenty Global Problems, Twenty Years to Solve Them* (New York: Basic Books).

Ruggie, J. G. (2007) 'Global Markets and Global Governance: The Prospects for Convergence', in S. Bernstein and L. W. Pauly (eds) *Global Liberalism and Political Order: Toward a New Grand Compromise?* (Albany: State University of New York Press).

Ruggie, J. G. (2009) 'Note on ISO 26000 Guidance Draft Document' www.busi-ness-humanrights.org/Documents/Ruggie-note-re-ISO-26000-Nov-2009.PDF

Russell, A. L. (2006) 'Telecommunications Standards in the Second and Third Industrial Revolutions', *The Journal of Communications Networks*, 5(1), 100– 106.

SAI (2010) 'Benchmarking Social Responsibility: Comparing ISO 26000 and SA 8000,' *SAI e-Newsletter*, June www.sa-intl.org/index.cfm?fuseaction=Page.view Page&pageId=760&parentID=479&nodeID=1

Shanahan, S. and Khagram, S. (2006) 'Dynamics of Corporate Responsibility,' in G. S. Drori, J. M. Meyer and H. Wang (eds) *Globalization and Organization: World Society and Organizational Change* (Oxford: Oxford University Press).

Smith, J. G. (2001) 'Globalizing Resistance: The Battle of Seattle and the Future of Democracy', *Mobilization*, 16(Spring), 1–19.

Smith, J. G. (2005) 'Globalization and Transnational Social Movement Organizations,' in G. F. Davis, D. McAdam, W. R. Scott, and M. N. Zald (eds.) *Social Movements and Organization Theory* (Cambridge: Cambridge University Press).

Smith, J. G. (2008) *Social Movements for Global Democracy* (Baltimore: Johns Hopkins University Press).

Smith, J. G., M. Karides, M. Becker, D. Brunelle, C. Chase-Dunn, D. della Porta, R. I. Garza, J. S. Juris, L. Mosca, E. Resse, P. Smith, and R. Vazquez (2007) *Global Democracy and the World Social Forum* (Boulder, Colorado, Paradigm Publishers).

Stremlau, J. (2009) *Opening Remarks at the International Conference on the Nigerian Elections,* Brown University, 11 December.

Sturén, O. (1980) *Responding to the Challenge of the GATT Standards Code.* Speech to the American National Standards Institute, Washington, DC, March.

Sturén, O. (1997) 'Decade by Decade,' in J. Latimer (compiler) *Friendship Among Equals: Recollections from ISO's First Fifty Years* (Geneva: ISO Central Secretariat).

Tamm Hallström, K. (2004) *Organizing International Standardization: ISO and the IASC in the Quest of Authority* (Cheltenham: Edward Elgar).

Tarrow, S. (1998) *Power in Movement: Collective Action, Social Movements, and Politics*, 2nd ed. (Cambridge: Cambridge University Press).

Tepper Marlin, A.(2006) 'Setting the Standard for the Global Economy', *Ashoka Innovation Conversations.* sic.conversationsnetwork.org/shows/detail3226. html.

Tepper Marlin, A (2009) *Interview with Honor McGee.* New York. 18 August.

Tepper Marlin, A. and Tepper Marlin, J. (2003) 'A Brief History of Social Reporting', *Business Respect,* 51(9 March) www.businessrespect.net/page. php?Story_ID=857

Tilly, C. (2004) *Social Movements, 1768–2004* (Boulder, Colo.: Paradigm Publishers).

Trentmann, F. (2008) *Free Trade Nation: Commerce, Consumption, and Civil Society in Modern Britain* (Oxford: Oxford University Press).

Undheim, T.A. (2008) *Leadership from Below* (Raleigh, N.C.): Lulu.com.

Undheim, T.A. (2009) *The Standards Landscape in 2020.* 'Trond's Opening Standard.' 27 May blogs.oracle.com/trond/

Verman, L. C.(1973) *Standardization, a New Discipline* (Hamden, Conn.: Archon Books).

Webb, S. and Webb, D. (1920) A *Constitution for a Socialist Commonwealth of Great Britain* (London: Longmans, Green, and Co.).

Weber, S. (2004) *The Success of Open Source* (Cambridge, Mass.: Harvard University Press).

Wirth, D. A. (2009) 'The International Organization for Standardization: Private Voluntary Standards as Swords and Shields', *Boston College Legal Studies Research Paper,* 173, 4 February.

Yates, J. (1989) *Control through Communication: The Rise of System in American Management* (Baltimore: Johns Hopkins University Press).

Yates, J. and Murphy, C.N. (2006) 'From Setting National Standards to Coordinating International Standards: The Formation of the ISO', *Business and Economic History On-Line* 4 www.h-net.org/~business/bhcweb/publications/BEHonline/2006/yatesandmurphy.pdf

Yates, J. and Murphy, C.N. (2008) 'Charles Le Maistre: Entrepreneur in International Standardization', *Enterprises et Histoire,* 51(June), 10–57.

8
Standard-setting, Certifying and Benchmarking: A Governmentality Approach to Sustainability Standards in the Agro-Food Sector

Marcel Djama, Eve Fouilleux and Isabelle Vagneron

The proliferation of sustainability standards

The last two decades have witnessed a considerable rise in the use of public and private voluntary standards, especially in the agro-food sector (Fulponi, 2006; Henson, 2008; Fouilleux, 2010). Three successive waves of standards can be identified. All three of these concern standards dealing with 'sustainability'.

The first wave of these standards was social-movement oriented, that is launched by producers, consumers and/or NGOs promoting alternative practices such as organic agriculture or fair trade. Despite a strong link with 'niche' markets and a historical connection with social critics, these standards have been gaining market share over the past two decades: an increasing number of products labelled 'sustainable' are today sold on supermarket shelves. According to some, these standards increasingly resort to tools from the 'neoliberal box' (Guthman, 2008), signalling the takeover of social criticism by market values and economic competition (Raynolds, 2004), particularly in the case of organic and fair trade labelling.

A second wave of standards emerged in the 1990s, in the form of business-to-business (B2B) food safety standards targeting the mainstream market. GlobalGap and the International Food Standard (IFS) are two examples of mainstream standards launched by European retailers to ensure a minimum level of food safety in food chains, elaborated on a product-by-product basis. Although voluntary from a formal point of view, these standards rapidly became *de facto* mandatory: they are increasingly required by European retailers and may hence be considered as barriers to entry to the European market (Henson, 2008). Although they initially focused on food safety issues, retailer standards increasingly tend to include broader sustainability claims, including either social or environmental arguments.

A third category of voluntary standards has been increasingly visible since the early 2000s. These standards are midway between early social movement oriented standards and retailer standards in the field of food safety. They share with organic and fair-trade standards a series of social and environmental preoccupations, and with B2B standards their private dimension and their mainstream market target. Their main specificity, however, lies in their organizational structure: they are produced through multi-stakeholder initiatives (MSI), which are presented as their main source of legitimacy. Both their membership and their governance structures include a variety of actors directly or indirectly involved in the food chain: producers, crushers, exporters, manufacturers, banks, industries, the retail sector, social and environmental NGOs. Such standards exist for a wide range of agricultural products, including coffee (Common Code for the Coffee Community, 4Cs), tea (Ethical Tea Partnership, ETP), palm oil (Round Table on Sustainable Palm Oil), soy (Round Table for Responsible Soy, RTRS), sugarcane (Better Sugar Cane Initiative, BSCI), cotton (Better Cotton Initiative, BCI) and biofuels (Round Table Sustainable Biofuels, RSB). MSI standards and their governance structures have given rise to a large literature in which they are variously designated, depending on the perspective of the authors, as 'non-state market driven governance systems' (Bernstein and Cashore, 2007); systems of 'transnational private governance' (Graz and Nölke, 2008) or 'transnational rule making organizations' (Dingwerth and Pattberg, 2009).

This growing body of literature aims at better understanding the emergence and/or the evolution of these standards and at making sense of their proliferation at both the national and international levels. The initial trend was to interpret private voluntary standards as an institutional response to an objective need for regulation in a context of economic globalization and to the inability of states and international organizations to rise to this challenge. More recent studies go beyond such a simplistic and functionalist explanation. A first group of works emphasizes the impetus provided by multinational companies, which develop proactive strategies to avoid or neutralize contestation by social movements (Braithwaite and Drahos, 2000; Haufler, 2003) or to transform the symbolic capital of reputation into a competitive advantage (Potoski and Prakash, 2005; Fuchs and Vogelmann, 2008). In this approach, reputation, information and competition between firms are seen as the main drivers for the development of sustainability standards. Another body of work emphasizes the increasing role and political clout of social movements, leading to formation of an international civil society. Social movements' capacity to organize and mobilize (mainly through development of communication networks) enables some to mutate into genuine political entrepreneurs (Keck and Sikkink, 1998; Fiorini, 2000).

Going beyond market-based analyses and social-movement-based approaches, a third category of studies tends to emphasize the weight of political dynamics in devising private instruments of regulation, echoing the works of Karl Polanyi (1983) on the social and political embeddedness of the market and its re-working by the American proponents of the 'New Economic Sociology' (Granovetter, 1985; Fligstein, 1996).[1] For example, Bartley (2007) interprets private regulation as an outcome of broader conflicts about power in the apparel and forest sectors. By placing actors at the core of his analysis, he stresses the needs of both interested actors within the market (segments of firms), and entrepreneurial actors in the organizational field (NGOs, governments), for the emergence of private regulatory initiatives. Departing from the traditional approach that draws on single-sector case studies, Bartley and Smith (2010) emphasize the highly interconnected nature of standard-setting organizations and consider certification as a general model of governance. In this paper, we follow this path but instead of mainly focusing on similarities and isomorphism (which tends to overlook tensions and political conflicts), we analyse sustainability standards as tools explicitly designed for coping with such tensions and conflicts.

Our aim is to take the political dimension of standards much more seriously into account, by explaining the ideas and discourse on which sustainability standards and multi-stakeholder devices are founded, as well as their institutional and technological bases, and the mechanisms through which a minimal coherence and an 'instable compromise' are maintained among actors involved at both the micro, meso and macro levels. In doing so, the paper looks at sustainability standards through the lens of governmentality. The first part of our analysis focuses on the dimension of managerialism embedded in the different activities related to sustainability standards. Using the example of the RSPO, the second part of the analysis emphasizes the key role played by consultants in the standard-setting process and in consensus building. We then underline the role played by certification bodies in reproducing and translating managerial logic within the sustainability standards realm. In the fourth section, we analyse the strategies elaborated by the International Social and Environmental Accreditation and Labelling Alliance (ISEAL) in benchmarking and harmonizing voluntary standards, and the difficulties this involves. The main empirical sources used include: written documents from the organizations analysed, data gathered through participant observation in various RSPO, RTRS and ISEAL meetings and in other conferences on voluntary standards, and interviews with actors involved in standard-setting organizations and certification bodies.[2]

Tracing managerialism in sustainability standards: a governmentality approach

Institutional theory has become the major lens through which organizational processes are analysed. Grounded in this theoretical framework, most works on sustainability standards and in particular on multi-stakeholder initiatives (MSIs) focus on organizational dynamics and legitimacy issues (Bäckstrand, 2006; Bernstein and Cashore, 2007). The (successful) quest for external legitimacy is identified as the main political rationale of private standard-setting organizations and the core explanation of their proliferation. This perspective borrows strongly from an influential article by Di Maggio and Powell (1983) analysing why organizations within a given field adopt similar structures, cultures and outputs to enhance their legitimacy.

According to these authors, pressures towards homogeneity (or isomorphism) result from coercive, mimetic and normative forces. Coercive forces are defined as the external pressures exerted by governments or regulatory bodies to adopt the structures that they favour. Mimetic forces are pressures to copy other organizations' activities and/or structures. Normative forces highlight the influence of professional communities. They capture the ways in which organizations are expected to conform to standards of professionalism, and to adopt structures and practices considered as legitimate by relevant professional communities. According to Di Maggio and Powell (1983, p. 150), 'this typology is an analytical one (...) while the three types intermingle in empirical settings'.

Basing themselves on Di Maggio and Powell's framework and using their concept of 'organizational field', Dingwerth and Pattberg (2009) provide an explanation of the proliferation of private organizations for transnational rule making over the last decade and a half. These are described as 'remarkably similar in their organizational design, processes, and rhetoric, even where such similarities are costly' (*ibid*, 2009, p. 708). While their work highlights important features of these organizations' dynamics, it fails to address some major political dimensions of sustainability standards. Indeed, most scholars interested in multistakeholder initiatives have shown a peculiar lack of interest in exploring concrete dimensions of governance and questions related to how it is operationalized: *how* are these organizations actually governed (Dean, 1999); *how* are the conflicting or antagonistic behaviours of stakeholders transformed into cooperative attitudes; *how* can different views, ideas and agendas coexist within an organization and *how* can organizations with such properties proliferate?

Our own argument is that a better understanding of the political dimension of sustainability standards requires an analytical shift from a focus on processes of external legitimation to one on internal governance dimensions. This is precisely what a governmentality perspective enables: unlike most institutional narratives, it allows the analyst to investigate how governing is accomplished in practical and technical terms.

The notion of governmentality underlines a radical transformation in how power is exercised – namely, as an articulation between forms of knowledge, power relations and processes of subjectivation (Foucault, 1978/2001, 2004a). Foucault's (2004a, pp. 111–112) definition of governmentality is a dynamic one:

> the ensemble formed by institutions, procedures, analyses and reflections, the calculations and tactics that allow the exercise of this very specific, albeit complex, form of power – which has as its target population, as its principal form of knowledge political economy and as its essential technical means apparatuses of security.[3]

The notion of governmentality also signals a historical movement of transformation of the Western State that is marked by 'the pre- eminence over all other forms (sovereignty, discipline and so on) of this type of power which may be termed government, resulting in the formation of a whole series of specific governmental apparatuses, and in the development of a whole complex of knowledge' (*ibid*).

Through this perspective, Foucault analyses the development of liberalism and neo-liberalism as specific modes of government based on knowledge and techniques aimed at limiting formalized government practice and at adjusting it to 'natural' market mechanisms (Foucault, 2004b). In this evolution, traditional forms of authority (based on hierarchical command) are replaced by new disciplinary apparatuses (based on expertise and techniques) that enable 'government at a distance' (Miller and Rose, 1990; Lascoumes, 2004).

In this chapter, we focus on two related dimensions of governmentality: political rationalities and technologies of government. Political rationalities refer to the ideas, principles, values and knowledge that frame an object of government: what should be governed, and the way it should be governed. Technologies of government capture the actual tactics and tools used to govern. According to Foucault, political rationality and technologies of government go hand in hand, insofar as the idea of government is not restricted to knowledge, but rather designates a whole sphere of activity. As observed by Miller and Rose (1990, p. 8), 'if political rationalities render reality into the domain of thought (...) technologies of government seek to translate thought into the domain of reality'.

This overlap between knowledge and technology is a central feature of advanced liberalism, which as Rose (1993) indicates gives a pivotal role to expertise and to technologies of government. Rose isolates four characteristics of 'advanced' (neo-)liberalism as governmental activity: the mobilization of knowledge resulting from social sciences to govern human conduct; the use of techniques which aim at creating autonomous individuals whose actions are aligned to the goals of governing authorities; the mediation of experts who act as a relay for governing at a distance; and a constant questioning of the activity of government, aimed at rendering advanced liberalism both more legitimate and more effective.

In reference to this framework, we focus on the political rationalities and the technologies at work in the making of sustainability standards. We postulate that sustainability standards are not only emblematic of the art of governing in the age of advanced liberalism, but also act as a vehicle for the international circulation of values, knowledge and technologies that we define as managerialism. The term 'managerialism' has emerged in recent years to designate the collection of knowledge and practices initially intended for corporate management but now systematically aimed at increasing the efficiency of collective action, irrespective of the object or the entity concerned (Townley, 2002). The main characteristic of managerialism is a set of techniques which are supposed to be universal in nature and can be adopted by any organization. Focusing on managerialism as a technology for governing sustainability standards means that we will consider sustainability standards as 'a set of practices, knowledge, measures and institutions whose aim is to manage, govern, control and guide – in what claims to be a useful sense – the behaviour, acts and thoughts of people' (Agamben, 2007, p. 28).

The past twenty-five years have witnessed a considerable extension of the scope of application of corporate management, whose constituent rationalities and practices have spread into both the public sector (Ferlie, 1996; Pollitt and Bouackaert, 2004; Le Gales and Scott, 2008) and the world of NGOs (Lewis, 2001; Roberts *et al.*, 2005). NGOs' managerial turn became visible in the 1990s, characterized by: the adoption of knowledge and practices developed within corporate and 'New Public' management; the adoption of concepts coming from the accounting world (accountability, transparency and effectiveness), as well as through the development of a distinct professionalized field – with its own private training institutes, consultants, handbooks specifically dedicated to NGO management and others. The trend towards professionalization is today reinforced by a proliferation of training programmes on NGO management in European and North American universities. Meanwhile, donors (both state agencies and private foundations) also serve as a relay for managerialism (Roberts *et al.*, 2005).

As observed by Boltanski and Chiapello (1999), the dissemination of a managerial model prioritizing the autonomy, initiative and responsibility of individuals with a view to improve individual and collective performances results from a dual transformation. There has been a transformation of capitalism itself, as seen in the decline of the hierarchical model of the Fordist organization and its replacement by new forms of networking. There has also been a transformation of management techniques, which now re-appropriate the repertoire of intellectual and social criticism articulated by the labour movement, previously considered as alien. These ideological changes in management help us to understand its dissemination, in particular within organizations founded on philosophies of action and cultures *a priori* hostile towards hierarchy. In particular, these changes shed light on the conditions which may have facilitated the proliferating connections between the corporate world and NGOs, as in the case of MSIs.

Beyond this analysis mainly related to the ideological dimension of the transformation of management, the role of new instruments, or the instrumental dimension of organizational change, must be underlined. In the case of sustainability standards, three main neo-liberal technologies of government appear to be crucial features: 'consensus-formation', audit and benchmarking. *Consensus* may be considered as a technology of government, insofar as it does not result from debate or negotiation (unlike compromise), but rather has the effect of neutralizing debate. As Rancière (2005, p. 8) reminds us, consensus is a 'machine of power' which aims at imposing a vision, a way of presenting facts and a direction for their interpretation.

While consensus formation relates to the internal construction of the legitimacy of sustainability standards, *audit* – the instrument for control of compliance with standards – enables measurement and verification of the extent to which obligations have been translated into visible practices and results. However, as stressed by Power (1997), audit techniques are far from neutral: they entail new practices and transmit new political and moral rationalities. In particular, they propagate new forms of subjectivity, transforming beings in self-managing units whose actions and practices are measurable. Audit thus shapes the behaviours of individuals and organizations through a new regime of visible (self-) responsibility and control. In sum, audit, which is mostly delegated to accredited independent certification bodies, relates to the external legitimacy of standards.

Finally, as underlined by Larner and Le Heron (2004), *benchmarking* is about comparisons that give distinct and even disparate practices and organizations a 'like with like' status. 'It is this ability, to make the "incommensurable commensurable", that allows economic space to be represented as global' (*ibid*, p. 214). Benchmarking is crucially incarnated in the world of sustainability standards by the ISEAL Alliance, an organisation which develops meta-codes of conduct and identifies global best practices in standard setting and implementation. Thus it relates to what can be thought of as lateral integrity of the managerial rationality.

These technologies are clearly complementary both to each other and to the new managerial rationality as it is defined by Boltanski and Chiapello (1999), that is based on and reproducing autonomy, initiative and responsibility. More precisely, they confer to the managerial political rationality respectively an internal, external and transversal –or lateral- consistency. This chapter is aimed at illustrating both the content and the complementarities of these technologies of government. The third section provides an illustration of the crucial feature of consensus building in standard-setting, the fourth section highlights the role of audit and certification and the fifth section describes benchmarking and related activities by ISEAL.

Governing standard setting: the roundtable on sustainable palm oil case

In this section, we demonstrate the pivotal role of managerial rationalities in standard setting, using RSPO as a case study. RSPO is a multistakeholder initiative, which aims at mitigating the potentially negative social and environmental impacts of palm oil production. It is a voluntary business-to-business initiative, targeting the mainstream market. For a number of previous years, NGOs had been criticizing the negative impacts of palm oil production: destruction of South-East Asian primary forests; erosion of biodiversity; threats to endangered species such as orang-utans, whose habitat is being destroyed; and expropriation by plantation firms of communities living on land converted to palm cultivation.

The initiative was launched in 2001–02 by the WWF (formerly the World Wildlife Fund, now the World Wide Fund for Nature). In 2003, a first roundtable gathering of different stakeholders was organized in Malaysia.[4] 40 participants agreed to a joint declaration to implement and promote a sustainability standard for the production of palm oil. Early in 2004, the RSPO became an association under Swiss law, with its head office in Zurich, a secretariat in Malaysia and a liaison office in Indonesia. A governance mechanism was established, coordinated by an Executive Board with 16 members elected for two years and representing different stakeholders (cf. Table 1).

Table 8.1   Allocation of seats on RSPO's executive board

Sector	Number of seats
Oil palm growers	4*
Palm oil processors and/or traders	2
Consumer goods manufacturers	2
Retailers	2
Banks / investors	2
Environmental / nature conservation NGO's	2
Social / development NGOs	2

Note: * The college of growers or producers is divided into four components, who are allocated one seat each: the Malaysian planters; the Indonesian planters; planters from the 'rest of the world'; and smallholders.

The main decisions are made at plenary meetings during an annual general assembly to which all members are invited. Members have the opportunity – before the annual general meeting – to submit motions on which votes will be held. The Executive Board examines applications for membership, implements decisions made during plenary meetings, organizes working groups, and manages finances.

Since the first RSPO roundtable (RT1), six annual roundtables and five general meetings have been organized. In 2004, RT2 launched the process of defining the principles and criteria for sustainable palm oil production. In 2005, RT3 adopted the principles and criteria that had been proposed and implemented a two-year pilot phase for their empirical validation following tests with volunteer firms. RT4 and RT5 (in 2006 and 2007) implemented the procedures for third-party control and auditing. RT4 and RT5 also discussed how smallholders should be taken into account, and how generic principles and criteria should be adapted to national contexts. In 2008, RT6 approved the sustainable palm oil certification mechanisms. To date, 11 RSPO certificates have been issued to companies.

In this light, the RSPO initiative is usually presented as a success story. Indeed, in the space of a few years, RSPO has succeeded in instituting a complete cycle of regulation, from establishment of rules to definition of control and traceability procedures for certified products. At the same time, RSPO's membership continues to grow – a sign of increasing success, in particular with planters and the industry. Finally, RSPO remains unchallenged by any would-be alternative standard. It thus exemplifies the successful institutionalization of a certification scheme, as described by Bernstein and Cashore (2007). As already mentioned, our aim in this chapter is not only to underline this institutionalization, but also to analyse how this particular standard-setting device – and standard – was constructed and elaborated in practice. In the multi-stakeholder context of RSPO, this means describing two dimensions of how managerialism unfolded: the crucial role of experts, and the techniques that are mobilized to frame the debates and neutralize potential conflicts.

Consolidating NGO–industry partnerships: consultants as intermediaries

The story of RSPO began in 2001 when the Swiss office of the WWF commissioned a consultant to identify opportunities for developing a partnership with the industry with a view to establishing and implementing sustainable criteria for the production of palm oil. This consultant, a former professor of management in a Dutch university, left higher education to create a consulting firm specializing in building NGO–industry partnerships for sustainable development, in particular in the agro-food sector. Following a request by the WWF, the firm organized an initial meeting in London in 2002, during which representatives of downstream industries (distributors, processors and end-users of palm oil), private banks and public European development banks, consulting firms specializing in environmental issues and WWF (the only conservation NGO present) sketched the outline of a collaboration. In fact, this initial contact meeting defined the guiding principles of the future 'initiative on sustainable palm oil', promoted 'practical', 'viable' and 'controllable' sustainability criteria and proposed a 'pragmatic' solution based on commercial imperatives. Standards, it was agreed, were to be developed through an approach involving all the stakeholders and designed to encourage a common understanding of sustainability criteria among them.

Consultants also play a major role in standard setting. In the case of RSPO, the consulting firm ProForest was hired by the Executive Board to shape and facilitate the process through which the content of the standard was to be defined – in terms of 'principles, criteria and indicators'. As ProForest stated in the preamble to a methodological document:

'The development of standards is a complex and specialist task and should be co-ordinated by a facilitator. The facilitator should ideally have experience of facilitation together with a credible understanding of oil palm and direct experience of developing criteria for natural resource management' (ProForest, 2004, p.6).

Besides its auto-promotional dimension, this formula summarizes precisely the tasks that ProForest has been undertaking in RSPO.

ProForest was founded in 2000 and is headquartered in Oxford. It specializes in implementation of sustainable development strategies and provides advice on 'responsible' management of natural resources, in the forestry and agri-food sectors in particular, as well as in the field of conservation. Its founders come from the environmental audit and certification business. They were centrally involved in developing criteria for the 'Forest Stewardship Council', the pioneer in forest certification. But ProForest was not alone in acquiring expertise in this area. As early as 1998, the MNC Unilever defined indicators for sustainable palm oil production which it would test through pilot projects on its own plantations and through a number of suppliers. Meanwhile in 2000, the Swiss supermarket chain Migros also developed a programme based on criteria for sustainable palm oil production, which it intended to impose on its suppliers – drawing on the expertise and reputation of WWF and ProForest. Respectively, these would establish its criteria and monitor and certify their implementation by suppliers.

Thus, previous collaboration explains the participation of ProForest in a meeting in London in 2002 to launch the sustainable palm oil concept. The criteria defined by the WWF and ProForest for Migros were based on experience these two organizations had gained during the FSC process, adapting them to the technical operating conditions of palm oil plantations. The Migros standard incorporated the basic principles which later would be adopted by the RSPO (transparency, compliance with the law, good agricultural practices, environmental and social responsibility). It also defined an action plan to formulate mechanisms for adapting generic criteria to local contexts and to encourage learning. Shortly after the first Roundtable in 2003 – which aimed at enlisting producers – the organizing committee of the first roundtable commissioned two studies from ProForest, one concerning debates on the relations between deforestation and the expansion of palm oil plantations (the issue) and the other concerning mechanisms for establishing standards for sustainable palm oil production (the solutions) (cf. ProForest, 2003a; 2003b). From February to March 2004, a document (ProForest, 2004) was circulated among members of the provisional RSPO board, presenting a first draft of the standard (principles and criteria)[5] and a methodology for pursuing their further development through a multi-stakeholder framework.

These draft documents produced by ProForest remain the foundation of the standard (principles and criteria). A comparison between the first draft and the final version approved by the stakeholders reveals no substantial changes. Thus, the development of RSPO standard indeed illustrates mimetic isomorphism at work. The standard-setting process was based on experiences gained from an existing organization rather than reinvented. However, the practical reason for this was that a single consultant had a pivotal role in both FSC and RSPO (cf. Dingwerth and Pattberg, 2009). Seeing this process in terms of the role of consulting firms, and their preferred techniques, leads us in a different analytical direction to conventional narratives emphasizing unspecified pressures to copy as the source of mimesis.

Socializing standards: technologies at work

As we have seen, the contributions of most stakeholders mostly consisted in approving the direction already taken by consulting firms and a pioneer group including WWF, Unilever and Migros. This does not mean that underlying the RSPO programme was a Machiavellian strategy imagined by these actors. Instead, although specific outcomes remained uncertain, the different possibilities were all shaped in advance by specific political rationalities and tools. The multi-stakeholder standard-making process can be seen as one where stakeholders are enrolled or socialized in specific technologies which facilitate both the standard's construction and its ownership, rather than as a real decision-making process. This is another instance where the know-how developed by consulting firms comes into play. Two main 'tactics of power' at work can be observed here: the first is based on the central role given to the principle of consensus, while the second relates to propagation of a rhetoric of pragmatic and short-term solutions as a means of neutralizing controversy.

In line with the multi-stakeholder nature of RSPO, a Criteria Working Group (CWG) gathering 25 selected members from all sectors was established in 2004.[6] Its mission was to define principles and criteria over a 12 month period in accordance with a 'transparent' and 'public' procedure. With this in mind, two physical meetings of members were scheduled together with a public consultation phase.[7] In relation to the decision-making process to be adopted by the CWG, ProForest emphasized the need for consensus in order to facilitate ownership of decisions by all stakeholders.[8] The parameters of this deliberative procedure – especially the very limited time allocated to the CWG to define the standard – neutralized controversies and encouraged participants to concentrate on points formulated by the technical consultant who supplied the information used by the group and also 'facilitated' and 'chaired' the discussion. For the stakeholders, it was less a case of debating the criteria than evaluating their operationality, and whether they incorporated the interests the stakeholders represented.

As a participant in the CWG stated: 'We approved the proposals of ProForest in aggregate. Our task was to work towards a consensus. If we hadn't succeeded in obtaining a consensus, we would have voted. I don't know how we did it, but we always avoided a vote.'[9] Consensus here is a crucial element of the managerial dynamics at work in the RSPO. It was the main mechanism facilitating ownership of the standard and successful construction of the 'NGO-Industrial Complex' (Gereffi *et al.*, 2001) around it. It was made possible by the mobilization of apparently neutral intermediaries (that is, with no visible links to any of the parties concerned) whose credibility stemmed from their expertise and past experience. The former enabled objectives to be formulated which, in their operational form, could be handled by plantation managers. The latter conferred credibility on the social and environmental objectives proposed.

Another way used to achieve consensus was to confine deliberation on sensitive issues to specialized working groups or committees. For example, a Biodiversity Technical Committee was created in 2009 for a period of two years to improve the principles and criteria for the conservation of biodiversity. The aim of the committee was to make proposals based on feedback from the first audits conducted in plantations applying for RSPO certification[10] as well as on appraisals by the 'biodiversity community' (conservation NGOs, private consultants and academics). The committee also had responsibility for suggesting research topics in order to increase knowledge on sensitive issues. In practice, as documented in the minutes of the committee's meetings[11], only immediately operational solutions were adopted, while those requiring time for further investigation were rejected. The influence of managerial rationalities could be noted again. Scientific knowledge was marginalized in favour of the expertise of consultants, as found in proposals for 'practical' and 'economically acceptable' solutions that could be implemented in the short term.

In this section we have highlighted some micro-political features of standard setting in the case of RSPO. We have stressed the pivotal role of consultants in facilitating the building of NGO–industry partnerships, defining the architecture of the standard, organizing the approval of standards through a technology of consensus building, and in neutralizing potential conflicts. We now turn to other engines of standards rationalization, namely the certification business and the meta-representation of standards and standard organizations at the transnational level.

Certification as a core business

As underlined in our introduction, standard setting initiatives are multiplying, while their scope is constantly broadening. Although quite diverse, implementation of most sustainability standards shares a common feature: control through third-party certification. This common feature, that can be viewed as another sign of advanced liberalism, based on a Benthamian surveillance philosophy, requires the deployment of specific technical expertise in auditing and traceability protocols.

In the agri-food sector, the history of certification bodies is closely related to that of the organic sector. Throughout Europe and the USA, the principles of organic agriculture were initially defined – and compliance with them verified – by organic farmer associations such as the Bio-Dynamic Agricultural Association, Agrocert, CCOF, Demeter, the Soil Association, Suolo e Salute, etc. In France, the federation of local associations, Nature et Progrès, first elaborated written technical specifications for organic farming. Verification of compliance of production practices with organic principles was then carried out by local committees of producer and consumer representatives.

In the 1980s, the first national (public) organic standards emerged. In 1991, EEC Council Regulation 2092/91 established the first pan-European organic standard and redefined control procedures and practices. This involved first, translation of the movement's environmental concerns into easily verifiable requirements (to allow auditability); second, making third-party certification mandatory; and third, forcing pioneer organic farmer groups to separate their production and verification activities to avoid conflicts of interest. Subsequently, no fewer than 40 organic certification bodies (CBs) were registered in the 1990s in Europe alone. By 2009 the number of CBs accredited to inspect and certify organic standards had reached 488 worldwide (*Organic Standard,* 2009). This may be partly explained by the rapid expansion in the market for organic products. Although some CBs were linked to pioneer organic farmer associations (for example, Naturland, Soil Association, Demeter) that continued to develop their own organic standards with their own certification requirements, mostly concentrated on inspection and certification to public organic standards only.

The commercial success of organic farming drew the attention of large commercial quality control and compliance services providers such as SGS, Control Union, Bureau Veritas and others, who all established organic certification capacity by one means or another. For example, Control Union entered the organic certification business in 2006 through acquiring the Dutch Skal International. The proliferation of sustainability standards has tended to favour CBs with large resource bases and to encourage growth and consolidation strategies. Emblematic of this evolution, large CBs such as SGS are now well connected and play a crucial role in the 'community' of sustainability standards (Bartley and Smith, 2010).

More recently a number of the pioneer CBs have aimed to become 'one-stop shops' for certification by gaining accreditation to an array of standards (public and private organic, GlobalGap, Utz Certified, Starbucks, ISO, HACCP, IFS, BRC, FSC and others). This may be understood partly as a competitive strategy allowing customers to be offered as many options as possible, and partly in terms of reputational innovation. Ability to certify to a wide array of standards shows the CB's organizational competence and that of its team of inspectors. However, there is a trade-off since for CBs multiple accreditations are costly and time-consuming (for example, translating standards into new languages, training of inspectors, document preparation and more). As a consequence of this, some CBs develop partnerships with others based on a strategy of specialization in either a geographic location or a type of accreditation.[12]

Simultaneously, several CBs have started to develop their own standards in areas where competition in standard setting had been limited or absent. The examples include: Ecocert (cosmetics, ethical trade, organic detergents.), IMO and Soil Association Certification (ethical trade); BioAgricert (ethical trade, energy economies); IMC (catering). Fair trade is quite emblematic of this new standard-setting strategy, with Ecocert, Soil Association and IMO developing their own ethical standards to challenge the monopoly of FLO International and FloCert in fair trade standards. They have been recently followed by Bio Agricert (operAequa) and SCS (Certified Fair Labor Practices).

However, to limit discussion of the role of certification bodies to that of merely providing certification services is to miss the main point. CBs are crucially involved systematically both in supplying external

Table 8.2 Range of certifications offered by leading certification bodies

	Organic			Food safety		MSI		
	EU	NOP (USA)	JAS (Japan)	Global Gap	IFS	MSC	FSC	RSPO
Bureau Veritas (Qualité France)	✓	✓	✓	✓	✓	✓	✓	✓
Control Union	✓	✓	✓	✓	✓		✓	✓
IMO Control	✓	✓	✓	✓	✓		✓	✓
SCS		✓		✓		✓	✓	✓
SGS	✓			✓	✓	✓	✓	✓
TÜV					✓		✓	
Ecocert	✓	✓	✓	✓	✓			

Source: Authors' own research.

legitimacy to standards, and in their adaptation to concrete circumstances. Thus they play the role of translation and transmission belts between the different stakeholders including consumers and potential producers.

First of all, CBs occupy a central role in shaping the market since auditing enjoys the '(...) the power to connect, disconnect and provide legitimacy in the market.' (Ouma, 2010). Second, their intermediate position between standard makers and standard takers, and the associated expertise, gives them a powerful position as translators and gatekeepers. In the certification process, CBs are responsible for the *de facto* operationalization of criteria and indicators in an array of circumstances and with an array of different kinds of operators. Certification procedures are not operationally standardized, although they are checked during the accreditation process, although they are themselves subject to ISO standards. This leaves space for negotiating what may be crucial aspects of standards in the process of their implementation, as well as for arbitrary/discretionary decisions. Third, as already noted, the frontier between standard setting and standard certification is increasingly blurred: many CBs are involved in both functions (albeit in formally distinct guises), while some NGOs traditionally engaged in defining sustainability standards (Utz Certified, Rainforest Alliance) now also partake in certification. Utz Certified has a history as a setter of standards for sustainable commodities (tea, coffee, cocoa), but at the same time now *'offers traceability systems for RSPO-certified sustainable palm oil'*.[13] Utz is also preparing to certify soy traceability systems (RTRS). Rainforest Alliance sets sustainable agriculture standards for a wide range of commodities (tea, coffee, fruit, cocoa, flowers, ferns and others) and now also acts as a certifier for FSC under its Smartwood programme.

Certification thus exists as an important relay for managerial logic in relation to sustainability standards. First, it builds on a type of managerial expertise – the audit – that both shapes the content of standards and confers external legitimacy based on trade on them. Second, it reinforces managerialism within standard setting by implicitly deselecting or devaluing standards which are not easily subjectible to audit. Third, certification contributes to the managerialization of NGOs – as illustrated by the cases of several pioneer organic farming organizations, Utz Certified and Rainforest Alliance – and to formalizing their interactions with the business community. Fourth, certification transmits managerial practices to operators implementing the standards, through a process of performance-related negotiation. Finally, the harmonization of certification and inspection activities (formally based on ISO/IEC Guides 65 and EN 45011) supplies an additional degree of common managerial coherence to decentralized and competing standards (Mutersbaugh, 2004). This type of 'lateral' coherence is also achieved in a more direct way through the existence of ISEAL, as we shall see in the next section.

Proliferation of standards: benchmarking and scaling-up by ISEAL

As actors in the field often like to mention, the increasing number of voluntary initiatives in environmental and social labelling has created a 'need for dialogue' and for 'sharing experiences'. Among the various networks that have arisen as a result, the International Social and Environmental Accreditation and Labelling Alliance (ISEAL) is of a special interest due to its formal organizational status and widening recognition in the field of sustainability standards.

The original impetus for ISEAL came in 1999 from four standard-setting organizations – FSC, IFOAM, FLO and MSC. These had a common wish to collaborate and to be represented in governmental and inter-governmental forums. While the main objective of ISEAL, which was formally registered as a not-for-profit enterprise in 2002, is 'To create a world where ecological sustainability and social justice are the normal conditions of business', ISEAL also presents itself as 'the global hub' or 'the global association for the social and environmental standards movement'[14] as a result of constituting 'a community of practice incorporating expertise in standard setting, accreditation, certification, auditor training, producer capacity building, and in a range of policy issues'.[15]

All these roles are played out by ISEAL not only by promoting voluntary standards in the public arena (including in relation to international organizations), but more particularly by promoting specific procedures targeted at the production and dissemination of 'good' – best-practice – voluntary standards. This means standards which are 'transparent, open and inclusive', and based on multi-stakeholder procedures. In other words, not only does ISEAL promote sustainability standards, its aim is also to contain the proliferation of standards, to promote harmonization and above all to upgrade existing standards to a higher level of quality, through benchmarking against best practices.

To this end, ISEAL has developed meta-standards ('codes') defining a range of procedures, which are both meant to assure the conditions for standards to promote sustainability and for harmonization among standards to take place. Benchmarking against these meta-standards is promoted in four distinct areas through special documents: a Code of Ethics, a Code of Good Practice for Setting Social and Environmental Standards, a Code of Good Practice for Assessing the Impacts of Social and Environmental Systems, and a Verification Code. Needless to say, all these meta-standards have been – or are being – established through the type of procedures promoted by the organization, that is voluntariness, inclusiveness, participation, public consultation, consensus-building.

The first code developed by ISEAL is short and very general. The *Code of Ethics* proposes a 'vision for (ISEAL) membership' based on collaboration, trust, knowledge sharing and common beliefs: 'Member (organizations) share a sense of common purpose, built on trust that leads to a high level of collaboration and learning. Members participate actively in sharing, exchange and knowledge building resulting in a vibrant and engaged community'[16]. However, the main meta-standard promoted by ISEAL is the *Code of Good Practice for Setting Social and Environmental Standards*[17]. This prescribes the main steps for developing sustainability standards and provides general rules concerning their 'structure and content'. Rather symbolically, the only documented references mentioned in this document are the WTO Agreement on Technical Barriers to Trade and the ISO/IEC guides for standardization, both of which refer to standards in general rather than sustainability standards as such.

Clearly reflecting a core belief in the virtue of procedures – as already noted, one of the main dimensions of managerialism – this code lays down guidelines on the standard-setting process. Only some of these are summarized here. Fostering inclusiveness is presented as a central principle, by requiring, for example, 'that participation and decision-making reflects a balance of interests' and that 'meaningful opportunities to contribute' are provided to all 'interested parties'. Second, public consultation is also identified as a critical requirement for good standard setting and revision, including 'at least two rounds of comment submission by interested parties, where necessary'. Third, the need 'to strive for consensus' appears as another central principle, although the code also mentions that 'it is important that the standard setting organization has a documented decision making procedure in cases where voting is required and makes an explicit effort to inform interested parties of this procedure before the start of the standard development or revision process through their public summary'.

The code refers constantly to accountability, transparency and verifiability (standards 'shall be structured to allow for monitoring and evaluation of progress...avoid language and structure that may create ambiguities in their interpretation', and so on). In addition, in line with the objective of avoiding proliferation of standards, the code insists on the need for standard setters to have clear 'terms of reference' including a review of potentially overlapping standards and a 'justification for the need' of a new standard. Standard setters are also supposed to inform one another when developing new initiatives.

In this process of further shaping and framing voluntary standard systems, ISEAL is currently working on two additional meta-standards. One is the *ISEAL Code of Good Practice for Assessing the Impacts of Social and Environmental Standards Systems*, aimed at helping standard-setting organizations to assess 'the effectiveness of their various activities'. Launched in 2009 and adopted in June 2010, discussion about this code focused on which impacts of standard systems should be measured and on how to ensure comparability of results. It is worth noting that such a highly political matter was dealt with through the specification of best practice procedures (choosing an 'appropriate scope' for evaluation, defining a scale, ensuring 'transparency', fostering 'broad participation' again[18]) rather than designating what parameters should be assessed. The last meta-standard is the so-called *Verification Code*. Its release is planned for 2012 and it will aim at defining best practices in auditing, certification and accreditation.

ISEAL membership is officially divided into three categories based on degrees of compliance with ISEAL codes (full members, associated members and affiliated members). This structure also defines a benchmarked path of progression for organizations within ISEAL. 'Full members' include standard setters and accreditation bodies complying with the ISEAL Code of Ethics and the ISEAL Code for Standard Setting.[19] 'Associate members' have committed themselves to comply with ISEAL's codes and are on the way to become full members.[20] 'Affiliate members' are organizations that subscribe to the ISEAL Code of Ethics and are interested in participating in ISEAL *'primarily as an information sharing and awareness raising exercise'*. Organizations that have declared their intention to become associate members belong to this category.[21]

As a consequence of its growing and increasingly diverse membership, ISEAL has come to shield divergent, competing and sometimes even antagonistic interests. Competition between standards occurs in terms of differences in the areas where claims are made (environmental, health-related, labour, hygiene), as well as within the same area of claim, between standards with different level of ambition, such as between FSC and PEFC in the case of forests. Furthermore, different standards may assume different underlying definitions of sustainability, with organic standards at one end of the spectrum and the Roundtable on Sustainable Biofuels and the Better Sugar Cane Initiative at the other. Although this type of tension has existed within ISEAL since its inception – for example, between IFOAM and FLO on the one hand and Rainforest Alliance on the other[22], the gap between founding members and later recruits is increasing as the number of sustainability standards grows. Central among the topics likely to prevent bridge-building between the various definitions of sustainability at stake is that of genetic engineering. But tensions between standards setters belonging to ISEAL are also evident regarding the different ways that compliance is recognized. For example, some standards do not define any 'pass or fail criteria' for compliance, but rather focus on progress or improvement ('commitment to constantly tend towards better practices'). Despite being officially explained in terms of budgetary reasons, we may wonder if the withdrawal of IFOAM from ISEAL in May 2010 is not also partly related to this type of tension.

In such a context, making the choice not to deal directly with the *content* of the standards (objectives, criteria, underlying definition of sustainability), but rather to concentrate on governance structures and procedures is clearly a way to limit tensions and optimize lateral consistency and legitimacy between members. In this sense, the faith in procedure embodied in ISEAL can be interpreted as another means of depoliticizing the sustainability debate. If, up to now, ISEAL's procedural strategy seems to be successful, it might become more difficult to maintain in the near future. Tensions are likely to increase over the short and medium term, due to ISEAL's desire to expand further and to increase its visibility and representation.

Conclusion

The vast majority of research dealing with sustainability standards focuses on their institutional design and legitimacy. These studies produced new insights about how these institutions have become central sites for the design and implementation of governance. However, this literature fails to address the concrete process of governing. To overcome these limits, we have proposed an alternative research agenda based on a governmentality approach, which puts at the core of the analysis the values, knowledge and technologies of power that frame sustainability standards. Our aim is to show how existing techniques of neoliberal governance 'shape the thinkable and hence the actable' (Guthman, 2008, p. 1242). As we have illustrated, sustainability standards are dominated by a neoliberal political rationality, characterized by three main managerial technologies of government: 'consensus-formation', audit and benchmarking.

Consensus formation relates to the internal construction of the legitimacy of the standard, and at the same time to the internal consistency of managerial rationality. As we have underlined in describing the emergence and setting of the RSPO standard, consensus formation rests upon consultants' know-how and expertise. These actors play a pivotal role in both gluing NGO–industry partnerships together and shaping the content of standards. This is against a background where the political authority of some hegemonic players (a handful of retailers, agri-food firms and NGOs) clearly challenges the usual 'democratic' narrative emphasizing the importance of giving equal weight to all stakeholders in standard-making. *Audit*, which is mostly delegated to accredited independent certification bodies, relates to the external legitimacy provided to standards by managerial rationality. As we have shown, as sustainability certification became a growing business in the sector, the number of certifiers proliferated as has the range of services they provide, illustrating what Mutersbaugh calls the growth of a 'transnational economy of inspectability' (2005, p. 391). Finally, we have illustrated how the activity of *benchmarking* is endorsed by the ISEAL Alliance as a response to the proliferation of (at least potentially divergent) sustainability standards. The development of meta-codes of conduct and best practices in standard setting and implementation can also be seen as building a lateral –or transversal- consistency based on disseminating a common managerial rationality. As the three empirical parts of this chapter have shown, these technologies of government serve to neutralize conflicts among stakeholders. They can thus be seen as the means of depoliticizing the sustainability standards realm.

Standards today are designed as much – if not more – to fulfil managerial criteria (for example, the 'auditability' of principles) than to solve specific environmental and social problems. Furthermore, the circulation of managerial technologies through consensus-building, auditing and benchmarking contributes to the diffusion and reinforcement of a shared depoliticized culture among actors with backgrounds in different activities and professions. The rise of a 'market for sustainable development' – through the growing demand for services and expertise in facilitation, capacity-building, empowerment, verification and certification – also actively contributes to the development this depo-liticized culture. But while managerial technologies aim at neutralizing conflicts, it remains an open question whether sustainability standards succeed in pacifying the confrontation between corporate actors and social movements on social and environmental issues. Outside the realm of sustainability standards at least, it seems more obvious than ever that conflicts – and thus politics – have never ceased.

Notes

1 See Guthman, 2007.
2 This work was carried out with the financial support of the Agence Nationale de la Recherche (ANR) under the 'Programme Agriculture et Développement Durable, project Normes' (ANR-06-PADD-013).
3 For Foucault, 'apparatuses of security' go beyond the coercive institutions – such as the police and armed forces – and encompass all kinds of knowledge, surveillance and intervention devices targeting the population: e.g. social sciences, statistics, public health, welfare policies, urban planning, etc.
4 The organizing committee consisted of WWF (the only NGO); the firms Anglia Oils, Migros, Sainsbury, Unilever and Golden Hope; and the Malaysian Palm Oil Association.
5 The terms 'standard', 'principles and criteria' and 'criteria' are used inter-changeably by RSPO participants. In its 'Discussion paper...' (ProForest, 2004) ProForest used the term standard, but later a correction proposed by one of the parties who replacing the term 'standard' by 'criteria' was intro-duced.
6 The Criteria Working Group was made up by ten representatives from the growers; five from the 'Industry and Investors Colleges; five from environ-mental NGOs and five from social and development NGOs.
7 The first meeting of the CWG was held in October 2004 prior to the open-ing of RT2 in Jakarta. The second meeting was held from 15–18 February 2005 in Malaysia. Between these two meetings the members of the group communicated by e-mail.
8 'Decisions of the Criteria Working Group should be made by consensus. Although this is perhaps the most difficult and time-consuming system, it is a process that leads to greater ownership of decisions by all stakeholders.' (Proforest, 2004, p. 7)
9 Interview with JCJ, Bali (Indonesia), 16 November 2007.
10 The first RSPO audits were conducted in 2008.
11 In the Minutes of the 2nd Biodiversity Technical Committee (BTC) meeting, 13 June 2009 (Jakarta) it is reported that an ecologist suggested 'a review of existing papers/plans for riparian zones'. Members of the BTC replied that they rather should consider 'immediate action *sans* the need for a review/framework approach, and only methodologies/recipes/instruction on how to manage'.

12 For example, a CB with accreditation to a given standard but no office in a given country will subcontract inspection in this country to a CB with a local office but no accreditation to the standard.
13 www.utzcertified.org (accessed February 2010).
14 www.isealalliance.org Patrick Mallet's presentation of ISEAL's Code of Good Practices, (accessed June 2010).
15 Strategic Plan, 2009–2013, p.4.
16 www.isealalliance.org (accessed June 2010).
17 Quotations are from Version 5.01 (April, 2010).
18 *Code of Good Practice for Assessing the Impacts of Social and Environmental Standards System*, Version 1.0, May 2010.
19 Fairtrade Labelling Organization (FLO) International, International Federation of Organic Agriculture Movements (IFOAM), Forest Stewardship Council (FSC), International Organic Accreditation Service (IOAS), Marine Aquarium Council (MAC), Marine Stewardship Council (MSC), Rainforest Alliance, Social Accountability Accreditation Service (SAAS), Social Accountability International (SAI), Union for Ethical BioTrade (UEBT), and UTZ CERTIFIED Good Inside all belonged to this category in January 2010 (www.isealalliance.org). IFOAM withdrew from ISEAL in March 2010.
20 In this category we find: the Common Code for the Coffee Community (4C) Association, Accreditation Services International (ASI), the Alliance for Water Stewardship (AWS), the Better Sugarcane Initiative, the Center for Resource Solutions (Green-e), the Global Footprint Network, the Roundtable on Sustainable Biofuels (RSB), RugMark International, the World Fair Trade Organization (WFTO), and the WWF Aquaculture Dialogues www. isealalliance.org (accessed June 2010).
21 GlobalGap and PEFC are in this category www.isealalliance.org (accessed June 2010).
22 Interviews, ISEAL members, February 2010.

References

Agamben, G. (2007) *Qu'est-ce qu'un dispositif?* (Paris: Rivages Poches / Petite bibliothèque).

Bäckstrand, K. (2006) 'Multi-Stakeholder partnership for sustainable development: rethinking legitimacy, accountability and effectiveness', *European Environment*, 16, 290–306.

Bartley, T. (2007) 'Institutional emergence in an era of globalization: the rise of transnational private regulation of labour and environmental conditions', *American Journal of Sociology*, 113(2), 297–351.

Bartley, T. and Smith, S.N. (2010) 'Communities of practice as cause and consequence of transnational governance: the evolution of social and environmental certification' in M.L.

Bernstein, S. and Cashore, B. (2007) 'Can non-State Global Governance be legitimate? An analytical framework', *Regulation and Governance*, 1(4), 347–371.

Boltanski, L. and Chiapello, E. (1999) *Le nouvel esprit du capitalisme* (Paris: Gallimard).

Braithwaite, J. and Drahos, P. (2000) *Global business regulation* (New York: Cambridge University Press).

Dean, M. (1999) *Governmentality : power and rule in modern society* (London: Sage publications).

Di Maggio, P. and Powell, W. (1983) 'The iron cage revisited: institutional isomorphism and collective rationality in organizational fields', *American Sociological Review*, 48(2), 147–160.

Dingwerth, K., and Pattberg, P. (2009) 'World politics and organizational fields: the case of transnational sustainability governance'. *European Journal of International relations*, 15(4), 707–743.

Fouilleux, E. (2010) 'Les standards volontaires. Entre internationalisation et privatisation des politiques agricoles' in: B. Hervieu, N. Mayer, P. Muller, F. Purseigle and J. Remy (eds) *Les mondes agricoles en politique. De la fin des paysans au retour de la question agricole* (Paris: Les Presses de Sciences Po).

Ferlie, E. (1996) *The new public management in action* (Oxford : Oxford University Press).

Fiorini, A. (2000) *The third force. The rise of transnational civil society* (Washington DC: Carnegie Endowment for International Peace).

Fligstein, N. (1996) 'Markets as politics: a political-cultural approach to market institutions', *American Sociological Review*, 61, 656–73.

Foucault, M. (1978) 'La Gouvernementalité' in M. Foucault *Dits et écrits vol.2* (ed. 2001) (Paris: Gallimard).

Foucault, M. (2004a) *Sécurité, Territoire, Population. Cours au Collège de France (1977–1978)* (Paris: Seuil).

Foucault, M. (2004b) *Naissance de la biopolitique. Cours au Collège de France (1978–1979)* (Paris: Seuil).

Fuchs, D. and Vogelmann, J. (2008) 'The power of TNCs in transnational environmental private governance' in J-C. Graz and A. Nölke (eds) *Transnational private governance and its limits* (London: Routledge).

Fulponi, L. (2006) 'Private voluntary standards in the food system: The perspective of major food retailers in OECD countries', *Food Policy*, 31(13), 1–13.

Gereffi, G., Garcia-Johnson, R. and Sasser, E. (2001) 'The NGO-Industrial complex', *Foreign policy, July–August*.

Granovetter, M. (1985) 'Economic action and social structure: the problem of embeddedness', *American Journal of Sociology*, vol. 91(3), 481–510.

Graz, J-C. and Nölke, A. (eds) (2008) *Transnational private governance and its limits* (London: Routledge).

Guthman, J. (2007) 'The Polanyian Way? Voluntary Food Labels as Neoliberal Governance', *Antipode*, 39(3), 456–478.

Guthman, J. (2008) 'Thinking inside the neoliberal box: the micro-politics of agro-food philanthropy', *Geoforum*, 39, 1241–1253.

Haufler, V. (2003) 'New forms of governance: certification regimes as social regulations of the global market' in E. Meidinger, C.Elliot and G. Oesten (eds.) *The Social and political dimensions of forest certification* (Remagen: Forstbuch).

Henson, S. (2008) 'The Role of Public and Private Standards in Regulating International Food Markets', *Journal of International Agricultural Trade and Development*, 4(1), 63–81.

Keck, M. and Sikkink, C. (1998) *Activists beyond borders: transnational advocacy networks in international politics* (Ithaca, NY: Cornell University Press).

Larner, W. and Le Heron, R. (2004) 'Global benchmarking. Participating 'at a distance' in the globalizing economy', in W. Larner and W. Walters (eds.) *Global governmentality: governing international spaces*.(London: Routledge).

Lascoumes, P. (2004) 'La gouvernementalité: de la critique de l'Etat aux technologies du pouvoir', *Le portique*, 13–14, Foucault : usages et actualités http://leportique.revues.org/document625.html

Le Gales, P. and Scott, A., (2008) 'Une révolution bureaucratique britannique? Autonomie sans contrôle ou 'freer markets, more rules'', *Revue Française de Sociologie*, 49(2), 301–330.

Lewis, D. (2001) *The management of non-governmental development organizations : an introduction* (New York: Routledge).

Miller, P. and Rose, N. (1990) 'Governing economic life', *Economy and Society*, 19(1), 1–31.

Mutersbaugh, T. (2004) 'Serve and certify: paradoxes of service work in organic-coffee certification, *Environment and Planning D – Society & Space*, 22(4), 533– 552.

Mutersbaugh, T. (2005) 'Just-in-space: certified rural products, labour of quality and regulatory spaces', *Journal of Rural Studies*, 21, 389–402.

Ouma, S. (2010) 'Global standards, local realities: Private agrifood governance and the restructuring of the Kenyan horticulture industry', *Economic Geography*, 86(2), 197–222.

Polanyi, K. (1983) *La grande transformation. Aux origines politiques et économiques de notre temps* (Paris, Gallimard) [1ère édition 1944].

Pollitt, C. and Bouckaert, G. (2004) *Public management reform: a comparative analysis* (Oxford: Oxford University Press).

Potoski M., Prakash, A. (2005) 'Green clubs and voluntary governance: ISO 14001 and firm's regulatory compliance', *American Journal of Political Science*, 49(2), 235–248.

Power, M. (1997) *The Audit Society: rituals of verification* (Oxford: Oxford University Press).

ProForest (2003a) *Palm oil, Forests and Sustainability* (Oxford: ProForest) http://www.proforest.net/objects/publications/round-table-discussion-paper-1.pdf

ProForest (2003b) *Defining sustainability in oil palm production: an analysis of existing sustainable agriculture and oil palm initiatives* (Oxford: ProForest) http://www.proforest.net/objects/publications/round-table-discussion-paper-2.pdf

ProForest (2004) *Discussion paper on the development of criteria to define sustainable palm oil*, Final draft, 22nd February 2004. (Oxford: ProForest) http://www.rspo.org/PDF/RSPO%20Oil%20Palm%20Criteria%20Discussion.pdf

Rancière, J. (2005) *Chroniques des temps consensuels* (Paris: Seuil).

Raynolds L. (2004) 'The Globalization of Organic Agro-Food Networks', *World Development*, 32(5), 725–743.

Roberts, S.M., Jones J.P. and Fröhling (2005) 'NGOs and the globalization of managerialism: a research framework', *World Development*, 33(11), 1845–1864.

Rose, N. (1993) 'Government, authority and expertise in advanced liberalism', *Economy and Society*, 22(3), 283–299.

Townley, B. (2002) 'Managing with Modernity', *Organization*, 9(4), 549–573.

9
Multi-stakeholder Initiatives for Sustainable Agriculture: Limits of the 'Inclusiveness' Paradigm

Emmanuelle Cheyns

Introduction[1]

In a context of increasing criticism, initiatives aimed at creating sustainable standards for environmentally sensitive agricultural commodities (coffee, cocoa, palm oil, soy, biofuels, sugar cane, cotton and others) have been developed through a process of Roundtables.[2] These so-called 'multi-stakeholder' initiatives (MSIs) provide 'open' participation/negotiation mechanisms bringing together, on a global scale, economic operators from the agri-food sectors concerned (national and multinational producers, buyers, wholesalers, banks, distributors) and from local and international social and environmental NGOs (Fransen and Kolk, 2007).

These private and voluntary initiatives are based on a rationale focusing on government failure, particularly in the South, to assume responsibility for environmental goods. They base their legitimacy on their capacity to ensure the balanced representation and participation of 'all categories of stakeholders' within participatory and inclusive processes by means of dialogue and a desire for consensus.[3] The participation of all stakeholders, and thus a wide range of interests, is at the heart of a new form of legitimate action that forms part of a broader liberal model of building a coalition of interest groups. In the fields of management science and consulting, MSIs have been supported by works on 'partnered governance' promoting the inclusion of a wide range of operators, particularly private operators, in the task of regulation (Zadek and Radovich, 2006; Glasbergen, 2006). The authority of the resulting coalitions stems from the fact that, in this particular domain, it speaks on behalf of a large number of voices; that it has identified all the pros and cons and provides a broader perspective; and that it favours sharing knowledge and expertise among stakeholders (Jenkins *et al.*, 2002; Boström, 2006).

The criticism traditionally levelled at MSIs concerns the unequal resources and competences of the participants and the asymmetric balance of power which inevitably follows (Fransen and Kolk, 2007), for example, between the organizations of the North (which take the key positions of governance) and the South (Reinicke *et al.*, 2000), between local NGOs and international industries or NGOs and others.

In this chapter, we intend to extend this criticism by analysing the nature and functioning of MSIs using tools from the field of the French 'Sociologie pragmatique', and more specifically the sociology of 'regimes of engagement' (Thévenot, 2006, 2007b). These works demonstrate a number of different ways in which people can be engaged with regard to their environment, from the most public to the most familiar forms, by highlighting three regimes of engagement. The first aims to qualify a common good ('justifiable engagement') and involves a 'moral subject'[4] in a pluralist perspective[5] (Boltanski and Thévenot, 2006/1991). The second is that of 'functional and strategic engagement', more familiar to the social and political sciences, where the environment is dominated by 'stakeholders' asserting interests. The third regime is that of 'familiar engagement', where people can operate by maintaining personalized attachments and relations (Thévenot, 2006). These three regimes of engagement are on an even footing in terms of value and legitimacy. Understanding participation therefore involves examining its mechanisms and their capacity to provide a number of elements enabling participants to make themselves heard and to operate not only within a plurality of stakeholders (the founding authority of the MSIs), but also within a plurality of principles of justice (qualifying the common good from a pluralist perspective) and of attachments (in terms of proximate surroundings) with a view to interacting in the plural (Richard-Ferroudji, 2008).

The results presented here are based on participatory observation between 2003 and 2009 within the RSPO (Roundtable on Sustainable Palm Oil) and RTRS (Roundtable for Responsible Soy), in Asia and Latin America[6]. They are also based on interviews with participants and non-participants in Europe, Brazil, Argentina, Malaysia and Indonesia (NGOs, plantation firms, industry, foundations and sponsors, consultancy firms, certifiers, family producers and 'local communities' in Indonesia).

We will examine the manner in which these Roundtables frame the legitimacy and engagement of actors and question their capacity to include participants other than 'stakeholders'. We further show how these mechanisms lead to a form of de-politicization[7] of standards in that they focus action on 'strategic engagement'. In the first section, we will present the central figure of the stakeholder and what this figure generates in terms of substitutions with regard to representation. We will then show how the strategic engagement targeted by the MSIs disrupts the qualification tests for the common good and results in the exclusion of participants, in particular local and smallholder communities who wish to debate principles of justice. Finally, we will demonstrate how forms of knowledge and language norms linked to strategic and functional engagement exclude those people affected locally through their personal attachments. These results all call into question the paradigm of inclusion.

Prevalence of the interests format and of liberal voluntary capacities

Inviting 'stakeholders' to participate in Roundtables presupposes that participants are identified with some specific interests and are endowed with proactive voluntary capacities. These characteristics led to the first wave of exclusions of participants and gave rise to processes of substitution of representation.

The stakeholder: a central participating figure

In the RSPO and RTRS, the status of members and the principle of representativeness deployed are founded directly on the concept of the stakeholder, who is the central participating figure. In the RSPO, therefore, it is essential to belong to one of the seven categories of stakeholder stipulated in the statutes to be a member of the association[8]: 'growers, processors and traders, consumer goods manufacturers, retailers, banks and investors, environmental/nature conservation NGOs, social/developmental NGOs'.[9] Governments and research institutions are not seen as stakeholders of the same order. They may enjoy the status of affiliated member or observer which gives them the right to attend annual general meetings without the voting rights accorded to the other (ordinary) members.

Each stakeholder is expected to play the primary role of defending the specific interests of his/her category. It is in part for this reason that research institutions are not granted the status of ordinary members.

Well, research institutions do not really *have a direct interest in palm oil* production and trade. They do not adopt a formal and decisive position. But they are welcome to participate! (Interview with Social NGO, NL)

The division of labour in the defence of interests is closely linked to the traditional distinction in the field of sustainable development between the so-called environmental, social and economic pillars and refers to specialization among NGOs. Even if the roles are gradually becoming more complex, social NGOs are expected to contribute to defending social interests, environmental NGOs to environmental interests, industry to economic interests and so on.

We also play a specific role, so we do not really deal with social issues. We only focus on biodiversity and conservation aspects because there are other social NGOs which handle social aspects. And of course we discuss with them. (interview with Environmental NGO, NL)

If WWF, which deals with the environment, says it's OK, then it's OK [concerning the criteria of sustainable palm oil]. We (the industry) aim to earn money and increase our profits. (interview with Board of Oil and Margarine Producers, NL)

Very often during the debates, the stakeholders are grouped by category, referred to as 'interest groups'. In the main working groups, with a strong emphasis on decision making, the principle of balance is defined by the number of seats allocated to each interest group. In RSPO, this is particularly the case with the Executive Board (16 seats allocated to the seven categories of stakeholders) and the Criteria Working Group whose members established the sustainable palm oil specifications (25 people divided into four interest groups referred to as 'constituent groups'). In this last working group, the procedure stipulated that each interest group should discuss the criteria 'which directly relate to their own constituent group'.[10] Industry therefore discusses economic criteria, social NGOs discuss social criteria, and so on., even if at other times the procedure provides for exchange of views between groups. Legitimization of the Roundtables is thus founded on the capacity of the participants to defend an interest and belong to an interest group and its own capacity to facilitate the 'balanced' representation of interest groups.

Participation is also based on a 'voluntary' capacity which should enable stakeholders to take their place in the process on their own initiative. Participants decide to participate in Roundtables (by registering for conferences, offering to participate in working groups, applying as members of the association) or are co-opted (encouraged to participate by their networks). As stakeholders, the participants by implication enjoy and use strategic and bargaining capacities.

To communicate, it is particularly important 'not to be shy', to know the others' plans, 'to understand the stakes', 'to be proactive', to stick up for oneself (contrary to the 'victim' figure who is disqualified), 'to lobby, 'to intervene', or 'to make the first move'.

Asked about what restricts the participation of 'smallholders'[11] in the RSPO, a Dutch certifier mentioned the voluntary capacities necessary to negotiate and provide information on the required format, that is the expression of a preference rather than a public justification ('I want that!'):

> I mean the Dutch are very direct: 'I want that!' Faced with this, you need to be able to resist, not to be shy. [...] For directors of Indonesian companies, it's different: they have travelled, they are used to negotiating, to speaking with other cultures, for example European cultures (interview with a certifier, NL).

Some elements are clearly strategic: drawing up the agenda of the annual Roundtables, appointing experts to the working groups, and others, are tasks conducted by restricted groups, such as the Executive Board or the Organizing Committees in which the initiators of the Roundtables play an important role. Appointing members of some restricted working groups ensures a decisive role for their networks and for access to information. In the case of the group responsible for defining the criteria for sustainable palm oil, co-optation led to top-down representation. The 25 'experts' responsible for developing the criteria for sustainable palm oil were all selected by the Organizing Committee and, while throughout the entire process they were supposed to consult stakeholders within their category, they do so using lists which they drew up themselves, generally by calling on their networks. Similarly, the positions of hosts/coordinators and rapporteurs of the 'world café' debates and parallel workshops are potentially strategic and perceived as such by certain participants to influence or focus the debates.

Substitution of representation

These expectations *vis-à-vis* participants give rise to a certain number of exclusions and raise problems concerning the imperative of equal participation incorporated in the notion of balanced representation.

First, individuals or groups which are not part of the initiators' networks informed are excluded and those which are not organized in the form of interests groups have no genuinely recognized legitimacy: 'If you are an individual[12] you are invisible' (Social NGO). This was the case for 'smallholders' and 'local communities' during the early years of the RSPO process.

The absence of smallholders from the negotiations, despite the fact that they are responsible for 30% of global palm oil production, was long justified by certain participants in terms of the lack of a corresponding interest group, or by their 'inability' to provide visible representation for larger groups: 'it is too early for an association of smallholders to be present on the RSPO Board [on which a seat is reserved for it] as they must be able to consult and represent all smallholders, whereas this is far from being the case at present' (interview with Board of Malayan planters, 2005). In light of these criticisms, social NGOs decided to organize smallholder participation more directly and the order was given to create an interest group: 'There are a million smallholders, so how do you go about selecting them? Some try to represent their interests or to organize them according to a specific interest, like Sawit Watch tries to organize them to come to the conference and participate' (interview with Social NGO).

Second, those participants who do not take their place at their own initiative, in particular if they belong to little-recognized groups, then risk seeing their representation replaced by other participants. In a certain number of restricted working groups (like the Criteria Working Group), smallholder and local community representation is thus entrusted primarily to social NGOs and consultancy firms. In larger or more open arenas (plenary sessions, parallel workshops, 'world cafés' and others), their representation is partly substituted by every category of stakeholder present, talking about 'the case of smallholders', taking decisions concerning them or presenting points of view articulated as expressions of their interests. This may involve industrial firms in the value chain, plantation companies, certifiers and bankers, a fact which may appear paradoxical in light of the divergence between their own interests and those of the people on whose behalf they speak. This substitute representation of smallholders, in particular by plantation companies, is nothing new in the history of the development of palm oil which has long pigeon-holed smallholders in a position of objects of assistance (Cheyns, 2005).

For certain members, the absence of local communities and smallholders may pose a problem for the legitimacy of the process as seen from the outside, although their participation is still perceived as a question of individual responsibility: 'Yes, the absence of smallholders in the RTRS affects its legitimacy, but they didn't want to come[13]; the RTRS is open!' (Interview with Dutch consultancy firm). Beyond the non-recognition of their capacity to act autonomously (prolonging 'assistance'), it is their capacity to take their place in the arena which is undermined. This process can be seen in all domains of the Roundtables, whether it is a case of occupying the debate in the workshops or being the first to take the floor during the short periods of debate in the plenary sessions.

What is worth noting is that smallholders themselves counterpose another vision of plural discussion to that found in the Roundtables, in particular a vision which provides for equal shares of time in discussion, allowing each participant to speak his/her mind in a more drawn-out process. Hence, an Indonesian smallholder expressed his disappointment at the length of debates compared to the number of participants present and at the organization of the right to speak:

> The debate times in the plenary sessions are too short. When the room is full like that [500 participants], you need 30 minutes of questions. Here, there were only three questions. And after that, you have to leave time for people to answer. Even if it takes several hours to answer, the time needs to be allocated [...] Second, there are no 'rules': one person asks a question and the others don't have the chance [to do so].
> -What rules would be good, for example?
> -OK, for example, we sit down in groups: the smallholders [sit] here, the NGOs here, the planters here. So you can see who is who. You can see who is asking a question. And whoever is chairing the meeting should allow every group to speak. That way, all the groups speak in every session during debates' (Interview with an Indonesian farmer, smallholders group).

These proposals underline the disparity between the rules of debate where each participant must assert a place and those where there is a mechanism responsible for allocating a place to everyone (in this case the chairperson, but also through the physical distribution of participants in the room).

Participation is thus based on a voluntary capacity and a disposition to negotiate (articulated in terms of representing interests) whereby each individual is responsible for 'finding a place', at the risk of seeing representation substituted by others. This capacity reflects participation in a liberal format of engagement, excluding consideration of suitability of the mechanism to embrace a wide range of participants or forms of engagement other than that of 'stakeholder'. In particular, we will see that the mechanism has difficulty in incorporating participants wishing to discuss the principles of justice, or describe their personal attachments and adverse circumstances they have suffered in their real lives.

The challenge of qualifying the common good

'Strategic engagement' is founded on voluntary capacity, individual intention, choice, the project, interests and strategy to achieve certain goals and objectives. In this section, we will see that communication among participants takes the form of a choice that privileges 'promoting an opinion' and involving several parties with the aim of balancing these different individual preferences (Thévenot, 2006; 2011a). By favouring this regime of engagement, MSIs suppress another form of engagement desired by certain participants, that is a vision of qualifying a common good. In this regime of 'justifiable engagement' (Thévenot, 2006; 2007b) the environment is no longer understood as a means of satisfying a need, rather it is described and justified in terms of principles of justice by participants who, in this process, are endowed with moral capacities. The challenge for the MSI mechanism therefore concerns its capacity to take account of a wide range of voices focussing on the recognition of a pluralism of principles of justice (Thévenot, 2006; Richard-Ferroudji, 2008). It is this capacity which will be studied in this section.

Urgency and fear of disagreement

Urgency, expediency or justice?

A quality expected of the participants is that they engage in action in a 'practical' manner in order to find a quick and effective solution.

> Here, it is different from an 'ecological foot print' or scientific approach. Scientists can spend years finding an ideal solution which may, furthermore, prove to be inapplicable. The RSPO is not a scientific approach but a multi-stakeholder approach, i.e. what is the best we can do at present so that everyone can implement it? We are not dealing with the absolute or the ideal; we are looking for a practical solution (Interview with a representative of a Board of Industrialists, NL).

The formal absence of governments in the decision-making processes of these Roundtables is correspondingly justified by the organizers in terms of their 'difficulty in taking quick decisions': 'the aim is to bypass or shortcut decision-making in order to speed up the process of resolving the problem' (Interview with Social NGO, NL).

The desire to keep industry on-board and the principle of urgency leads to the position of the 'pragmatic' (in the usual sense of the word) or 'realist' participant being legitimized, including from the point of view of leading NGOs. This position is presented as being one which will facilitate dialogue between NGOs and industry.

> Ideally, you would say "stop soy production". But pragmatically, that is not going to happen. There are too many interests. If they make money with soy, companies are not going to stop. So NGOs need to be pragmatic and establish a set of criteria allowing them to continue working while at the same time saving part of nature or certain social values. That is the balance you try to find (interview with Environmental NGO, NL).

At the level of interests, this type of participant is contrasted with the 'idealist' who would aim for a common understanding of the problem and, more specifically, would endeavour to qualify what is just or fair. It leads to the debate between visions and definition of a common good being put to one side in favour of negotiating on the basis of existing solutions.

> I have my heart, and I think a lot of nice things have to be done. But we are also in a hurry. So I do not have time to wait for all people to be educated and understand and analyse the problem, blah blah blah. And there are solutions (interview with Environmental NGO, NL).

This position is associated with a justification of disparities in multi-stakeholder participation, despite the latter being at the heart of the claimed legitimacy of these mechanisms: 'Small-scale producers are not involved in the RTRS. [...] I mean we want poor people to be well represented. But how do you ensure this is the case? It's very hard. I am afraid we are a bit more pragmatic. It is not ideal, but we have to move' (interview with Environmental NGO, NL). This disparity is presented as a desire for a balance between two requirements, that of acting quickly and achieving desired ends without being bound by the rules of what is 'just', and that of legitimacy, which inevitably raises the question of what is 'just': 'The challenge for any multi-stakeholder process related to sustainable commodity production is to strike the right balance between the needs of expediency and legitimacy' (Pi Environmental Consulting, 2005). 'Expediency' refers to the idea of quick, useful and necessary action even if it is not necessarily fair; it similarly includes a sense of self-interest which runs contrary to that of justice. We clearly see here the difficulty in handling the notion of justice, which is necessary to the idea of legitimacy and yet brushed aside by the argument of 'pragmatism'.

Refocusing on the subject

In the Roundtables, the notion of stakeholder incorporates a requirement of operationality and refocusing on a specific, precise and circumscribed subject – in this case the sustainability of palm oil or soy. An intervention by one participant during an RTRS workshop is indicative of the tensions created by this refocusing:

> The problem is not only soy, it is more complex. The entire agricultural model must be discussed. We must talk about the agricultural model of maximum profitability which pushes small-scale farmers to sell their land and farmers to migrate! ... And government representatives should be present.

These remarks were brushed aside by the coordinator who reiterated the rules: 'Our discussion here must stay within the framework of a private initiative aimed at proposals concerning soy!' (Workshop Coordinator, consultancy firm, NL).

The necessary operationality leads to participants being sidelined if they attempt to refocus the debate on broader issues, implying a moral and political burden and an extension of the good considered. This is the case, for example, with certain NGOs who articulate a stance on so-called 'global issues' considered to be 'too political' – in particular issues linked to the living and work conditions of migrants on plantations, use of GMOs, agricultural production methods or food consumption patterns (what we might agree to change in our methods of consumption, what type of agriculture we want for tomorrow) and so on. It is another reason why governments do not enjoy the status of ordinary member, because their mandate extends to topics considered to be too broad[14] (such as regulation of land rights).

Incorporating several parties: negotiating a list of criteria

Although the RSPO targets a 'better world' and promotion of sustainable palm oil[15], the participants interviewed agree that there have been no debates, even within the smaller groups, on definition of sustainability or the type of common goods aimed at.

> We have very few debates concerning the principles and very few discussions concerning the long-term visions. For example, what will the level of demand be in 20 years? Should we produce palm oil or something else? Thinking about development in relation to the world in general, they don't even do that at the G8! (Interview with a member of the Working Group defining criteria on sustainability).

The tasks of defining and evaluating sustainability are implemented following a method which is very fashionable in the field of sustainable development: that of 'Principles, Criteria, Indicators'[16]. In the case of the RSPO, this method involves in practice drawing up lists of criteria for sustainable oil (39 criteria) without becoming bogged down in discussion of principles where the political dimension gives rise to fears of disagreements which might prove to be too great.

'This method provides the possibility not to frighten people from the outset. You agree first at a general level, you do not go into details. You are not fighting. [...] You need a commitment from the industry' (interview with Environmental NGO, NL).

Avoiding debate on the major principles of sustainability helps to eliminate tension: 'What is sustainability? One will disagree. It's too long. Nobody has the same vision!' (interview with environmental NGO). In particular it helps to avoid exposing divergences among the participants concerning issues of justice[17]. Instead there is a concentration on listing criteria where the interests of all groups can be served by each proposing their own criteria (environmental criteria for the environmental NGOs and so on). Similarly, decentralization of discussions on criteria to interest groups is justified as a solution which helps avoid strong tensions from surfacing. In particular, it can prevent fundamental divergences from being revealed.

In this process, the actors depict compromise as a negotiation reminiscent of 'sharing a cake'. Irrespective of whether or not they can envisage making the cake bigger, they have to surrender part of their potential gain.

How do you define negotiation?
I go there, and I am of the opinion that biodiversity loss should be stopped. And then there are farmers and they tell me 'that is all very fine, but I want to develop, I want to cut the forest to set up a farm and make a living'. And then we sit down, talk to each other, and come to a decision that allows him to cut maybe part of this forest, and conserve the rest, or whatever. So that's negotiation (interview with Environmental NGO, NL).

Furthermore, the goods to be negotiated take the form of opinions and preferences, a fact which we will examine next.

Organising the debate: a market place for ideas and opinions

In the Roundtables, common goods are constituted, and given public expression, in terms of the negotiable opinions and interests of a 'liberal public' (Thévenot, 2007a). Disagreement is then re-formatted as a choice between options (Thévenot, 2011a). Public discussion incorporating several parties thus creates markets for opinions and preferences. This is the implicit aim, for example, of the 'world cafés' and 'open space technology', new discussion technologies suggested by consultancy firms and widely used in the context of the Roundtables.

The world cafés are forums for discussion in small groups of about ten people organized of several short rounds (20 minutes). At each new round, the participants break up and form new groups. The aim of the promoters of this concept[18] is to establish a format for discussion reminiscent of 'conversation', a creative exploration ('play, experiment, and improvise') and the development of a collective intelligence based on the numerous encounters: 'link and connect ideas', 'allow for a dense web of connections'.[19]

In open space technology[20], the groups are all placed in a circle in a large room with no physical separation between them. The participants move from group to group to take part in discussions as they wish with no specific plan, in a room where the centre remains empty in order to create the conditions necessary for encounters as the different participants move round. The aim of this technique is to break away, momentarily, from planned action in order to embrace the excitement of the game, listen to contrasting opinions while connecting them through the creation of a 'market place' where human exchanges and ideas can be found (Owen, 1997).

The so-called 'two feet' rule asks for 'fluttering' mobility: 'if you are neither learning nor contributing, use your two feet and go somewhere more productive' (Owen, 1997). Symbolized by the image of a butterfly, the rule encourages participants to move from one group to another according to their focuses and their curiosity, while the image of the bee illustrates that the action involves 'pollinating' ideas from group to group. Furthermore, the process is directed by another rule: 'Whatever happens is the only thing that could have happened'. This rule should help to free the participants 'from major anxiety' (Owen, 1997) since the severe constraints weighing on the search for ideal solutions or the integration of the future are relaxed: 'this principle keeps people focused on the here and now, and eliminates all of the could-have-beens, should-have-beens or might-have-beens'.[21]

These meeting technologies are connectionist and aim to increase the interactions between people over a short period of time. The search for solutions focuses on the creation of a 'web', a multi-stakeholder market place for ideas and opinions. The diversity of the participants and the speed of the exchanges more often than not lead to lists of opinions being produced or choices being made between the different options provided. The questions examined in the world cafés, for example, aim to confirm choices ('what are the strengths and merits of the RSPO certification procedure?'), work on the choices of options using technical documents prepared in advance ('debate on certification systems and verification options' using a document prepared by a consultancy firm) or make suggestions concerning specific and technical questions ('how can smallholders be trained?'). The compartmentalization and specialization of the questions do not require participants to envisage a common horizon focusing on issues which engage the common good. The initiative allows the 'pressure' on participants to be relaxed in terms of moral responsibility. The principle 'Whatever happens is the only thing that could have happened' emphasizes this idea of detachment from moral requirement or from stakes which weigh on the future in order to focus on the present and the set of opinions which, when connected, should produce solutions.

An oppressive[22] regime of strategic engagement

These characteristics, proper to the regime of strategic engagement, create other conditions for the exclusion of participants.

Disqualifying local communities and family producers

Encouraged and supported by NGOs to join the Roundtable in 2005, local communities and smallholders approached the RSPO as a political arena to debate and make the international community aware of problems linked to their living conditions, in particular to their (lack of) land rights. However, they were systematically disqualified from introducing these themes in plenary sessions, on the pretext that they were 'off the topic'.

They should try to express themselves more constructively. When we hear them speak, we don't have any desire to help them. [...] They talked about land rights every time, it was very repetitive and it was not the topic of the discussion. [...] They create more negative energy rather than positive (interview with Board of Industrialists, NL).

The procedural and strategic engagement expected from participants opposes the desire of local communities and smallholders to talk about justice.

In the side events [bilateral negotiation in the wings of the official conference], where we negotiate with a company, it is as if we have to whisper. We want to talk in public in the plenary sessions and other scenes. The most interesting thing for us is to talk about justice, freedom. They should allocate more time [in plenary sessions] to talking about how farmers live and give firms less opportunity to make presentations (interview with an Indonesian family farmer).

The way in which these groups raise political issues in the arena – 'giving farmers justice' with regard to land rights and considering the people locally affected – contrasts with the technical rationality generally applied within the framework of the Roundtable:

What do you mean by: 'We [WWF] are not political'?
Other NGOs demonstrate clear political involvement. For example, Greenpeace are politically involved in social issues. And I agree with this. But our role (WWF) is to ensure industry wants to talk. [...] We also protect local communities, but we still want do it in a very formal way. For example, if you look at the local communities: you say 'it should be clear whose land is it'. Because it is not clear, to be fair. So you do not say: 'you must protect the communities!' It is a general statement. Everybody should agree with what you propose (interview with WWF, NL).

In practice, tackling the debate in terms of 'it should be clear whose land it is' reduces the land issue to questions of obtaining deeds and legal rights, thereby strengthening the position of the plantation companies in the conflicts.[23] Local populations fight for rights which are not clearly recognized in their countries, such as customary rights. If these were examined in the Roundtable, this would entail an open debate with a political dimension focusing on sharing use of land, recognition of local rights and local agricultural practices, thus highlighting different visions of the common good.

Finally, in addition to being ignored on the pretext of their deviating from the topic at hand, smallholders are also disqualified during their interventions through accusations of 'militancy'. The first public intervention of an Indonesian smallholder during a plenary session of 4th Annual Conference of the RSPO led to other participants castigating the speaker as an activist who had usurped the identity of 'real' smallholders. Somewhat taken aback, the smallholder in question, far from backing down, went directly up to the chairman of the Roundtable saying, 'look at my hands, these are the hands of a farmer!' as proof of his authenticity.

From pluralism to the closure of criticism: arbitrating the common good

In petitioning for the principles of justice to be discussed, smallholders openly disagreed with the definition of sustainability which was agreed on during the first meetings between the leading NGOs and industry, even before the Roundtables were launched (Cheyns, 2009). In the pragmatic positioning already mentioned, this definition naturalized the increasing demand for oil or soy: 'The industry only works on production, and they say: 'we just produce what is required. We take it for granted that soy is needed' (interview with environmental NGO, NL).

This resulted in an agreement that it was appropriate to produce soy or palm oil in large quantities to meet demand, but only on non-forest land. This in turn affirmed the agro-industrial production models already in place for more than 50 years: improved yields, intensification, mono-crop farming, (bio-)technologies and so on. The fact that GMOs seeds were accepted by environmental NGOs in the 'responsible soy' specification of the RTRS illustrates this desire to channel agriculture in the direction of forest conservation without challenging its productive and economic logics. By the same token, other production models envisaging integration of agriculture with nature (systems of combined or diversified crops, such as agro-forestry), as well as traditional or family agriculture, were discarded.

In denouncing 'domestic'[24], 'market' and 'industrial' orders, and instead demanding 'civic' orders of worth[25], family producers attempted to propose an alternative definition of sustainability in their interventions, both in the RSPO and RTRS. This definition was, however, sidelined; a real discussion of principles of justice was perceived as threatening dissolution of the 'community of participants'. Thus in the RTRS, the Federation of Family-based Agricultural Workers of Southern Brazil (FETRAF-SUL) opposed the model of mono-crop farming and use of GMOs, which 'reduce the autonomy of family farmers', while denouncing 'domestic' and 'market' subordination to companies. The Federation demanded diversified agriculture and increased equity in the distribution of wealth and land. Similarly, in the RSPO, Indonesian family producers demanded a revision of the price-setting formula for sales of palm bunches and more autonomy with a revision or an end to contracts binding them to plantation firms. Both these demands were put to one side or not considered. In the case of the RTRS, the members of the Organizing Committee requested the Federation to allow the questions of 'monoculture vs. diversity' and 'GMOs vs. non-GMOs' to remain 'outside the scope of Roundtable debate' due to the fact that 'divergences between these production models are too wide' (interview with Fetraf-Sul). In the RSPO, 'civic' justifications focusing on solidarity (sharing of returns by means of price revision) and greater smallholder autonomy were displaced by proposals closer to the liberal grammar of civic rights equality put forward by the NGOs and accepted by industry.[26] Its criteria's social principle therefore includes the rights of workers, the right of local communities to give 'free, prior and informed consent' before establishing new plantations on their lands, the right to a minimum wage for workers and outlawing of discrimination based on 'race, caste, national origin, religion, disability, gender, sexual orientation, union membership, political affiliation, or age'.[27] While it is recognized by family producers, this vision is far removed from dealing with social and economic inequality – that is, access to and sharing of resources.

Hence, promotion of a consensus based on 'industrial' rationality and depicting expressions of differences between the participants as threatening a break-up of the Roundtable led to its political element being reduced. Reformatting disagreements in terms of a choice of options enabled industry and NGOs to continue to meet, whereas this was rarely the case in the past. Some arguments and people were nevertheless excluded by this process.

From detached opinions to real lives

In addition to coming to an agreement with regard to their interests, NGOs and international industries share common types of expert knowledge and managerialist dispositions, as well as forms of language corresponding to strategic engagement. This shared grammar of strategic and functional engagement finds it difficult to recognize the legitimacy of local knowledge and of participants who engage with outsiders in terms of recounting their real lives and most familiar attachments. This creates further conditions of exclusion. It is also through language of this kind that smallholders and local communities, in some circumstances, express their desires for justice and report the adverse conditions that they suffer. Intensified production models and the expansion of large plantations by allocation of new blocks of often occupied land has a negative impact on their daily life and 'proximate goods'[28] – impacts that do not lend themselves to expression as 'detached opinions'.

Tensions and exclusions focusing on forms of knowledge

The Roundtables engage participant knowledge which is, for the most part, founded on biology, agronomy and management and which can be seamlessly incorporated into a regime of strategic and planned engagement. Interventions in the plenary sessions are based on a type of evidence which is 'industrial' in nature in that it makes use of statistical data, graphs, histograms and macro-economic or macro-environmental variables. This knowledge enters into conflict with other knowledge, in particular that of smallholders and local communities who, in the context of the Roundtables, put forward other types of argument or evidence which are monographic in nature in that they are based on the presentation or documentation of cases: reports on disputes, specific first-person case histories and so on. *A priori*, this type of argument has no less value than 'industrial' evidence, although in the case of the Roundtables, it is not accorded any legitimacy.

> People do not like it when smallholders take the floor in debates because they use this forum to express complaints about a particular case. (...) They have long stories. It is difficult to contribute to the discussion, there is this tension between people expressing their own problems and raising issues that are of general interest to the discussion. (...) Participants do not think it is relevant (interview with a Social NGO, NL).

This dichotomy of knowledge is also expressed in a differentiation of local from global knowledge. Thus, according to the RSPO Executive Secretariat, smallholders could not present their points of view directly in the plenary session as their vision was 'too local' in nature:

Even if they could make a presentation in the plenary session, the problem remains that the smallholders could not answer the subsequent questions as they are not fully aware of all the technical aspects, they do not have a global vision, for example concerning greenhouse gases. They do not have a sufficiently broad vision of the problem. They will simply present their own case.

This viewpoint prevails generally across most participants, who feel that the 'local' vision of smallholders does not enable them to be involved in international debate. To quote a certifier: 'They only know their job, not the market demand, EU politics and so on. They have never travelled'. Nevertheless, none of these participants questions their own limitations, in particular in obtaining access to local situations or in representing people affected in their daily lives or familiar contexts. Conversely, small-scale farmers claim a different form of legitimacy in the Roundtable process, as embodying 'practical' knowledge that they feel is very scarce among the majority of the speakers and which they contrast to 'theoretical' knowledge disconnected from reality:

Some people only talk about their [theoretical] knowledge. They are only interested in making a good presentation, irrespective of whether or not it is possible to achieve it! It is just theory. Someone might be good in theory but he has no practical experience. I have seen a lot of people like that in the RSPO. If I prepare a presentation I will use a PowerPoint, but it will be based on practice (interview with an Indonesian family farmer).

The Roundtable mechanism's inclusiveness is therefore called into question, in that it favours or even exclusively recognizes a single form of knowledge – knowledge based on 'international expertise' – to the detriment of local knowledge.[29]

Tensions and exclusions focusing on language norms: 'Speaking from the heart'

'Roundtable-speak' or the language of the Roundtables is also a language softened by 'liberal civility' (Thévenot, 2008), which permits pluralized interaction without confrontation. The 'professional style' recognized in this context is a technical one which avoids major confrontations and favours indirect formulations and a certain degree of caution. Some criticize it as a 'technocratic' or 'bureaucratic' style or describe it as 'an NGO style' or 'United Nation-speak' (Consultant, NL).

> The NGO style does not allow conflicts. It is a very indirect, polite, diplomatic style. Proforest [consultancy office in London] is highly professional. It has a highly conflict-shy politically correct style (...). Highly antagonistic issues remain hidden in cautious formulations or are postponed (interview with a consultant, NL).

Personal detachment, predominant in public arenas, is the rule. It assumes a capacity to transform personal attachments into opinions or interests that will fall into a field of 'sharable' choices (Thévenot, 2008; 2011a). Contrary to the local communities which express a strong sense of attachment, the representatives of international NGOs transform their personal attachments, such as a passion for wild or mystical nature into opinions better suited to the format, such as the need to sequester carbon stocks or into macro-environmental arguments focusing on the emission of greenhouse gases.

Emotion and affect are sidelined as linguistic deviations. The strong attachments expressed by local communities embarrass the participants, who find the public interventions of these communities 'too emotional' or even 'aggressive'. On the other hand, smallholders and local communities want to put an end to the 'techno-speak' which hides political objectives and to ensure 'truthful dialogue' among the participants where they must be 'honest, sincere and speak from the heart':

> In the RSPO, there must be no lies: all the parties must be able to adopt *good* strategies. If the RSPO exists, it is because of the negative effects. The RSPO must come from the heart. That is what I think because I have seen a lot of people make presentations [in the plenary sessions]. They don't speak from the heart. Some of them lie (interview with an Indonesian family farmer).

For farmers, this true language must be capable of integrating emotions or more direct stances, even if this means appearing 'hard' or 'shocking' to some participants: 'It is best to speak from our hearts. There is no need to speak with sugar on our lips when in our hearts and in reality, it's not sweet' (interview with an Indonesian farmer).

From detached roles to real lives

Finally, tension exists between the participants' capacity to play and change roles and the capacity to recognize people as they are affected in their real lives.

Most international participants have only a very limited knowledge of the living conditions of 'local minorities', often in remote and very inaccessible locations; they are more accustomed to major hotel chains and conferences in cities throughout the world. The Roundtables primarily emphasize the capacity to be mobile and not remain rooted in a particular territory, living in a 'connectionist' world (Boltanski and Chiapello, 1999), as crystallized in the figure of the 'manager'. In this world, isolated, local, deeply-rooted, attached participants are 'small fry' in the eyes of the 'big fish' deemed capable of detachment and connection.

We thus observe a high turnover rate in the Roundtables with participants leaving to be replaced by successors the following year or changing the institution they represent (for example, leaving an NGO to join a consultancy firm, a certification body or an advisory body working within the Roundtable and vice-versa, moving from one NGO to another and so on). This capacity to change rationale and position by shifting from one institution to another illustrates the capacity of the participants both to play and to change roles. It also underlines the capacity for detachment (abandoning deep-rootedness) which is in stark contrast to the attachment of 'local' figures such as family producers and local communities who defend rights while putting their local daily lives at risk, without being paid by one or another international institution.

> The difference between them and me is that they are here as part of their job whereas I am here to defend our very lives, and we aren't paid for that.' 'Look at Dr. A. for example. He has a professional style. He is just here to pick up his salary. He walks in like a salesman, taps the microphone and says 'Thank you!' He starts by saying 'Anyone would think that my theme is sustainable and so am I because this is the fourth time that I have made a presentation to the plenary session of the RSPO (interview with an Indonesian family farmer).

While smallholders had, without success, asked to speak at the plenary session for a number of years, the person referred to as Dr. A. in the previous interview had made three previous presentations 'concerning smallholders' without belonging to this category. We see here the frustration and indignation of the farmers at being prevented from expressing themselves in the plenary sessions when they want to describe their real lives, and finding their place instead taken by people 'who come to pick up their salary' or to play a role without engaging with their daily life and material fate.

Legitimacy conferred through detachment is challenged by local figures themselves who rather refer to the importance of people's consistent truthfulness and convictions:

> I liked the world cafés. I preferred to follow the same people during the 'three rounds' to hear their comments on the different themes, to see if they were genuine or liars; because in the world cafés, you can say one thing at one table and something different at another [at the next round]. I am Arifin, a smallholder. When I change tables, I am still Arifin, a smallholder. But I was curious to see if this was true for the others? Perhaps they are Arifin here and someone else at another table, talking here on behalf of a firm and there as a farmer. That's just an example to show that people can change their positions, their opinions. Here you agree about greenhouse gases and there you have a totally different opinion. It is a question of strategies. In the end, the final report back will tell the world: it is our input and it is a multi-party process. This is just a hypothesis, because there is very little criticism in the inputs (interview with an Indonesian family farmer).

In addition to lucidly highlighting the feeble opportunities for expressing criticism and the 'strategic positions' taken by most participants in the world cafés, this participant expresses the importance of the 'genuineness' of the person. He echoes the doubts of Bühler (2002) concerning the legitimacy of the participants who have no deeply-rooted attachment for the place or who have not experienced marginalization and exclusion and 'who might not have to account with their life histories'. This author recommends re-scaling participation beyond the local level and replacing justice and dignity ('recognition of what you are and respect for what you are') at the heart of participation, with a view to rethinking the issue of inclusion. These proposals may serve as an antidote to forms of manipulation, instrumental rationality or consensus which do not reflect what participants really think or are too far removed from the fate of the people who engage in the process with their life stories.

The results presented here reflect tensions between different regimes of engagement. We have noted the desire of local communities and smallholders to talk about justice 'from the heart', in a context where convictions are disqualified or more specifically considered as a form of 'militancy' or 'idealism' which has no place at the Roundtables. We have also underlined their desire for genuineness which assumes that everyone's life history will be considered. These two forms of engagement oppose the format of choice where options are detached from the individual who chooses them (Thévenot, 2011b).

Conclusion

An initial conclusion of this paper, which echoes Thévenot's analysis of 'Governing by standards' (1997; 2009), is that these multi-stakeholder initiatives, based on strategic action and debate between options and interests, stifle engagement in the qualification of a common good. Under the pressure of urgency and pragmatism, the opportunity for open political debate at these Roundtables is rejected. At the same time, the functional and strategic engagement that is institutionalized hides from participants the fact that a politics is implicit in the elaboration of choices made. In the final analysis, we clearly see the conservation of an agro-industrial model of agriculture founded on a 'market-industrial' compromise and the predominance of a 'civic rights' rather than 'solidarity' approach to social principles. The dual problem of the impossibility of open political debate and designation of the decisions taken as objective, since they are technical, leads us to talk about (de)politicization, the brackets reminding us that this increased technical content is in no way apolitical.

The principle of inclusion remains a real challenge, because not all participants are geared towards the format of strategic action and because some of them refer to other forms of legitimacy or engagement which are not accommodated. There is a rejection of the legitimacy of participating figures other than that of the 'stakeholder', in particular that of the 'moral subject' or 'attached person', which reproduces the conditions of unequal or asymmetric participation.

These multi-stakeholder initiatives, which form part of a broader liberal political model of a 'coalition and balance of interest groups and power', are developed against the explicit risk of a 'tyranny of the majority' (Thévenot, 2001). Nevertheless, while speaking for a large number of voices and ostensibly founded on the principle of inclusion, they find it difficult to introduce pluralism in defining the common good. They also experience difficulties in taking account of personal attachments, and thus in opening up to people affected in their real lives.

Notes

1 The research reported enjoyed the support of the National Research Agency (Agriculture and Sustainable Development Programme, 'NORMES: Governing by standards and standardisation mechanism in sustainable agriculture' project, 2006–2009). I would like to extend my particular thanks to Laurent Thévenot for his valuable comments during the research, Philippe Barbereau with whom I conducted a number of interviews (section three) and all of my colleagues in the 'Normes' project. I would also like to thank Benoît Daviron, Audrey Richard-Ferroudji, Eve Fouilleux and Peter Gibbon who read and commented on the initial draft of this paper.

2 The Roundtable on Sustainable Palm Oil (RSPO) created in 2003, the Roundtable on Responsible Soy (RTRS) from 2005, the Better Sugar Cane Initiative (BSCI) and Better Cotton Initiative (BCI) from 2006, and the Roundtable on Sustainable Biofuels (RSB) in 2008.

3 www.rspo.org

4 By moral, we understand 'the expectations weighing on each person which guide his or her engagements according to a vision of what is fair or what is good' (Pattaroni, 2001).

5 That is, with reference to different principles of justice.

6 The annual soy (RTRS) conferences are held in Brazil, Argentina or Paraguay and mainly bring together European and South American actors. The annual palm oil (RSPO) conferences are held in Indonesia, Singapore or Malaysia and mainly bring together European, Malaysian and Indonesian actors (the last two countries contribute 85 per cent of global palm oil production).

7 I use the term 'political' in the sense of 'life in the City' as defined by Pattaroni (2001): coordination of individual activities with a view to constructing a 'good' collective.

8 The two Roundtables have an official status of international association (under the Swiss legal code).

9 Official statutes, RSPO.

10 Procedural note, RSPO.

11 'Smallholder' is a term used by the participants in the Roundtable to designate family producers farming small areas.

12 In the sense of 'not represented by a category of stakeholders'.

13 On the day of the interview, the interviewee referred to the federation FETRAF-SUL, which represents family agriculture in southern Brazil and which decided to withdraw from the RSPO, and to the fact that during an entire period, no other association came to represent family agriculture.

14 Interview with RSPO participants and the Dutch Ministry of Agriculture.

15 The aim of the RSPO is to 'promote the growth and use of sustainable palm oil [...] for a better world' (www.rspo.org).

16 The method involves establishing the general principles of what sustainable palm oil is, which then give rise to a certain number of criteria. A principle consists of several criteria, for example Principle 6, 'Responsible consideration of employees and of individuals and communities effected by growers and mills' consists of 10 criteria (1: the social impacts linked to the plantations are identified by participatory means and give rise to plans for reducing the negative impacts; 2: there are open and transparent

methods of communication between mills and local communities). The indicators guide the data entered which, more often than not in a combined form, facilitate measurement of whether or not the criterion has been achieved.

17 For example, the economic pillar has been translated through criteria for the economic viability of agricultural production by the interest group representing industry, whereas public consultation by internet indicated other possible conceptions which were nevertheless not considered (in particular a principle of equity or sharing value enabling small-scale farmers to undertake long-term investments) (Cheyns, 2009).

18 www.theworldcafe.com

19 *Ibid.*

20 www.openspaceworld.org This concept was formalized by the US consultant Harrison H. Owen.

21 *Ibid.*

22 In reference to the analytical framework presented by Thévenot (2009).

23 From a legislative point of view, it is difficult for indigenous populations and local communities to obtain access to land deeds and, in certain cases, the legal implementation framework is not yet in place (for example for collective lands) (Le Bihan *et al,*. forthcoming 2010).

24 In terms of paternalistic (and exclusive) contract farming arrangements.

25 The market, domestic, civic and industrial orders of value refer to different principles of justice (Boltanski and Thévenot, 2006/1991).

26 This difference is illustrated by Thévenot and Lamont (2000) in a comparison between use of civic equality (legal rights) definitions in the United States *vs.* solidarity definitions in France.

27 RSPO document, 'Principles and Criteria' 2007.

28 Proximate goods refer to ease, personal convenience or affects. They are expressed here in personalized and localized relations with people and objects (Thévenot, 2006).

29 As reported by Bülher (2002) in her analysis of mechanisms for engaging the Zapatistas in Mexico.

References

Boltanski, L. and Chiapello, E. (1999) *Le nouvel esprit du capitalisme* (Gallimard, Paris).

Boltanski, L. and Thévenot, L. (2006) [1991] *On Justification: Economies of Worth*, transl. by C. Porter, 1st French edition 1991 (Princeton: Princeton University Press).

Boström, M. (2006) 'Regulatory credibility and authority through inclusiveness: standardisation organizations in cases of eco-labelling', *Organization*, 13(3), 345–367.

Bühler, U. (2002) 'Participation 'with Justice and Dignity': Beyond the 'New Tyranny'', *Peace, Conflict and Development*, 1, 16.

Cheyns, E. (2005) 'Family agriculture and the sustainable development issue: Possible approaches from the African oil palm sector. The example of Ivory Coast and Cameroon', *OCL. Oléagineux corps gras lipides*, 12(2), 111–120.

Cheyns, E. (2009) 'Naturalisation marchande, rationalité technique et (dé-)politisation du bien commun. Les standards agricoles 'durables' dans les *Initiatives multi partie prenante* in INRA, SFER, CIRAD 3èmes Journées de recherches en sciences sociales, 9, 10 and 11 December 2009, Montpellier, France.

Fransen, L.W. and Kolk, A. (2007) 'Global Rule Setting for Business: A critical Analysis of Multistakeholder Standards', *Organization*, 14(5), 667–684.

Glasbergen, P. (2006) 'The partnership paradigm: Governance between trust and legitimacy', in *Proceedings International Planning History Society Conference*. New Delhi, India.

Jenkins, R., Pearson, R., and Seyfang, G. (2002) *Corporate responsibility and Labour rights*. (London: Earthscan).

Le Bihan, E., Cheyns, E. and Jiwan, N., (forthcoming 2010) *Local practices in relation to the RSPO standard: Reinforcing the application of FPIC*, Cirad and Sawitwatch, Policy Brief.

Owen, H. (1997) *Expending Our Now: The story of Open space technology* (San Francisco: Berett-Koehler).

Pattaroni, L. (2001) 'Le geste moral: perspective sociologique sur les modalités du vivre ensemble', *Carnet de Bord*, 2, 67–77.

Pi Environmental consulting: Vellejo, N. and Hauselmann, P. (2005) *Multistakeholder Governance: A brief Guide* (Suisse).

Richard-Ferroudji, A. (2008) *L'appropriation des dispositifs de gestion locale et participative de l'eau. Composer avec une pluralité de valeurs, d'objectifs et d'attachements*. Thèse en Sociologie (EHESS, Paris).

Reinicke, W.H., Benner, T., Witte, J.M., Whitaker, B, and Gershman, J. (2000) *Critical choices: The United Nations, Networks, and the future of global governance*, Ottawa, International Development Research Centre.

RSPO (2007) 'RSPO Principles and Criteria for Sustainable Palm Oil Production. Including Indicators and Guidance', October 2007..

Thévenot, L. (1997) 'Un gouvernement par les normes; pratiques et politiques des formats d'information' in B. Conein and L. Thévenot (eds.) *Cognition et information en société*, Paris, Ed. de l'EHESS, *Raisons Pratiques 8*, 205–241.

Thévenot, L. (2001) 'S'associer pour composer une chose publique' in J.N. Chopart *et al*, (eds) *Actions associatives, solidarités et territoires* (Saint Etienne: Publications de l'Université de Saint Etienne).

Thévenot, L. (2006) *L'action au pluriel. Sociologie des régimes d'engagement*, Paris: La Découverte.

Thévenot, L. (2007a) 'Reconnaisances : avec Paul Ricoeur et Axel Honneth' in A. Caillé (eds) *La quête de reconnaissance. Regards sociologiques* (Paris: La Découverte).

Thévenot, L. (2007b) 'The plurality of cognitive formats and engagements: moving between the familiar and the public', *European Journal of Social Theory*, 10(3), 413–427.

Thévenot, L. (2008) 'Sacrifices et bénéfices de l'individu dans un espace public libéral', *Cahiers d'éthique sociale et politique*, 5, 68–79.

Thévenot, L. (2009) 'Governing life by standards: A view from engagements', *Social Studies of Science*, 39(5), 793–813.

Thévenot, L. (forthcoming 2011a) 'Bounded justifiability. Three constructions of commonality in the plural' in P. Dumouchel and R. Gotoh (eds) *Bounds and*

Boundaries: New Perspectives on Justice and Culture (Cambridge, Ma.: Cambridge University Press).

Thévenot, L. (forthcoming 2011b) 'Métamorphose des évaluations autorisées et de leurs critiques. *L'autorité incontestable du gouvernement par l'objectif'*, in G. De Larquier, O. Favereau, A. Guirardello (eds) *Les conventions dans l'économie en crise.*

Thévenot, L., and Lamont, M. (2000) 'Exploring the French and American polity' in M. Lamont M. and L. Thévenot (eds.) *Rethinking comparative cultural sociology: Repertoires of Evaluation in France and the United States* (Cambridge: Cambridge University Press).

Zakek, S. and Radovich (2006) 'Governing collaborative governance: Enhancing development outcomes by improving partnership governance and accountability', *Accountability and the corporate social responsibility initiative*, working paper 23. Cambridge, MA: John Kennedy School of Government, Harvard University.

10
Competition, 'Best Practices' and Exclusion in the Market for Social and Environmental Standards

Stefano Ponte and Lone Riisgaard

Introduction

Private standards in agro-food value chains have evolved considerably over time, in relation to the functions they perform, their institutional structure, the issues they seek to regulate, and the way this regulation is exercised. As established standards have evolved, new standards emerged regulating new issues or new combinations of issues. The proliferation and development of private standards has been accompanied by a growth in the number of institutions and actors setting standards and assessing conformity, including standards-setting bodies, auditors, and certification and accreditation agencies (NRC, 1995; Hatanaka *et al.*, 2005) and by the emergence of an audit 'industry' and an audit 'culture' (Power, 1997; Busch and Bain, 2004; Henson and Humphrey, 2010; Loconto and Busch, 2010). Such developments have been particularly marked in relation to standards focusing on social and environmental issues.

Increasingly, private actors such as corporations, NGOs and industry associations are involved in negotiating standards for producers, labour and the environment, and for monitoring compliance to these standards. This new form of governance has expanded rapidly across industries of interest to critical Northern consumers such as garments, toys, forest products, agricultural products, chemicals and electronics – and is now overlapping with more traditional public regulation of social and environmental issues (Gereffi *et al.*, 2001; Utting, 2005; O'Rourke, 2006). Private governance through standards remains highly disputed, particularly since the intended positive impact on producers, workers and the environment is by no means guaranteed, or even assessed. Standard initiatives have been criticized for implementing a Northern agenda on Southern producers and workers, for not being sensitive to local specific conditions, and for providing consumers with a false sense of problem solving (Barrientos *et al.*, 2003; Utting, 2005; O'Rourke, 2006; Blowfield and Dolan, 2008). Others, however, argue that such private initiatives are more efficient than traditional labour or environmental regulation and, moreover, suit current global production systems (see for instance Bernstein, 2001).

In addition to the multiplication of social and environmental standards, a parallel development has taken place on what are considered the 'best practices' for governing standard themselves (the setting, revision, management and certification of standards). New 'roundtables' (for sustainable soya, palm oil, biofuels) and 'stewardship councils' (such as the Aquaculture Stewardship Council) are currently being developed in accordance with the so-called new 'virtues' of transparency, inclusiveness, consensus and accountability (see also Djama *et al.* this volume; Cheyns this volume). Such best practices are inherited and adapted largely from the experience of the Forest Stewardship Council model and have been subsequently codified by the International Social and Environmental Labelling Alliance (ISEAL) – a body which sets norms for sustainability standard setting (see Bernstein and Cashore, 2007; Djama *et al.* this volume).

Overall, the literature on sustainability standards suggests that 'best practices' in the governance of standards and specific forms of governance (for example, the multi-stakeholder form) are becoming more common. It also suggests that competition is leading to a 'race to the bottom' in the field of standard content and to a differentiation between standard organizations that focus on market size and those that focus on high standard content. The two aspects may even be mutually reinforcing, as standardization of governance practices and forms makes standard content even more the focus of competitive dynamics among different initiatives. While these are important and relevant considerations, we argue that this picture needs critical engagement, disaggregation and further clarification. In this chapter, we will engage in three sets of questions:

(1) *Does competition among different standards matter in determining standard content?*

We question whether the general proliferation of standards is really leading towards a 'race to the bottom' in standard content. We also question whether there is a clearcut differentiation between different kinds of standard organizations in terms of a tension between size and principles. In order to do so, we place external competition (between standard initiatives) in the context of the possibility that standard initiatives experience the tension between achieving size and principles *internally*. This internal tension can be the manifestation of conflict between stakeholders that promote high standard content (environmental NGOs and experts, fish management consultants, labour specialists) and stakeholders that seek to achieve commercial success (supply chain managers, brand/label managers, marketing consultants). It can also be the manifestation of conflicts within standards initiatives between groups promoting different kinds of standard content (environmental versus social/labour issues).

(2) Does 'best practice' pressure in standards governance lead to improved practices?

While we do not question the observed trend in the literature towards standardization of 'best practice' in standard governance, we also examine whether and how such practices are adopted, especially by 'early movers', and with what consequences. As other chapters in this volume show, even when best practices are adopted, the process of negotiation can be managed in ways that marginalize critical voices and disadvantaged groups (Djama *et al.* this volume; Cheyns this volume).

(3) Is a 'race to the top' in standard content a positive outcome for the inclusion of Southern suppliers?

This aspect is particularly important in the context of North–South competition for the supply of certified products. Although higher labour standards in production may be a worthy goal *per se*, they tend to improve Northern competitiveness in relative terms in sectors where there are both Northern and Southern suppliers. Therefore, while attempting to raise labour standards may be relatively uncontroversial in cocoa or oil palm plantations (produced only in the South), it may have counterproductive outcomes in, for example, cut flowers (where Southern producers compete with Northern producers). Similarly, requiring demanding fishery management procedures may lead to environmental gains, but it may also disadvantage Southern fisheries.

In order to address these three sets of issues, we examine the development of social, labour and environmental standards in two sectors: capture fish (excludes aquaculture production) and cut flowers. The two sectors share some important similarities – they both handle high-value fresh products; the value of trade of both products has increased dramatically in the past 20 years; and in both cases imports from developing and emerging economies constitute roughly half of total consumption by value in Northern countries. This last feature allows us to examine whether the tensions between the interests of different stakeholders may reflect differences in the interests of Northern and Southern producers.

The two sectors also have important differences that we will use analytically to address the three sets of questions posed above. *Capture fish* is a sector characterized by low competition – here one initiative (the Marine Stewardship Council, established in 1997) was established in the context of an open field and only one main referent in terms of best practice in standard governance in the realm of natural resources (FSC, the Forestry Stewardship Council, started in 1994). MSC has been able to maintain a governance structure that is more corporate-style and less inclusive than is the case for FSC, even though it has formally adopted 'best practices' in standard governance in more recent years. It has also maintained a quasi-monopolistic situation in the market for sustainable fish. *Cut flowers* is a sector where a large number of parallel initiatives (including several multi-stakeholder initiatives) were implemented in a relatively short period of time (late 1990s–early 2000s), thus defining a context of high competition from the start and strong influence from best practice expectations, especially from the mid-2000s onwards.

The research jointly presented here is the result of two individual projects on sustainability standards in capture fisheries (Ponte) and cut flowers (Riisgaard). The projects involved interviews with representatives of standards initiatives, certifiers, auditors, representatives of local industry associations, exporters, processors and producers in Europe (both sectors), East Africa (both sectors) and South Africa (fish). Details of methodologies used in the various contexts are available in Ponte (2008), Riisgaard (2009a; 2009b) and Gibbon *et al.* (2010).

Background

A large literature on sustainability standards in agro-food and forestry products has emerged in the past decade or so. It has focused on the development of principles, on standard implementation, on the ethics and governance of standards, on the industry of consultants, auditors, and certifiers that has emerged around standards and on their institutional features (see, among others, Busch, 2002; Raynolds, 2004;

Hatanaka *et al.*, 2005; Henson and Reardon, 2005; Muradian and Pelupessy, 2005; Pattberg, 2007; Swinnen, 2007). The literature has also examined how states respond differently to the voluntary features proposed by standard initiatives (Cashore *et al.*, 2004; Gale and Haward, 2011) and how voluntary standards are in constant need to achieve, maintain and manage legitimacy to exert authority (Bernstein and Cashore, 2007; Tamm Hallström and Boström, 2010).

In relation to best practices, much of the literature argues that despite the wide adoption of the new virtues of standard making and management, the technical systems which are to implement these standards do not necessarily lead to inclusiveness of Southern and/or disadvantaged actors and to appropriate standard content in relation to local conditions (Fransen and Kolk, 2007; Gupta, 2008; Ponte, 2008). In particular, a tendency has been noted for end results to focus more on environmental protection than on socio-economic effects (Klooster, 2005; Mol, 2007).

Recent work has started to look at how different standard initiatives compete and/or cooperate to enrol producers, other value chain actors and stakeholders (such as environmental NGOs), and at how such competition and/or cooperation impacts the content of these standards. As a point of departure in this literature is the observation that, in many agro-food products, a wide range of standard schemes have developed in parallel to set, promulgate and implement standards aiming to achieve more or less the same ends. Abbott and Snidal (2006) term this *parallelism*, describing the sometimes competitive, sometimes cooperative relations among independent standard schemes working within roughly the same issue area. The existing literature on parallelism tends to argue that despite the emergence of various forms of cooperation among standards initiatives, the competitive elements of parallelism are leading to a 'race to the bottom' in terms of standard content. Macdonald (2007), for example, argues that the landscape of competing standard schemes opens up a large discretionary space in defining the substance and scope of how social and environmental issues are tackled in production. According to Macdonald, such discretionary space allows multiple systems to coexist in parallel with 'high' standard content only being achieved by those participating in 'niche' supply chains. This position seems to support the notion that competition among standards leads to a race towards the lowest content in standards within mainstream markets. Raynolds *et al.* (2007) and Mutersbaugh (2005) reach similar conclusions, arguing that standards that seek to raise ecological and social expectations are likely to be increasingly challenged by competition from those that seek to simply uphold current standards.

Other authors also look at how different standards organizations strategically place themselves in the marketplace. Ingenbleek and Meulenberg (2006) examine the strategies that standard organizations pursue to put their sustainability objectives into practice. In their comparison of ten sustainability standard schemes, they find that many strategic differences between schemes can be traced back to two types of standard organizations: those weighing principles over size, and those weighing size over principles. The most essential difference is thus found in the trade-off between the principles of sustainable production and the size of the programme, that is the number of farmers that adopt the standard. Ingenbleek and Meulenberg argue that standard schemes follow either a differentiation or a lowest cost strategy when targeting markets. In a differentiation strategy (pursued by schemes that weigh principles over size), a standard scheme enables primary producers to differentiate themselves from mainstream producers on the basis of sustainability and to communicate this is to the end consumer. Standard organizations that weigh size over principles apply lower sustainability requirements in their standards, and thus require relatively lower investments from farmers than differentiators. Farmers producing under such standards add value to retailing and or processing firms because they increase their brand image and protect these firms to some extent from the attacks of action groups. However, these standards are not communicated directly to the end consumers.

As mentioned earlier, this picture needs critical engagement, disaggregation and further clarification. In the next three sections, we address the three sets of questions highlighted in the introduction to this chapter: (1) whether external competition among different standards and/or internal competition between different stakeholders within a standard initiative matters in determining standard content; (2) whether 'best practice' pressure in standards governance leads to improved practices; and (3) whether higher standard content leads to inclusion or exclusion of Southern suppliers.

The Marine Stewardship Council ecolabel for capture fisheries

The ascendancy of the Marine Stewardship Council (MSC) initiative, its continued domination of the sustainable fish market, and the specific content that its standard incorporated cannot be understood in isolation from the history of influence and the preferred tools used by conservation NGOs in fisheries. While ocean conservation has been a key preoccupation in some NGOs (especially Greenpeace) for a long time, it was only in the 1990s that mainstream international conservation groups, such as the National Audubon Society and WWF, began to focus on fish work. Previously, such groups had paid attention mostly to the terrestrial environment and to the wellbeing of marine mammals rather than fish (Sutton and Wimpee, 2008). Conservation groups faced an industry that had a stronghold over US and international fishery management. They were well aware that governments and international organizations had overseen the collapse of cod fisheries in New England and Canada and the depletion of other important marine stock such as Atlantic bluefin tuna. As a result, in the mid-1990s they started to turn towards market-based mechanisms to address these problems. This took place first via campaigns against consumption of specific species and then via the development of certifications and eco-labels, sustainable sourcing guidelines and advisory lists for consumers (Boots, 2008). As they adopted less confrontational methods, conservation NGOs started to see business as a partner in their efforts, and thus also became more aware of its commercial imperatives. This paved the road for the establishment of a compromise between moderate environmentalism and commercial imperatives which is the base of MSC's current success.

As part of the process of building such compromise, in 1995 WWF began discussions with Unilever on how to tackle sustainability in fisheries. WWF's entry point was one of conservation. Unilever was at the time the world's largest frozen fish buyer and processor, and its main preoccupation was the risk of not being able to source fish in the future for its dominant frozen food business. In 1996, the director general of WWF and Unilever's chairman agreed to collaborate in the creation of a new organization called Marine Stewardship Council (MSC), partially inspired by the FSC that had been established in 1993 also under the influence of WWF. Assisted by a giant public relations firm, WWF and Unilever took the idea on a tour of eight workshops. They convened two drafting workshops in 1996 and 1997, whose participants included the 'Who's Who of fisheries science and management' (Sutton and Wimpee, 2008, p. 408; Tamm Hallström and Boström, 2010). The socio-economic aspects of fishing were given much less attention. MSC was formally established as an NGO in London in 1997 under the chairmanship of John Gummer, a conservative MP and former UK fisheries and environmental minister. In 1999, MSC severed its ties to WWF and Unilever, and in 2000 it certified its first two fisheries.

Despite the development of other seafood ecolabels, MSC remains by far the dominant player in this field, giving it a quasi-monopoly both in the *supply* market (in terms of number and coverage of certified fisheries) and in the *demand* market (market share among fishery ecolabels used by retailers and branded manufacturers).[1] At the time of its establishment, MSC did not have any substantial supply competitor that certified a wide range of sustainable wild-capture fisheries. Yet, given the time and resource consuming certification process, in its first years of operation it certified only a few fisheries – and only two of which were of commercial significance (Alaska salmon in 2000; and New Zealand hoki in 2001). By 2006, it had certified 15 fisheries, including two new important ones (Alaska pollock in 2005; and South African hake in 2004). In terms of demand competition, at that time, MSC-certified products faced no competition in the market, but had significant commercial presence at the retail level only in the UK, Switzerland and Germany – with some presence in the US, France and other European countries (Ponte, 2008).

If we fast-forward to March 2010, we find a dramatically altered situation. Supply coverage has increased to over 62 certified fisheries, another 130 undergoing assessment and 40–50 under confidential pre-assessment. According to MSC, this translates into over 7 per cent of the world's total wild harvest (MSC, 2010a). On the demand side, 3800 products now bear the MSC label in 62 countries, for an estimated retail value of USD 1.5 billion (MSC, 2010b). At the retail level, in addition to early adopters such as Sainsbury in the UK, Whole Foods in the US, and Migros and Coop in Switzerland, the most important developments have been Wal-Mart's commitment in 2006 to source all its fresh and frozen fish from MSC certified fisheries, and commitments of various nature by Carrefour, Target, the Dutch Retail Association, Marks & Spencer, Aldi, Lidl and Metro. MSC fish products are increasingly used in foodservice as well, including by Sodexo (the leading foodservice provider in North America and a major player elsewhere) and a small number of restaurant companies (MSC, 2010b).

Given the low level of competition from other sustainability standards in capture fisheries, in the rest of this section we focus on the internal dynamics of MSC to ascertain what key factors shaped its governance structure and the content of the MSC standard (question 1). This is accompanied by an analysis of how MSC played strategically in the field of 'best practice' development to minimize changes in its governance structure (question 2) and a discussion of the exclusionary consequences for Southern players (question 3).

Internal dynamics: governance structure and expert knowledge

One of the main reasons MSC managed to grow quickly and to maintain a quasi-monopoly in the market for sustainable fish certifications lies with the specific governance structure it developed. Even though MSC had been fashioned after the FSC, the latter is an open-member organization, while the MSC structure is significantly different and more corporate. FSC is governed by a General Assembly, where voting power is divided equally between Northern and Southern countries (Tamm Hallström and Boström, 2010). The FSC general assembly itself elects the Board of Directors that is accountable to FSC members. MSC was established as a foundation, but evolved to a multi-stakeholder organization. Its managerial structure was designed to insulate the Board of Trustees (whose members are nominated, not elected) from the political influence of civil society actors (Gale and Haward, 2004; 2011; Tamm Hallström and Boström, 2010). Gale and Haward (2011) argue that the WWF, having learnt from the FSC experience, decided to promote a less inclusive and more efficient governance structure for MSC that could keep up with a fast-moving business environment. This very insulation resulted in commercial success, but it also meant that MSC in its formative years was only partly responsive to the needs of Southern fisheries.

In 2000, MSC revised its governance structure. Alongside the Board of Trustees, its executive decision-making body, two groups reporting to it were created – the Technical Advisory Board and the Stakeholder Council, with the former being the most influential (see Tamm Hallström and Boström, 2010). This way, MSC moved towards a structure that is now more common among multi-stakeholder initiatives (usually including a board, one or more technical committees and a stakeholder council), but managed to do so without altering the overall top-down governance structure (the Board of Trustees is not elected and is not accountable to the Stakeholder Council) and by maintaining the predominance of certain fields of expert knowledge (and the equilibrium between them) over others. The Technical Advisory Board (which provides advice on technical, scientific and quasi-judicial issues to the Board of Trustees) includes 14 members: eight of these are fishery assessment and/or management scientist; the remaining are experts on chain of custody, certification and fish processing – no economists or other social scientists are members. The Stakeholder Council represents specific interests grouped under three categories represented by 32 individuals. The 'public interest' category has ten members, mostly from environmental groups, but also including a few donor representatives, academics and policy makers. The 'commercial and socio-economic category' includes 18 members, all from companies and industry associations (thus representing commercial interests, not broader civil society concerns). The third category, 'developing world' has only four members (three academics and a consultant).

The dominance of fishery management scientists and of marketing, logistics and chain of custody experts both in the formative years and in the configuration and consolidation of governance structures has allowed MSC to establish an internal balance between moderate environmentalism and commercial imperatives, at the cost of social/labour issues and of Southern interests. MSC has explicitly avoided being involved in the certification of socio-economic aspects of fisheries.

Strategic engagement in the formation of best practice in standards governance

In its formative years, MSC was able to grow without altering its corporate structure and tightly controlled field of participation because it was not subjected to pressure to adopt 'best practices' in standard governance. Such guidelines were developed some years after its establishment in 1996. But even in later years, MSC was able to apply governance reforms in narrow ways because it was itself strategically engaged in co-designing such best practices – in both capture fisheries and in social and environmental standards initiatives more broadly. While the MSC standard drew from the existing FAO Code of Conduct for Responsible Fisheries (FAO, 1995; see also Hosch *et al.*, 2011) in terms of content, 'best practices' in terms of due conduct and diligence in ecolabelling did not actually influence MSC – rather, best practices were themselves based on the MSC model (Willmann *et al.*, 2008). In 1998, FAO convened a technical consultation to develop guidelines for ecolabelling of fish with the objective of establishing basic principles to avoid discrimination of groups of producers and fisheries and to foster harmonization of criteria and procedures, and mutual recognition of different ecolabels. The final text of such guidelines was approved by FAO in 2005 (FAO, 2005).

What is interesting in this regard is that MSC in its standard development process actually ran foul of some of the key provisions that are now included in the guidelines – especially in relation to non-discrimination. First, having been established before the FAO guidelines, MSC does not obviously need to work retroactively on inclusivity and transparency in standard *setting*. Second, MSC has certified a very small number of developing country fisheries (see below). Yet, when MSC declared that its system would be fully consistent with the FAO guidelines,[2] only two organizational 'refinements' were deemed to be needed: separating the accreditation of certification bodies from MSC's standard setting functions; and creating independence between the objections process and the certification programme. Its recent adoption of a Risk-based Framework (RBF, see below) only allows some flexibility (and only in special circumstances) in interpreting developing country data within a largely unchanged certification system – thus MSC interpreted the opening provided by FAO guidelines for special treatment of developing country fisheries in a very narrow way.[3]

Another set of 'best practices' that applies to social and environmental standard governance more generally is the 'Code of Good Practice for Setting Social and Environmental Standards' by ISEAL. We examine this code here because MSC has been a key actor within ISEAL. ISEAL is an association whose members are social and environmental standard-setting and accreditation organizations. It aims at developing guidance for and strengthening the effectiveness and impact of these standards. Its roots stem from a meeting held in 1999 by MSC, FSC, the International Federation of Organic Agriculture Movements (IFOAM) and Fairtrade to discuss the possibility of closer collaboration among standard setting organizations. ISEAL has developed a code on standard setting, has just finalized a 'Code of Good Conduct for assessing the impacts of social and environmental standards' and has also started working on a 'Code of Good Conduct for verifying compliance with social and environmental standards'. These are voluntary codes that members comply with to meet a 'minimum bar' requirements in the respective areas of standard setting, impact assessment, and verification (see also Djama et al. this volume).

MSC needs to comply with the code on standard setting only when it revises its standard. MSC would not have been qualified as conforming to some of the provisions of the code at the time it developed its own standard. The code on impacts, finalized in 2010, tells managers of standard organizations how to set up a monitoring and evaluation process to assess whether they achieve their goals. Given the mixed record on attributing positive environmental impacts to the MSC standard (see Ponte, 2008), this could be seen as creating more problems for MSC than the code on standard setting. Yet, all the code on impacts demands is for managers to seek *improvements* in the effectiveness of their standard to achieve their goals and to improve the evaluation system itself. The code does not suggest in what timeframe goals and outcomes need to be reconciled, nor does it indicate what size gap between expectations and reality is acceptable.

Implications for Southern suppliers

As mentioned above, in the early years of operation MSC did not pay much attention to developing country needs (Constance and Bonanno, 2000; Ponte, 2008). Representatives from developing countries were only invited to one consultative meeting in London. Out of about ten workshops that were carried out to present the initiative to various fisheries, only one took place in a developing country (in an upper-middle income country where several large-scale industrial fisheries operate). As a result of the kind of standard that was developed within this context, by 2006 only three fisheries had been certified in developing countries and two fisheries were undergoing certification. All five fisheries were located in upper-middle income countries. As of early 2010, there were still only three developing country fisheries holding a certification (including a very small fishery in a low-income country), while only five developing country fisheries were undergoing certification. Almost half of all MSC certifications took place between January 2009 and March 2010, but much of this growth can be attributed to Nordic fisheries (some of which are of very large size, such as Norwegian herring).[4] Interestingly, these had fought against the establishment and growth of MSC in the 1990s and early 2000s.

In the mid-2000s, MSC did start to recognize that its standard and certification procedures were not geared towards the realities of developing country fisheries, especially small-scale and data-deficient ones. A special programme (MSC Developing World Fisheries Programme) was set up to improve the awareness of MSC in developing countries and to develop guidelines for the assessment of these fisheries. Under such a programme, MSC also started an initiative called 'Access for all fisheries' which includes the development of a 'Risk-based Framework' (RBF). The RBF aims at developing guidance for certifiers on the use of 'unorthodox' information on fisheries, such as traditional ecological knowledge. It aims at using a 'risk-based' approach to qualitatively evaluate fisheries when 'scientific' sources of information are not available. In 2007, this led to the approval by the MSC's Technical Advisory Board of the 'Guidelines for the assessment of small-scale and data-deficient fisheries'. The guidelines were piloted in seven small-scale data-deficient fisheries, six of which are based in developing countries (one of which has been subsequently certified).

MSC documentation clearly claims that the environmental 'bar' has not been lowered with the introduction of RBF.[5]

The RBF was then included in a new 'Fisheries Assessment Methodology' (FAM), the main aim of which was to simplify the assessment structure, minimize variability of application of the standard and streamline the fishery assessment process for all certification. The number of indicators was trimmed from 70 to 31 and fisheries using FAM have cut down their assessment period dramatically and face lower costs of certification (MSC, 2010c, p. 2). The application of the new FAM is likely to be one of the key factors behind the recent increase in the number of fisheries that obtained certification, but this has not altered the number of certified Southern fisheries so far.

Interim conclusions

The evidence summarized in this section suggests some partial conclusions that relate to the three questions posed in the introduction: (1) in a context of low external competition, MSC devised a standard that in terms of content can be seen as relatively 'high' on environmental issues, but that excludes social issues altogether; this was the result of a particular internal configuration of expert knowledge embedded in MSC's governance structure; (2) as an early mover in the realm of sustainability standards, MSC was not subjected to 'best practices' when it was writing the standard and setting up related institutional structures; it played a key role in later devising such best practice guidelines, and eventually applied a narrow interpretation in reforming its standard governance system; (3) a relatively high standard content led to the exclusion of the majority of Southern suppliers from certification.

Sustainability standard initiatives in cut flowers

The cut flower industry is a particularly interesting example of the proliferation of a multitude of standards which seek to regulate the social and environmental conditions of production, and thus it is an ideal case study to question some of the propositions of the parallelism literature highlighted in the introduction. The character of cut flower production and trade has set the frame for some highly criticized working conditions in the industry. The largest developing country exporters (Kenya and Colombia) in particular have been favourite targets for campaigns demanding better environmental and social conditions both locally and in Europe and North America. In 2006, developing countries supplied

22 per cent of EU imports of cut flowers and foliage and 60 per cent of US imports, and their share is increasing.

The seasonal nature of the cut flower trade, with demand peaking at European/US festivals such as Valentine's, Mother's day and Easter and lowest demand during the Northern summer, makes labour demand in production highly uneven. Seasonality is a major force behind the employment of large numbers of temporary workers at times of peak demand. The increase in sales to large retailers has further intensified the need for a flexible workforce to meet the ever-changing requirements of retailers, whose orders are often adjusted on the day of delivery (Hale and Opondo, 2005; Riisgaard, 2009a). The perishability of the product means that workers often have to work long hours to complete critical tasks such as harvesting and spraying, but it is the heavy use of chemicals that constitutes the main health hazard to workers and the surrounding environment and communities.

Differently from capture fish, the cut flower standards arena is characterized by a high level of competition among different initiatives. For this reason, in this section we focus on these external, rather than internal, dynamics to assess whether competition leads to a race to the bottom in terms of standard content (question 1). We also analyse which 'best practices' in standards governance have been adopted, to what extent, by whom and in what circumstances (question 2). Finally, we look at the implications of both for the exclusion or inclusion of Southern suppliers (question 3). We focus on standards that are present in the EU market, since this is where we see the largest proliferation of standards and thus patterns of competition and adoption of best practices can be analysed fruitfully.[6]

The dynamics of parallelism in a competitive standards market

The industry has reacted to the criticized working conditions in the South by adopting a range of parallel private social and environmental standard initiatives since the mid-1990s (see Table 1). Initially, the codes mostly covered technical issues such as chemical usage and environmental management. The social components of codes relating to workers' welfare and rights are a more recent addition (Barrientos et al., 2003). The majority of standard initiatives have been conceived and formulated in Europe, but in recent years a variety of initiatives have also been developed in producer countries and the US. Cut flower export trade associations in Kenya, Uganda, Zambia, Zimbabwe, Ethiopia, Ecuador and Colombia have all developed their own standards. In all, at least 20 different social and or environmental standards (international and national) exist for cut flower export (CBI, 2007; Riisgaard, 2007; 2009a).

Certification of growers to social and environmental standards is often a requirement from buyers and since different buyers demand different standards, it is not unusual for producers to hold multiple certifications. The flower sector is one where a large number of initiatives emerged in a relatively short period of time (mid 1990s–early 2000s), thus defining a context of high competition from the start both in relation to demand and supply. Complex arrangement and different types of cooperation have also developed with strong influence from best practice expectations on standard governance – especially from the early-2000s onwards.

The market share of certified flowers in the European market is much higher than for capture fish. A rough estimate is that between 50 per cent and 75 per cent of flowers imported into the EU adhere to one or more standards. Of the standards aimed at the EU, Milieu Programma Sierteelt (MPS), Global-GAP and retailer codes are by far the biggest in terms of number of producers certified. It is not known how many producers are certified to Global–GAP or retailer codes, but any producer exporting to British retailers will have to be certified. MPS has almost 4,000 certified growers – although most to their environmental or GAP schemes only, not their social standard. MPS is owned by the Dutch flower auctions and growers,[7] while Global-GAP was initiated by a group of large European retailers.[8] Those standards that are communicated through a consumer label comprise a much smaller proportion of the market.[9] However, the share of consumer labelled flowers has been rising quite rapidly over the past few years. The standards (aimed at the EU market) that communicate through a consumer label tend to be collective standards and include the Fairtrade Labelling Organizations International (FLO), Fair Flowers Fair Plants (FFP) and Flower Label Programme (FLP).

A first wave of standards that emerged in the flower industry was mainly set by buyers or producer groups and tended to focus on environmental issues, be weak on social concerns and rely mainly on internal monitoring. These included MPS (in 1995), FLP (in 1996), Kenya Flower Council (KFC) (in 1998), FlorVerde (in 1998) and several retailer codes.

However, the development in 1998 of two multi-stakeholder base codes, the International Code of Conduct for the Production of Cut Flowers (ICC) and the Ethical Trading Initiative (ETI), started to put pressure for higher social standards. The ICC was created by a coalition

Table 10.1 Social and environmental standards in cut flowers

Standard	Standard origin and type	Release	Characteristics	Cooperation dynamics
Selection of Northern industry standards				
GlobalGAP (flowers and ornamentals)	Coalition of European supermarkets. Business to business standard.	2003	Good agricultural practices with a small section on worker health, safety and welfare.	MPS-GAP, KFC and Florverde have been benchmarked and recognized as equivalent.
Milieu Programma Sierteelt (MPS)	Dutch growers and auctions. Business to business standard.	1995	Environmental management (MPS A, B, C) with optional social qualification MPS-SQ and MPS-GAP	MPS-SQ is based on the ICC code and MPS-GAP is benchmarked to Global-GAP. MPS-A + MPS-SQ benchmarked and accredited to FFP.
Fiore Giusto	Italian NGOs, unions, flower growers and exporters. Consumer label.	2007	Environmental certification system	Benchmarked to the ICC and accredited to FFP.
Selection of Southern industry standards				
Kenya Flower Council (KFC) Code of Practice	(KFC) Association of Kenyan flower exporters. Business to business standard.	1998	Environmental and social certification system	Benchmarked to Global-GAP. Has endorsed the HEBI code and has a recognition agreement with Tesco produce code from 2006.
FlorVerde	Asocoflores (association of Colombian flower growers). Consumer label.	1998	Environmental and social certification system.	Benchmarked to Global-GAP.

Continued

Table 10.1 Continued

Standard	Standard origin and type	Release	Characteristics	Cooperation dynamics
FlorEcuador	Expoflores (association of Ecuadorian flower growers). Business to business standard.	2005	Environmental and social certification system.	
Multistakeholder and NGO consumer labels				
The Fairtrade Labelling Organisation (FLO) (flowers and plants)	Fairtrade labelling organizations and fairtrade producer networks. Consumer label.	2006	Principles of fairtrade including a fairtrade premium administered by a joint body consisting of workers and management.	Until 2006, fairtrade flowers were certified by Max Havelaar requiring FLP or MPS-SQ certification.
Flower Label Program (FLP)	German importers and wholesalers, NGOs and trade unions. Consumer label	1996	Environmental and social certification system.	FLP was a business-to-business code between German importers and Ecuadorian producers In 1999 it turned into a multistakeholder label based on the ICC code.
Fair Flowers Fair Plants (FFP)	Union Fleurs (the International Floricultural Trade Association), NGOs and unions. Consumer label.	2005	Environmental and social labelling scheme.	Based on certification to standards equivalent of the ICC plus MPS-A.

Rainforest Alliance (flowers and ferns)	Environmental NGOs. Consumer label	2001	Certification system for conservation of biodiversity and sustainable livelihoods

Multistakeholder base codes (no certification system)

International Code of Conduct for Cut Flowers (ICC)	A coalition of European NGOs and the International Union of Food and Agricultural Workers (IUF)	1998	Base code with criteria on labour conditions and basic environmental criteria. Has guidelines on participatory implementation and monitoring.
The Ethical Trading Initiative (ETI)	An alliance of UK companies, NGOs and trade unions	1998	Social base code (not restricted to cut flowers).
The Horticultural Ethical Business initiative (HEBI)	Kenyan flower growers and labour NGOs	2003	Base code on social accountability for the flower industry based on the ETI and the ICC.

of European NGOs and unions and aims at guaranteeing that flowers have been produced under socially and environmentally sustainable conditions. It was influent on improving the social aspects of European standards for cut flowers. ICC formed the centrepiece of a campaign to regulate work and employment in flower production. Initially, importers in Germany were targeted, with success, to accept the ICC. Shortly after the German campaign, the Dutch MPS initiative was targeted and this led after several years of discussions to the development of the social module of MPS (MPS-SQ), which is also based on the ICC (Riisgaard, 2009a). Finally, a criterion for certification to the FFP label (see below) is conformity with the ICC.

The ETI is a UK initiative developed by a consortium of companies, trade unions and NGOs to promote and improve the implementation of corporate codes of practice which cover supply chain working conditions. Most UK supermarkets do not only have their own codes but are also members of the ETI. Supermarket members include: ASDA, the Co-Op Group, J Sainsbury, Marks & Spencer and Tesco. The ETI has been able to exert pressure on retailer codes, particularly in relation to having codes incorporate the ILO core conventions on labour rights. ETI was also instrumental in the establishment of the Kenyan multi-stakeholder code HEBI (the Horticultural Ethical Business Initiative) in 2003 (Hale and Opondo, 2005; ETI, 2005).

Thus, the ETI and ICC codes have formed the basis for the social content of a range of mainly European-based standards. Exceptions to this trend are standards that emerged in the US and the Global–GAP standard for flowers and ornamentals. But this is not too surprising, since US flower standards have not been subjected to the same pressure to raise social standards and Global–GAP product-specific standards are all modelled on the common GAP code.

Of particular interest in this context is the attempt to harmonize existing standards under a new consumer label named Fair Flowers Fair Plants (FFP). FFP was developed by Union Fleurs (the International Flower Trade Association uniting national producer, importer and traders organizations) with the collaboration of NGOs, labour unions and other standards initiatives, particularly MPS and the Flower Label Programme (FLP). FFP as a consumer label was launched in 2005 and is so far present in ten European countries in supermarkets, florists and flower chains. It has developed a new label which is based on existing standards that have been benchmarked to the criteria of FFP. To be able to sell under the FFP label growers need to be certified to a standard that is equivalent to both the ICC base code and to MPS-A (a Dutch environmental standard). This approach in theory makes it possible to unite different standard schemes while only communicating one harmonized label to the consumer.

From the beginning FFP has aimed at combining 'size' with 'principles', which is what MSC claims to have achieved in capture fisheries. But FFP has had to attempt that in a much more competitive situation. Their size strategy has been to campaign extensively among European flower outlets. As a result, success has been noticeable in relation to *demand* competition, with 197 traders and 4,227 sales outlets signing up to FFP. In terms of *supply* competition, the expectation was that multiple standards would benchmark to the FFP criteria and that FFP would be able to capture producers that were already certified to these other standards. This strategy, however, so far has only really succeeded with growers certified to MPS.[10] Thus, competition still characterizes the market for consumer labels for flowers in the EU market (FLO, FLP and FFP).

Overall, continuing competition in the market for standards for cut flowers has not led to a 'race to the bottom' in standard content – to some extent the contrary has happened with two influential base codes helping to raise the bar. Some standards organizations do prioritize size growth, while others do focus on raising the bar of standard content. But some standard initiatives clearly aim at achieving both size and a relatively high standard content. In particular relation to standards in cut flowers, the trend towards partial modularization/harmonization plays against a differentiation strategy, and in practice most standards are trying to capture the mainstream market, not just a niche.

Best practices and standards governance

As in other agro-food sectors, best practice pressure on standard governance arose from both outside and within the cut flower industry. The same two multi-stakeholder base codes that put pressure on improving the social content of standards (ETI and ICC), were also behind the pressure to adopt 'best practices' in standards governance – both in terms of promoting a multi-stakeholder form and in terms of participation and transparency. They affected mostly consumer labels, and especially those developed in the 2000s, but much less so business to business standards and codes including Southern grower association standards.

ETI was particularly active behind the establishment of the Kenyan HEBI social code. HEBI was formed because – despite the existence of initiatives that address labour standards on cut flower farms – a number of workers' rights violations persisted on these farms (ETI, 2005). The main problem seemed not to be the content of the standards, but the way in which compliance was assessed. At that time, many organizations were using their own auditors with little transparency or involvement of external, independent stakeholders. What set the HEBI standard apart from most other social standards are the detailed instructions concerning how to implement and audit the standard using participatory social auditing methods. The methodology also involves independent auditing and audit shadowing by (and in consultation with) civil society organizations (HEBI, 2005).

The HEBI code has been endorsed by both the Fresh Produce Exporters Association of Kenya (FPEAK) and the Kenya Flower Council (KFC), the two Kenyan business associations with flower grower members. However, it appears that the endorsement in practice does not entail adoption of the participatory auditing methodologies developed by HEBI. Indeed, the auditing procedures of the FPEAK and KFC standards remain modelled on international technical audit procedures, which are not participatory in nature. This way FPEAK, KFC and ETI retail members have been able to be seen as acting to redress civil society calls for more participatory governance structures while in practice not changing anything substantial. Moreover, recently HEBI seems to have ceased to function.[11]

The ICC includes guidelines aimed at making standard governance more inclusive and at ensuring meaningful participation of workers, local organizations and labour unions (ICC, 1998). Somewhat similar to the HEBI initiative, the participatory implementation and monitoring procedures were designed to secure that the standard would also have an effect on more embedded rights issues such as discrimination and freedom of association – issues where other standards had fallen short. In 1999, the Flower Label Programme (FLP) standard was turned from a business into a multi-stakeholder initiative aligned with ICC recommendations. And, unlike the case of the HEBI initiative, the ICC has been adopted in various standards initiatives with the inclusion of the participatory implementation and monitoring procedures – although in different variations. For example, MPS did this by creating MPS–SQ, an add-on which has its own participatory but separate governance structure and implementation procedures. It did so without changing either the governance structure, content or implementation procedures of MPS-A,B,C (the core MPS standard which is not optional). Overall, best practice pressure in the flower sector has resulted in more participatory governance structures among European standards with consumer labels but the larger business to business standards as well as Southern grower association standards have been only marginally affected.

Implications for Southern players

The experience of FFP suggests a story of a relatively demanding standard leading to Southern exclusion, along the lines of the MSC experience examined earlier in this chapter. In FFP, of the 159 flower growers certified in 2010, 134 are situated in the Netherlands and 27 in developing countries. Consequently 'scaling up' in this particular initiative has so far mainly reached Northern (particularly Dutch) workers and workplaces. Furthermore, before FFP came into existence there was a market (small but growing rapidly) for socially-labelled flowers, which the Dutch growers were not able to enter because of restrictions inherent in existing labelling schemes and because they are obliged to sell through the auctions where product differentiation by a label was not possible before the advent of FFP.[12] For European but particularly Dutch growers, FFP offers an opportunity to enter and compete in the market for flowers differentiated by a sustainability label, which earlier was restricted to Southern producers.

Other consumer labels for flowers are aimed exclusively or particularly at Southern producers and thus provide product differentiation opportunities specifically for Southern growers. One of these, the Flower Label Programme has 54 certified producers of which 47 are in developing countries. The label is aimed almost solely at the German florist market where it has around 3 per cent of market share.[13] The Fairtrade label for flowers is devoted exclusively to developing country producers and currently has 51 certified producers.[14] In relation to business to business standards, most Southern producers in the major exporting countries are certified to a national standard governed by the national grower associations. Some of these are benchmarked against Global–GAP[15] but even where the national standards are not benchmarked, many producers are GAP certified. The Dutch MPS standard currently has 117 certified Southern producers amounting to less than 3 per cent of the total number of certified farms (not too surprisingly since it was established as a standard for the Dutch flower industry).

Interim conclusions

The evidence summarized in this section suggests a second set of partial conclusions that relate to the three questions posed in the introduction: (1) continuing competition in the market for standards for cut flowers has not led to a 'race to the bottom' in standard content; some standards organizations have indeed prioritized size over growth, while others have focused on raising the bar of standard content; but other initiatives clearly aim at achieving both size and a relatively high standard content; (2) best practice pressures have resulted in more participatory governance structures in relation to consumer labels, but have not fundamentally affected larger business to business standards and Southern grower association standards; (3) one initiative (FFP) that has sought to raise the bar of standard content led to the inclusion of mainly Northern suppliers; other consumer labels are aimed exclusively or particularly at Southern producers, thus have not had exclusionary effects; and in business to business standards (which have a relatively 'low' standard content) many Southern producers in the major exporting countries have been able to successfully obtain certification.

Conclusion

In this chapter, we examined how 'governing through standards' takes place in two agro-food sectors of particular significance for developing countries – capture fish and cut flowers. In both sectors, developing country producers face not only increasingly demanding standards on environmental impact, social/labour issues, but also competition from Northern producers. We explored how competition (or lack thereof) in the market for standards, internal competition among different expert knowledge groups, and pressure from the establishment of 'best practices' in standard governance affect standard content, governance practices and the inclusion of Southern suppliers. We set out to question three main aspects arising in the existing literature on voluntary standards in the agro-food sector.

(1) We questioned whether competition among different standards matters in determining standard content, whether the general proliferation of standards is leading towards a 'race to the bottom' in standard content, and whether there is a clear-cut differentiation between different kinds of standard organizations in terms of principles and size. The analysis carried out in this chapter suggests that the level of competition in a market for standards does not seem to matter much. There is no sign of a general 'lowering of the bar' in terms of standard content, neither in the low-competition sector (capture fish) nor in the high-competition sector (cut flowers). In cut flowers, the base codes have actually helped raise the bar of standard content not only in niche markets but also in mainstream ones. There are also attempts to 'modularize' standards, so

that it is possible to build on a base code and then add modules on social conditions of production, and at developing comprehensive and mutually recognized standards with higher overall content. We have also shown that *internal* dynamics of competition within standard initiatives can be important. Due to space limitations, we could only carry out this kind of analysis in relation to MSC. Although MSC has avoided lowering its standard on environmental issues in the presence of low external competition, it did so in very specific ways. During its formative years of the late 1990s, MSC was able to achieve an internal equilibrium between environmental and commercial expertise and a fairly narrow representation that excluded social issues and meaningful Southern representation. At the very beginning, Unilever chose to work with WWF instead of Greenpeace in co-founding MSC exactly because it was more pragmatic and business friendly. MSC was able to insulate itself from more critical civil society pressure, shape its standard content to the need of Northern industrial fisheries, and market its label and certification system aggressively both with fisheries and buyers. It also resolutely fought any attempt to include social and labour issues in its standard. The recent adoption of a new 'Fishery Assessment Methodology' allowed MSC to claim a relatively high bar for its standard content while at the same time facilitating the achievement of more numerous and quicker certifications of (Northern) fisheries, thus catering to commercial concerns related to increased demand by retailers and processors for sustainable fish.

(2) We questioned whether there is an actual link between the spread of 'best practices' in standards governance and a 'race to the top' in terms of actual practice. We showed that the development of best practices in standards governance in the 2000s led to mostly cosmetic changes in first-generation standards. These standards in essence were able to avoid the 'stakeholder acrobatics' that newer standard initiatives need to go through (see Tamm Hallström and Boström, 2010; Cheyns this volume; Djama *et al.* this volume). Second-generation standards, and among these consumer labels especially, have had to adopt (or be seen to have adopted) best practices in standard governance more seriously. There are clear moves to make auditing more participatory, for example, but with limited uptake so far. Overall, best practice pressure in standards governance has affected mostly consumer labels, and especially those developed in the 2000s, but much less so business-to-business standards that are not communicated to the consumer. These latter standards are neither participatory in their governance structure nor in relation to implementation and monitoring procedures.

(3) We questioned whether a race to the top leads to positive outcome for the inclusion of Southern suppliers. Our conclusions on these points are more tentative, but still potentially disturbing. The case study of MSC suggests that relatively high standard content (and complex managerial requirements) led to the marginalization of Southern fisheries. In cut flowers, one of the higher-end standard labels on social and environmental conditions of production in cut flowers (FFP) has also mainly certified Northern producers and actually opened up Northern producer (particularly Dutch) participation in the market for 'fair' labelled flowers, where they now compete with Southern producers. This suggests that in markets where Northern and Southern producers compete, a higher standard content can be deleterious for the inclusion of Southern suppliers unless the standards specifically target certification of Southern producers and /or adopt specific measures to ensure inclusion.

Comparing two sectors with different levels of standard competition has allowed us to conclude that competition in the market for sustainability standards is not a problem *per se*. What is important is to understand how different levels and kinds of external competition, internal competition among different stakeholders, and best practice pressure are put into play with each other. This chapter has just started to scratch the surface of the complexity of this phenomenon. As sustainability standards proliferate in the agro-food and forestry sectors and move into the mainstream, important questions on standard content and governance remain unanswered, especially in relation to how they affect inclusion of Southern players. Further research is needed in this realm, covering a wider set of systematic comparisons of different sectors. What is also needed is a better understanding of whether there are intrinsic differences between designing and managing standards with a largely environmental focus (such as MSC) and those that are focused on (or have a substantial component of) social and labour issues.

Notes

We are most grateful to Stephanie Barrientos, Peter Gibbon and Allison Loconto for their useful comments on earlier versions of this chapter. Stefano acknowledges the support of the Danish Social Science Research Council and Lone the support of the Danish Development Research Council.

1   Other labels and certifications are either species-specific and/or location-specific (e.g. the Australian Southern Rocklobster Clean Green Program, the Salmon Safe label, the Flipper Seal of Approval for tuna, the Marine

Ecolabel Japan), or relate mainly to aquaculture, rather than capture fisheries (Global Aquaculture Alliance, GlobalGAP, various organic labels) (see Corsin *et al.* 2007). The only other existing label that includes capture fisheries (also from developing countries) is 'Friend of the Sea', but it is still small. Naturland is also developing a certification system for sustainable fisheries.

2 See 'Leader in fishery certification and eco-labelling announces 100 per cent consistency with UN guidelines', MSC Press release, available at http://www.msc.org/html/ni_241.htm.

3 The FAO Code of Conduct for Responsible Fisheries allows for special consideration to be given to small-scale fisheries (Para. 29) and for the use of less elaborate methods for stock assessment (Para. 32). They also recognize that there are management measures in small scale fisheries that can achieve adequate levels of protection even when there is uncertainty about the state of the resource (Para. 32) (FAO 2005). On the one hand, the wording of the FAO guidelines suggests that only *ad hoc* cases can be considered, not a *specific* verification system to be applied in developing countries (and/or to small-scale, data-poor fisheries in general). On the other hand, one could read parts of Para. 32 of the guidelines as a justification for adopting special standards (not only verification systems) in relation to specific cases.

4 See www.msc.org

5 See www.msc.org/about-us/standards/methodologies/fam/msc-risk-based-framework

6 Most standards are aimed either at the EU or the US market and the two sets of standards differ in history and content. While flower standards emerged in the mid 1990s for the EU market, standards aimed at the US flower market appeared later. Standards aimed at the US market are not very stringent on social issues but focus mainly on environmental concerns.

7 These farmers produce more than half the flowers sold in the EU. In February 1995, MPS turned into a national association of all the Dutch flower auction houses, the Federation of Agricultural and Horticultural Organizations, Netherlands and the Glasshouse Cultivation (http://www.my-mps.com/asp/page.asp?sitid=437).

8 Retailers sell an estimated 25–30 per cent of flowers in the EU (CBI, 2007).

9 No exact figures exist, but an estimate puts their market share between 5 per cent and 10 per cent depending on the country. This estimate is based on figures from the Flower Label Programme (which has a 3 per cent market share in Germany) as well as on estimates provided by representatives from Fairtrade Labelling Organization and Union Fleurs.

10 MPS was a key player in FFP from the beginning. Certification to an MPS-A equivalent standard is a condition for being benchmarked to FFP.

11 According to several board members, the performance and long term viability of HEBI is questionable, particularly due to lack of funds since external donors have pulled out. While the reasons for this are complex, according to civil society representatives from HEBI some actors are trying to eliminate HEBI slowly by not using it, by being reluctant to participate in meetings and by saying that they endorse HEBI while in practice only adopting small parts of it (Riisgaard, 2010).

12 The Dutch flower auctions (with an estimated 40 per cent market share of flowers in the EU) have since 2007 started indicating FFP certification at the clock front and in their supply systems. This is the first time that auction buyers are able to differentiate products that are certified to a consumer label (CBI 2007; Riisgaard 2009b).

13 Interview 2008 and www.fairflowers.de

14 http://www.fairtrade.net/annual_reports.html

15 It is not known how many cut flower producers are certified to GLOBAL-GAP globally, nor the percentage of Southern producers. But it should be noted that both KFC and Florverde has been benchmarked and recognized as equivalent.

References

Abbott, K. and Snidal, D. (2006) 'Nesting, Overlap and Parallelism: Governance Schemes for International Production Standards', Memo prepared for the *Alter-Meunier Princeton Nesting Conference*, Princeton, February.

Barrientos, S., Dolan, C. and Tallontire, A. (2003) 'A Gendered Value Chain Approach to Codes of Conduct in African Horticulture', *World Development*, 31, 1511–26.

Bernstein, A. (2001) 'Do-it-yourself labor standards: While the WTO dickers, companies are writing the rules', *Business Week*, 74.

Bernstein, S. and Cashore, B. (2007) 'Can non-state global governance be legitimate? An analytical framework', *Regulation & Governance*, 1, 347–371.

Blowfield and Dolan (2008) 'Stewards of virtue? The ethical dilemma of CSR in African agriculture', *Development and Change*, 39, 1–23.

Boots, M. (2008) 'Advancing the global marketplace for sustainable seafood: The Seafood Choices Alliance', in T. Ward and B. Phillips (eds) *Seafood Ecolabelling: Principles and Practice* (Oxford and Ames (IA): Wiley-Blackwell).

Busch, L. (2002) 'Virgil, Vigilance, and Voice: Agrifood Ethics in an Age of Globalization', *Journal of Agricultural and Environmental Ethics*, 16, 459–477.

Busch L. and Bain, C. (2004) 'New! Improved? The Transformation of the Global Agrifood System', *Rural Sociology*, 69, 321–46.

Cashore, B., Auld, G. and Newsom, D. (2004) *Governing through Markets: Forest certification and the emergence of non-state authority* (New Haven: Yale University Press).

CBI (2007) 'CBI Market Survey: The Cut Flowers and Foliage Market in the EU' (Rotterdam: CBI).

Constance, D. and Bonanno, A. (2000) 'Regulating the global fisheries: The World Wildlife Fund, Unilever, and the Marine Stewardship Council', *Agriculture and Human Values*, 17, 125–139.

Corsin, F., Funge-Smith, S. and Clausen, J. (2007) 'A qualitative assessment of standards and certification schemes applicable to aquaculture in the Asia–Pacific region', RAP Publication 2007/25. (Bangkok: Asia-Pacific Fishery Commission and FAO).

ETI (2005) 'Addressing labour practices on Kenyan flower farms', Report of ETI involvement 2002–2004. (Ethical Trading Initiative).

Fransen, L.W. and. Kolk, J.E.M (2007) 'Global Rule-Setting for Business: A Critical Analysis of Multi-Stakeholder Standards', *Organization*, 14(5), 667–684.

FAO, Food and Agriculture Organization (1995) *Code of conduct for responsible fisheries* (Rome: FAO).

FAO, Food and Agriculture Organization (2005) *Guidelines for the ecolabelling of fish and fishery products from marine capture fisheries* (Rome: FAO).

Gale, F. and Haward, M. (2004) 'Public accountability in private regulation: Contrasting models of the Forest Stewardship Council (FSC) and Marine Stewardship Council (MSC)', paper presented at the *Australasian Political Studies Association Conference*, University of Adelaide, 29 September – 1 October.

Gale, F. and Haward, M. (2011) *Global Commodity Governance: State Responses to Sustainable Forest and Fisheries Certification* (Basingstoke and New York: Palgrave Macmillan).

Gereffi G., Garcia-Johnson, R. and Sasser, E. (2001) 'The NGO-Industrial Complex', *Foreign Policy*, 125, 56.

Gibbon, P., Ponte, S. and Lazaro, E. (eds.) (2010) *Global Agro-Food Trade and Standards: Challenges for Africa* (Basingstoke and New York: Palgrave Macmillan).

Gupta, A. (2008) 'Transparency Under Scrutiny: Information Disclosure in Global Environmental Governance', *Global Environmental Politics*, 8(2), 1–7.

Hale A. and M. Opondo (2005) 'Humanising the Cut Flower Chain: Confronting the Realities of Flower Production for Workers in Kenya', *Antipode*, 37, 301–23.

Tamm Hallström, K.T. and Boström, M. (2010) *Transnational multi-stakeholder standardization: Organizing fragile non-state authority* (Cheltenham and Northampton (MA): Edward Elgar).

Hatanaka, M., Bain, C. and Busch, L. (2005)'Third-Party Certification in the Global Agrifood System', *Food Policy*, 30, 354–369.

HEBI (2005) 'Participatory Social Auditing. A guide for new auditors (2nd DRAFT) First edition February 2005'. Available at http://www.hebi.or.ke/pa-awareness.pdf

Henson S. and Humphrey, J. (2010) 'Understanding the Complexities of Private Standards in Global Agri-Food Chains as They Impact Developing Countries', *Journal of Development Studies*, 46, 1628–1646.

Henson, S. and Reardon, T. (2005) 'Private Agrifood Standards: Implications for Food Policy and the Agrifood System', *Food Policy*, 30, 241–253.

Hosch, G., Ferraro, G. and Failler, P. (2011) 'The 1995 FAO Code of Conduct for Responsible Fisheries: Adopting, implementing or scoring results?' *Marine Policy*, 35, 189–200.

ICC (1998) 'International Code of Conduct for the Production of Cut Flowers' http://www.flowercampaign.org/fileadmin/documenten-EN/code-en.pdf

Ingenbleek, P. and Meulenberg, M.T.G. (2006) 'The Battle Between "Good" and "Better": A Strategic Marketing Perspective on Codes of Conduct for Sustainable Agriculture', *Agribusiness*, 22, 451–473.

Klooster, D. (2005) 'Environmental Certification of Forests: The Evolution of Environmental Governance in a Commodity Network', *Journal of Rural Studies*, 21(4), 403–417.

Loconto, A. and Bush, L. (2010) 'Standards, techno-economic networks, and playing fields: Performing the global market economy', *Review of International Political Economy*, 17(3), 507–536.

Macdonald K. (2007) 'Globalising Justice within Coffee Supply Chains? Fair Trade, Starbucks and the Transformation of Supply Chain Governance' *Third World Quarterly*, 28, 793–812.

Mol, P.J.A. (2007) 'Boundless Biofuels? Between Environmental Sustainability and Vulnerability', *Sociologia Ruralis*, 47(4), 298–315.

MSC (2010a) 'MSC: Fishery commitment growing worldwide' (London: MSC).

MSC (2010b) 'MSC: Commercial commitment growing worldwide' (London: MSC).

MSC (2010c) 'MSC Annual Report 2008/09' (London: MSC).

Muradian, R. and Pelupessy, W. (2005) 'Governing the Coffee Chain: The Role of Voluntary Regulatory Systems', *World Development*, 33(12), 2029–2044.

Mutersbaugh, T. (2005) 'Fighting Standards with Standards: Harmonization, Rents, and Social Accountability in Certified Agrofood Networks', *Environment and Planning A*, 37, 2033–51.

NRC (1995) 'Standards, Conformity Assessment and Trade', Washington DC: National Research Council.

O'Rourke, D. (2006) 'Multi-stakeholder Regulation: Privatizing or Socializing Global Labour Standards?', *World Development*, 34, 899–918.

Pattberg, P.H. (2007) *Private Institutions and Global Governance: The New Politics of Environmental Sustainability* (Cheltenham: Edward Elgar).

Ponte, S. (2008) 'Greener than thou: The Political Economy of Fish Ecolabeling and its Local Manifestations in South Africa', *World Development*, 36(1), 159–175.

Power, M. (1997) *The Audit Society: Rituals of Verification* (Oxford: Oxford University Press).

Raynolds, L. (2004) 'The Globalisation of Agrofood Networks', *World Development*, 32(5), 725–34.

Raynolds L.T., Murray, D. and Heller, A. (2007) 'Regulating Sustainability in the Coffee Sector: A Comparative Analysis of Third-party Environmental and Social Certification Initiatives', *Agriculture and Human Values*, 24, 147–63.

Riisgaard, L. (2007) 'What's in it for Labour? Private Social Standards in the Cut Flower Industries of Kenya and Tanzania', *DIIS Working Paper* 2007/16 (Copenhagen: Danish Institute for International Studies).

Riisgaard, L. (2009a) 'Global Value Chains, Labor Organization and Private Social Standards: Lessons from East African Cut Flower Industries', *World Development*, 37, 326–340.

Riisgaard L. (2009b) 'How the market for standards shapes the market for goods: sustainability standards and value chain governance in the cut flower industry', *DIIS Working Paper* 2009/07 (Copenhagen: Danish Institute for International Studies).

Riisgaard L. (2010) 'The political economy of private social standards in the cut flower industry', in P. Gibbon, E. Lazaro and S. Ponte (eds) *Global Trade and Agro-food Standards: Challenges for Africa* (Basingstoke and New York: Palgrave Macmillan).

Sutton, M. and Wimpee, L. (2008) 'Towards sustainable seafood: The evolution of a conservation movement' in T. Ward and B. Phillips (eds) *Seafood Ecolabelling: Principles and Practice* (Oxford and Ames (IA): Wiley-Blackwell).

Swinnen, J.F.M. (ed.) (2007) *Global supply chains, standards and the poor. How the globalization of food systems and standards affect rural development and poverty* (Wallingford: CABI).

Utting, P. (2005) 'Corporate Responsibility and the Movement of Business', *Development in Practice*, 15, 375–88.

Willman, R., Cochrane, K. and Emerson, W. (2008) 'FAO Guidelines for eco-labelling in wild-capture fisheries', in T. Ward and B. Phillips (eds) *Seafood Ecolabelling: Principles and Practice* (Oxford and Ames (IA): Wiley-Blackwell).

11
The Local Instrumentality of Global Standards: How Mexican Indigenous Communities Use FSC Certification to Foster a Furniture Production Network

Dan Klooster

Introduction

According to common narratives, the North-South dynamics of certification are mainly determined by the decisions of actors rooted in the North, especially standard-setting bodies and the Northern retailers which dominate commodity chain governance. Even certification systems such as organic and Fair Trade, in which Southern stakeholders were initially influential, are said to become increasingly determined by Northern standard setters and buyers as certification becomes more mainstream. In this chapter, in contrast, I argue that global certification systems affect Southern production in complex ways, with outcomes that are shaped by conjunctural events and the agency of actors in specific regions. In Mexico, forest certification helped bring together conservationist and developmentalist organizations in a national network promoting both better forest management and better business management through improved production processes. In the Southern Mexican state of Oaxaca, forest certification also created possibilities for network formation. It helped bring together community forest enterprises, NGOs, government agencies, small carpentry workshops and local consumers in the shared tasks of sound forest management, rural development and socio-environmentally preferable consumption. In this case, third-party certification governs production by creating a category of 'sound forest managers' which helps to enrol disparate actors in a network promoting sound forest management, rural development and furniture production.

Forest certification as governance

About 8 per cent of the world's forests have been certified by the Forest Stewardship Council (FSC) and by the Programme for the Endorsement of Forest Certification schemes (PEFC), the two major certification systems. A number of minor certification systems covered a few more million ha of forests. By June 2010, 225 million ha of forests were certified under the PEFC system and 134 million ha under the FSC system, with about 3 million ha certified by both systems. FSC is the main system in the global south. Only Chile has more PEFC certified forests than FSC certified forests and in most Southern countries, PEFC is absent (Oliver and Kraxner, 2009. Environmental organizations prefer the FSC over the PEFC, which is usually perceived as an industry-led alternative to the more rigorous FSC (Gale, 2002; FERN, 2004).

Previous analyses have pointed out first, that forest certification governs production directly, through the application of standards, and second, that forest certification is a governance tool used by actors in commodity networks, especially retailers in buyer-driven commodity networks seeking a 'hands-off' mechanism for managing their supply chains (Bass *et al.*, 2001; Morris and Dunne, 2004; Klooster, 2005, 2006; Newsom *et al.*, 2006; Stringer, 2006). A third view, that certification creates possibilities for the formation and maintenance of production networks, is more recent.

From the first perspective, forest certification governs production because it standardizes the practices managers apply to their forests. The FSC emerged as an international organization in 1993, with members from forest industries, social groups and environmental organizations. These stakeholders eventually agreed to ten core principles and 56 criteria that inform FSC management standards, including a growing number of national and regionally-specific interpretations of these principles and criteria (FSC, 2002, 2008). Basically, the standards prohibit conversion of forests to other land uses, require that the rights of workers and indigenous peoples be respected, and require the identification and management of culturally important sites, sacred sites and high conservation value forests. Independent, accredited auditing firms inspect management plans, visit forests and consult stakeholders such as forest workers, surrounding communities and environmental authorities to determine if management upholds the FSC standards. Corrective Action Requests (CARs) specify actions required to demonstrate compliance with the standards. Annual audits monitor compliance with CARs and continued adherence to the FSC's principles and criteria (see public summaries posted to SmartWood, 2009; Newsom *et al.*, 2006; Mutersbaugh and Klooster, 2010). Auditors also issue chain of custody (COC) certificates to wood processing firms allowing them to label the products they manufacture from certified wood.

Forest certification standards move producers towards better environmental and social practices. Unfortunately, it is not always clear that certification provides forest managers with benefits commensurate with costs. Although governments, NGOs and even wood buyers sometimes subsidize certification costs under the FSC model, forest managers are responsible for the costs of inspections, audits, complying with CARs and modifying their forest management practices.

In the second perspective, forest certification becomes a governance tool used by actors in a commodity chain, or network. For scholars examining the political economy of production along global commodity chains, governance helps explain coordination in commodity production. Frequently, powerful firms dominate specific stages of production and shape the behaviour of their upstream suppliers and/or downstream retailers. Understanding these governance structures becomes increasingly important as systems of production become globally fragmented and less affected by the regulation of nation states (Gereffi, *et al.*, 2005).

When production processes are conceptualized to include both furniture manufacturers and fashion magazines (Leslie and Reimer, 2003), or supermarkets and ethical campaigners (Freidberg, 2004), or forest product retailers and environmental campaigners (Klooster, 2005), the concept of governance becomes more diffuse. Standards, codes and certification systems increasingly regulate ethical business practice in such networks (Mutersbaugh, *et al.*, 2005; Klooster, 2006; Hughes, *et al.*, 2008). Forestry is no exception. Midst, economic globalization and social movements expressing concerns over deforestation and the rights of forest-dwelling peoples, Forest Stewardship Council certification contributes to reshaping the regulatory context of forestry and creating 'new dynamics of international forestry production, trade and investment' (Stringer, 2006, p. 703). Environmentalist organizations have frequently pressured influential retailers such as B&Q and Home Depot to carry certified wood products by threatening to associate their brand names with forest destruction (Conroy, 2007; Klooster, 2005).

Eager to protect brand names, retailers required their suppliers to certify. Similarly, the WWF organized big retailers and wood processors to form buyers groups, later called Global Forest and Trade Networks, and these became important sources of demand for certified wood products (Bass, *et al.*, 2001; Taylor, 2005).

In these cases, certification is an instrument of retailer power because it outsources supply chain management procedures in a way which makes producers responsible both for making expensive changes in management and also for documenting and validating those changes. Home Depot, for example, proudly points out the number of suppliers it has brought into the FSC system, and IKEA will accept FSC certification as evidence of meeting its own corporate responsibility standards. In South Africa, B&Q pushed its suppliers to certify their forests (Morris and Dunne, 2004; Klooster, 2005, 2006). In such cases, powerful retailers protect their brands from association with forest destruction through a mechanism that shifts costs of compliance and verification onto producers who receive no guarantees of sales or better prices. Other actors in the network may also drive forest managers to certify. Certification is a requirement for communities to hold forest management concessions in buffer zones of the Maya Biosphere Reserve in Guatemala, for example (Finger-Stich, 2003).

Both of these perspectives suggest that Southern forest managers are likely to face significant barriers to certification, and may bear disproportionate costs from it. Compared to most Northern regions, Southern forest management practices tend to be less bureaucratized, less paper-intensive, therefore more likely to incur documentation costs in the process of becoming certified. In addition, since the South tends to have greater biodiversity than the North, Southern management areas are more likely to have High Conservation Value forests requiring additional management specifications. Most Southern forest producers are relatively marginal to Northern markets; Northern forests supply most of the North's demand for forest products and 75 per cent of the chain of custody certifications given to wood processing firms are in Europe, the US and Canada (FSC, 2010).

Not surprisingly, rates of adoption of forest certification in the South are lower than in the North. About 80–90 per cent of certified forests are in the northern hemisphere, where two thirds of the world's roundwood is produced. Western European countries have certified 53 per cent of their total forest area, North America 38 per cent, Oceania 5 per cent, and Africa, Asia and Latin America only about 1 per cent each (Oliver and Kraxner, 2009). Most certified forests are temperate and boreal;

tropical and subtropical forests make up only 13 per cent of the certified area (FSC, 2010).

In an emerging third view, certification facilitates network formation and maintenance, with contingent and site-specific results. For Eden (2009), forest certification supports the work of network governance, where governance is understood as a shift from government regulation to network regulation with various actors creating new spheres of authority and new mechanisms to provide and maintain public goods. In Eden's analysis, the FSC forms a 'credibility alliance' across environmentalist, forester, policy and business spheres. This work points out the constantly provisional character of the network giving legitimacy and efficacy to forest certification. Environmental governance depends on the continued commitment of disparate actors (Eden, 2009). Similarly, for Klooster (2010), debates over changes to FSC standards are constrained by tradeoffs between rigour of the standard, legitimacy to consumers and environmental NGOs, and acceptability of the standards to forest managers (Klooster, 2010). Once established, however, certification practices and labels accomplish work in production networks; they enable scientific knowledge and best practices in forestry to travel across geographical space and between wood producers, manufacturers and consumers, with network effects (Eden, 2009).

Studies of the governance role of forest certification are needed in specific regions. Eden's (2009) work suggests the utility of understanding how network actors use the 'boundary object' of certification in their own work, and this requires regional specificity. There is also the question of rural development in the global South, with its inter-related questions of livelihood, cultural diversity and the maintenance of biological diversity. The ways in which ethical campaigning and media attention are regionally embedded means that that there is a great deal of spatial variation in the ways in which these factors affect production network governance (Hughes, *et al.*, 2008). How do ethical claims help to govern production networks in places like Mexico? In the case of Oaxaca, for example, how do community forest management organizations use of certification to make the conservation implications of their production visible, to build networks, and to promote their community forestry enterprises?

To answer these questions, I consulted an extensive literature on the growth and impact of certification in Mexico, and conducted extensive open-ended, often repeated, interviews and observations among community forestry enterprises, community members and managers, NGOs and government officials, using a snowball sampling strategy, during almost a year of residence in the city of Oaxaca, southern Mexico, in 2007 and 2008.

Creating space for community forestry in Mexico: the role of certification

In Mexico, FSC certification has been part of a broader campaign to maintain economic space for community forestry as a viable strategy for conservation and rural development. Community forest management often produces rates of forest conservation that are higher than for protected areas in the same region (Klooster, 2003; Bray *et al.*, 2007, 2009), and much higher than non-managed forests which are often beset by illegal logging, forest fires and conversion to agriculture. This observation is consistent with the perspective of productive conservation, which holds that activities such as community forestry are an effective avenue for forest conservation because they encourage the active participation of forest inhabitants in the conservative management of a resource that is valuable to them.

Productive conservation is especially important in Mexico, where most forests belong to *ejidos* and agrarian communities, in which village members own forests and range lands as collective property. These *comuneros* and *ejidatarios* have the legal authority to appoint communal presidents and other representatives and to manage their common property lands in accord with federal regulation and the agreements of their village assemblies. Forest communities typically have few productive assets other than their forests; community forestry is also important because it provides income, rural employment and produces local social capital. It is an important rural development strategy which also conserves forests.

Initially, Mexican advocates of the community forestry sector became interested in certification in the early 1990s, when the North American Free Trade Agreement (NAFTA) was imminent and it was feared that imports would displace community forest producers after market liberalization. Certification, it was hoped, would create a niche for forestry in the same way that organic and fair trade had created a niche for Mexican coffee growing cooperatives. Government and NGO promoters hoped that certification would mitigate the trade deficit in forest products, provide access to export markets at premium prices, play a role in decreasing illegal logging, and improve community organization for forestry (Anta Fonseca, 2004; Gerez Fernández and Alatorre-Guzmán, 2005; Taylor, 2005; Klooster, 2006). The productive conservation implicit in certification especially appealed to pro-campesino NGOs and grassroots organizations because preservationist groups wanted to expropriate community lands to declare nature reserves. (Interview with Yolanda Lara, of the NGO Estudios Rurales y Asesoria (ERA A.C.) 8 November 2007.)

One of the first NGOs to promote certification in Mexico was the Consejo Civil Mexicano de la Silvicultura Sostenible (CCMSS), a Mexican NGO formed with support from multilateral donors to promote the community forestry sector within Mexico. The CCMSS organized some of the earliest Mexican evaluations in Oaxaca and the Yucutan peninsula in 1994. In 1997, a national union of community forestry organizations (UNOFOC, Unión Nacional de Organizaciones de Forestería Comunal A.C.) promoted certification to community leaders, foresters, and government officials. Using funds from a small grant from the North American Fund for Environmental Cooperation (NAFEC), a NAFTA parallel organization, UNOFOC funded evaluations in *ejidos* in several regions of Mexico. In 1999, using development assistance from the UK and Swiss governments, the Mexico office of the World Wide Fund for Nature (WWF) financed certifications as part of their campaign to support community forest stewardship in Mexico. The InterAmerican Foundation, the Ford Foundation, the MacArthur Foundation, Packard, WWF and the German, and UK agencies for technical cooperation (GTZ and DFID) also contributed to certification in Mexico between 1995 and 2001 (Madrid and Chapela, 2003; Anta Fonseca, 2004). In a few cases in Northern Mexico, private companies promoted the certification of their wood suppliers. Various sectors of the Mexican government also supported certification. Starting in 1998, the Proyecto de Conservación y Manejo Sustentable de Recursos Forestales en México (PROCYMAF), a programme of the Mexican Government partly funded by World Bank loans, promoted certification, as did several state governments and the federal government's Programa Nacional de Desarrollo Forestal (PRODEFOR), which covered many of the costs associated with certification.

Communities adopted certification for a variety of reasons, including community interests in having an external review of their professional forest managers, intrinsic desires to improve forest management, and expectations for more favourable treatment from government agencies. To a large extent, however, forest managers were disciplined by hope. They adopted forest certification and complied with its standards with the hope of seeing economic benefits (Klooster, 2006). Following steady growth over the course of a decade, a significant minority of communities in Mexico adopted forest certification. By 2009, 31 operations managing over 707,000 ha of forests were certified under the FSC system (Rainforest Alliance, 2009). Certification had little direct impact on market share or prices, however. Initially, there was almost no domestic demand for certified wood. Although there was a growing demand for certified wood in European and US markets, community forest enterprises faced significant hurdles in accessing these markets. Some Northern Mexico communities were able to sell some of their highest quality certified pine boards to be used as moulding by companies participating in supply chains for US companies, but elsewhere, especially in Oaxaca, forest communities were usually unable to meet buyers' demands for large volumes, stringent physical quality standards such as humidity, prompt delivery and low prices (Klooster, 2005, 2006).

Meanwhile, community forestry continued to be threatened by competition from cheap imports and from illegally harvested wood, which undercut prices for responsible producers who have higher costs due to investments in forest management, compliance with regulations, and taxes (Zuñiga and CCMSS, 2007a, 2007b; Zuñiga, 2009). Even in the legal market, relatively high costs of logging and transportation also make Mexican wood much more expensive than Chilean imports (Barrera, 2007). Imported Chinese furniture sells cheaply even in geographically isolated places like Oaxaca (Martinez, 2008).

To address the limited economic benefits from certification, community forest advocates and promoters in government and NGOs attempted to facilitate the market benefits of certification in various ways. With funding from USAID, philanthropic organizations, and private companies, the international environmental NGO, Rainforest Alliance, created the international programme TREES (Training, Extension, Enterprises and Sourcing) to help certified communities and businesses in marketing their forest products and improving business skills and production practices. Especially where price premiums for certified wood are missing, TREES helped certified community forest enterprises benefit from certification with technical assistance to help them add value to their wood harvest. It promoted value-adding activities such as reducing waste, finding uses for waste wood, developing better administrative procedures, training workers in better milling practices, improving board classification procedures, increasing the efficiency of wood transformation, and searching for new market opportunities (Interview with Juan Manuel Barrera, director of TREES for the state of Durango, 21 November 2007; see also Klooster, 2006).

Programs such as the World Bank Community Forestry Project (Procymaf), the Value Chain Programme (Cadenas Productivas) of the National Forest Commission, and state rural development agencies also invested directly in various aspects of forest-linked production chains. These agencies worked independently, often giving preference to certified producers, to make sector-wide investments to improve the physical quality of wood. For example, they helped fund the installation of wood drying kilns to control humidity and reduce the subsequent warping of boards. They also took steps to improve the managerial capacity of communities by promoting the professionalization of management. Meanwhile, the Mexican office of Greenpeace lobbied the federal government to induce domestic demand through preferred government purchases.

Certification helped make visible the conservation value of well-managed forestry; so it played a role in fostering a national network that promotes production among certified community forestry agencies. Certification helped to create a network with members as disparate as Mexican Greenpeace, the World Bank, USAID, Mexican federal and state forestry departments, international environmental NGOs like the WWF and the Rainforest Alliance, local NGOs, forest communities, and even domestic businesses with an interest in export markets.

In the Southern Mexican state of Oaxaca, certification also aided the formation of a similar network. This regional case more clearly shows the importance of associated events and the active roles of community forest management organizations in forming a network and using it to develop wood furniture manufacturing capacity in Southern Mexico.

Certification and network building in community furniture production in Oaxaca

Oaxaca is a state about the size of Switzerland, with 3.5 million inhabitants, many of whom are indigenous peoples of more than a dozen different ethnic groups. Rates of rural poverty are generally high. A state rich in forests of pine, it exports boards and imports furniture. It is also a leader in community forestry. About 130 communities and *ejidos* had logging permits in 2005 (Gobierno de Oaxaca, 2007). Many of these are successful at managing their forests well while providing employment and income for their communities and regions. Some of these communities have adopted a business-oriented management style with professional business managers who serve at the will of communities. Many of these communities face multiple barriers to regional and national competitiveness, especially those that produce low volumes of wood, have sporadic production, or high extraction costs due to remoteness, topography and limited infrastructure. Many also manage their businesses using a traditional *cargo* system in which a community member is elected to a poorly compensated or unpaid management position for a short period of time – often a year or two. These conditions make it difficult to maintain stable business relationships with private businesses or other community forest enterprises, or to maintain a long-term strategy of improving infrastructure and worker skills.

Nevertheless, over more than a quarter century of community forestry, many communities have acquired and learned to operate sawmills, although most of these use outdated equipment and have room for improvements in sawmill efficiency and board quality. A few communities have acquired state-of-the-art sawmills, resin distilleries and furniture factories. Oaxaca communities have also taken on greater forest management responsibility over time and have improved their forest management skills and practices. Oaxaca is now a leader in forest certification, with nearly a dozen community forest enterprises certified, or in the process of getting certification, contributing about 10 per cent of the volume of wood legally harvested in the state.

Certification in Oaxaca can be said to govern forest production directly through the application of standards, because it leads to modifications in forest management practices. Frequently, auditing firms award certification with requirements – called Corrective Action Requests (CARs) – that specific management improvements be made within a given timeframe. Most certifications in Oaxaca were accompanied by 10 or more CARs. These CARs require communities to modify their forest management plans to take into account the needs of threatened and endangered species, to map priority areas for conserving animal habitat, and to establish procedures to monitor species diversity as logged sites regenerate (see public summaries posted to SmartWood, 2010; Mutersbaugh and Klooster, 2010).

Certification did not create immediate markets, however. Certified communities sold their logs and boards to the same kinds of clients at the same prices as before (Klooster, 2006). Furthermore, when promoters connected certified communities with export markets, low volumes, physical requirements, lack of infrastructure and high prices precluded sales. Certification did not play a role in buyer-driven governance in Oaxaca. Oaxaca is not currently part of global value chains for wood products.

Faced with a deficient market for certified wood, community forest advocates and promoters in government and NGOs attempted to facilitate the market benefits of certification. Oaxaca NGOs such as ERA A.C. attempted to coordinate a number of community forest enterprises in order to meet high-volume orders, but was unsuccessful. A federal rural development programme, Alianza para el Campo, funded 14 million pesos worth of sawmill and woodkilns in 2003, disproportionately among Oaxaca's certified communities (Interview with Pedro Vidal Garcia Perez, former communal president, government forest sector promoter, and Mexican TREES director, 14 April 2008). TREES came to Oaxaca in 2004 and provided technical assistance to help certified forest managers add value to their wood harvest by utilizing unused wood, by developing better administrative procedures, by training workers in better milling practices, by improving board classification procedures, by increasing the efficiency of wood transformation and by searching for market opportunities. For example, with the support of consultants from TREES, one small Oaxaca community increased its sawmill efficiency from 154 to 193 board feet per cubic meter of wood entering the sawmill. Processing efficiency also increased, from 2,500 to 4,500 board feet per day (Interview with Juan Manuel Barrera, Durango TREES director, 21 November 2007). Certified communities often received preferential access to government and NGO financing for capital equipment and skills improvement.

By 2005, investments in logging enterprises, forest management, wood-drying kilns and the evolution of managerial capacity left a handful of communities ready to try furniture manufacture. Ixtlan de Juarez had recently invested in a door-making factory, which could also be used for furniture manufacture. Pueblos Mancomunados was also beginning to make furniture using refurbished equipment in an improvised, but flexible industrial space. Ixtlan's forests had been certified for several years. Although Pueblos Mancomunados was traditionally a logging community, it was not at the time working its forests due to a dispute with one of its eight member communities, and was not certified. It purchased certified wood from other indigenous communities, however.

Ixtlan was the first community with furniture manufacturing capacity, but it needed demand for its product. The Oaxaca office of the governor and the state forestry department came together with Ixtlan and Pueblos Mancomunados to develop a market for wooden school furniture produced in Oaxaca. Governor Ulises Ruiz had campaigned with the promise of forest sector development, and so there was a confluence of factors (Interview with Alberto Belmonte, business manager for Ixtlan de Juarez. 25 February 2008). The school furniture contract was an initiative of the three communities and Rainforest Alliance, which includes staff from Smartwood and TREES, but the governor made it happen. Certification was a selling point (Interview with Pedro Vidal Garcia Perez Mexican TREES director, 14 April 2008).

Beginning in 2005, the governor's office facilitated a contract with the state department of education (Instituto Estatal de Educación Pública de Oaxaca-IEEPO) for school furniture produced in Oaxaca from Oaxacan wood, displacing the annual purchases of steel and plastic furniture manufactured outside the state. At the insistence of people in the state small business section of the state Secretariat of the Economy (Pequenas y Medianas Empresas – PYME), the contract was divided between the community forestry sector and the Association of Furniture Making Firms of Oaxaca (Asociacion Oaxaquena de Empresas Fabricantes de Muebles – AOEFM). Most of the association's members are small firms comprising independent family carpentry workshops which joined together to improve their administrative processes, to participate in the school furniture contract and to become eligible for PYME funding programmes. State and federal PYME programmes provided 20 million pesos of financing to the 13 member firms of the association, each composed of a half dozen or more carpenter partners.

The exact distribution of the school furniture contract is set by a committee that includes the state agriculture and forest development agency (SEDAF), the IEEPO, the teachers' union, and both the Oaxaca and Federal Secretariats of the Economy. At first, the community forestry sector was composed of the communities of Ixtlan and Pueblos Mancomunados. In 2006, however, a third community forest enterprise, Textitlan, acquired furniture-making ability with a custom-built furniture factory. The school furniture contract was then divided 20 per cent for Ixtlan, 20 per cent for Pueblos Mancomunados, 10 per cent for Textitlan, and 50 per cent for the carpentry firms of the Association of Oaxacan Furniture Making Firms. In 2007, the volume of furniture ordered was reduced again, and divided the same way.

The three communities took the first step towards forming a consortium during a period of crisis in 2006, a major event in the history of network evolution. During that second year of the school furniture contract, the city of Oaxaca became convulsed in social protest against the governor and his actions to suppress a strike of teachers. Hundreds of barricades fragmented the city and the communities were unable to deliver furniture to the state education department. Months passed and the conflict showed no signs of ending. Desperate, they decided to make other kinds of furniture and look for other markets (Interview with Manuel Garcia Ignacio Nunez, Pueblos Mancomunados furniture factory manager, 21 April 2008).

The communities agreed to open an outlet store literally across the street from a barricade, in a building newly available for rent near the Oaxaca City offices of Pueblos Mancomunados. The initial relationship was a gentleman's agreement between the business managers of the three community forest enterprises. Production lines were re-arranged to produce residential furniture using many of the parts already manufactured for school furniture. The three factories coordinated their production to offer various lines of dining room, living room, kitchen, bedroom and office furniture. TIP eventually became the registered brand name for furniture based on the first letters of the names of its members: the zapotec communities of Textitlan, Ixtlan, and Pueblos Mancomunados (Interview with Manuel Garcia Ignacio Nunez, Pueblos Mancomunados furniture factory manager, 21 April 2008). There was also concern about the growing importance of the potential competition from the organized carpenters, who were receiving support from the Secretariat of the Economy and competing for the school furniture contract (Interview with Pedro Vidal Garcia Perez, TREES director 14 April 2008).

After several months of successful sales, the communities decided to formalize their relationship through an *integradora*, a kind of legal consortium designed to raise the competitiveness of small and medium sized businesses by providing services to its members such as financing, financial administration, marketing, joint purchasing, and joint sales (PYME n.d.). The Integradora Comunal Forestal de Oaxaca S.A. de C.V. (ICOFOSA) was legally formed in February 2007. It brings community forests, community sawmills, community furniture factories, factory outlet stores, and a brand name under integrated administration (Figure 11.1).

Through their *integradora*, the communities share their knowledge and varying areas of expertise. They also reduce the costs of experimenting, because the risk of new activities is divided by three. Furthermore, the consortium has the capacity to respond to high-volume orders from major retailers. In addition, the *integradora* is a liaison between the communities and government agencies; it is effective in accessing government funding opportunities. ICOFOSA applied for funding from the national forest commission and Procymaf for market studies and training for sales personnel, for example. Based in part on the results of those studies, ICOFOSA opened two more TIP stores in Oaxaca.

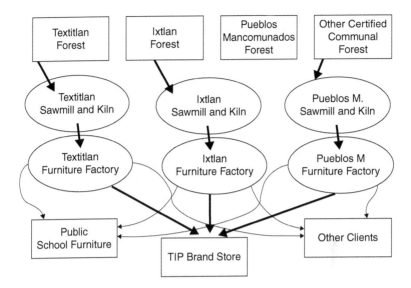

Figure 11.1 The ICOFOSA consortium linking certified communal forests to a shared furniture brand and retail outlet

Not shown are the sales of boards, which continue to provide the main source of revenue for each communal forest enterprise. Due to an internal conflict between its member communities, Pueblos Mancomunados does not currently log its own forests, but instead buys wood from other certified community forest enterprises in Oaxaca.

The administrative council of ICOFOSA consists of a president, initially the Pueblos Mancomunados business manager, a treasurer, initially the business manager of Ixtlan de Juarez, and a secretary, initially the business manager of Santiago Textitlan. Store managers and salespeople were then hired. In this way, ICOFOSA brings together business operations of three large indigenous communities. Santiago Textitlan has 4,000 inhabitants and 650 *comuneros*. Forestry there directly provides 250 jobs. In Ixtlan de Juarez, there are 4,500 inhabitants and 384 *comuneros*. Forestry directly provides 284 jobs. Pueblos Mancomunados is a commonwealth of eight communities comprising 15,000 inhabitants and 1,200 *comuneros* where forestry directly provides 300 jobs. *Comuneros* are community members formally vested with rights of voice and voting in the community assemblies which make decisions about the use of communal resources, including the forests they own collectively. Assuming five family members per *comunero*, ICOFOSA directly benefits 11,170 rural Oaxacans.

Communities are independent within ICOFOSA. Individually, communities continue the sale of boards, serving clients in Oaxaca, elsewhere in Southern Mexico, Mexico City and as far north as San Luis Potosi. They sell most of their high grade wood as kiln-dried boards. Only 30 per cent of their boards go to furniture factories, and furniture makes up only 20 per cent of total sales. Each furniture factory has three main sales outputs: school furniture, wholesale buyers and the TIP factory outlet stores. In 2008, the three TIP stores in Oaxaca city sold between 450 and 500 thousand pesos every month, on average. To decrease reliance on a few large orders, such as school furniture, ICOFOSA is working to increase the number and location of TIP outlets (Interviews with Jesus Paz, ICOFOSA manager 8 March 2008, and Manuel Ignacio Garcia Nunez, Pueblos Mancomunados factory manager, 21 April 2008).

In the meantime, however, ICOFOSA members are in the difficult transition from sellers of boards to manufacturers of furniture, with many new processes to master, new customers to please, and debts to pay. In this context the school furniture contract is particularly important because it provides economies of scale. In 2008, Ixtlan's order for school furniture was for 14,000 pieces of furniture in six models. TIP, in contrast, bought 3,000 pieces of furniture in 30 or 50 models, so the profit rate for school furniture is twice that for TIP furniture (Interview with Alberto Belmonte. Business manager for Ixtlan, 25 February 2008).

ICOFOSA is the product of a network with disparate actors. The most important actors in the network are the managers, leaders and community members of Textitlan, Ixtlan, and Pueblos Mancomunados. But the actors in the state government who promoted the preferential purchase of school furniture are also important, as are the numerous organizations that facilitated ICOFOSA's acquisition of skills and productive infrastructure. The total investment in furniture factories and wood-drying kilns is about 50 or 70 million pesos (exchange rate: 11 pesos to the US dollar). There were important technical assistance, grants and loans on favourable terms from the World Bank community forestry project (Procymaf), federal programmes including the forestry development programme (Programa de Desarrollo Forestal Prodefor), the National forestry department (CONAFOR), a federal rural development programme (Alianza para el Campo), The shared risk trust fund (El Fideicomiso de Riesgo Compartido – FIRCO), Trust Funds for Rural Development (Fidiecomoso FIRA), the federal Secretariat of the Economy (SE), the national commission for the development of indigenous peoples (La Comisión Nacional para el Desarrollo de los Pueblos Indígenas – CDI), the Oaxaca State Agriculture and Forest Development Secretariat (Secretaria de Desarrollo Agropecuario y Forestal – SEDAF),

USAID, and TREES. The indigenous communities were not mere objects of development actions undertaken by these financial supporters, however. About 70 per cent of total investment came from community funds earned from forestry and loans to the communities. Several observers pointed out that funding was difficult to get in the beginning of the process, but once success was evident, more organizations wanted to be associated with the experience.

Certification is an important element in the network-building strategies of community forest enterprises. When I asked ICOFOSA business managers about the role certification has played in the growth of TIP and ICOFOSA, they answered that 'we are making it play a role'. Certification has not added any value on its own, they explain. The furniture price is still set by the quality of the wood and the manufacturing process, not whether it is certified. Instead, certification brings with it significant costs. Among their customers, 'the culture of certification in the state is still missing' they told me.

One way the communities take steps to make certification play a role is by promoting certification in the institutional market for school furniture. Ixtlan and Pueblos Mancomunados lobbied the government to demand certified wood in the school furniture contract. Business managers from the communities gave PowerPoint presentations on certification to an influential teachers' union and to representatives of the governor's office, for example. The first year of the contract, it was only a requirement that the wood came from Oaxaca. The second year, that it came from well-managed forests, which essentially meant it was from communities either certified or in the process of getting certified. The third year, certified, but without chain of custody certification. For 2009, the communities were considering asking for the COC requirement as well (Interview with Alberto Belmonte, business manager for Ixtlan de Juarez. February 25, 2008). Suggestions to require that school furniture be made of certified wood also came from forest sector promoters in CONAFOR and SEDAF, the federal forest department and the state agriculture and forest development programme. Suspicions that one of the member firms of the AOEFM was using Chilean wood to manufacture school furniture reinforced the idea that certification should be a requirement of the school furniture contracts.

Certification also helped enrol actors in the networks that produced the ICOFOSA consortium and the broader production network for certified furniture. It did the work of identifying environmentally sound forest management (see Eden, 2009), making it easier for the communities forming ICOFOSA to cooperate with each other, since their shared value of sound forest management was externally validated. When Pueblos Mancomunados, which cannot log or certify its own forests because of an internal land dispute, lagged in acquiring a chain of custody certification for its sawmills and furniture factory, the other members of the consortium pressured them to speed up the process.

Certification also makes it easier for environmental organizations and government agencies to support community forestry as a form of productive conservation. With certification, politicians and rural development agencies can promote 'sound forest management' at the same time as they promote wood furniture production. Without it, they would be vulnerable to charges of subsidizing 'forest destruction'. The actors involved in the school furniture contract saw certification as a way to avoid illegally cut wood and support the best forest managers in the state. Without this guarantee of certification, it was thought, promoting forestry could damage the environment and rural society, instead of improving them.

Certification was especially important for enrolling the *integradoras* of small carpenters in the school furniture production network. Unlike forest communities, AOEFM firms do not have their own sources of wood and are often suspected of supplying themselves with illegally cut wood or imported wood. The requirement to use certified wood, therefore, is a form of value chain governance of great importance to state forest managers and government buyers of furniture who were initially opposed to the participation of carpenters in the furniture supply network because of the potential association with illegal logging. It is also of interest to the community forest enterprises of ICOFOSA who were able to discipline their competitors while promoting their own interests as suppliers of certified boards. When making school furniture, AOEFM firms buy boards from certified producers, especially Textitlan and others in ICOFOSA (Figure 11.2).

The carpenters of AOEFM now make use of the certification discourse to differentiate themselves from cheap imports and from furniture produced by other carpenters. According to Raúl Mingo Gómez, secretary of the AOEFM, 'we have established our presence with quality furniture, with certification' (Martinez, 2008).

However, certification does not yet have a clear role in the important task of enrolling consumers in the certified furniture production network. A market study conducted for ICOFOSA interviewed 475 people in commercial areas of Oaxaca City. Although 80 per cent claimed to

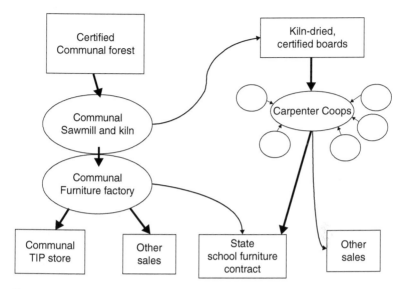

Figure 11.2 The supply network of certified furniture production in Oaxaca

know something about forest certification, only 30 per cent of those related the idea to forest conservation. Most thought it had to do with the durability of furniture. A handwritten note on a copy of the market study in the offices of the National Forestry Commission, says that forest certification is good, but the selling points for furniture in the local market are quality and price, not certification (Perez Ramirez, 2007).

Nevertheless, TIP is working to make certification play a role in its efforts to build a brand. As TIP tries to convince consumers of the value of their brand, their promotional materials make increasingly explicit the socio-environmental qualities of their products. Stickers on some of the furniture in the showroom display the FSC tick-tree logo, with the text 'this product is made with kiln-dried wood from the certified forests of Ixtlan de Juarez'. A banner hangs at the back of the store displaying the FSC and Rainforest Alliance certification stamps and the text 'When you buy products with the FSC logo you are supporting responsible forest management around the world'. Banners behind furniture displays show indigenous children and pine seedlings and explain the meaning of forest certification. TV and other news reports also carry the idea that TIP furniture protects forests and provides livelihood for rural Oaxacans (Figure 11.3).

Figure 11.3   Furniture display in the TIP factory outlet store, Oaxaca City, 2009
Certification supports the community consortium's efforts to brand its products as socially and environmentally preferable.

Conclusion: global certification fosters the creation of local networks

At the forest level, certification clearly governs forest management. It bans some existing practices and requires additional ones. In Oaxaca, forest certification has removed a toxic fungicide used in sawmills and required improvements and documentation of issues such as habitat management and species monitoring.

The forest certification label attaches the quality of 'sound forest management' to wood even after it leaves the forest gate and is transformed into wood products. This visibility and traceability makes it a useful tool for other forms of commodity network governance. Forest certification also supports the value chain governance goals of buyers. It serves as a hands-off tool for buyers to govern their suppliers. It protects them from negative publicity related to upstream suppliers. However, in places such as Oaxaca, Mexico, where high prices and low volumes put forest producers at the margin of global commodity chains, this governance aspect of certification has little effect. Buyers do not drive certification in areas where they have no suppliers.

A fuller understanding of the way certification governs production requires looking beyond these types of relatively direct North-to-South impacts of standards. The Oaxaca case illustrates a third type of 'governing through standards'. This chapter showed how forest managers and their supporters used forest certification to enrol other actors in a network that constructed a market for furniture made from certified wood.

Community forest managers made use of certification to facilitate cooperation within their consortium, to gain a preference in government purchases of school furniture, to enrol other actors in the network and to enrol buyers in their markets. They are proactively using certification in a broader branding strategy to conquer space in a market, enhance the value of wood and capture that value for rural development and sound forest management. They are using certification to create value by branding their furniture as socially beneficial and environmentally sustainable.

Rural development promoters also made use of forest certification to identify their support for investments in the wood processing chain as parts of strategies to promote sound forest management – not as part of chains promoting clandestine logging or forest degradation. In this way certification has facilitated changes in production processes because certified communities were more likely to receive investments such as wood kilns and milling equipment from state and federal development funds, and capacity building from the TREES programme.

Similarly, environmentalists made use of certification to promote productive conservation; it broadens their palette of possibilities for achieving their goals. Forest certification makes visible a common interest among these disparate actors in a commodity network. It facilitates their cooperation in a set of activities that improved forest management, increased the efficiency of sawmills and new, value-adding processes such as wood-drying kilns, furniture factories and even a brand based on socio-environmental values. In this way, certification helps produce a network that promotes productive conservation through value-added forest-based enterprises. Certification helped to leverage qualitative changes in production patterns, but these were co-determined by local, strategic actors – especially community forest managers.

Note

I am grateful to a Florida State University sabbatical and a Fulbright-Garcia Robles Fellowship for defraying costs of fieldwork in Oaxaca, Mexico, during 2007 and 2008.

References

Anta Fonseca, S. (2004) Forest Certification in Mexico http://www.yale.edu/forestcertification/symposium/pdfs/mexico_symposium.pdf (accessed 29 June 2007).

Barrera, J. M. (2007) Certificación y competitividad en ejidos y comunidades forestales de México. Durango, México: 59.

Bass, S., Thornber, K, Markopoulos, M. D., Roberts, S. and M. Grieg-Gran (2001) *Certification's Impacts on Forests, Stakeholders and Supply Chains: A report of the IIED project: Instruments for sustainable private sector forestry* (Stevenage: Earthprint) http://www.iied.org/psf/publications_def.html (accessed 22 August 2003).

Bray, D. B., Merino-Pérez, L. and Barry, D. (eds.) (2005/2009) *The Community Forests of Mexico: Managing for Sustainable Landscapes* (Austin: University of Texas Press).

Bray, D. B., E. Durán Medina, L. Merino Pérez, and J. M. Torres-Rojo. (2007) 'Nueva Evidencia: Los Bosques Comunitario de Mexico', Mexico D.F., Consejo Civil Mexicano para la Silvicultura Sostenible A.C.

Conroy, M. E. 2007. *Branded! How the 'certification revolution' is transforming global corporations* (Gabriola Island, Canada: New Society Publishers).

Eden, S. (2009) 'The Work of Environmental Governance Networks: Traceability, Credibility and Certification by the Forest Stewardship Council', *Geoforum*, 40, 383–394.

FERN (2004) 'Footprints in the forest: Current practice and future challenges in forest certification' https://www.wwf.de/imperia/md/content/pdf/waelder/footprints.pdf (accessed 15 March 2004).

Finger-Stich, A. (2003) 'Community Concessions and Certification in the Maya Biosphere Reserve' in E. Meidinger, C. Elliott, and G. Oesten (eds.) *Social and political dimensions of forest certification* (Remagen-Oberwinter Verlag).

Freidberg, S. E. (2004) 'The ethical complex of corporate food power', *Environment and Planning D: Society and Space*, 22(4), 513–531.

FSC (2002) 'FSC Principles and Criteria for Forest Stewardship', Retrieved 31 July 2009 from http://www.fsc.org/fileadmin/web-data/public/document_center/international_FSC_policies/standards/FSC_STD_01_001_V4_0_EN_FSC_Principles_and_Criteria.pdf

FSC (2008) 'FSC and Biodiversity – 2. High conservation value forests (HCVF) – Taking special care of particularly conservation worthy forests', Retrieved 31 July 2009 from http://www.fsc.org/152.html

FSC (2010) 'Global FSC certificates: type and distribution: June 2010' http://www.fsc.org/fileadmin/web-data/public/document_center/powerpoints_graphs/facts_figures/Global-FSC-Certificates-2010–05-15-EN.pdf (accessed 14 June 2010).

Gale, F. (2002) 'Caveat Certificatum: The case of forest certification' in T. Princen, M. Maniates, and K. Conca (eds) *Confronting Consumption* (Cambridge: The MIT Press).

Gereffi, G., Humphrey, J. and Sturgeon, T. (2005) 'The governance of global value chains', *Review of International Political Economy*, 12(1), 78–104.

Gerez Fernández, P. and Alatorre-Guzmán, E. (2005) 'Challenges for Forest Certification and Community Forestry in Mexico' in D. B. Bray, D. Barry, and L. Merino Pérez (eds) *The Community-Managed Forests of Mexico: Managing for sustainable landscapes* (Austin: University of Texas).

Gobierno de Oaxaca (2007) *Programa Estrategico Forestal del Estado de Oaxaca, 2007–2030*, Oaxaca, Gobierno de Oaxaca.

Hughes, A., Wrigley, N. and M. Buttle. (2008) 'Global production networks, ethical campaigning, and the embeddedness of responsible governance', *Journal of Economic Geography*, 8, 345–367.

Klooster, D. (2003) 'Campesinos and Mexican forest policy during the 20th Century', *Latin American Research Review*, 38, 94–126.

Klooster, D. (2005) 'Environmental certification of forests: the evolution of environmental governance in a commodity network', *Journal of Rural Studies*, 21(4), 403–417.

Klooster, D. (2006) 'Environmental Certification of Forests in Mexico: The political ecology of a nongovernmental market intervention', *Annals of the Association of American Geographers*, 96(3), 541–565.

Klooster, D. (2010) 'Standardizing Sustainable Development? The Forest Stewardship Council's plantation policy review process', *Geoforum, 41(1)*, 117–129.

Leslie, D. and Reimer, S. (2003) 'Fashioning furniture: restructuring the furniture commodity chain', *Area*, 35(4), 427–437.

Madrid, S., and Chapela, F. (2003) 'Certification in Mexico: The cases of Durango and Oaxaca' in A. Molnar (ed.) *Forest Certification and Communities: Looking forward to the next decade* (Washington DC, Forest Trenes), Annex 3.

Martinez, R. (2008) 'Industriales chinos comercializan muebles en la entidad, advierten Las Noticias Voz e Imagen de Oaxaca' online. Oaxaca, Mexico: online.

Morris, M. and Dunne, N. (2004) 'Driving environmental certification: its impact on the furniture and timber products value chain in South Africa', *Geoforum*, 35(2), 251–266.

Mutersbaugh, T. and Klooster, D. (2010) 'Environmental Certification: standardization for diversity', in S. Lockie and D. Carpenter *Agriculture, Biodiversity and Markets* (Earthscan).

Mutersbaugh, T., Klooster,D., Renard, M.C. and Taylor, P. L. (2005) 'Quality certification as rural governance: What is at Stake (Editorial)', *Journal of Rural Studies*, 21(4), 381–388.

Newsom, D., Bahm, V. and Cashore, B. (2006) 'Does forest certification matter? An analysis of operation-level changes required during the SmartWood certification process in the United States', *Forest Policy and Economics*, 9, 197–208.

Oliver, R., and Kraxner, F. (2009) 'Certified Forest Products Market 2008–2009', in United Nations (ed.) *Forest Products Annual Market Review 2008–2009*, 111–124.

Perez Ramirez, A. N. (2007) 'Estudio Para el Desarrollo de la Imagen Corporativa TIP Muebles Como Marca de la Integradora Comunal Forestal de Oaxaca S.A. de C.V.', Oaxaca, PROCYMAF II.

PYME. (n.d.) 'Empresas Integradoras (definicion)', Retrieved 30 January 2010, from http://www.contactopyme.gob.mx/integradoras/definicion.html

Rainforest Alliance (2009). 'Listado de ejidos forestales certificados FSC en México', Retrieved 16 December 2010 from http://www.ccmss.org.mx/modulos/biblioteca_consultar.php?folio=258

SmartWood. (2010). 'Certified Forestry Operation Summaries (Mexico)', Retrieved 16 December 2010 from http://www.rainforest-alliance.org/forestry/certification/transparency/operation-summaries-mex (accessed 14 December 2010).

Stringer, C. (2006) 'Forest certification and changing global commodity chains', *Journal of Economic Geography*, 6, 701–722.

Taylor, P. L. (2005) 'In the Market but not of it: Fair Trade Coffee and Forest Stewardship Council certification as market-based social change', *World Development*, 33, 129–147.

Zuñiga, I. and CCMSS. (2009, 01/27/2010) 'Nota Info 22. Balanza comercial forestal 2008', from http://www.ccmss.org.mx/modulos/biblioteca_consultar.php?folio=252

Zuñiga, I. and CCMSS. (2007a, 01/27/2010) 'Nota Info 15. El combate a la tala ilegal en México', from http://www.ccmss.org.mx/modulos/biblioteca_consultar.php?folio=176

Zuñiga, I. and CCMSS. (2007b, 01/27/2010). 'Nota Info 16. El mercado ilegal de la madera en México', from http://www.ccmss.org.mx/modulos/biblioteca_consultar.php?folio=185

12
Conclusion: The Current Status, Limits and Future of 'Governing through Standards'

Stefano Ponte, Peter Gibbon and Jakob Vestergaard

Standards and the re-articulation of governance

The Washington consensus era that started at the end of the 1970s was characterized by liberalization and deregulation. The gradual shift towards a post-Washington consensus (from the late 1990s onwards) entailed a major reversal of attitudes towards regulation, with more focus on transparency, participation and standards of good practice. The ambition of limiting government regulation as much as possible has been replaced with efforts to spread a set of governance practices where standards play a major role. But this shift does not mark a move from market-oriented policies back towards the dirigisme that prevailed between the 1940s and the late 1970s. Rather, the role of states has been re-articulated in the context of a wider set of governance modes, where a larger range of actors operate, private forms of authority are on the rise, and where the state is sometimes charged with ensuring that a range of standards defined elsewhere is met in public and private sectors (Vestergaard, 2009). Moreover, standards do not represent a *lassaiz-faire* approach to regulation. They are part of a re-articulation of governance of economy and society in which the locus of regulation shifts, and the style of regulation is moderated, rather than one where regulation disappears. Thus, what we have examined in this book is more aptly captured by the concept of 'governing through standards', rather than 'governing through markets' (cf. Cashore *et al.*, 2004). Standards mark a governance field characterized by a complex configuration of deregulation and different modes of re-regulation. It is a political field that poses itself as de-politicized.

Conceptually, governing through standards is also different from what much of the literature refers to as 'global governance'. It rarely involves attempts to define and impose one or few global standards and institutions to manage them. Among the case studies included in this book, the closest attempts to establish global standards have been made in banking and especially financial reporting, with mixed results in terms of uptake and often contradictory results. While standards are seen by others as part of the emergence of a so-called 'global public domain' that includes private and public actors debating, contesting and taking action on the provision of 'global public goods' in various domains (Ruggie, 2004), we rather see them as part of a complex 'spaghetti bowl' (to borrow Bhagwati's term) of often 'issue-specific' governance efforts that are tendentially international but rarely truly global. Governing through standards is characterized by an intricate overlap of diverse settings and forums, a widening range of public and private actors (beyond corporations, business associations, NGOs and government to include also professions, epistemic communities and expert groups), different types of regulation and self-discipline, and a wide array of more concrete technologies of government. Therefore, standards are part of multiple, overlapping, fragmented and contested terrains of governance that have international implications geographically, but that are not necessarily embedded in global institutions nor constitute global governance *per se*. The chapters in this collection examined sectoral and individual elements of this messy conglomerate from the often overlapping perspectives of governmentality and political economy (see the Introduction to this volume).

Standards as technologies of government

Several chapters in this collection see governing through standards as a key neo-liberal technology of government. This is because standard-making arises from practices of consensus-making, the voluntary enrolment of private actors, and often the cooperation of the public and private sectors. Devolved self-implementation, self-monitoring and self-reporting are main features of such standards, even if these are accompanied by certain external controls. These are all 'practices of the self' that legitimize standard organizations and allow 'governing at a distance' of their subjects.

In Chapter 6, Gibbon and Henriksen analyse the development of quality management standards in the US and UK military industry from an explicit governmentality perspective. These standards were the precursors of authoritative civilian quality standards (first in the UK and then internationally as in the ISO 9000 series) – and hence arguably of neo-liberal standards generally. Gibbon and Folke examine the transformation of these technologies away from traditional forms of sovereign power and disciplinary mechanisms such as surveillance and external inspection as they travelled across the Atlantic between 1960 and 1980. They argue that although other governmentality work has examined standard-based practices, they have not necessarily analysed the actual standards they are based upon and the changes these underwent over time, as if these technologies are available 'off-the-shelf' in forms compatible with the neo-liberal project. Such an analysis, however, draws attention to the link between material interests and the recasting of standards in neo-liberal forms.

In Chapter 5, Humphrey and Loft examine international standards for financial reporting, including the related processes of accounting and auditing. In this field, private and public authority are interconnected in complex ways and a key role is played by the auditing *profession*. International standards on auditing are based on principles rather than rules or a set of instructions, therefore 'professional judgment' by auditors is important. The auditing profession exercises some discretion in how it applies standards, a space where it reclaims 'self-regulation' as its *raison d'être*. In Chapter 8, Djama, Fouilleux and Vagneron highlight how certification agencies play a similar role in relation to sustainability standards, where they are important relays and translators of a managerial logic. They operationalize criteria and indicators included in standards in many different settings. They are translators and gatekeepers between standard makers and takers. In both cases, this creates an interpretive space that undermines consistency of results from auditing and certification. It may also open possibilities for interpreting such inconsistency as the result of political considerations. As a result, pressure is mounting both in financial auditing and certification to harmonize procedures and narrow the space for interpretation. In Chapter 10, Ponte and Riisgaard show that this pressure has been clearly articulated in relation to the Marine Stewardship Council label and is also reflected in the difficulties facing widespread implementation of 'participatory auditing' (a technique opening up even more discretionary space) in the cut flower sector.

In Chapter 7, Murphy and Yates examine the role of professions from a slightly different angle. They provide a historical analysis of the 'social movement of engineers' that is behind the setting of voluntary standards, such as the ISO 26000 standard on organizational social responsibility.

They show that consensus-based standard setting (see also Chapters 8 and 9) needs to be understood in relation to the role played by *epistemic communities*. Participants in standard setting processes are not just representatives of particular stakeholders or defenders of the interests of specific firms as a more traditional political economy approach would have it, but are part of professional groups that share knowledge and set criteria for validating new knowledge. Yet, epistemic communities do have structural features: Murphy and Yates argue that they tend to be more powerful when more of their members hold key roles in government, perform important functions within powerful firms, and/or when they draw from the most dynamics sectors of a time.

Furthermore, members of standard committees or networks are not only part of sectoral or technical communities, but also of an epistemic community of 'standard setters' – which has been around for more than a century. In this community, Murphy and Yates argue, there is less cohesion than in others because some key issues such as criteria for validating new knowledge about standard setting, who should be part of the community, and the level of consensus needed, were never completely resolved (although ISEAL strives to play a role in this direction in relation to sustainability standards – see Chapters 8 and 10). The common conviction among these professionals that humanity can benefit from their standard-setting knowledge qualifies them as an 'epistemic social movement' seeking broad utilitarian outcomes, efficiency and welfare. Due to the transnational nature of standard work, such movement takes a network form (see also Chapter 11 where standards are sources of network formation in a more localized setting) and is focused on a particular process – standard setting by consensus.

In Chapter 8, Djama, Fouilleux and Vagneron continue the analysis of *consensus building* as pertaining to a set of technologies of government identified collectively as *managerialism*. Through the study of multi-stakeholder initiatives in social and environmental standard making, they show how these techniques and attached expert knowledge are mobilized to frame debates and neutralize potential conflicts. They analyse ideas and discourses on which these ideas are built, the role of process consultants and the institutional and technological instruments that are mobilized to manage unstable compromises and foster consensus. Key experts in this process provide knowledge on how to achieve a wished outcome (consensus) and how to prop up sectoral technical knowledge that is focused on short-term and pragmatic solutions. Djama *et al.* argue that the rise of managerialism in NGOs that took place in the 1990s encompasses new or increasingly widespread technologies of government – auditing, benchmarking and consensus-building. Auditing, they argue, (along with Power, 1997) is not a neutral and apolitical instrument of verification, but rather propagates new forms of subjectivity based on self-management. Benchmarking, which is comparing practices against a baseline, can be seen as providing 'lateral integrity of the managerial rationality' (p. 191). Consensus building, they point out, is a technology of government that does not result from debate or negotiation (which would lead to compromise). It has the effect of neutralizing debate. These three technologies are seen as both reinforcing each other and as building a managerial rationality based on autonomy, initiative and responsibility. They neutralize conflicts among stakeholders (to different degrees) and depoliticize the realm of sustainability standards making.

Djama *et al.* also highlight other strategic components in the process of consensus building which are usually the fodder of political economy analyses – the importance of early movers and 'initial contact meetings' (see similar processes in Chapters 4, 9 and 10). Focusing on the Roundtable on Responsible Palm Oil, they show how an initial meeting in London in 2002 resulted in setting the guiding principles of practicality, viability and pragmatism *before* the formal start of the roundtable process. Such meeting was organized by a consulting firm specialized in building NGO–industry partnerships. Attending were industry actors (except primary producers), banks, WWF and consulting firms specialized in environmental issues. One of these firms played a key role in the subsequent writing of the first draft of the standard. Most importantly, the standard was eventually accepted throughout the process of Roundtable meetings without any substantial changes from the first draft. Thus, the contribution of stakeholders was mainly one of 'approving the direction already taken by consulting firms and a pioneer group' (p. 195). This was the result of the socialization of specific technologies that facilitated the construction of the standard and its management in specific ways. Consensus building, quick deliberative procedures that placed time pressure on stakeholders, and the striving to find pragmatic and short-term solutions played a key role in this respect. This meant that instead of assessing the criteria set by the consultant, stakeholders were only evaluating their operationality.

Djama *et al.* show that other kinds of knowledge were marginalized to the advantage of the expertise of consultants, leading to adopting immediately operational solutions and dropping those that required more time for investigation. This trajectory is similar to the one chronicled in Ponte and Riisgaard in Chapter 10, where they highlight the environmental–managerial compromise reached by MSC in its early stages, its focus on pragmatic solutions and the exclusion from the standard of difficult areas, such as the social and work conditions of fishery production. These experiences suggest that standards – following again the quality management model – are increasingly about fulfilling managerial criteria rather than solving concrete problems (in this case social and environmental ones).

In Chapter 9, Cheyns argues that *participation* and its management is central to understanding how multi-stakeholder initiatives operate. Through the analysis of 'regimes of engagement' (Thévenot, 2006), she examines how actors are engaged in relation to their environment. Building on earlier convention theory, Thévenot's approach expands the range of possible modalities of engagement that are recognized in this theory from 'justifiable engagement' to also cover 'strategic engagement', where stakeholders assert interests, and 'familiar engagement' where they operate by maintaining personalized relations. Cheyns applies this framework to explain the manner in which two Roundtables on sustainable palm oil and sustainable soy frame the engagement of actors and exclude participants that cannot be characterized as 'stakeholders'. Cheyns argues that these Roundtables focus on strategic engagement that leads to depoliticization and the exclusion of those who engage through their personal attachments (local communities, familial engagement) and those who wish to engage in relation to principles of justice (justifiable engagement).

The framing of the figure of 'stakeholder' is particularly important in this context because it defines the principle of representativeness (see also Pattberg, 2007). In the initiatives examined by Cheyns, stakeholder categories are defined (leaving out those that do not 'fit'), a balanced representation in terms of number of seats allocated to each category is sought, and participants are expected to be proactive, assertive and direct, and articulate their position in terms of representing category interests. The moral subject or 'attached person' does not match with the stylized figure of a legitimate participant. Individuals and groups that are not part of the 'initiators' network' are excluded or marginalized. The absence of adequate smallholder representation in the palm oil roundtable, for example, is justified by claims that smallholders are not capable of organizing themselves, lack resources, and/or are unable to achieve unitary representation – and, as a result, their interests are defended by proxy by others. Also, the format of discussion in plenary sessions does not allow participants to engage in discussing principles of justice, nor to describe their personal attachments and situations that they experience as producers. A strategic engagement, based on urgency, expediency, pragmatism and necessary action suppresses the other two possible forms. One of the key technologies of government in this context is the organization of debate in terms of a market where different opinions (rather than disagreements) can be negotiated. 'Open space technology' and 'world cafés' are two of the formats observed by Cheyns – they are connectionist, aim at increasing interactions and seek to create a network quickly. Questions are compartmentalized and specialized, keeping a common vision out of the picture and relaxing the need for moral responsibility – all of which leads to a trajectory that is perceived as 'natural' by stakeholders.

These roundtables engage the knowledge of biology, agronomy and management – seamlessly incorporated in a regime of strategic and planned engagement. Similarly, in the case of MSC, Ponte and Riisgaard show how fish biology, fishery management, logistics and industrial fishery knowledge take the lead, while data-deficient, small-scale fisheries and socio-economic aspects of fishing are left behind. Cheyns shows that in Roundtables, industrial knowledge based on statistics, graphs and variables enters into conflict with monographic, local, and lived experience of smallholders and communities, which are not accorded any legitimacy. Although smallholders can bring in practical experiences, it is practical solutions that are valued, which are based on international expertise. In Cheyns' words, 'roundtable-speak ... [allows] pluralized interaction without confrontation' (p. 227), where the lived experiences of farmers and their emotional statements are deemed to be out of place.

Standards and their effects

The contributions to this collection are also concerned with the political economy of standards in terms of examining the strategies behind their setting and management, the configuration of actor interests and alliances, inclusion and exclusion dynamics, and (re)distributive and substantial effects. While all chapters previously mentioned are also concerned with these issues via the examination of the material (in addition to the ideational, normative and discursive) effects of programmes and technologies of government, we highlight here the lessons arising from chapters (and parts of chapters) that focus on more direct strategic, structural and interest-based dynamics.

Chapters 2, 3 and 4 show that the internationalization of banking has placed severe limits on domestic regulation of capital adequacy ratios and created the opportunity of competitive advantage for banks based in countries with lower ratio requirements. Pressure by US financial regulatory agencies led to the addressing of capital adequacy ratios (and later on, other aspects of banking) through a multilateral standard-making initiative rather than international regulation or the coordination of different domestic regulations. These chapters show that the Basel I accord on banking standards was one of the instruments that attempted to address regulatory arbitrage. But it soon became clear that it was too crude and rigid. Also, many observers argued that the realities of the financial sector made government technologies outdated and government not well equipped to regulate banks. This led to pressures to adopt more self-regulatory instruments and to the Basel II accord.

In Chapter 2, Young shows that Basel II standards set requirements for a much broader and complex set of parameters in banking, involving a much more intensive utilization of banks own internal practices. He argues that the gradual process from Basel I to II constituted a passage from a developmental state approach based on active intervention by regulators to a neoliberal regulatory state, where the basic frame of action is set by international standards, but where both regulators and banks were able to exercise considerable discretion in carrying out regulatory processes.

In Chapter 3, Vestergaard and Højland highlight three instruments in Basel II that ended up being pro-cyclical in their effects, instead of stabilizing the financial sector as originally intended. First, value-at-risk models were included in Basel II as a form of calculating market risk. These models work as long as market fluctuations remain 'statistically normal', thus excluding 'extreme events'. The financial crisis has unveiled the limits of calculability of such risk. Second, the adoption of 'mark to market' accounting principles (valuing assets at current market value instead of at historical acquisition prices) exposed bank balance sheets to fluctuations that went along with the market. In a boom period, this meant lower risk weighting and capital requirements, thus fuelling further credit expansion and asset market inflation. Third, the separation of banking and trading books (with the latter subject to lower capital requirements) encouraged the proliferation of securitization, where non-tradable loans (such as mortgages) were aggregated in pools and securities were issued on the basis of such pools. This was meant to redistribute risk of a bank to other banks and non-bank investors, thus reducing risk overall. As the recent historical record shows, it did the exact opposite.

In Chapter 4, Lall shows that the instruments highlighted by Højland and Vestergaard assumed their particular content in Basel II as a result of the Basel process' regulatory capture by large international banks. These banks exploited personal links with committee members to secure 'first-mover' advantage in the standard setting process. They managed to extract rents at the expense of smaller banks and ultimately undermined the stability of the international financial system. By arriving at the negotiating table first, they exerted influence to shape outcomes that later tended to be self-reinforcing. Lall argues that as more resources were invested in the Basel process, the costs of abandoning early decisions increased.

Two other chapters deal explicitly with the intended or unintended distributional effects of standards. In Chapter 10, Ponte and Riisgaard examine how 'governing through standards' takes place in two agro-food sectors of particular significance for developing countries – capture fish and cut flowers. In both sectors, developing country producers face not only increasingly demanding standards, on environmental impact, social/labour issues and (in fish) on food safety, but also competition from Northern producers. They explore how competition (or lack thereof) in the market for standards and pressure for the establishment of 'best practices' in standard governance affect standard content, governance practices and the inclusion or exclusion of Southern suppliers – in the context of a literature arguing that competition among standards is leading to a 'race to the bottom' in terms of standard content. Ponte and Riisgaard suggest that there is actually no sign of a general 'lowering of the bar' in terms of standard content, neither in the low-competition sector (capture fish) nor in the high-competition sector (cut flowers). In cut flowers, so-called base codes have actually helped raise the bar of standard content not only in niche markets but also in mainstream ones. There are also attempts to 'modularize' standards, so it is possible to build on a base code and then add modules on social conditions of production, and at developing comprehensive and mutually recognized standards with more demanding content.

Ponte and Riisgaard's chapter, along with Chapters 8 and 9, show that the *internal* dynamics of competition within standard initiatives are important. During the formative years of MSC in the late 1990s, it was not subjected to competition from other standards in its field. This allowed MSC to achieve an internal equilibrium between environmental and commercial/managerial expertise and a fairly narrow representation that excluded social issues and meaningful Southern representation. MSC was able to insulate itself from more critical civil society pressure, shape its standard content to the need of Northern industrial fisheries, and market its label and certification system aggressively both with fisheries and buyers. It also resolutely fought any attempt to include social and labour issues in its standard. New procedural fixes are allowing it to claim both a relatively 'high bar' for its standard content while at the same time facilitating the achievement of more numerous and quicker certifications of (mostly Northern) fisheries, thus catering to commercial concerns related to increased demand by retailers and processors for sustainable fish. Ponte and Riisgaard also show that the development of best practices in standards governance has led to mostly cosmetic changes in first-generation sustainability standards that were developed in the 1990s. Overall, best practice pressure in standards governance has affected mostly second-generation standards (and consumer labels among these) that were developed in the 2000s. Finally, they argue that 'a race to the top' in some standards is entailing the exclusion of Southern suppliers, especially in markets where Northern and Southern producers compete.

In Chapter 11, Klooster argues that existing standards can be used locally, in certain circumstances, in ways that create new networks and forge new local and regional markets. Klooster argues that the representations in much political economy approaches to standards, where key decisions made in the North place barriers to entry on Southern players and standardizes forestry practices more generally, are only part of the picture. Klooster shows that global standards, such as FSC, are shaped by conjunctural events where they 'touch down', and that local actors have more agency than meets the eye. In Mexico, FSC certification facilitated the emergence of a national network promoting better forestry and business management. In the Mexican state of Oaxaca, forest certification rather than leading to exports created alternative and more sustainable networks of forest management and furniture production. Community forest managers made use of certification to facilitate cooperation within their newly created consortium, to gain preference in government purchases, to enrol other actors in their network and to find new markets for timber use, including a broader branding strategy and value addition. Rural development promoters used certification to promote sound forest management through supporting investment in wood processing. Environmentalists used it to promote productive conservation. Klooster's findings suggest that while forest certification does govern production directly where exports are dependent on it, it also operates in more indirect and unexpected ways through local and regional commodity networks. This may signal that the political economy literature on standards may be too obsessed with distributional issues in a narrow way.

Has 'governing through standards' reached its limits?

In this book, we have shown how standards are re-articulating the governance of economy and society. They are not instruments of deregulation *tout court*, but are part of a proliferation of governance practices that facilitate acting 'at a distance' and at the same time discipline subjects (people, organizations and states) and promote self-regulation. Such standards are based on 'voluntary enrolment' of private and public actors, are often built upon practices of consensus making and normally operate through self-reporting, inspection, certification and accreditation. Governing through standards is a configuration of deregulation in some domains and different modes of re-regulation in others. When maintained within a narrow space of interpretation, it promotes rule making that poses itself as de-politicized. Attempts to widen such interpretive space are fought against under the guise of ensuring replicability and consistency.

Professions, epistemic communities and expert groups play a key role in setting and managing these standards, expanding the range of key actors beyond corporations, governments and NGOs. The enrolment of these 'new' actors has the profound effect of framing negotiations, compromises and consensus in a de-politicized domain. Sometimes it is sectoral or issue-specific knowledge imbued in the legitimacy of expertise that is enrolled, at other times process-management skills and specific standard-making and management abilities. Thus, in addition to important structural differences in endowments, access to resources and ability to draw on influential networks, differential abilities to shape outcomes are also contingent on more subtle games of enrolling one expert group or kind of expert knowledge instead of another, using specific formats of negotiation and consensus-building processes, and legitimating specific modes of engagement instead of others. Strategic tools used in this realm include quick deliberative procedures that place time pressure on stakeholders, narrow identification of stakeholder categories, the elimination or minimization of residual categories of stakeholders, the prioritization of pragmatic and short-term solutions, and heavily managed forms of participation and 'voicing'. These techniques, strategies and processes are taking place in an increasingly number of realms of economy and society and are reaching deeper aspects of these realms.

But the contributions to this book also indicate that in some realms governing through standards may be reaching its limits. Despite the dynamism of standard making and management, it is becoming clearer that standards are unable to substantially address some of the more complex social and environmental problems and systemic financial risk. Also, as many sustainability standards arose as a consequence of social pressure and activism, sustaining such pressure in the long term poses serious challenges. Despite these emerging signs, the chapters of this book suggest that so far there has been no rethinking of the voluntaristic nature of these standards, their efficacy in delivering on their stated objectives, and their limitations in dealing with systemic risk and complex phenomena. Efforts in this area have been limited to trying to substitute standards which are putatively better or more complex, and to making standard setting, management and certification follow best practices in the field.

The chapters on banking showed that governing through standards has had no measureable effect on stabilizing the banking sector and finance more generally – as a matter of fact, it has been a factor that facilitated the onset of the contemporary financial crisis. Despite its lofty objectives, the current Basel III process of revising banking standards seems to have fallen prey of the same mechanism of regulatory capture of Basel II. Therefore, rather than a return to more traditional regulation and external supervision, and the inclusion of effective anti-cyclical measures, a much more diluted set of standards is likely to be enacted.

Best practices in multi-stakeholder initiatives are being used to subtly manipulate participation and the space and modalities of expression of voice from weaker actors. While this may make such standards more likely to succeed in terms of wider adoption by business, such processes do not bode well for the achievement of intended results. Certification for sustainable fisheries (under the MSC label), for example, has shown no clear and demonstrable effect on fish stocks, and has excluded developing country fisheries from certification so far. Internal reform of the MSC system has focused on facilitating smoother, faster and more harmonized processes of certification, not on setting up dedicated certification systems for artisanal, data-deficient fisheries. Efforts to make cut flower standards more demanding are leading to more favourable market outcomes for Northern, rather than Southern, growers. ISO's decision to change the ISO 26000 standard from an auditable management system standard to an advisory guidance standard is not a good sign for its potential efficacy either.

While participation and consensus building have been used tactically in multi-stakeholder initiatives to validate decisions made by a smaller group of early entrants, such technologies of government may be failing at the meta-standard level. As indicated by Djama, Fouilleux and Vagneron, ISEAL's codes of good practices on standard setting, on assessing the impacts of standards and on verification, are being developed in the context of an increasing gap between the founding members and newer standard initiatives on what constitutes sustainability and on how compliance is recognized (pass-fail versus 'constant improvement'). This signals a limit to what the consensus-building process can achieve (and IFOAM's recent exit from ISEAL may signal this), despite the fact that the ISEAL codes do not deal with standard content but with governance and procedures.

These observations suggest an increasing distance between standards objectives and real objects of standardization. They also indicate that the more 'managerialism' triumphs, the less inclusive standard processes will be. Also, while multi-stakeholder initiatives may be neutralizing conflict within their boundaries, these conflicts will continue outside their confines. While not achieving a stated objective may not be necessarily transmitted as 'failure' (as long as 'improvements' are taking place) to consumers and other audiences of standards, we wonder how long such posturing is politically tenable.

The limitations of governing through standards may not be confined to failure of achieving intended effects. In some realms, claims have been made suggesting that the complexity of issues at stake may have reached the limit of calculability and governability through standards. Recent discussions on catastrophic risk and the management of complex phenomena suggest that other, more open-ended processes are being established alongside standards, including new protocols to engineer for diversity and adaptability, 'enactment' processes and 'open systems' embracing instability, spontaneity and self-organization (Hinchliffe *et al.*, 2007; Collier, 2008; Massumi, 2009; Higgins and Larner, 2010b; Aradau and van Munster, 2011). Others have also asserted that complexity is being increasingly addressed through subjective and personalized modalities, rather than 'objective' and systemic or 'scientific' modalities, as celebrities permute into 'expert celebrities' and endorse or guide consumption choices for sustainability or other good causes (Richey and Ponte, 2011). Within standards themselves (for example, in the area of information technology), more flexibility demanded by certain expert communities is being counteracted by others whose expertise is in bureaucratized standard setting itself. The extent to which any of these developments are truly novel, or represent partial repetitions of earlier narratives and conflicts, remains unclear, as does whether standards themselves will be able to accommodate the pressure for more open, adaptable systems or whether these can grow outside the realm of standards. Historically, the feasibility of governing through standards has often been played out in this overlapping field. This time, however, some of the actors are new, including not only powerful corporations, governments and different professions, but also international NGOs, new groups of experts and new sources of non-expert 'inspiration'. A final question concerns whether a return of traditional regulation is likely. Some observers see new space being re-established for the role of traditional public regulation, given that large emerging economies where most manufacturing is now taking place have increased their capacity (if not their will) to exercise control over production practices under their jurisdiction (cf. Mayer and Gereffi, 2010). And indeed in some fields, regulation to simplify the banking business model and achieve a clearer separation between actors would be more beneficial than devising 'better standards'. But our optimism in this realm is limited, and rather than a return to traditional regulation, what we may be witnessing is a further refinement of standardization. In what ways this refinement will take place should be part of an agenda for future research.

References

Aradau, C. and van Munster, R. (2011) *Politics of Catastrophe. Genealogies of the Unknown* (London and New York: Routledge).

Cashore, B., Auld, G. and Newsom, D. (2004) *Governing through Markets: Forest certification and the emergence of non-state authority* (New Haven: Yale University Press).

Collier, S.J. (2008) 'Enacting catastrophe: preparedness, insurance, budgetary rationalization', *Economy and Society*, 37(2), 224–250.

Higgins, V. and Larner, W. (2010b) 'From standardization to standardizing work', in V. Higgins and W. Larner (eds) *Calculating the Social: Standards and the reconfiguration of governing* (Basingstoke and New York: Palgrave Macmillan).

Hinchliffe, S., Kearnes, M.B., Degen, M. and Whatmore, S. (2007) 'Ecologies and economies of action–sustainability, calculations, and other things', *Environment and Planning A*, 39, 260–282.

Massumi, B. (2009) 'National Enterprise Emergency: Steps Toward an Ecology of Powers', *Theory, Culture & Society*, 26(6), 153–185.

Mayer, F. and Gereffi, G. (2010) 'Regulation and economic globalization: Prospects and limits of private governance', *Business and Politics*, 12(3), Article 11.

Pattberg, P.H. (2007) *Private Institutions and Global Governance: The new politics of environmental sustainability* (Cheltenham: Edward Elgar).

Power, M. (1997) *The Audit Society: Rituals of verification* (Oxford: Oxford University Press).

Richey, L.A. and Ponte, S. (2011) *Brand Aid: Shopping well to save the world* (Minneapolis: Minnesota University Press).

Ruggie, J.G. (2004) 'Reconstituting the global public domain – Issues, actors, and practices', *European Journal of International Relations*, 10(4), 499–531.

Thévenot, L. (2006) *L'action au pluriel. Sociologie des régimes d'engagement* (Paris: La Découverte).

Vestergaard, J. (2009) *Discipline in the Global Economy? International finance and the end of liberalism* (London: Routledge).

Index